AIR FORCES
Escape & Evasion Society

PRO LIBERTATE AMBULAVIMUS

TURNER PUBLISHING COMPANY

May 8, 1945. Lt. Murray is set to leave his Dutch friends in Muiden, The Netherlands, after liberation from the Nazis. The original caption for this picture was printed in Dutch—"Met 'N Bootje Genomen En Met 'N Motor Gegaan"—translated, it means, "He came in a little boat and left on a motor." (Courtesy of Claude C. Murray)

TURNER PUBLISHING COMPANY
The Front Line of Military History Books
P.O. Box 3101
Paducah, Kentucky 42002-3101
(502) 443-0121

Air Forces Escape and Evasion Staff:
Ralph K. Patton
Lt. Col. Clayton C. David (Ret.)

Turner Publishing Company's Staff:
Editor: Kelly O'Hara
Designer: Trevor W. Grantham

Library of Congress Catalog
Card Number: 91-075228
ISBN: 1-56311-034-2
ISBN: 1-68162-189-4

Limited Edition. Additional books may be purchased from Turner Publishing Company.

Air Forces Escape and Evasion

Editorial note: The material for this book was typeset as submitted, with a minimum of editing. As such, the Publisher is not responsible for historical or geographical inaccuracies.

Message From The Chairman

No publication can do justice to the stories of the Evaders and the Helpers represented in this book, but the publication you have in your hands is a small sample of frightening adventures now told in a calm, mature manner by a unique group of men and women bound together by an indefinable bond forged almost 50 years ago.

America's airmen were under orders to evade capture, if possible, should they be shot down; most tried; some did not. Allied nationals were under no such orders, their actions were voluntary, some spontaneously came to the aid of fallen airmen, some turned them in to the Gestapo. A number of America's airmen lost their lives in trying to evade capture, or escape from capture. Thousands of the nationals of occupied lands ended up in concentration camps or were executed for their activities on behalf of the men represented in this book.

The following incredible stories are true and the names and places are real. We the survivors are trying to say "We will never forget" those who didn't make it, as well as those who helped us to make it. AFEES is dedicated to this task, this is the "raison d'etre" of AFEES.

Ralph K. Patton
Chairman of the Board

Dedication

This book is dedicated to our "Helpers", the thousands of foreign nationals, who risked their lives to come to the aid of the Allied fliers shot down over enemy occupied countries, most of us during World War II. It is dedicated to the hundreds of brave men and women of the Resistance who were tortured and executed by their occupiers, because they were Helpers. It is also dedicated to those of our Helpers who survived long periods of detention and torture in Nazi prisons and concentration camps.

The penalty for aiding Allied airmen was well known, but this did not deter our Helpers from taking the risks. We, the survivors salute those who paid the ultimate price. We vow to make known to future generations that these brave men and women made the supreme sacrifice to insure our freedom, as we fought together for the freedom of all.

Clayton C. David, President
Air Forces Escape and Evasion Society

History of the Winged Boot

Some call it the "Flying Foot" or the "Winged Foot", but the Royal Air Force who issued this badge in the Western Desert, June 1941, named it the "Winged Boot." The following is an extract from the book, *Customs and Traditions of the Royal Air Force*, by Squadron Leader P.G. Hering, published in 1961 by Gale & Polden, LTD, Aldersot, Hants, England:

The exploits of aircrew who walked back to their bases after bailing out of their aircraft, being shot down or having force-landed whilst operating over enemy-held territory during the Desert campaigns in the Middle East, were responsible for the initiation of another highly respected war-time badge. Because their return to their squadrons was of necessity much later than that of their more fortunate comrades, they were heralded as a new "corps d'elite" and became known as "later arrivals". As their numbers increased their experiences became legend and eventually a mythical Late Arrivals "Club" came into being, and with it a badge.

A winged boot was designed by Wing Commander (later Group Captain) George W. Houghton, who was at the time the Senior R.A.F. Public Relations Officer in the Middle East. He obtained the permission of Lord Tedder (then Air Officer Commanding-in-Chief, Middle East) to issue each late arrival with the badge to wear on his flying suit or uniform. The innovation captured the imagination of the war correspondents, who enthusiastically reported the origin of the badge and the experiences of its wearers. In addition to his badge, each late arrival was given a "club" membership certificate on which was recorded the circumstances making him eligible for membership, and the words: "It is never too late to come back."

According to the Royal Air Forces Escaping Society Press Officer, Bryan Morgan: "The membership of this Society was exclusive to the Middle East, it was never available in this country (England) and it doesn't exist any more.

In 1943 when American airmen of the U.S. 8th Air Force started to return to England after having been shot down over enemy occupied territory, some unknown American evader started to use the Royal Air Force "Winged Boot" as a symbol of his having evaded capture and having "walked home." This symbol of evasion was never authorized to be worn on U.S. uniforms in the ETO therefore evaders wore it under the left hand lapel on their tunic or battle jacket. One of the first stops an evader made after being released by Air Force Intelligence in London was usually a visit to Hobson and Sons in London to have them make a "wire badge" "Winged Boot".

When the Air Forces Escape and Evasion Society was formed in June 1964, it was decided to use the "Winged Boot" as the center piece of the AFEES logo. As an extension of this, we approached Hobson and Sons in London to make several items with the original "Winged Boot" in metallic thread from the original dies.

There is no official "Winged Boot" organization or club therefore eligibility for wearing it is ill defined. AFEES is the only known organization that uses the "Winged Boot" as a logo or symbol. *Editorial note: Originaly entitled "The True Story of the Winged Boot". By Claude C. Murray and Ralph K. Patton.*

Air Forces Escape and Evasion Personal Experience Stories

The Le Grain family, one of hundreds of European families who helped American airmen evade capture. (Courtesy of Joseph Perry.)

ESCAPE FROM FRANCE!
THE STORY OF JAMES E. ARMSTRONG

James E. Armstrong was a pilot stationed in England before the invasion of Europe by Allied troops in World War II. It was September 6, 1943. He was returning from a mission to Stuttgart, Germany when his plane was shot down in occupied France. He parachuted safely, but one crew member was killed.

Armstrong suffered a sprained ankle in the jump but was not seriously injured. After getting water from a ditch, he spotted a Frenchman and showed him the phrase sheet from his escape kit. The man told the 21 year-old pilot to get in the woods. He hid in the woods for 10 days and the Frenchman brought him food twice a day.

Using a compass shaped like a pocket watch and a silk map, the young first lieutenant started walking towards Paris. Two days after he left Normandy, he came to a village near Paris called Trielsur-Seine where he was sheltered in a home. A doctor treated him for burns on his hand and face and then took him by train to his Paris apartment. Members of the French Resistance picked him up and took him to the suburb of Drancy.

In Drancy he and two Americans and an Englishman who had been shot down stayed in a home and were provided with false French identity cards. Armstrong was given the name of Jean Riber, occupation, butcher. By the end of October, the first of several attempts to escape to England was made.

The escape plan called for a PT boat off the coast of Quimper to take about a dozen Allies to England. It failed, as did several other attempts. Each plan was ingenious but failed for various reasons. Each time a plan failed, the airmen were taken back to Paris by train. Once they were supposed to meet a guide in Carcassonne who was to take them out across the Pyrenees Mountains. When they got to Carcassonne the guide was not there.

There were many close calls on the train rides back to Paris. The guide would keep the men moving from one car to another to evade the Germans.

On another escape attempt, the plan was to make a break Christmas night, 1943 by boat. Armstrong waded out to the boat but the mission was called off. He got another boat on January 21. The tides were quite high and the plan called for the men to wait for it and to rise and fall, then drift out under a bridge. As they drifted under the bridge they were told to "halt", but continued on past a German fortress. They drifted out into the bay and crossed the English Channel.

There were 31 in a less than 30 foot fishing boat with sails and a motor. Everyone was seasick. It carried a crew of two sailors, 12 Allied airmen and 19 Frenchmen who were going to join the Free French in England. There was a storm and the Channel was rough. Even the British Navy wasn't going out. After two nights and a day, the boat landed at Falmouth in Cornwall, England.

Armstrong was taken to London for interrogation. There he learned that two of his crew had returned by way of Spain.

Armstrong was sent back to the United States and eventually became pastor of the New Covenant Church in Thomasville, Georgia.

ATTACKED BY BANDITS!

By Robert Augustus

On April 12, 1944, on the way to bomb a fighter field at Zwickau, Germany, Bomber Group, 445th, consisting of 12 B-24s, was suddenly attacked by approximately 100 Me109s. At first we thought it was a fighter escort since they were due to join us at that time 1:30 p.m. Our plane, *Nine Yank and a Jerk*, was flying low left in the "Purple Heart" element. The navigator, Lt. Hermanski, gave the first alert as we were being attacked by several bandits at 12:00 level. Lt. Sam Schleichkorn, our pilot, gave me permission to lower the ball turret, then all hell broke loose. They were coming at us in all directions, and it became necessary to restore order on the intercom.

During the attack the starboard waist gunner and I damaged or destroyed two fighters. Being in the ball turret and unable to see what was happening, I was unaware that we had suffered several hits. When the intercom and the power went out, I decided it was time for me to leave the turret. I manually returned the turret to a position where I could crawl back into the plane. When I opened the turret door I was greeted with a wall of flames. The plane was on fire, and it appeared that everyone had left. I managed to get up in to the waist area only to discover that the radio deck, where I had left my chute, was in flames. Somehow, despite the flames, my chute was all right.

After recovering my chute, I went over to the starboard gun and fired one last burst at the fighters lined up on a 24 next to us. As I turned to go out the escape hatch, I saw my tail gunner, Sgt. Marty Clabaugh, stumble out of the tail turret, and he was completely on fire. I started to go to him when I realized he was beyond help, and the plane was going into a dive. I put my chute on and dove out the hatch.

I waited to open my chute until I felt I had cleared the immediate combat area. As I drifted down I could see that I was going to land in the middle of a herd of cows. Since I had no training in the proper way to maneuver a chute, I was reluctant to try. Somehow I missed landing on any of the cows, however I made a direct hit on a cow flop. Having had to leave my shoes behind in the plane, I severely damaged my right ankle upon landing. Gathering my chute from among the cows I limped, hopped and ran to the edge of a woods

nearby and buried my chute under some leaves.

Going further into the woods I found a suitable place to hide, catch my breath, and examine my situation. I found that besides the damaged ankles I also had burns on my face and hands. It was that this point that I heard someone running nearby. I looked around and saw another guy from my group going in a big hurry. I yelled and he came over to my hiding place.

We discussed our situation and decided to wait until near sundown and then head for France. While we were waiting we heard voices singing and people laughing. As the noise came closer, we looked up from our hiding place and saw in the distance a group of young people carrying baskets, having a great time. We noticed that as they moved along they would occasionally drop something out of the baskets. When they were out of sight and the area appeared safe to move around, we left our hiding place to go and see what they were dropping. We discovered that what they had been dropping were sandwiches wrapped in brown paper. We picked up a couple of the sandwiches and went back to our hiding place to have our first food in Belgium.

We then went down to the edge of the woods where we saw a farmer plowing his field. As he got near where we were hiding, I stepped out of the woods and asked him our location. I'm afraid my combination of high school French and English did not work as he waved his arms about and shouted what sounded like "les allemands" and turned around and went away. It wasn't until weeks later that I found he telling us that the Germans were in the area.

As it started to get dark, we headed out of the woods in a southwest direction. We soon came upon a paved two-lane road heading in the same general direction. We decided to walk on the road since it was easier, and we could always jump into the woods if necessary.

As we continued walking, the woods started to thin out and were replaced by farmland. As it began to get light, we went off the road and found a haystack into which we crawled to get some sleep.

Later in the morning we walked across the field to the farmhouse and knocked on the door. When the farmer answered the door, he knew that we were American airmen. He invited us in to meet his family and to sit down and eat. His wife found some clothes for us to wear and a pair of shoes for me. After eating they gave us a road map and pointed out that we were south of Liege. The wife gave me something for my burns and a piece of cloth to wrap around my swollen ankle. They both appeared nervous and anxious for us to leave. We took the road map, our escape kit, and hit the road for France.

We felt safe in our farm clothes and decided to walk on the road during the day. The next afternoon after walking through a small town, a boy on a bike went by whistling the French national anthem and dropped a bag of food. We held on to the food until we came to a small stream where we stopped and ate our lunch and drank some water. It was almost sundown so we agreed to stay there until morning.

The next morning we started out and two days later we found ourselves nearing the border. It was here we had our first encounter with the Germans. As we were walking through a small town near the border, we turned a corner and came face-to-face with a group of German soldiers marching through the town in the middle of the street. Pete and I were both smoking cigars when we saw them and by the time they had marched by, we had chewed the cigars down to the last two inches. We walked to the end of town and out in to a field overlooking a woods where we had a good laugh and a sigh of relief. By now we were hungry, so we headed for a house at the edge of the woods.

It was at this house that we made our first mistake. We did not notice, at first, the telephone lines into the house. We knocked on the door and a well-dressed, middle-aged woman answered the door. We explained, in our French-English, that we were hungry and would like some food. She instructed us, in English, to wait and she would bring some food. I had a funny feeling about her and looked and saw the wires and told Pete I felt we should get the hell out of there. We ran into the woods in a due west direction. Maybe it was imagination, but we both swear we heard dogs. After we had run for a long time we suddenly came out onto a field overlooking a river. On a path running beside the river was a girl leading a herd of cows. She looked up as we came running down the hill and motioned for us to get among the cows. As we edged our way in among the cows she continued to move them along towards a town at a bend in the river. When we reached the town she took us to a house where we were given a glass of wine and told to wait. In a few minutes a woman appeared and told us not to worry we were among friends.

We had dinner and some wine before climbing into the most comfortable bed ever created. The next morning after breakfast, we met two men who told us it was too dangerous for us to stay there and we would be moved that night. Two different men came that night and took us to a loft where we were placed under armed guard. They told us they were the French Maquis, and they could not help us until our identity was confirmed. The next morning we were taken out to the yard and our pictures were taken.

After about 10 days in the loft under an armed guard, we were awaken one morning by the same two men who had brought us. They told us that we were indeed who we said we were and were now members of the French Maquis. We were taken that night to a bedroom on the second floor of a house in the town. We stayed there for a few days until one night when two different men came and took us back to the woods. We were told that we were going to build a shelter in the side of the hill. The men had axes, shovels and wire with which we were to build this shelter. The next morning we started to build this new home of ours. There Pete, myself, and four Frenchmen were digging into that hill, cutting down and hauling trees and shrubs and not understanding what anybody was saying. It was like something out of a Marx Brothers movie. When finished it contained a bed made out of logs, wire and brush that slept five and could not be seen from 50 feet away.

We were informed that our place was to be operated as an outpost for the main body of the Maquis which was located deeper in the woods. Later, other people were brought in to the camp including an R.A.F. gunner and a British agent. It was here that I was given a code name, "the little man with a pipe", and I.D. card, and a work card. the cards carried the fictitious name of Louis J. Busse, born in Flanders, and worked as a clerk in Liege for the Atlas Construction Company.

We were still here in June when the invasion took place. Soon after that they moved Pete to some place else, and I never saw him again. After Pete left I was moved to the main camp of the Maquis. There was a fire fight with a German Panzer unit that resulted in a large number of casualties to the Maquis. The commander of the Maquis, a French Foreign Legion captain, suggested I leave along with an R.C.A.F. gunner and an American pilot who had just been shot down. We took his advice and headed back in to Belgium.

As we left the woods and got onto a paved road, we noticed a uniformed man on a bicycle headed our way. He stopped and asked for our papers. I handed him mine but the others, not having any, were in deep trouble. Red, the R.C.A.F. man, asked me if he was armed. When I replied "no", Red suggested we the kill the s.o.b. Hearing this, the man quickly let us know that he was a forest ranger, a member of the Belgium Underground and would help us.

He then took us to a farmhouse where I was treated for trenchfoot and scabies by a local doctor. His treatment consisted of rubbing my skin raw with a scrub brush and painting it with some kind of foul smelling lotion. The trenchfoot was taken care of by putting my feet in a bucket of boiling spinach juice. We then were taken to a monk's house where we had another close call.

While we were in the monk's garden, we could see some German soldiers on bikes coming toward the farm. We immediately jumped behind some bushes and aimed our only gun, a 38 revolver, at them. Fortunately they were only after eggs and stayed near the barn and soon left. From there we were split up, with Red going alone and the pilot and I eventually ending up in a burgomaster's house. The pilot was then taken away and I was left with the burgomaster. Soon after I, too, was moved.

My next stop was with a very nice couple and their dog in a town called "Salt Les Spa". I did not spend too much time with them; however, they did give me a new suit of clothes and new shoes.

After that I was moved to a lovely town called Theux near the German border. I stayed with a woman and her nine-year-old son. Her husband had been beaten by the Gestapo in front of her and his son and dragged off to a concentration camp. This woman and boy were two of the bravest people I have ever known. We lived upstairs over the dress shop she owned. The shop was part of a row of shops and homes that butted up against each other. The people next door were also members of the Underground. The door connecting the two houses was sawed in half, like a Dutch door, so that I could escape to the basement next door should it be necessary.

The Germans were carrying stolen loot in cabbage wagons every night to their warehouse at the edge of town. One night two German soldiers stopped and knocked on the door demanding they be let in for the night. As I looked out from the edge of the window, I could see her open the door to the two soldiers. As they stuck their guns in her stomach she put her hands on her hips and defied them. She also was shouting a lot of German and French words that I have no idea what they, were but the meaning was clear enough for the soldiers to leave. I had a gun; however, to use it would have brought every soldier in the town. She came back in, and we each had a glass of cognac.

After I had been there for a while, I awoke one morning to the sound of gunfire and bombs. P-47s were attacking the warehouse and the roads outside of the town. The roar of the tanks could be heard in the distance. There were several loud explosions in and around the town. In the afternoon the sound quieted down, and you could hear the rumble of approaching tanks. It was all over and American tanks were coming down the hill toward the blown up bridge that separated them from the town.

The next morning I said goodbye to all those wonderful people as we toasted each other with wine and whatever else was available. During the six months I had a price on my head: $10,000 or get someone out of a concentration camp. Never once was I turned over to the Germans. God bless them all.

DOWN OVER BLECHAMMER, GERMANY

By T/Sgt. Royce F. Austin
460th Bomb Group, 761st Bomb Sqdn.

After bailing out and evading once before, I had difficulty getting back on flight status. I asked to be sent back to my squadron. I told them I would stow away on a plane if they didn't put me back on crew. I had to go see Colonel Babb. I said that I wasn't caught, and they didn't know that I was over there being as I had escaped. Colonel Babb finally let me go back to a crew upon my discharge from the hospital (I had spent nearly a month in the hospital with a fractured leg as a result of my first bailout over Vienna). I was placed on a crew who had lost their nose gunner on a mission. I flew 31 more missions with my new crew, until our misfortune on a direct hit (oil refineries & marshalling yards) over Blechammer, Germany on December 2, 1944.

We were hit by flak over the target with a direct hit in the bomb bay. The first run over the target looked good but our Wing Commander Colonel Bertrum C. Harrison said, "Not good enough boys," so he had us do another run over the target, (no flak then). When we made a second run, all Hell broke loose. I will never forget Colonel Bertrum C. Harrison (who later made General & Wing Commander of Loring A.F.B., Maine). After taking a direct hit in bomb bay, I was the toggelier and dropped the bomb, right through the bomb bay doors. We had one Propaganda 100# bomb and the rest were 500# bombs.

We got a direct hit in bomb bay into the tanks in the wings. Took out the catwalk, and raw gas was going all over. I asked the pilot what we were going to do and he said, "We're bailing." I got out of nose turret and started throwing armor plating, etc. out the nose wheel door. I broke up the Norden bombsight with my .45cal. automatic. The Engineer Sturbush got down out of the Martin turret. He had flak through his legs and arms. He grabbed a fire extinguisher and put out the fire on the oxygen on flight deck, then he passed out. We hooked a static line onto his rip cord. I was first to go out the nose wheel door after grabbing a first aid kit off the wall and hooking it on my D ring. After I went out I pulled my ring and held onto it, but nothing happened. I threw away the ring and pulled out my pilot chute and reeled out some silk; then it caught. I hadn't seen anyone else come out by that time. When I landed it was around 12:00 noon, and I landed right

by the side of a house with a thatched roof. This time I landed right, and fell over backwards into the fence of this woman's house. I cut about half of my parachute and stuffed it inside my jacket. I gave the woman whose house was there the rest of it and the life jacket. They were starting to feed me but someone came running into the house yelling "Ruska-Ruska." They then acted like they didn't want anything to do with me. There were four horsemen galloping down the other side of the valley (later to find out they were Russian Kosaks). So I took off up a woods road and dug into a hole in the side of a bank. I pulled brush into the entrance and laid there until about 5:00 p.m. At 4:00 p.m. it was dark and I heard shooting and saw a house burning down in the valley where I had come from. (I later found out it was the woman's house where I was. They had found half of the parachute and life jacket).

While dug in I opened the escape kit and cut holes on inside of lining on coveralls and rolled up the $5.00 - $1.00 bills, also the file and compass. Took one of the silk maps and used it for a "Babushka" on my head as I lost my flying helmet on the way down. I waited until about midnight and started in an easterly direction. In the morning before daylight, I got in under the firs and cut some branches and lined a place to sleep, made a mound and covered it with snow. I wrapped up in my parachute and tried to sleep but it was real cold.

My second crew: Pilot, Lt. Beam; Co-Pilot, Lt. Joe Gorskiga (never heard from after bailout in Poland); Navigator, Lt. Bradford; Bombardier, Lt. Castell; Eng. S/Sgt., Homer Sturbush (had reunion with him in 1988, 40 yrs.); Radio, S/Sgt. E. Kelly; Tail-gunner, Sgt. Shepard (deceased); Ball, Sgt. Austin Stubus; Waist-gunner, Sgt. Robert Dmythyshyn (spoke fluent Polish).

I traveled this way for about three days, and then I saw

Royce F. and Imogene Austin with their wedding dress made of his parachute. (Courtesy of Royce F. Austin)

a whole lot of soldiers (approx. 500) looking for me. I found another hole and pulled more brush over me and laid there. The fourth day I came upon a small village about 8:00 a.m. I walked right down the middle of the street toward the church. There was no one in sight. I saw a small kid behind a house and I said to him "Americanski." He disappeared into the house and out came with an old fellow (about 70 years). He spoke some English as he said he worked in the coal mines in Pennsylvania before he got caught in the revolution in Russia. He took me into the house and told me they would prepare a meal as I told him I had not eaten in four days. He spotted the first aid pack on my belt and said that a Polish soldier had been shot four days prior and wanted to know if I was a doctor. I told him "no" but that I had medical aid training. They took me over to the soldier and I looked at the wound. He had been shot in the right chest and it went right through his shoulder. Both sides were black. I told the woman to heat some water and I cleaned the wound, cutting away the black skin. I gave him a morphine shot and had three more left in the kit. I put in sulfanilamide powder and wrapped him in a tight compress. I gave them instructions on how to use the morphine every four hours if he had pain. After I had fixed him up, he sat up in bed and put his arms around me with tears streaming down his cheeks. (I often wonder if he lived; they are tough people). They took me back to where the meal was prepared. Chicken, potatoes, cheese, bread, soup, milk, etc. They also brought in a young girl who could speak seven different languages. They wanted me to marry her and stay there to be the Justice of the Peace (which was the greatest honor of a town). At that moment the door opened and there was a commotion outside and in came six Kosaks with stein-guns. The old man who spoke English told them, "He's Americanski," but they paid no attention to him. They took me prisoner and took me by wagon, by walking and by truck to Premiscel, Poland where they put me in a stockade with Germans although not in with them. I was questioned for six days, and all they got from me was name, rank and serial number. They brought in my navigator, Lt. Bradford, and I jumped up and shook hands with him. They stopped their questions. They moved us to L'Wow, Poland. We stayed there until we were moved to Poltava, Russia. We then traveled to Siberia, Tehran, Iran, Tunis and back to Italy. I was back there in my base on Christmas Day and was first in line and guest with Col. Price that day for Christmas dinner. I was grounded and shipped back to the States in February 1945. Went to Miami, Florida and was sent to Washington, D.C. for interrogation for six days. Part of the parachute that I saved during my first bailout was turned into a wedding dress by my wife, Imogene, on March 18, 1945.

A Veteran's Special Mission

By John F. Barnacle

Everything seemed normal and routine, as 40 U.S. B-24 Liberator Bombers of the 450th "Cottontails" Bomb Group taxied to their respective holding positions near the end of the sloppy and soggy runway at the U.S. airbase in Mandura, Italy, preparing for take-off into a gray sky that cold, dismal morning of March 1944. Heavily defended aircraft assembly installations on Schwechat Airdrome in Vienna, Austria, were the selected target of a well-coordinated 15th Air Force military operation and strategic air strike.

One of the Liberator Bombers of the 450th Group never made it, developing engine problems over northern Yugoslavia, subsequently crashing on a mountain slope near the small village of Sanski Most, Yugoslavia.

Having to turn back from the target, a courageous young pilot, 1st Lt. Reaford C. McCraw of Fayetteville, Arkansas, struggled to control and stabilize the disabled plane in hopes of reaching home base in Italy, while anxiously seeking an alternate emergency landing site.

After ordering the crew to bail out of the stricken aircraft, while he, Lt. McCraw demonstrating near-superhuman strength, wrestled valiantly with the aircraft controls in a frantic and determined effort to stabilize the plane into a reasonably stable altitude, while attempting to keep the plane aloft at a near-level position long enough to allow the crew to safely exit the rapidly falling aircraft.

Despite his gallant, courageous and heroic effort, the plane plunged to earth carrying Lt. McCraw to his untimely death. Lt. R.C. McCraw paid the SUPREME sacrifice - he not only gave up his life defending his country - but he SACRIFICED his own life in order to save his nine other fellow crew members.

Staff Sergeant John F. Barnacle, the ball-turret gunner, was one of the nine airmen who safely exited the aircraft and parachuted to safety, landing in German occupied territory near the small village of Luski-Palanka, Yugoslavia.

After several hours of wandering on the ground, he was found and rescued by Marshal Tito's Partisan soldiers. Barnacle was fed, sheltered, and hidden in their homes, at great risk to themselves and their families. The Partisans also helped him to escape and evade capture by the Germans, taking him through the Underground network to Allied control, and eventually back to Bari, Italy.

Recalling the fateful day of the bailout, Barnacle remembers that his thoughts that day as morning turned into afternoon, were not of being a hero. He was mostly concerned about surviving. Thoughts of safely exiting the disabled aircraft and then escape and survival after reaching the ground, quickly flashed through his mind, as engine after engine on the B-24 sputtered and quit. At Lt. McCraw's instruction, Barnacle and crew bailed out as the stricken plane plummeted across the wispy-clouded sky near Zagreb in north-central Yugoslavia. For the next 48 to 72 hours, he had no idea of the fate or whereabouts of his fellow crew members.

Landing in snow drifts of four to six feet, deep in enemy-occupied territory, Barnacle realized that he could be picked up by Yugoslav Chetniks; he could be found outright by German soldiers who might shoot him on the spot or take him to a prison camp; or he could be found and recused by friendly and loyal Marshal Tito's Partisan forces.

Disabled and hobbled by a groin injury suffered in the jump which hampered movement, Barnacle, in much pain, was unable to move well. He sighted a small village off in the distance, but hesitated to go directly there, fearing certain capture should it be occupied by German troops.

Dispirited and near despair after wandering around for several hours, Barnacle was suddenly startled by the sharp crack of a rifle shot piercing the still, crisp mountain air and shattering the eerie silence, while resounding across the snow-covered slopes and hills; followed immediately by a loud, bombing and commanding voice - with words sounding like HALT or STOP. He instantly froze in his tracks. At the top of a ridge, at a distance of approximately 50 yards, appeared a huge figure of a man, advancing rapidly, but cautiously toward Barnacle, while pointing an unwavering rifle aimed straight at his head.

Barnacle, unarmed and vulnerable, was visibly shaken with trepidation of being shot. Instinctive reflex action, caused by apprehensive fear, prompted the instant uplifting of his arms, fully extended, as a signal of surrender, while his quivering body was tensed and ready to absorb the impact of a rifle bullet, should it be forthcoming. As the soldier neared closer, Barnacle was soon able to recognize the large red star on his titofka (Partisan cap). Barnacle was greatly relieved to learn that a Tito Partisan - a peasant farmer named Duro Novakovic, had found and recused him.

Novakovic took him to his two-room farmhouse in the village of Luski-Palanka, where he was fed, hidden and allowed to rest to recuperate from the groin injury. He shared a bed with the three minor children, two boys and a girl, sleeping in the same room with the entire family. Barnacle eventually was reunited with the surviving members of his crew several days later in the nearby village of Sanski Most.

The wreckage of the plane was found by Partisans and they recovered the pilot's body. The Partisans built a crude wooden coffin, and with their assistance, the crew members buried Lt. McCraw's body near the crash site. (Lt. McCraw's remains have long since been removed to a U.S. military cemetery in Italy, near Anzio. Over the years parts of the plane were stripped and used by Partisans, but a section of the wing was saved and later erected as a memorial/monument at the location of Lt. McCraw's former grave site near the plane's wreckage).

Guided by a young Yugoslav Partisan, a Captain Dan led the small group of airmen over deep snowy trails and narrow muddy roads, mostly at night as the area was surrounded by German troops and to avoid being strafed by German aircraft during daily sorties over the area. The group walked over 50 miles, walking at times in a zig-zag route, two-abreast in loose close-order formation, but frequently having to change to single file as terrain or circumstance dictated.

Tired, weary, hungry, suffering pain and discomfort and numbed by the bitter cold temperatures and frost-bite, the group arrived in the village of Petrovac, stopping at a house for food, medical attention and much needed rest. They learned that the house was a British mission, manned by a small contingent of British soldiers equipped with a short-wave radio that could make contact with Allied and U.S. forces in Bari, Italy.

The Yugoslav officer, Capt. Dan, was ordered to deliver the men to Marshal Tito's secret headquarters in a hidden cave in the mountains near Drvar. As the group prepared to leave, the British Army major, commanding officer of the mission, "pulled rank" and would not let them leave the mission. They had no choice but to follow orders given by a superior Allied officer.

After 21 days, many false alarms and aborted rescue attempts by U.S. and Allied forces, they were finally picked up and evacuated by a C-47 aircraft sent in under the cover of darkness. Intermittent gunfire was coming from German troops located in surrounding hills directed at incoming and outbound C-47 aircraft.

The experience and ordeal lasted 30 days, but stayed with Barnacle for a lifetime.

For 45 years, the retired Redstone Arsenal worker has thought many times about that mission and his harrowing experience, and contemplated yet another mission to Europe to return to Yugoslavia to find and THANK his rescuers.

With the help of Steve Galembush, an OSS/Navy veteran who had volunteered to parachute into Yugoslavia in 1944 to assist downed U.S. airmen, and who later lived and worked with the Partisans, and Mischko "Misa" Mirkovic, who was orphaned by the war and joined Tito's Partisans at 12 and later became a movie actor and Director of Belgrade TV and Radio, Barnacle received an official invitation from the U.S. Embassy in Belgrade, Yugoslavia to return for a visit. He and Steve left on September 16, 1989 to spend a week in Yugoslavia, visiting officials and dignitaries, Yugoslav (SUBNOR) war veterans, and the people in the villages where he had been in 1944. He also had the opportunity to visit the House of Flowers, located on the late President Tito's estate where Tito is buried, to lay a memorial wreath on the late president's tomb and to deliver a message of THANKS to the Yugoslav Partisans inscribed in a large memorial book kept in the anteroom of the House of Flowers. A memorial wreath was also placed at a Yugoslav War Memorial at Jasenovac, in memorium of all Partisan Freedom Fighters killed during the war.

SHOT DOWN OVER OCCUPIED FRANCE! THE STORY OF EUGENE BENNETT

Flying conditions were horrible on the morning of June 7, 1944, the day after D-Day, when Allied troops stormed the beaches of Normandy. Second Lt. Eugene Bennett of the 56th Fighter Group of the 62nd Fighter Squadron, 8th Air Force and the others in his P-47 Thunderbolt group didn't go out on D-Day. They left at 4:30 a.m. the next morning, loaded with frag bombs. It was dark, rainy, and miserable.

The primary mission of P-47 pilots assigned to the 62nd Squadron was to accompany B-17 Bombers on sorties out of England with targets in Germany, France and Holland.

Their mission that day was to hit German light bombers that had moved onto an airfield near Bernay, France. Because of the heavy cloud cover, Bennett and his fellow pilots couldn't find the target. The group pressed on, however, looking for "targets of opportunity." As they dropped to about 10,000 feet they spotted a convoy of

German tanks near Bazoches toward the Normandy front. As Bennett dropped down to make a pass, the tanks opened fire and his plane was hit. The oil lines were cut and the engine was on fire. Smoke engulfed the cockpit, ruling out any chance of trying to crash-land the plane. Bailout was the only option, a dangerous option, however, especially at such a low altitude.

Bennett used his dive bomb air speed to pull the plane up to a greater altitude. When the plane stalled he kicked the right rudder and slid open the P-47's razorback canopy. Bennett dove towards the wing in hopes of avoiding it and dropped between it and the tail. The Thunderbolt crashed and burned on a field between him and the German tanks. Bennett parachuted safely and hit the ground running.

Wet, discouraged and scared, the young pilot, a veteran of 29 combat missions, quickly hid his equipment and found cover in a haystack. It was 7:30 in the morning and he felt very much alone as he watched his fellow pilots turn and head back to England.

After a few hours in the haystack, Bennett approached a French farmhouse, but as he crouched behind cover to check it out he saw a steady flow of German trucks passing by and realized it was a German army moterpool depot. He hid behind some hedges until he saw a young Frenchman approaching on a bicycle. The young American spoke no French but managed to communicate and hitch a ride on the handlebars. After about two miles, at an intersection, the Frenchman pointed to a dirt road and Bennett started walking.

He walked three or four miles, jumping for cover from time to time to avoid being seen. He came to another intersection. In the center stood a statue of St. Christopher. It was 4 p.m. The pilot was tired and hungry. He sat down at the statue. He was disgusted and lost.

Just then a man and a boy pushed their bicycles through the intersection. Bennett tried to communicate with them, but they wanted no part of him and kept moving, out of sight. There was a loud whistle and the man came back and motioned for the pilot to come quickly. They walked together to a house in a nearby village where he had his first food.

Others came in excitedly and told him he would have to leave. They took him to an orchard out back and gave him a quilt for cover as it was raining. That night they came with more food. During the night Bennett could hear the constant coming and going of trucks. It was a German army motorpool.

The next morning another Frenchman took him to another farm where he was given shelter in an isolated smokehouse. If caught in the smokehouse, it would not have implicated and endangered his helpers. The French helpers brought him food and wine under the cover of darkness.

On June 11th, another Frenchman, a member of the Resistance, came with civilian clothes and a bicycle for Bennett. His name was Dick Chadburn and he spoke English.

Chadburn had helped other downed American pilots and he advised Bennett to act deaf and dumb if they encountered Germans. They rode the bikes to the LePortier family farm in the village of Courteilles, Putanges. The young pilot, being a farm boy, himself from Pennsylvania, adapted quickly to life on the farm. He stayed and worked there for three weeks, but the ruse was exposed one day when a German Gestapo stopped by the farm for fresh eggs. He realized Bennett was not French and rushed to the house screaming at the LePortiers. Bennett hid under the porch. The Germans did not find him, but vowed to return.

He hid out for a few hours in a cornfield then biked with another Resistance member to the Le Metz farm, 20 kilometers south near Ranes. Here he was taken in by the Buffons.

Le Metz served as a local headquarters for the Resistance. Ammunition, machine guns, radio equipment, etc. were dropped at night by British Lancaster Bombers, guided to the farm by red flashlights. With the supplies, Bennett and the others would make mines to blow up trucks and bridges.

On August first, Rene and Jean Buffon awoke him and told him to get moving, the Germans had discovered who they were and what they were doing. The trio took off, pursued by Germans and their dogs. After running for two days they stopped at a Resistance member's home. The Buffons

George F. Bennett

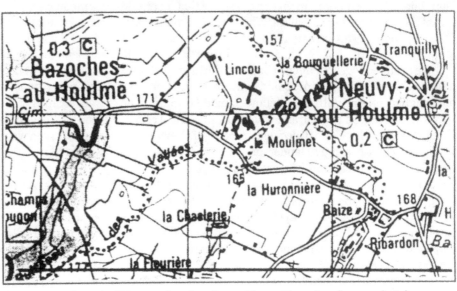

This map of Occupied France pinpoints Bennett's position when he was shot down.

were worried about their family back at the farmhouse so they backtracked to Le Metz. A white towel on a stone fence warned Bennett that Germans were close by so he hid in a field behind the house. Later he was moved to the next village.

Jeannette Buffon was tortured by the Germans and Mr. and Mrs. Georges Buffon had been interrogated. Their barn was burned.

During his stay at Le Metz, another American pilot was shot down and rescued. Originally placed in different locations, the two pilots were reunited the first week of August by the Resistance. They were taken out of Le Metz to a shelter they built out of wheat sheaves. They came out of hiding when Patton's Third Army tanks rumbled by on the way to Paris, August 6.

The two pilots were flown back to England and debriefed. Bennett returned to the U.S. in October of 1944 and became a flight instructor to young French pilots learning to fly the P-47 in combat.

FROM THE DIARY OF BOB BLAKENEY FOGGIA MISSION—16 AUGUST 1943

By Robert W. Blakeney

Bob Blakeney and his crew crash landed on a beach in Reggio Calabria, Italy on August 16, 1943. They were returning from a mission over Foggia. Five crew members survived the crash - Lt. Carl S. Hagar, S/Sgt. Henry R. Farley, S/Sgt. "Rene" Dones; S/Sgt. John M. Hess and S/Sgt. Bob Blakeney. Lt. Hagar was badly burned and Sgts. Hess and Farley were bleeding from head wounds and many cuts. Italian soldiers picked them up and held them as prisoners. Blakeney and the rest of his group were sent through many towns in Italy, experiencing vicious treatment and starvation until they reached Sulmona prison camp. They remained there until their escape in October. Following is an account of their escape.

One day in October, it appeared that there weren't too many guards on the corners of the wall, and somehow, the gate did not appear to be closed. About late afternoon, maybe early evening, all 16 to 18 of us wandered toward the gate. We flung it open and all raced to some nearby woods and then up the side of the mountain. While we were running up the side of that mountain east of the camp, we heard gunfire. Whether it was aimed at us or perhaps others who were trying to escape out the gate, I don't know. We were all too busy breaking the mile record going uphill.

We grouped together at one point and decided we'd have a better chance if we split into pairs, or into threes. There was one English soldier with us, a fellow named Graham, who was from Lowell, as I recall, and who had joined the Army in Canada. John Hess and I decided to pair off. Farley and Dones went with a Sgt. Henderson (or Glenn Hickerson) from Texas. The rest split into small units, as well.

By this time it was getting or was dark. John and I kept going to the top of the mountain where the woods were thick. We kept moving most of the night and slept little. By the next morning, we were hungry as we had taken no food with us. But we wanted to stay in the mountains for better cover and we did so the rest of the day.

That evening, I remember, we were so hungry that when we came upon a farm area, we dug out some potatoes and ate them raw. We also took some tomatoes and ate them. We had no matches to start a fire, but we didn't want to light one anyhow. We had raw potatoes for three to four days and some tomatoes. Later on, when we came onto some fig trees, we ate many figs. Unfortunately, diarrhea followed.

It is difficult now to remember the days thereafter, but primarily figs and tomatoes were our diet. Both of us were sick once each, so we had to stop and hole up for 24 hours or so. We never saw any of our group again.

One night, we were so hungry, we approached a farm house. We had been out about six or seven days by this time. I remember talking in French to the Italian at the house and getting some bread. We decided not to sleep in his barn, but rather, in the pile of hay (with mosquitoes) in the field. John woke me later during the night, told me that he saw the Italian leave the house and seemed to head toward the village. John figured he was going to turn us in, so we got up and ran again for as long as we could.

Our compass was the sun. Although we heard rumors in the prison camp that the Allies had invaded north of Rome and from the east coast to Italy, we felt our best bet was to head south as directly as possible. Although we did most of our walking during the dark, we marked some area as south during the day, and we did our best to go that way in the dark.

Both of us had bad diarrhea a few times. We lost considerable weight as well. We lived mostly on the figs, tomatoes and water.

One evening, we stopped at another farm house. There was only a man and his wife there, both seemed to be in their 50s or early 60s, so we felt safe. We watched the house for a while, but because we were so hungry, we approached it. I again spoke to them in French. They gave us some hot goat's milk cheese. It was delicious. They gave us some bread, as well. Also, we took some bread with us for the next day. They seemed like nice people, but we did not dare too stay long. We kept going.

Every night we slept on the ground or in some rocky areas. We stayed up in the mountains as best we could. We did very little walking in daylight to avoid being seen.

Finally, we reached a town near Campobasso. It was named Ilesi. The first night we made our observations near a farm house. We saw considerable German troop movement at night, by truck. They were going up a road toward Campobasso. We tried to count the trucks, but couldn't get close enough to see or to count the troops in those trucks.

Outside the town of Ielsi was a farmhouse. An old Italian farmer appeared to live there, so when he was alone in the field working, we went up to him. He spoke a little broken English and understood what we were saying to him. We did not tell him we were escaped prisoners; however, we only told him that we had been shot down. He told us he had a son in Chicago and last he heard, his son was in the American Army. We knew this farmer only as "Sam".

We were so hungry and tired, and he seemed so sincere, that we stayed close by, but in the woods, for three days. His wife was afraid the Germans would find us in the house, but she still baked bread for us, and even gave us chicken once. We also got back to the macaroni - all of it was great. I think we had some more goat's milk cheese there, and again it was great. This family, as well as a few of their neighbors next door, were very good to John and me.

Come the day we had to leave, John and I felt better with some solid food in us. We knew the Germans were doing considerable moving and we heard exchanges of artillery every now and then, so we knew our lines had to be close by. We told Sam we were going and he insisted that his nephew (or son - I don't recall) would show us the way to the front lines. This guy had been in the Italian Army but had come home while we were there. He wore a sidearm.

We started out after we had seen a German patrol of about six to eight soldiers several hundred yards away. We now foolishly had civilian clothes on. We were sitting on a hill with this guy when suddenly we heard artillery booming ahead of us and behind us. We apparently were in the middle of a battle. It seemed that the shells raining down were getting closer to us. I turned to our hero guy who was going to show us the Allied lines, but he was running back toward the house! John and I came close to laughing.

We then moved forward, toward where we figured our guns were. We stopped at a farmhouse, again an elderly man and his wife, and we asked for some water. But as she was giving us water, she spotted a German patrol and unfortunately, she screamed "Tedeschi".

We looked, saw, and ran like Hell. But we heard no gunfire. Nevertheless, we put plenty of distance from that place before we stopped to rest. We were now on a hillside with a wide open field in front of us and woods beyond that field. We hesitated, thinking this field had to be mined, but we knew we HAD to cross it.

I took out the prayer book and read a prayer to the Blessed Mother. I then gave the book to John, told him to read the same prayer. This he did even though he was not a religious person.

We then ran as fast as we could across that open field - about 100-200 yards wide - no gunfire, no mines. When we reached the woods, we rested. There were empty cans of food with German markings scattered about, but we touched nothing. We kept going through the woods and in the distance, saw another farmhouse. I peeked around the corner of that house while John stayed back in the woods. I saw guns, but just the heads of some soldiers minus their helmets. I went back to tell John, and to work out our next action.

For awhile, we did nothing, waited until the elderly Italian lady came to the back of the house for reasons unknown. We quietly asked her who the soldiers were. Again, my French came in handy and I learned from her that the soldiers were CANADIANS!

I had John stay in the woods because he had real blond hair. With the name of "Hess", he'd surely be mistaken for a German before I would.

I walked back with the woman and shouted out, "Je suis American". And I kept yelling it.

One of the soldiers answered back in English, so I explained we were escaped prisoners, my buddy was back in the woods. Then John came out and I recall one of the Canadians remarking it was a good thing John did not come out first!

We were now safe. We made it to the Canadian 5th Army. Shortly thereafter, we talked with Major John MacDonald, Canadian Army, but who lived in Hartford, Connecticut. And we stayed with them for three days and nights, giving them all the information we had about German movements and locations.

Next, we were given a ride back to American Headquarters. Ironically, it was back to Foggia, where we had bombed when we were shot down. The ride back was on a motorcycle - the first and only time I've ever been on a motorcycle.

After briefing and interrogation by American officers, we were told that several other prisoners had made it back to Foggia a few days before us. We were clothed and fed - good to be back in uniform again. Then we were taken to the Foggia Airport where we boarded a C-47, I think, and were flown back to Tunis. We asked the pilot if he could fly over Reggio Calabria where our plane went down. He did! We saw only the tail section left of our plane. The rest had been burned to ashes.

This was the end of our story from 16 August 1943 to sometime in the October-November period of 1943. We were given a 20 day leave in London and were decorated by General Eaker. I got home in time for Christmas, 1943.

NIGHT INTRUDER BOMBER CREW
By Eugene B. Boward

Near midnight on 11 November 1944, I collected my flight gear for my 51st and last A-20 Havoc Bombing mission. This was to be a night intruder attack on the last remaining bridge over the Po River in northern Italy. I was with the 86th Squadron, 47th Bomb Group, 12th Air Force. Ours was the only American unit engaged in these single-aircraft night attacks on German convoys, troops, guns, airfields, etc. My previous night missions had ranged from pure "milk runs" to insane nighttime low-level raids.

That night I would fly for the first time with a close friend, S/Sgt. Schultz (top turret gunner) and his pilot, Lt. Wright, with Lt. Dowdell as bombardier-navigator.

Take-off was routine and we climbed on-course toward our assigned target area. There was little ground activity as we crossed the "front lines". Two 40mm guns (German and American) were dueling with tracer ammunition. The German gun ignored us; however, a short time later we took light, but accurate, flak and I was certain our A-20 was hit, though there was no evidence of damage.

Later, as we neared the northern end of the Apennine Mountains, I again heard our plane take a hit, but this time there were no tracers or exploding flak. None of our crew reported any flak. I was uneasy as I mentally pictured a Luftwaffe Night-Fighter hanging back in our blind-spot and lobbing 20mm ball ammunition our way, with no visible evidence that it was there. Unlikely, but...?

I was looking over my 50-caliber Browning toward the pitch-dark mountains below when Lt. Dowdell reported excitedly that we were losing altitude rapidly. The pilot, Lt. Wright, confirmed this and stated he could not hold altitude, even with wide-open throttle.

As a precaution, I began pulling my machine gun from the escape hatch to stow it against the side of the aircraft just as Lt. Dowdell salvoed our bombs. The gun's storage latch did not function and the gun fell back downward on three attempts before finally remaining latched. I was shaken because Schultz and I could not get out the hatch with that gun in place. Just as I completed my task, Lt. Dowdell came over the intercom with "Bail out! Bail out!" and the plane rolled violently.

Glancing backward I saw Schultz's turret seat drop and I rolled forward and out into the darkness, pulling my rip-cord immediately. I fell down through a tree for the easiest landing imaginable. My knees never bent, but I did land in a small, cold, stream.

Schultz and Dowdell landed hard in open areas and both sustained some back or leg injury. We three (Lt. Wright was killed) got together within two days with a British major who was stationed behind the lines for liaison with the Italian Partisans. The major arranged for us to live-in with an Italian family. Later he sent a message to us to prepare to walk back through the German-held territory and front lines on November 19th-20th.

We had a grueling 30-hour walk over partially snow-covered Apennines with a large group of Partisans, plus three other American airmen, two escaped P.O.W.s (American and New Zealander), and six or eight German G.I.s who also wanted to be on the Allied side of the front lines. During that time we were twice involved with German patrols. Before the first patrol could catch us, a German (Austrian) captain, now with the Partisans, invited our German pursuers into a wine shop and got them all drunk. The next patrol, encountered just as we were passing through the front lines, shot-up our group, but none of the Allied or German G.I.s were hit.

During this last patrol encounter I (who was in full American uniform) was asked by Partisans to walk in front of our group so that our own U.S. troops would not shoot us up by mistaking us for the enemy. With the exception of Lt. Gianechi and me, all of our big group went around behind the mountain ridge to escape the German rifle-fire, consequently, we two found ourselves way out in front and all alone. Lt. Gianechi, (escaped P.O.W.) asked me to accompany him in an attempt to contact our American troops. So we proceeded, and without further trouble made contact with the 92nd Infantry Division around 1330 on November 20th. We asked the Infantry commander at the nearest command post to alert his troops for arrival of a large group of armed, but friendly, Partisans, evadees and others. They arrived OK about an hour or two later.

Lt. Dowdell, S/Sgt. Schultz and I completed our evasion in less than nine days. We rejoined our squadron and were sent home around Christmas, 1944. The memo below was given to us before we were sent home:

Department of Army Memo
Restricted
Heaquarters
Army Air Forces Personnel Distribution Command

Subject: Security of Military Information   1 September 1944

To: All AAF Personnel Returning from Theaters

1. The Commanding General, AAF, has directed that the following information be disseminated to you immediately upon your return from theaters:

   a. While in this country it will be easy for you to talk indiscriminately about your recent experiences and thereby be responsible for the enemy's getting a better shot at your friends and comrades who are still in the thick of things.

   b. It will be natural for you to want to talk to your family and friends about your experiences and for them to urge you to do so. It will also be natural for the enemy agent to pick up all the information he can from your talk.

   c. Some of our units have already been ripped apart because the enemy intelligence has been able to put our plans together from small bits of information. This information was given out, in conversations such as you will be tempted to have, by military personnel like yourselves, who did not realize they were disclosing information of importance. The enemy is as greatly benefited by information disclosed by you as he is by information disclosed by one who is an enemy.

   d. However, it is possible to talk in general terms about the "show" you have been through, without giving aid to the enemy. To do this your talk must be confined to:

   (1) General description of the countries you have been in.
   (2) Discussion of the peoples of those countries, their customs, habits, etc.

   But remember that this is for conversation only. Any of this information, if to be used for a press release or newspaper story or over the radio, must be cleared through Public Relations. (If you are a returned escapee, evadee, or internee, even clearance through Public Relations will not protect you in the event of any violation of security. All returned escapees, evadees, and internees are reminded of their special instructions in this connection).

   e. *YOU MUST NOT*, under any circumstances, give information to anyone -wife, parent or friend, which would:

   (1) disclose the number of troops in the area from which you have come, or their disposition or equipment;
   (2) disclose the size or type ships of the convoy or its escort which accompanied you, or its route;
   (3) indicate the facilities, present or in construction at ports, cities, or camps in which you have been;
   (4) disclose new equipment being used in the field;
   (5) disclose the tactics being employed or your idea concerning what future tactics will be or should be employed;
   (6) indicate the geographic locations of APO numbers;
   (7) disclose the designations of units in the field.

   f. *DO NOT ENGAGE* in political or other discussions concerning our Allies. Remember that the Russians and the English stemmed the Axis tide before we entered the war, and they and the French and others are our **Allies**. *DO NOT* start criticisms of our friends.

   g. An alert, persistent and capable enemy intelligence system exits. No bit of information is too small for its use. Your loyal friends will understand, if, when they question you, you say "I can't talk about the details of that show yet". Their sons and brothers will be safer as a result, and you will be fulfilling your continuing obligation to the men you have left behind.

By command of Major General Harmon:

A TRUE COPY:

Henry M. Bailey
Colonel, Air Corps
Chief of Staff
Herbert Henderson
Captain, AC

Night Intruder Bomber Crew. (Courtesy of E. B. Boward)

Broadcast:
From the BBC London, England
Recorded By "War Report" 27.1.45

SS MEN AND FORTRESS CREW

Cue Material: This is the story of the crew of *Little Joe Junior*, a Fortress which developed engine trouble when bombing Hanau. First one engine began to throw oil, which slowed the whole plan up and just after she reached the target area, flak hits put another engine out of action. The Fort managed to bomb its target successfully and then turned for home, badly slowed down and losing height; the bomb bay doors were jammed in the open position and one oxygen system was leaking, but the pilot was determined to make for friendly territory.

This is the story of the co-pilot, 2nd Lt. Herbert Drumheller of Pottstown, PA, the ball gunner, Staff Sergeant Nicholas J. Peters of Wyandotte, MI, and the tail gunner, Staff Sergeant Clarence W. Gieck of Long Beach, CA, all members of the 8th U.S. Air Force.

Peters: We were limping for home and for quite a time everything was quiet - there was no flak and no sign of Jerry fighters, but suddenly our No. 2 engine started vibrating badly and the vibrations shook the whole ship. The pilot tried to throw the prop off by making a series of violent maneuvers, but then flak started picking us up and the pilot gave the order to prepare bail out. In spite of all this our pilot remained perfectly cool and very alert; his evasive action was perfect. He'd fly along until he thought the enemy had got the range and fired, and then he'd turn to another course, and sure enough, the flak would burst just where we'd been. He did this over and over again; if it hadn't been for his skill

we'd have been blown out of the sky. Finally they were putting up such a barrage that evasive action was too risky, so we got the order to bail out. The flak was very heavy now, and one of our other engines was reported by the waist gunner to be on fire. We were now pretty low, in fact about 11,000 feet, and we were being fired at by 20mm cannon as well as the heavy stuff. The first three men bailed out; then I jumped out the waist door and at the same time Gieck, the tail gunner, went out the tail door. Gieck, you got down before me, you tell them about that drop.

Gieck: For the first two minutes we were shot at by small arms fire and 20mm. Sitting in our chutes and looking down we could see little red sparks and white puffs below us, it sounded like popcorn. We could see the three boys who'd jumped before us high above in the sky, still coming down, but they were going to come down too far behind the German lines. We were glad to see the rest of the crew had now bailed out of the plane.

The co-pilot hit the ground first and due to the jar he got he couldn't get up until I had landed, got out of my chute and gone over to him. He was still lying there dazed. Then Pete landed and when Herbie, the co-pilot, had recovered, we three went into a huddle. We weren't sure where we had come down, we only knew the general direction of our lines. I had a small compass so we set out in that direction, walking west and hoping for the best. Suddenly from a thicket nearby we heard a voice call "Americanish", and that stopped us up very short! At first we thought we had run up against some French but when they called us towards them we saw they were Germans. There were two of them, one had a rifle and the other a pistol. Pete, you understand German, what did they say?

Peters: The younger German called out "Come on down here". We hesitated, but finally seeing that they weren't pointing their guns at us we went down into the thicket. One of them told me he was wounded in the left leg, so I bandaged it up for him. They hadn't had any water but they offered us bread and cigarettes. They told me that they had been in the thicket for three days, and we found out afterwards that they were SS men. I asked one if he knew where our lines were, and he pointed in the direction we'd been heading. "Are you sure?" I asked. "Well that's where the bullet that hit me came from," he replied.

I suggested we all try and make for the American lines, but they wanted to wait until after dark as they said the American boys over there were pretty trigger happy. They told us that the Americans knew they were in the thicket and when I heard that I said "Look here, we're going to get going now, if you want to you can come along with us." Gieck said we ought to have something to show we're friendly, so the Germans produced a big white sheet and Gieck tied this on a long stick, and so we all set off.

We made a pretty queer sort of party. We plodded through the snow, Indian file. I was first with the banner, then a German, then Herbie, then the second German and finally Gieck here. It wasn't too pleasant, all the time we could hear machine gun fire and shells were going over our heads in all directions. We spotted a town and made towards it hoping it was in friendly hands. Just as we were on the outskirts, we saw two Germans standing on the step of a house watching us, near the house was a German command car. We took all this in and did some fast thinking and trying not to show our desire to make a quick get-away, we skirted round the town. When we last saw the Germans, they'd turned and gone into the house. Obviously they had seen the Germans with us still carrying their weapons and not unnaturally thought we were being brought into town under armed escort. Lady Luck was with us! This was no place for us so we got out of town as fast as possible. Gieck took the lead now and he led us down the railroad track.

Gieck: We'd gone about three quarters of a mile down the track when we saw a G.I. helmet pop out of a hole and a very welcome American voice say "Drop the banner". We had walked in to one of our own patrols, and soon they guided us back to our own lines.

ESCAPE STORY OF FORREST S. CLARK

I was shot down on bombing mission to Lechfeld, Germany, 13 April 1944. We were just able to reach Swiss territory and I was interned with my crew in Adelboden and Wengen.

In mid-December 1944 I made a contact in Zurich who said he could get us to the U.S. Legation in Berne, and we could escape.

It was late December 1944 when we were taken to the border of France, and by arrangement with the French Underground guides, we walked over the mountains, across the border and barbed wire and eventually into France where we went to a pre-arranged meeting in a farmhouse.

We walked the next day toward Annecy, France. There was much sniping and some enemy holdouts in the area. There was still fighting and we skirted around the major battle, the Battle of the Bulge, that was raging up north.

We made an end run around these battles and managed to reach Annecy and then Lyons, France just before Christmas 1944. It was quite a Christmas celebration when we finally linked up with U.S. forces in France.

There were POWs and internees in our group. I was in

44th Bomb Group, 8th Air Force, as a radio-operator gunner, T/Sgt. I returned to the U.S. in January 1945.

LUCKY PARACHUTE SAVES AIRMAN'S LIFE
THE JACK CLIFFORD STORY

Lt. Jack Clifford was a veteran of 97 bombing missions in 13 months as navigator of a B-24 bomber in China when on his last bombing flight in May ended in bailout. (Clifford also was forced to bail out on his very first mission in China).

The crew had just strafed a convoy from a height of only 200 feet in the South China seas when his aircraft was severely damaged. A big hole was torn in the "Frendlim" and there were other holes in the wings. One crew member was badly wounded. All jumped out at about 6,000 feet over the top of a mountain in the dark.

Clifford was wearing "lucky" parachute number 13. The chute not only delivered him safely to the ground, it kept him warm during the first night after bailout. After landing, the only thing to do was to sleep in the open and it started raining. Clifford used his silk parachute for cover. His mother, Mrs. Paul C. Clifford of the Chicago area, believed the chute saved her son's life twice: during the landing and from pneumonia and sure death from exposure. The lieutenant brought the parachute home as a charmed souvenir of the war.

Although his crew was scattered over several miles, Clifford said they were reunited in a few days. The downed crew was reported as missing in action for about three weeks. During those weeks, they were making their way to their air base 300 air miles away, (twice as far by primitive trails).

The men were aided by friendly Chinese who fed them and gave them what clothes they could. In one village, kindly Chinese gave them a 14-course dinner as Chinese girls would wipe their faces with perfumed towels from time to time. The Chinese were very happy to see American soldiers and would often shoot firecrackers for the occasion.

TWENTY-FIVE YEARS AFTER . . . AN AMERICAN AVIATOR FINDS AGAIN IN VICHERES, THE BRACELET THAT HIS FIANCEE OFFERED TO HIM

(from a French newspaper)

Editorial note: In the interest of historical preservation, this article was typeset exactly as submitted. It retains the influences and perceptions of the original article that appeared at first printing.

It was June 7, 1944, an American fighter, which just flew over Nogent le Rotrou, was crashed by the German anti-aircraft over Vicheres. Fortunately, the pilot, though he was very much wounded, still could creep along and he had found a shelter to Mr. and Mrs. Marcel Rousseau's farm in the place named Touchebreau.

Wreckage of Couture Plane

Pictured here is the wreckage of the plane in which Lt. Robert Couture crashed in France June 7, 1944, D Day plus one. The picture was sent to Mr. and Mrs. Wm. Couture, Rice Lake, by the priest who befriended Lt. Couture while the local pilot was a guest of the French underground for three months.

In the farm a rejoicing was prepared, for the Rousseau's daughter was about to have her communion at the end of the week, and this was on Tuesday night. Mrs. Rousseau's plans were changed; there was no hesitation at all from Mr. and Mrs. Rousseau, what first had to be done was to save this soldier, at first by helping him and by hiding him.

The searches of the enemy began at once. The German soldiers questioned everybody in the neighborhood. Nobody had seen anything; nobody had heard anything. The priest of the village, Father Echard, said that he knew nothing about this trouble, though he was quite familiar with it. Each farm in the surroundings was searched, but Touchebreau.

He was looked after some days in the farm, his health grew better and after a moment, the pilot Robert Couture (his grandfather was a Canadian whose origin was French) was led to finish his healing to the house of another inhabitant of this region, Mrs. Houpillard, at the Point du Jour...there, he was nursed very carefully, and he was soon ready to join the "Maquis" of Freteval, which was not very far from Cloyes, but in the Loir et Cher, where he had to wait for the arrival of the General Patton's armies of the Liberation.

A travel organized in the States, for the persons in the situation of this pilot who are indebt to their French friends, permitted Mr. Couture to come, with his wife, and to visit the spot.

First he had met in St. Germain Mr. Lochouarn, who was also a young boy at the moment when Couture was in Freteval, and who had offered to him a photograph of his communion on which he had written his address. From there he came on Tuesday to visit his friends in this province of France. How moved they were and how great the joy was, when he saw Mr. and Mrs. Rousseau and the "little" Bernadette who is now Mrs. Houvet and has two children.

This meeting was a great entertainment in Touchebreau, where Father Echard and Mr. and Mrs. Houpillard were gathered with the Rousseau and Houvet families.

They visited the surroundings, they took photographs . . . the program included the traditional exchange of memories as well.

Among these souvenirs, one moved especially Mr. and Mrs. Couture; it was when Mr. Rousseau gave him the

From left, Mrs. and Mr. Rousseau, Father Echard, Bernadette Houvet, Couture, Percy, Dominque, Mr. Houvet and Philippe.

bracelet that Mrs. Priscilla Couture had offered to the young aviator before his departure, as they were engaged. The pilot had lost it in his terrible fall and Mr. Rousseau had discovered it and had kept it, waiting for the occasion to give it back to its owner.

This happy day brought a lot of joy as much in the hearts of our sympathetic fellow-country men as for their friends who live beyond the Atlantic. *Submitted by Robert Couture*

CAPTAIN HOWARD CURRAN—EVADEE: SEPTEMBER 12-18, 1944

510th Fighter Squadron, 405th Fighter Group

On September 12, 1944 the 510th Fighter Squadron, 405th Fighter Group, 9th Air Force was stationed at airfield A-64 near St. Dizier, France, which is 200 km/120 miles east of Paris.

On the morning of September 12, 1944 Captain Howard Curran of Pratt, Kansas, squadron operations officer of the 510th Fighter Squadron, 405th Fighter Group was flying on his 95th combat mission leading the squadron of 12 P-47 Thunderbolts on an armed reconnaissance mission over German occupied eastern France.

Captain Curran was also leading the squadron in the number of combat missions flown and was expected to be the first pilot in the squadron to fly 100 missions, return to the United States for a 30-day leave, then return to the squadron to fly a second tour.

Just east of Pont-A-Mousson on the Moselle River, about midway between Metz and Nancy, we observed a number of German artillery units firing on the advancing American troops that were west of the river. We immediately peeled off and went in to trail formation and started strafing these targets of opportunity. As usual we found the German anti-aircraft accurate and intense. In short order one of the flight

Capt. Howard Curran and his Thunderbolt, "Kansas Tornado".

leaders (Captain Charles Appel) said over the radio that his aircraft was badly hit and that he was heading west to friendly territory. He then left the area with his wingman. I found out later that he made it far enough west before he had to bail out and that he landed in liberated France.

The rest of the squadron continued to attack the German targets and then someone called over the radio that we were being jumped by German ME-109s. They had the advantage of surprise and altitude on us but we turned up and into them and were successful in shooting several of them down including one by Captain Curran. However, soon afterwards another ME-109, unseen by me, shot me down. Although I was on fire and dangerously low, I made a successful bailout. After one swing in the chute I hit the ground running as I knew I was in German held territory.

My bailout was observed by French civilians and they beckoned me by friendly gestures to join them. Although I spoke no French and they no English, we were able to understand each other by sign language with no trouble. They soon had me safely out of sight and into French civilian clothing. They also hid my chute.

I learned later that my principle French benefactor was a young man of about 25 years old whose name was Francois Lertex. They were all risking their lives to help me as the Germans would execute anyone caught helping a downed Allied airman. My bailout was also observed by the Germans and during the next few days I observed German soldiers that appeared to be looking for me.

Knowing that the Moselle River was nearby and that the Americans held the area west of the river, I was able to convey to the French that after dark I would swim the river back to friendly territory. They were against that idea and later that night I heard a loud exchange of small arms fire from the direction of the river. I assumed that an American patrol was trying to cross the Moselle River and were repulsed by the Germans. I soon gave up the idea of swimming the river, but decided that I would stay where I was and let the American troops come to me.

My French friends furnished me with food and shelter, but I was confined to the French residence where they were hiding me. After the exciting life of flying combat with a fighter squadron and enjoying the comradeship of fellow squadron members, this waiting to be liberated became boring.

The season was mid-September and the beautiful Indian summer weather was very enjoyable. It was also great flying weather, and I often heard and saw flights of P-47 Thunderbolts flying overhead. How I envied them.

The French residence included the usual walled courtyard and that is where I spent all my waking hours. The American artillery to the west and the German artillery to the east were continuous in firing their shells overhead. It didn't take long to be able to identify them by their sound.

One sunny afternoon as I and a couple of my new found friends were enjoying the warm sunshine in the courtyard a "short round" from the Americans landed just beyond us in the courtyard. Fortunately the concussion and shrapnel from the exploding shell fragmented away from us into the stone wall of the courtyard. Later we determined that it exploded less than 20 feet away from us. This was the only near miss that I experienced during the time I was an evadee.

One day my principle benefactor, Francois Lertex, produced a box camera and we had a third party take our photograph. After the war I received a copy of this photo by mail addressed to me c/o the U.S. Army and it had been forwarded by them to my home address. Francois Lertex is still living and currently resides in Nancy, France.

After six days of being M.I.A., the U.S. Army liberated the town and yours truly. They came from the south, having crossed the Moselle River a few miles south of Pont-A-Mousson. The Germans evacuated the town just ahead of them and offered no resistance. I, along with my French friends, were very glad to see them.

I was liberated by members of the U.S. Army 35th Division and it included many mid-western personnel like myself. Although I was dressed and looking like a French native, I had no trouble identifying myself as an American by use of my dog tags. I still remember that the first GI that I approached came from Kingman, Kansas which is only 30 miles east of my hometown of Pratt, Kansas.

After thanking and saying goodbye to my French benefactors I started walking south in the direction the American troops were coming from. As soon as I found an advance command post, I again identified myself and was furnished a jeep and driver to take me to the rear to higher command headquarters to be interrogated by Intelligence.

During the time that I was M.I.A. I had observed L-4s flying in the area as artillery spotters. Shortly after crossing the Moselle River by jeep over a pontoon bridge I spotted a field that these L-4s were flying from. I had the jeep driver pull in and after identifying myself for the third time that day, I asked them to fly me to A-64 at St. Dizier where my unit was located. I was overjoyed when they agreed to do this and I dismissed my driver and jeep. After a short flight (about 60 miles) in an L-4, we landed at A-64 and taxied up to the 510th Fighter Squadron operations center. The mission that had started six days earlier was ended, and I was back at home base.

Curiously several personnel whom I recognized watched as an apparent French civilian deplaned from the L-4 aircraft and approached the operations tent. When I was recognized I received a hilarious welcome back. No one on the mission had seen me bail out so there were lots of questions as to what had happened to me.

I was pleasantly surprised to be greeted by two former squadron pilots and personal friends who had been shot down weeks before and had returned from M.I.A. status during the past week while I was M.I.A. They were Captain Arlie Blood from California, who was shot down in May by anti-aircraft fire while strafing a troop train over the Brest Peninsula and Lieutenant Tom Hamilton of Miami, Florida, who was shot down in July on his 43rd mission near St. Lo, France. Both were known to have bailed successfully but their fate from then on was unknown until they returned from being M.I.A.

They were leaving in a couple of hours for Paris to be interrogated by Ninth Air Force HQ Intelligence before rotating back to the United States. Both were close personal friends and I was delighted to learn they had returned from M.I.A. status. I prevailed upon them to delay their departure until later in the afternoon and I would join them. It was

Capt. Howard Curran and French benefactor, Francois Lertex.

Ninth Air Force policy at that time to return all successful evadees back to the United States for re-assignment. So, late that afternoon the three evadees from the 510th Fighter Squadron, Curran, Blood and Hamilton, all original squadron cadre, departed A-64 at St. Dizier, France on the first leg of our trip homeward.

We were flown to Orly Field at Paris, France in a 405th Fighter Group Administrative UC-78 aircraft piloted by Lt. Jack Zeltwanger from Pennsylvania, another of the original 510th Fighter Squadron cadre.

EVADING CAPTURE!
By Lt. Col. Clayton C. David U.S.A.F. (Ret.)

In January 1944 US and British newspapers carried photographs of a foam doused B-17 called *Meathound* that had been flown back to England with only the pilot aboard. With two engines out, a fire in the left wing, and an explosion imminent, Lt. Jack W. Watson ordered his crew to bail out. Clouds prevented a view of the ground, but they knew they were approaching Amsterdam, from the east. Then, with only his life at risk in the plane, Watson made a choice to try for England rather than drop into coastal waters. Unknown at the time, fate dealt cruelly with some of the men who jumped: four would be carried MIA; four others became POWs, but the remaining crew member, co-pilot Clayton David, evaded capture. He eventually became the first of the 109 MIA's from the 303rd BG, who went down on 11 January, to escape from occupied Europe and to return to England on 25 May 1944.

Clayton's first and only parachute jump was perfect. He landed on a 50 ft. strip between the Zuider Zee and Kinselmere Lake near Durgerdam. Unseen by the Germans, he was spotted by the Piet Schouten farm family who hid him and passed him on to the Dutch Underground at Amsterdam. With the help of Joke Folmer, Jacques Vrij, Marianne Spierings - Slabbers, and many others, the Dutch-Paris line got him as far as Paris via Venlo and Maastricht, Holland, then to Brussels and finally Paris. There, while waiting with seven others to be escorted down the line to Toulouse, their Parisian helpers were arrested. Two by two, the men slipped from the church where they were hiding, into the street while the arrests were taking place.

It was about 2:00 pm when David and Kenneth Shaver, who had paired together, started their walk south from Paris. By nightfall, they had walked some 25 miles to a small village where they found a place to stay. The next day, the lady and two of her friends bought tickets and put Clayton and Ken on a train for Toulouse. They made many mistakes, had to get off for one night which was spent with the Gabriel Guillions at Bretigny, and on the third day jumped off a train at Pleaux, France, still in possession of their tickets. After walking across country in heavy snow, they were taken in by Rene and Anne-Marie Beffera for a period of three weeks. The food and lodging there was great, but the two were unwilling to wait for the invasion and liberation.

Mr. Beffera made the proper contacts and Rene Pontier secretly established their identity with Intelligence in London. They were then moved into a remote area with a group of the Maquis who received, hid, and dispersed air drops. A week later Clayton and Ken were on their way, again via train, for Toulouse. This time they were escorted by a man and woman, Jean and Paule Arhex. The two escapees became a part of the Maquis dispersal system which meant carrying two suitcases a piece which were filled with guns, ammunition, hand grenades, etc.

After an overnight stop in Toulouse, where the suitcases were left, the four continued by train to Pau where they were driven to the foot of the Pyrenees Mountains. There Ken and Clayton met their Basque guide who led them, a French courier, and a Spanish Civil War evader. They traveled through the mountains for three days and three nights before they stood waist-deep in snow at the top on the French-Spanish border. The guide pointed the route for the four to walk and to slide down the mountain into Spain, then he turned and headed back for his home in France. On the way down, the four separated, as their objectives were then different. It was well after daylight when David and Shaver were arrested while walking through a small Spanish village. They were interned for about five weeks before being taken to Madrid and then Gibraltar for a flight back to England.

Evading the Enemy-Vive La France
By William C. Dubose

It was about 3 p.m. on Saturday, June 17, 1944. We were flying over the beautiful green wheat fields and farms of northern France. Our mission that day was to glide two eleven second delayed action thousand pound bombs into a railroad bridge across the Somme River near Peronne. The purpose was to help cut the German supply lines leading to Normandy.

There were 48 of us on this mission. We were to take turns flying in elements of two about 100 feet above the water, release our bombs just as the target passed through our gun sight, pass over the bridge and make a sharp climbing turn to the left. Not far beyond the bridge, the river swept left, and on the right bank was a German airfield.

When our turn came, my flight leader, Capt. Don Penn and I dove down and flew along the river toward the bridge. We could see French people atop the high banks waving and cheering us on.

Apparently we were only about 10 seconds behind the aircraft ahead of us. As we lined up on the bridge, one of the bombs from the previous P-38 went off in the water far short of the bridge, and I could not help flying through the splash.

Don released one bomb instead of two so I quickly changed my trigger so I would also only release one bomb. My thought at that moment was that we were to make a second run. (Interesting how an incorrect assumption can change your whole life. No, I didn't go on to become a famous ace or pursue a flying career; maybe that's why I am alive and well today).

Don then advised our leader that one of his bombs had hung-up and would try to jettison it. He did this on a freight train some 10 to 15 miles away and blew hell out of it. I asked Don what I should do with my extra bomb. "Drop it on a target of opportunity," was his answer. I saw one sitting at the station of a very small village I later learned was called Chaulnes.

What an opportunity! Zip along just above the train and drop a thousand pound bomb into the cab. This was going to be the epitome of all boiler explosions. What fun for an immature kid who just turned 20.

Things went as planned for the first few seconds as I zipped along about 20 feet above the train. Then all hell broke loose. German flak positions on both sides of the tracks opened up on me. They couldn't miss. Shells flew through my wings and nacelles. Instantly, I triggered my guns and dropped the bomb, but it was too late. My plane was on fire and Don was screaming for me to bail out.

I pulled up, jettisoned the canopy, unhooked my seatbelt and decided to go out over the top because smoke was pouring into the cockpit. After I pushed myself up into the slip stream, I was pinned against the back of the canopy hanging half in and out of the plane. I couldn't move and just dangled there for a few seconds until my plane turned over into the dead engine and started down. A few seconds later I was pulled free. I saw the tail whip by and pulled the rip cord. My parachute opened with an explosion, and I saw my plane burning on the ground. I looked around to see where I was going to hit and tried to turn my chute so I would hit facing forward, but it was too late.

I slammed into a wheat field going sideways and broke and dislocated my right ankle and sprained my left. I hit with such force that my one-man dinghy was popped loose and spread all over the area. I pulled in my collapsed parachute and unhooked my harness. We had been told to bury it, but I did not have the strength, so I left it there and crawled about 30 feet to a dirt road.

At the top of a hedgerow on the other side I could see German soldiers running from the village of Chaulnes toward my plane which had hit about 100 yards from where I had landed.

I crawled back across the road into the wheatfield and headed toward some trees about a mile away. As I crawled toward the edge of the field, I saw two German soldiers running toward me. I thought they saw me, so I laid down. They got to the edge of the wheatfield and turned toward the road. Had they run straight ahead, they would have tripped over me.

At this point, I decided it was too risky to crawl across an open field, so I headed back to the hedgerow on the side of the road and hid myself with leaves and bushes. I looked at my watch; it was 3:15 p.m.

As I lay in that hedgerow, 40 German soldiers combed the area looking for me. A few came within five feet of me as they walked and drove along the road. Apparently they gave up the search after a few hours.

As evening approached, I could see the lights of a farm house several miles away. I decided that would become my destination. Perhaps the people who lived there would help me.

It did not get dark until after 10 p.m. (double daylight saving time). I decided it was safe to start crawling through the wheatfields toward the lights of that farm house. I hadn't crawled very far before I realized this was going to be a painful task. My green summer flying suit gave little protection to my knees.

Perhaps if I got to my feet and could find something to use as a cane, I could hobble to my destination. I saw a concrete power pole in the distance. I crawled to it and tried to pull myself to my feet. It was too painful. I could not put any weight on my ankles. I sat down, tore the legs from my flight suit and wrapped them around my knees. This gave me some relief.

As I crawled through the wheatfields, I tried to camouflage my path by crawling in and out of the fields in places that would be difficult for someone to follow. I was told later that some French people did follow my route, but it was not easy.

Late that night, I crawled to a spot where my hand reached out into empty space. I stopped and felt around for solid ground. There was none. Then I heard what sounded like German voices down below me. I slowly and cautiously backed away. Had I crawled up to the edge of a German flak position? I will never know.

As the early morning light appeared, I could see that straight ahead of me was the railroad line. Its bed was higher than the wheat so if I tried to crawl over it in the light, I could be seen for hundreds of yards in all directions. There went my plan to reach the farmhouse. Just as well, it still seemed to be several miles away.

My second plan was to turn left and head toward the village of Chaulnes. Perhaps I could find some friendly French people who would hide me.

By this time my knees were bleeding and every movement was painful. I decided to sit on my back-side and push myself along backwards using my hands to propel me. I did this from early morning until late that afternoon.

About 5 p.m. I reached a dirt road near the outskirts of Chaulnes. I sat in the wheat at the edge of the road. Finally, a woman and her young daughter walked by. I got to my knees so they could see me and yelled, "I am an American."

The woman was startled but kept calm. She grabbed her daughter's hand and pulled her along, apparently telling her not to look back at me or say anything.

Approximately 30 minutes later a man came walking down the road in my direction and seemed to be looking for me. I hollered at him and he came over, knelt down and spoke to me.

Using my French-English translation card from my escape kit, I was able to show him sentences that stated that I was an American airman, shot down, injured, thirsty, hungry and wanted to be hid. He was cautious and asked if I could speak German, Spanish or French. I was not able to speak any of these languages but from the little I had learned in high school, I could understand what he was getting at. He wanted to make sure I was not a German spy planted there to find out who were members of the French Resistance. He motioned for me to stay low in the wheat so I would not be seen; then he left.

Sometime later, two teenage boys came looking for me. One motioned for me to crawl across the road and follow them. I got across the road but was not able to crawl any further. One of the boys pulled me onto his back and ran about 100 yards down the road to a driveway leading into a farm. His father was waiting for us with a wooden wheelbarrow. They put me on it, put an old piece of carpeting over me and wheeled me back to the barn behind the house. In the corner of the barn was a pile of grain. Somehow, they pushed me up and over the crest so I was hidden between the grain and the wall. I quickly fell asleep.

Hours later when it was dark, I heard voices below and could tell someone was crawling up toward me. They brought me a piece of bread and a bottle of water. After I had eaten, they pulled me down and took me into the house. I was taken to a bedroom on the second floor where we attempted to communicate.

I do not recall how many people were there, but I do know they were concerned with my physical condition. One lady was from the local Red Cross. They called her "Madmoiselle Rouge." There was nothing she or anyone else could do to help my ankle.

They took what was left of my flight suit, my GI pants and shirt and gave me a sweat shirt and pair of pants to wear. I kept my wings and dogtags.

The next morning I was awakened and a man who could speak English appeared. He was a former World War I English soldier who had married a French lady and settled in France. They put me in his horsedrawn carriage, told me to lay down so I was hidden. I was then driven about ten miles out into the country to his farm.

He told me that their big beautiful home had been burned by the German occupation forces as they invaded France. They now lived in the servants quarters nearby. There was no room for me in this one bedroom house which they shared with their daughter. They had cleaned out a chicken coop for me.

Actually, the chicken coop was adequate. It was clean, had a cot and an end table and the chickens next door were noisy but good company.

While there, I was made to stand and hobble around with a cane as soon as the swelling went down. I am sure they were concerned about getting me mobile as soon as possible and moved somewhere else. Both my legs were black and blue all the way to my hips. I had really hit the ground hard!

Two weeks later, I was transported back to the village of Chaulnes and put into the care of the Edward LeBlanc family. They lived on the main street about two blocks from the railroad station where I had tried to bomb that train. The downstairs front of their house was a store. Their living quarters were behind the store and upstairs. I lived in a bedroom on the second floor.

The French had given me false identification papers and used the picture from my escape kit (we all carried our picture taken in civilian clothes . . . just in case we were shot down). My French name was Jean Pierre Dubose. I was supposed to be a friend of the family from the Normandy area who was deaf and mute . . . injured during the invasion of France.

The LeBlancs had neighbors sympathetic to the Russians who visited quite often unannounced. They would bring their map of Europe and discuss the latest positions of the Russian and American fronts. The LeBlancs were not sure their friends should know they were hiding an American flyer so every time they visited, I played the role of a deaf and mute person.

Papa LeBlanc was always testing me to make sure my act was convincing. One evening we were seated at the dinning room table. My back was to the door. The Russian family dropped in to discuss the latest position of the fronts. Papa walked in the door and dropped an empty metal bucket on the hard floor just behind me. The noise startled everyone. Luckily, I did not flinch an eyebrow or muscle.

They had a daughter, Suzanne, who was married but her husband was being held as a prisoner in Germany. The LeBlancs also had a son somewhere in North Africa with what was left of the French Navy.

The French insisted that I get out of the house occasionally to get some exercise. They got me a bicycle and we rode along the dirt road beside the flak positions so I could see my enemy. They also took me out to the hole in the ground where my P-38 had hit. I can assure you I was not enthusiastic about making these bicycle trips.

It was more interesting to watch the 100 regular German troops and 100 SS troops who occupied this village and manned the flak positions march down the main street every evening singing German songs. Apparently they did this to keep up their morale and show the French who was boss.

The day after the attempt to assassinate Hitler, there was a lot of confusion among the troops and some of the officers left town. The soldiers milled around the village discussing what they should do.

I stood at an open window upstairs in the back of the LeBlancs' house and watched three or four German soldiers standing on a road just behind their yard. They saw me watching and yelled something. I had no idea what they were saying so I just stood there. One of the soldiers pulled out his pistol and fired at me. I got the point and moved away from the window.

All the French families tried to feed me as best they could. I ate a lot of boiled tripe, strawberry sandwiches and chicken. The sanitary conditions were not the best and a few days before I was to be moved to another family, I got dysentery. It made me very sick and very weak. However, the French school teacher who was to take care of me for the next few weeks showed up and we took off on our bikes. I was so weak. I had to walk beside my bicycle and push it up any kind of incline.

On one of these walks up a hill, we were accompanied by a German soldier. My French school teacher friend and he talked all the way up the hill. I just played deaf and mute and was scared.

I lived with this family about two weeks and was told that I would be transported by car to another location. By the way, every move I made was north...the opposite of the direction I wanted to go.

This time I was picked up by two members of the French Resistance. In the car was an American B-17 gunner...my first contact in a long time with someone with whom I could really communicate.

As we drove north through the countryside we saw a group of P-47s strafing. Our driver immediately pulled into a farmyard and parked under some trees. We all ran for the house. Shortly after we got into the house, two truck loads of German soldiers drove into the yard and parked under the same trees. As the soldiers ran for the house, my new B-17 gunner friend and I were told to run out the back and hide behind an outhouse near the edge of a field. We hid there for what seemed like eternity, watching the P-47s strafe on one side of us and the German soldiers milling around in the house on the other. Finally, the P-47s left, the Germans left and we departed.

We were taken to the apartment of a Madame Heller in the village of Billy-Montigny. She was the head of the French Resistance in that area. She was Australian and her husband a Hungarian photographer. They had been caught in France when the Germans invaded France. Neither were French citizens but were forced to stay there during the war.

After waiting quite a while, a young man riding a bicycle showed up and motioned for us to follow him. He could see that I could hardly walk so he put me on the handlebars and drove several blocks. He told me to get off and walk straight ahead. He then went back to get my friend and in this manner shuttled us to the Brewers home on the edge of town. We were lucky no German soldiers were around or we would have been apprehended for being out after curfew.

Our new French host ran a brewery next to his home before the occupation. He was proud of all the things he had been able to hide from the Germans. He took us for a tour of his brewery and property.

Under the loading dock of his brewery was a secret entrance to an area where he had stashed hundreds of cases of champagne and a room where he kept his radio. Here he could listen to broadcasts from the BBC directed to the people of the French Resistance. Radios were outlawed by the Germans. Upstairs in one corner of his brewery, were stacked hundreds of cases of empty bottles. His car was hidden behind them.

The large garden of his home was beautifully landscaped. In the center he had poured a concrete slab. Next to it lay an unexploded 1000 pound bomb with the detonator still attached. He was going to stand it on the slab as a souvenir of the war. Next to his garage, in a wood pile, he had stored two British 200 pound unexploded bombs. Needless to say, we were not thrilled with the tour.

Madame Heller and her driver came by that afternoon to take us to our next destination. On the way, we picked up a typical looking Englishman, mustache and all. Madame Heller tucked our wings and dogtags in her bosom. My American friend and I sat on either side of the Englishman and asked him to look the other way whenever we passed any German soldiers.

We drove down one narrow dirt road beside hundreds of marching German soldiers. My friend and I made sure the Englishman was looking the other way. We came to a gate guarded by several German soldiers. The soldiers, the driver and Madame Heller spoke for a few minutes. Finally the guards raised the gate and we drove through. My heart was in my mouth!

Our destination was the home of the Mr. and Mrs. Dernancourt who lived in the city of Lens. Six other Allied airmen already lived with them. From that point on, the nine of us lived together in the rooms above their store which was located on the main street of this city.

By day, we played poker with our "escape money", sunned ourselves in the brick courtyard behind their house, shared by a pig, or watched the activity of the German soldiers from the windows upstairs. We all picked out pretty girls on the street whom we would like to meet when we were liberated. We also helped prepare the meals.

We ate a lot of soup which contained everything our hosts and their close friends could conjure up to put into the pot. We spent many hours grinding, peeling and stirring.

This is where I met Clifford O. Williams, a P-38 pilot from the 343rd Fighter Squadron. He had been shot down the same day that I got into the 55th Fighter Group. The nine of us consisted of two Australians, two Canadians, two Englishmen and three Americans. Madame Heller had also found places for about 14 other Allied airmen to live in the Billy-Montigny, Lens area of northern France.

One evening while all of us were sitting around the dining room tables eating, we heard a scream from the young teenage girl who was minding the store up front. She came running back to warn us that a German truck with many soldiers had driven up and parked in front of the store. We all thought that someone that turned us in and we would be taken prisoners and the French people shot.

As it turned out, the Germans had stopped to take hostages. They made it a point to take a husband or wife from a family...never both. They were put in the truck and taken off to be shot. This was shortly before we were liberated by the English 1st Army. The French were out every night blowing up bridges, killing German troops and cutting telephone wires. For several weeks, we could hear the explosions, see the flashes of light as the French Resistance did their thing . . . things like putting unexploded bombs onto carts and dragging them under railroad bridges where they hoped they would eventually explode.

It was interesting to watch the German troops retreat. For several days before the English 1st Army arrived, the Germans came down the main street heading north in every conceivable mode of transportation imaginable...trucks, cars, bicycles, horses, horse drawn carts, tanks, on foot, etc. This went on 24 hours a day.

Finally, the English 1st Army rumbled through with tanks and trucks and many troops. Everyone was out waving and cheering. Flags were flying and people were crying tears of joy. As the troops sped by, they threw us cigarettes and candy bars but would not stop.

When a convoy did stop, we spoke to them and they got word to their officers that we were Allied airmen and needed transportation back to Paris. This was arranged but it took a few days.

In the meantime, we were treated as heros by the townspeople, were given a banquet and asked to march in a liberation parade. In the parade with us were French collaborators. The women had their hair shaved and they were kicked and spit upon as they marched along. The pretty girl I had picked to meet after liberation was one of those women!

Several days later, several of us were put in a truck and taken north to the front lines where we were turned over to the American 1st Army. We spent one night in a German prison compound. It was just behind the lines and a place where the captured Germans were brought before they were sent south to prison camps. There were tough looking SS troops among them.

The next day we were put in a truck along with other Allied airmen who had been found along the way and driven back to Paris. There we were taken to the Hotel Maurice. This had been the German Army headquarters in Paris during the occupation but was now a place where all the evadees and escapees were brought to be interrogated. We spent two or three days here. Our false identification was taken and we were given a GI shirt, pants, pair of shoes and socks. I took a cold water bath, the first bath in three months.

We were flown by C-47 back to London. I was put into a tent hospital north of London where I spent another month or so. Every V-1 shot toward London seemed to pass over this location. It was another terrifying experience. I was flown back to the good old United States in November of 1944 and back to my home state of California. Again I was put in a hospital where they tried to repair my ankle.

FIFTY YARDS FROM THE GERMAN BORDER

Submitted by Frank W. Enroughty

The mission was to bomb an air base in Germany. The squadron of B-17s left the airfield near Norwich, England on March 21, 1945. All but one plane returned that day. The bomber flying left in the formation was hit by a shell and went down. There were 10 men on board. Seven, including ABC Enforcement Supervisor Frank Enroughty, made it back to the States.

"When the shell hit, two were injured in the plane. Everyone bailed out. I think one man was captured because I watched him until his chute opened. From that day to this I haven't seen or heard from any of them," Enroughty said.

After the plane was hit, Enroughty was lucky. He landed in a swamp and survived the crash without injury. The weather, which was in the 70's, was unusually warm for the second day of spring. He was equipped with a survival kit containing a map, compass, package of bouillon, water purification tablets and a chocolate bar that was so highly concentrated that you could not eat the whole thing at one

Aunt Agnes, daughter of Mr. van Mast, brought Frank food.

Anny and Ida also brought Frank food.

Mr. and Mrs. van Mast and Jonny.

The house Frank hid in on the van Mast farm.

time. "I ate from that chocolate bar for two days," he said.

Although he did not know exactly where he was, Enroughty knew that he needed to travel west, unseen, to get across the border. He traveled at night and slept in hiding places during the day.

"One day I hid under a bridge by a stream. It was in an open field with a horse. When the horse walked in the stream to get a drink, it got mired in the mud. I know that animal must have been in that field for a long time and it drank from the stream frequently, but it just happened that it got stuck the day I was hiding there."

He continued, "I knew that people would come to help it, so I took off across the field and hid in some bushes. Sure enough, a group of people showed up and pulled the horse out of the stream."

Enroughty still did not have a chance to breathe a sigh of relief. "One of the farmers had a German shepherd with him. The dog started toward the bushes and barked at me. He knew I was there, but that was about the time they finished with the horse and they called the dog away."

There was another close call for the first lieutenant before he reached the border. "I usually walked around towns and villages, but one night I walked through one. It was dark, and I almost walked right up on someone. I saw the glow of a cigarette just in time to avoid him."

When Enroughty was found, he did not realize he had made it safely across the border. "I was asleep in a haystack at the time. The man who found me knew who I was, but I didn't know who he was."

Enroughty's rescuer was a Dutch farmer named G.B.H. van Mast. He had purposely left stacks of hay on his farm to provide a hiding place for allies. Enroughty found one such haystack in a shed. When the farmer entered the shed, he found a jacket and a pair of boots. He tugged at the boots on the haystack and found the American pilot.

"I was armed and he was not," Enroughty said. "He did not speak English and I did not speak his language. We communicated with sign language. He set his watch ahead a half hour and pointed to it. I reckon he found out that I was hungry, so for some reason, I just let him go."

When van Mast returned, the shed was empty. Enroughty had left and was hiding nearby in some bushes.

"I trusted him, but I was afraid someone else might return with him. Instead, he came back with two sandwiches and a pot of coffee. You know, it was the first and last time I have ever eaten raw fatback, but you'd better believe I ate it then."

van Mast returned again later that afternoon. "He brought an English-speaking gentleman from the village. They advised me that they would take care of me if I would put on civilian clothes. It was dangerous for me. If the Germans had found me they would have classified me as a spy, but the Dutch were risking their lives to help me, too. They then hid me in a summer cottage. I stayed there about a week and worked on the van Mast farm in Buurse.

"On April 1, the English marched through the town. They were told about me and they came out to the farm and picked me up."

Enroughty has never forgotten the big-hearted family. "That last day, I sat down to dinner with them. About 10 to 12 people were seated at the table. When we finished, another group the same size sat down to dinner. I am not sure they were all van Masts, but it was a large family."

UNIFORM IN A MILK CAN
AMERICAN PILOT VISITS HIDING PLACE IN BUURSE

This story was written by the helping family of Frank Enroughty. It was originally written in Dutch, then translated by a friend of the family. We have reprinted this story exactly as it has been translated to preserve the charm of this original story. - Editor

On 28 March 1945 at 9:45 p.m. World War II ended for pilot Frank W. Enroughty from Richmond, Virginia (U.S.). The bomber in which he was second pilot was hit and took fire at a charge on a German airfield.

Everybody who was still alive, jumped out. Frank Enroughty - 26 years old - fell in a swamp, where he hided himself that day. He got a compass and knew he had to go in a western direction to arrive in the allied Netherlands. After a two days hiding and two nights walking, he arrived at a shed at the border of a forest. He had good luck for the shed, plenty with straw and hay for the convenience of other people, being in hiding, was a Dutch one. It belonged to G.B.H. van Mast, of the inheritance Harmolen in Buurse (Haaksberger).

TWO SHOES IN THE STRAW

Friday - after 15 years - van Mast and Enroughty met each other again and their greeting was very nice. They recognized each other directly and walked together to the place on the border of the forest, or about 1 1/2 mile from the farm. Mrs. Rebecca Enroughty, accompanying her husband and her friend, Mrs. Elaine B. Hughes, looked attentively when van Mast (with his hands) and Enroughty told about the circumstances the morning van Mast discovered the pilot in the shed. van Mast told the neighborhood was incommoded by marauders. He had crammed a shed with straw and hay and thought marauders could hide themselves there. On the top of the straw he saw a pair of brown shoes. He grabbed something - it was a fur-lined vest - and at once he looked in the barrel of a revolver. van Mast explained to the guest that he was "allright", and with his hands he told the pilot to be arrived in Holland. The past days Frank only had lived of a piece of choclat and had good appetite. He explained this to van Mast who put the hands of his watch half an hour forward, what meant he would come back at that time.

MILK AND BREAD

After half an hour van Mast came back to the shed with milk and buttered slices, but the pilot had disappeared. Enroughty had taken the certainty for the uncertainty. He was sure of the good intentions of van Mast, but not sure he wouldn't bring with him anybody who could bring the good escape from Germany to a bad end. The American had hidden himself in an adjacent bush, with his revolver in position. When he saw van Mast coming back alone he came out and enjoyed the milk and slices.

Enroughty didn't stay a long time in that uncomfortable hiding place. van Mast brought him to the summerhouse "ansje". He took care for civilian cloth and put his uniform in a milk-can, that the Germans, being in position round the farm, shouldn't suspect trouble.

Of the SS-man, deserted in the begining of the war and hidden there too he had nothing to fear, though he became flippant and asked the Germans in slang (he came from Munster) how "Adolf" was doing.

OUT OF THE MILK CAN

Everything went well for Enroughty. They didn't discover him. The only thing he had to do was to be silent in company. Mr. Wim Janmink was his interpreter. He gave Enroughty, who was working in the field one day, indications as much as possible. When Buurse was liberated British Servicemen were send for him. His uniform came out of the milk-can and Frank took place in the Allied Forces. But Frank would and should see again the place were he found hospitality and protection. Back in Buurse this week - he recognised everything: the shed were he hided himself, the summerhouse were he lived a week, and the hospitable people which took care for him and kept him out hands of the enemy. Frank and his wife do say they will never forget this all.

This translation was made by one of my aunt's friends in Holland. I have tried to copy it so that you will see the excellent English and spelling of my aunt's Dutch friend. Frank Enroughty

THE LAST ESCAPE THROUGH THE SHELBOURNE LINE

By Louis Feingold, Navigator, 8th Air Force

Mission #20. A successful drop on Ludwigshafen, Germany. Successful...until the plane was hit by enemy flak. Knocked out of formation, a straggler, the B-17 was attacked by seven German fighters. The only recourse was to bail out.

The navigator and his bombardier landed in an open field 60 miles north of Paris. Immediately, some local farmers came to their aid. Fortunately, the navigator remembered his high school French and became the unofficial translator. They hid in the woods until a man who spoke English appeared. Though they didn't know it at the time, this was their first encounter with the French Resistance.

The Frenchman arranged to meet the fliers that night at a nearby spot "where the wires cross the road." Could the Frenchman be trusted? Was he a collaborator? Will they be taken prisoner? The final consensus: It was the only chance they had.

That night the Frenchman returned whistling "It's A Long Way To Tipperary." They were safe. Both the navigator and bombardier breathed a sigh of relief.

Luck was with the two fliers. They made contact with the French Underground quickly; this greatly increased their chances of successfully escaping back to the comparative safety of England.

So began their journey along the Shelbourne Line, a Resistance route organized by two Canadians trained in escape operations. For a week the two fliers were smuggled from place to place, including a factory and a bakery, while the Germans scoured the area looking for them.

They were then led to the home of Odette and Gaston LeGrand in Clermont. There they met up with four other fliers. The LeGrands housed all six men for three weeks until they received the orders for four to move on. Before leaving for Paris the fliers were given fake identity cards: the navigator became a deaf-mute farmer.

Luck was with the two fliers. The navigator and bombardier were among the last men to escape along the Shelbourne Line before the route was closed down. The two remaining fliers, scheduled to leave four days later, never made it to England. They were captured by the Germans and remained prisoners of war until the liberation, a year-and-a-half later.

In Paris they hid for four more weeks, assuming a second false identity. Then, under the guidance of the Resistance, the two fliers moved along by train to Guingamp, in Brittany, about 200 miles west of Paris.

In Guingamp the fliers were smuggled to two houses before bedding down for the night. The next evening, the navigator and bombardier were told to walk down the street and wait until a truck stopped. They jumped in the back and stopped on every street corner until the truck picked up 17 fliers in all. The fliers were kept in an abandoned farmhouse on the coast for two days.

Then, on a moonless night, they were taken to Bonaparte Beach in Brittany. They slid down a cliff to the shore. A Resistance fighter flashed a signal to the sea. Soon four rowboats arrived. The fliers rowed in total darkness to an English ship waiting for them off the coast.

The navigator remembers waking up to the rising sun . . . the White Cliffs of Dover . . . and freedom.

Luck was with the two fliers. They were among the last group of Americans to escape in this secret manner. Operation Bonaparte was closed down shortly after the navigator's return to England.

BEHIND ENEMY LINES: WORLD WAR TWO'S LARGEST RESCUE OF MIAS
By Richard Felman

During World War II, I was one of over 500 American MIAs shot down over enemy occupied Yugoslavia and rescued by General Draza Mihailovich and his Chetnik Guerrillas. To this day it remains the largest rescue of American lives from behind enemy lines in history. Unfortunately, a foreign policy of appeasing post-war communist Yugoslavia has kept the details of our rescue from being released.

In 1944 I was a young lieutenant navigator with the Army Air Corps flying B-24 bombing missions over southern Europe. I was assigned to the 415th Bombardment Squadron (heavy), 98th Bombardment Group (heavy), 15th Air Force, stationed in Lecce, Italy.

Before every mission our bomber crews were briefed if shot down over Yugoslavia we were to stay away from Mihailovich and his Chetniks and seek out instead the men with the Red Star on their hats: Tito's Communist Partisans. Our latest Intelligence was reporting that Mihailovich was "cutting off the ears of American airmen and turning them over to the Germans."

Returning from a 250 bomber plane raid on the Ploesti Oil Fields in Romania, my plane was attacked by German ME 109s and 10 of our 11 man crew were forced to bail out from 18,000 feet over the Yugoslav Hills. (Our ball gunner, Thomas P. Lovett, Roxbury, Mass., was killed in the plane during the exchange of gunfire.) Shortly after landing I came face to face with General Mihailovich and his Chetniks. Not only did they not "cut off my ears and turn me over to the Germans" as Intelligence had warned, but many of their own people - fighters and peasants - were killed while protecting us from the enemy.

The Germans had counted our 10 chutes coming down and knew exactly where we were but could not get to us in the hills. They sent an ultimatum to Mihailovich demanding he turn us over to them or in retaliation they would burn down

611th Bomb Squadron, 400th Bomb Group, Charleston Army Air Base, SC beside their B-24, "Never a Dull Moment."

a village of 200 of their women and children. When Mihailovich refused, they carried out their threat. (47 years later I still carry the stench of their burning flesh in my nostrils.)

As the daily bombing offensive increased during the summer of 1944, more and more airmen were being shot down over Yugoslavia causing great concern to Major General Nathan Twining, the commanding general of the 15th Air Force Headquartered in Bari, Italy. At his direction, First Lieutenant George S. Musulin, AUS, Office of Strategic Services, headed a three member rescue unit that was blind-dropped at night deep into enemy territory with medical supplies, short-wave radios and a coded evacuation plan called "The Halyard Mission."

The only possible evacuation area we had was a narrow strip of land high on a mountain top that had been used for grazing livestock. Unfortunately, it was only 1800 feet long and much valuable time had to be lost lengthening it another 200-300 feet to meet the absolute minimum for C-47 operation.

Once that was done and 15th Air Force HQS was notified, on the night of August 9 and morning of August 10, 1944, they sent in stripped-down C-47 transports landing at five minute intervals to pick up the airmen while multiple waves of 25 P-51 fighters provided protective cover and carried out diversionary strafing attacks on the six German garrisons in the surrounding area. It was one of the most spectacular "air shows" of the entire war. Much credit for the success of the operation was attributed to the 10,000 Chetniks Mihailovich assigned to protect the area should the Germans decide to attack. All told, over 500 American and 200

August 10, 1944. B-24 crewmen on arrival at 15th Air Force Hospital in Bari, Italy after being evacuated from behind enemy lines in Yugoslavia. On landing, they were greeted by Lt. Gen. Nathan Twinning, 15th AF Commanding General. They were directed to maintain secrecy about the details of the rescue. (L to R): Lt. Richard L. Felman, Lt. Paul Mato. Lt. Richard Felman is wearing a Chetnik Guerilla hat.

July 31, 1944. General Mihailovich (see arrow) speaks to a group of American airmen shot down over Yugoslavia by Nazi Fighters. He expressed no bitterness at being abandoned by US and English Forces and asked only that we return to our Allies with the truth. The soldiers had been cautioned by US Intelligence sources that if captured by Mihailovich, he would "cut off their ears and turn them over to the Germans."

other Allied personnel were rescued in this manner during War World II. Ironically, even after our rescue, Allied "Intelligence" continued to report that Mihailovich was turning Americans over to the Germans.

Based on the same false Intelligence reports we got at our briefings, the United States and Great Britain no longer recognized Mihailovich and switched their support to Tito. This enabled the Communists to take over the country after the war and execute Mihailovich on the trumped up charge of collaborating with the Germans.

In 1948, two years after Mihailovich was killed by a Communist firing squad, President Truman acknowledged our nation's grave mistake and, on the recommendation of General Eisenhower, posthumously awarded Mihailovich the Legion of Merit, Degree of Chief Commander, for his material contribution to Allied victory and rescue of American airmen. For the first time in history, this high award and the story of our rescue was classified secret by the State Department so as not to publicize their colossal blunder or offend the Communist government of Yugoslavia by exposing this deception to their people.

Since that time, the rescued airmen have sought to express their gratitude to Mihailovich by petitioning Congress for permission to erect a memorial in his honor. In 1976 and 1977 the United States Senate granted them that permission, but the bills were defeated by State Department opposition. The Mihailovich Memorial Bill (supported nationally by the American Legion, Veterans of Foreign Wars and the Air Force Association) has been before Congress in every session since, but in the 1991-92 session, Congress is still being denied by the State Department and Yugoslavia.

In 1990, the head archivist at the Air Force Academy Library in Colorado Springs found it hard to believe there was no record of our rescue in their files. Our comprehensive documentation was welcomed, and we were assured that the future cadets will share with us one of the most glorious moments in the history of the United States Air Force.

The final chapter in our story remains to be written.

ESCAPE FROM ENEMY LINES
THE PAUL E. GARDINER STORY

Major Paul E. Gardiner was missing in action for 40 days after being shot down in his P-47 Thunderbolt, the *Huckle De Buck* June 18, 1944. At 26 years of age, Major Gardiner was the leader of his squadron, 9th Air Force. He flew 70 combat sorties and 49 missions before that day his ship fell victim of heavy flak.

On the day he was shot down, the major's squadron had been assigned to strafing some heavy enemy emplacements. Planes who were strafing flew at tree-top level, depending on the great speed of the ship, to make for poor targets of enemy anti-aircraft guns. The enemy usually tried to get the lead ship first as they knew it carried the squad's leader.

That day was no exception and the major's ship came under heavy attack. The rudder and tail controls were shot away by flak. Major Gardiner tried to maneuver the ship around in an effort to get back to Allied lines but was not

Maj. Paul E. Gardiner and his P-47 Thunderbolt fighter, "Huckle De Buck" as they appeared in action over France and Germany.

successful. When he saw his only chance was to bail out he started to climb out of the cockpit at about 800 feet.

Some of the major's safety harness got caught inside the plane as he was attempting to bail out. He could not get it loose and was standing there virtually tied to the spot as the ship was losing altitude. He pulled the rip-cord in his parachute and the speed of the plane caused the chute to pop open and jerked him free of the ship.

He saw the parachute open and then hit the ground hard. He broke some ribs in the jar and later found a bit of flak in his flesh but felt very lucky to be alive.

The airman managed to escape and evade for 40 days before finally reaching safety. He sings the praises of the men in his squadron. "The pilots were the best on earth," says Gardiner, "...our squadron was made up of the best men and finest fellows in the whole U.S. Army."

*The source for this story submitted by Paul E. Gardiner was *The Cherokee Republican*, September 15, 1944.

MY SEVENTH MISSION
By Ralph Hall

I was engineer, top turret gunner, with the Glenn Johnson crew. Our B-17 was hit with flak on mission to Bordeaux France, 5 January 1944. German fighters closed in on our ship over Brittany and our tail section came off. Seven bailed out. The plane crashed northwest of Kergrist Moeleu, near a forest. I ran south, after stomping my chute in a mud puddle. I lost my survival kit on the way out of the plane so I had no map or money to exchange for help. I gave away my rings and lighter (which had my nickname, Buck, on it). Later one of my crew members was shown it, and he knew I was being hidden. We lost both our tail gunner and ball turret gunner.

If my first chance to escape had worked, I would have beaten my crew back to England, February 1st or 2nd.

I learned this year, that it was to have been "Shorty" Gordon and group, with French helper Fan Fan on a large fishing boat with a sail. We were to meet a larger vessel in the ocean, but the boat started taking on water and on returning, it sank as we reached shore. The Germans were waiting for us, capturing several, but I walked a bit with Gordon and then started picking up rocks and putting them on a wall as if I was working there and I went out of sight once over the hill.

I walked all day following a railroad and late evening was taken in on a farm. Next day I walked, February 4th, my brother's birthday, and forded streams until I came to a red bank that I recognized. I went back to the farmhouse I had left; the Le Signes were surprised to see me again.

That night I was taken by a Frenchman with dark rimmed glasses to Douarnenez to the home of Mille Marguerite Seznec and her aunt, Taunte Marie, where I stayed from February until 22 August 1944.

At times I could hear Germans come into the building below my home and could see them on the street through my shuttered window.

On the day of the invasion, Marguerite returned home from work very excited. She had a radio for me to listen to BBC. Of course the volume had to be low.

Some of my early helpers never gave their names. Several I have heard from were Thepant, a farm family, Jegu, Pierre Dreau (Pierre Sebriel and Yves Lorenquer) two boys about my age who brought a bicycle for me to ride with them to Gouren. My big feet in wooden shoes had trouble pedaling 20 miles. We ran into several Germans along the way and hid in the bushes.

At one of the farms, there was a large fireplace with benches on either side and the men and myself were sitting when Germans knocked at the door. I was pushed under the bench but the Germans never came inside, lucky for me and that family.

After the bike trip to Gouren, I was taken to a Dr. Bariou, for a check up and a bath. He took me by car, in the floor covered with blankets, across town to the farm of Jean Marie Paulet - for a short stay and then on the other side of town to the farm of Jean Pierre Calvez. There I stayed several days along with an Indian who had escaped from Rennes. There we were put on a train to Rospordea, with a French guide, a boy of 15-16 years. At Quimper we were hidden overnight by a French lady who had a wine shop. From there we went to Douarnenez, where we were picked up by French police and put in jail for five hours. I told them my serial number, and when they found I was a U.S. airman, they wined and dined me. I was then taken to LeSigne farm for several days.

My stay in Douarnenez, at Seznec home lasted from February to August 22, 1944. One day a group of people, a French captain and several R.C.A.F. cadets along with Mon. Quebriac and Donald Chenney of Ottawa, Canada, R.C.A.F. cadet came in a 1936 Ford. When we arrived in Rennes, I made contact with the 3rd Armored Div. on August 26. We went on to Laval and on 30 August we left by plane, a C-47 with no parachutes on board. I was rather uneasy! I left France for England and came home on an Italian liner and landed in the U.S. in New Jersey on 12 October 1944.

French Helper, Marguerite Sezner

Ralph Hall in hiding during WW II.

The home where Hall lived during hiding. An "X" marks the room in which he stayed.

ALWAYS GRATEFUL

By Louis L. Haltom

My B-17 combat crew of the 96th Bombardment Group flew in an aircraft named *Boot Hill*. My aircraft was on its fourth mission, May 17, 1943. Our aircraft crashed at about 12:20 hrs., a beautiful sunny day in France. Our plane was badly damaged by flak, but we continued to stay in formation. We made the bomb run and dropped our bombs on our target, fulfilling the purpose, training and expense for our mission in WWII. There was never a thought to save ourselves. We were there to bomb the hell out of the Germans.

Soon after leaving the target, we lost power to the number 2 engine. We feathered it, but could not feather number 3. Unable to keep up with the formation, even though the group lead pilot slowed down for us, we slowly fell back and lost altitude. The German Fighters, FockeWulfs, were quick to sense our situation; two engines out, a ball turret that was not moving or turning or firing, came in with a force of ten. They fired into the belly of the ship, would roll over and come around and fire into the aircraft belly and wings.

It sounded like tearing shingles off a house. Our 96th Bomber Group had pulled away. We were smoking like hell; the radio operator was still firing and wounded. By this time the tail gunner's guns were frozen and the men believed to be dead; the waist gunners were shot up but still firing. As I recall the gunners shot down three or four fighters.

Our Bomber Group (96th) friends were yelling over the radio to bail out. At about 12,000 feet I decided it was not possible to make the coast and ditch. Sadly and reluctantly, I rang the bell to bail out.

We had hoped to fly 25 missions and return home together. The crew members in the nose bailed out first, then the navigator, the bombardier and a guest navigator and guest pilot. Lt. McGee, our regular assigned bombardier, was not with us as he was sick. As luck would have it, he was shot down with another crew two weeks before our return to England in August of 1943.

The crew members bailing out of the nose were captured as they landed on the ground near a small village. German soldiers were in all the towns. My tail gunner was dead, and I do not know if my co-pilot got out as he insisted on keeping the plane right side up for me to get out.

I started to the bomb bay and had to return to help right the ship. The tail of the plane came off about 2-300 feet before hitting the ground. Only this saved my waist gunner. One gunner had been flying without his parachute. The other gunner was helping him on with it, when the tail came off. They landed in trees and their lives were saved.

My leg was badly sprained, as while coming down I kept trying to count the parachutes to determine how many were still in the air. I hit the ground hard using a chest type chute. My assistant crew chief (ball-turret gunner) landed over the fence from me. He joined me and gave me Morphine in my leg. By this time the French farmers and families were running to us with wine/cheese and changes of clothes. They pointed the way to go, away from the direction of the Germans. My assistant crew chief helped me to limp away.

We moved away as far as we could and later hid out in some woods until night fall. That night we were contacted by the French Underground. The members were a mixed group, school teachers and farmers. They provided food, more clothes and arranged for us to be moved out of that area under a truckload of wood. We traveled some 20 to 30 miles to St. Quy where all of my crew (five) stayed with a wonderful lady and a little boy. Somehow she found food, cooked wonderful meals and had lots of cherry trees in the back yard. After two to three weeks, we moved to an older couple's home for a week or so. From there we were taken about 10-15 kilometers to the Count and Countess De Maudit's chateau.

The Count had already sailed away in a little sailboat and joined De Gaulle's staff in Africa. The Countess, an American born lady from New York City, grew up next door to Barbara Hutton, the Woolco heiress. The Countess (Betty) stated later that the Count told her to do nothing but to stay alive while the war was going on and he was away. The Countess stated that as a French woman and also an American born woman, she could not day by day see American crew members being shot down. For her to sit there and do nothing was unthinkable. She joined the French Underground and opened up her chateau to hiding out downed crew members.

Later in 1956, it was my sincere pleasure to return and visit briefly with the Countess and Count. She aided and assisted 65 crew members and by De Gaulle and Eisenhower, was given the Medal of Freedom, the highest award that can be made to a civilian.

While we were at the Countess chateau, we were waiting for things to cool off as the Germans were making an intense effort to locate more parachuting crew members as they were fading away.

The chateau had a large library of books. We would read until about 2 a.m. One morning we heard dogs barking at the gate. We looked out; German soldiers were there. We proceeded to the attic and hid between the floor and ceiling. The Germans left before midnight taking the Countess and maids to concentration camps in Germany.

After midnight we left the chateau. We vaguely knew how and where to return to the older couple near St. Quay. When we found the older couple, we knocked on their door. The lady opened the door and was literally scared to death when she saw one of us. She suspected that the Germans had caught us and forced us to lead them to their house. We told them what had happened. We spent one night there and then were moved over to the other side of town.

Later we were moved, via train, to Paris by a guide of the French Underground. In Paris we spent 10 days in an apartment with a French nurse and her husband and then were placed on a Red Cross train to a large city in South France. This was a Red Cross train for moving the children out of Paris.

From there a member of the Underground took us by car (using coal) to Foxe, France. There we were turned over to another member of the French Underground who started walking us to Barcelona, Spain, via Andora, Spain. We had nothing much to eat except once in a while, a cube of sugar, a little bread and some green apples.

We arrived by foot, some two weeks later at about 10 miles outside of Barcelona. We were given food, clothes and a razor for shaving, then via train/streetcar were taken to the British Consular. Then we were placed in the apartment of a consular clerk to await the arrival of a Madrid British Embassy officer to take us to Madrid. We could not be seen as we would have to have identity papers to be authorized to be in Spain.

After a month in Spain we were given identity papers and taken on a party of the town by an embassy officer. He paid for everything and we enjoyed a most wonderful evening.

About a week later, we were taken to Gibraltar by train and arrived at about 4 p.m., just in time for a pot of good tea. We spent about four days there. A C-47 with English crew flew us to London, arriving I believe on the 4th of August 1943.

My crew returned to the USA in October 1943. I became a test pilot for the B-29, which one year later I took to combat and flew a full tour of missions from Saipan, bombing Japan by day and night as a member of the 499th Bombardment Group, 20th Bomber Command under General Lensy.

The crew and I will always be grateful to the English and French people for the hospitality shown us.

AN ATTIC HIDEAWAY

By Clifford Hammock

The first person to reach him was Mme. Boullette, who was tending her sheep. She hid him in a barn in back of her house. Two weeks later, the Germans took over the village, so she moved him to a small attic room in her house.

There was no heat, so when the weather got cold, Marcel Hitou carried him to his house, even though there were ten Germans occupying his house. He slept on a cot at the foot of their bed for 74 days. Hitou thought he had safely left on a plane, but the plane couldn't land as the Germans had found their field.

He was carried by car to Paris where he met a young man with the French Underground who arranged for a passport and photo. He was taken to Mme. Payen at 20 Rue St. Lazare where he stayed over a month. Then on to another house where he met Paula. She was later captured.

A French lady went with him by train to southern France. There he met with four other men, who with two guides, walked across the Pyrenees into Andorra. This took three days and nights. By then, it was the last of January.

He traveled to Barcelona, Madrid and Gibraltar by truck and train. From there he flew back to England.

TAIL END CHARLIE BAILOUT!

By Gene Haner

I was co-pilot of a B-17 crew, 353rd Squadron of the 301st Bomb Group. November 7, 1944 we started on a mission to Vienna and encountered 100 mph head winds. Group commander chose to hit an alternate target - Maribor, Yugoslavia at around noon. We were to bomb the railyards, which were filled with troop trains carrying German troops north from Greece. To make sure no civilian injuries, we had to bomb visually. Group leader dropped our altitude from 30,000 to 20,000 ft. to ensure better accuracy. On our bomb run the target became obscured by clouds at the last moment, so the squadron leader chose to make a 360 degree turn over the target. They only had six anti-aircraft guns at Maribor, but the gunners had a chance to zero in on us with all that time over the target.

Our plane was the seventh in the squadron, so called *Tail End Charlie*, and we were hit hard with flak right after bombs away. One engine was shot out, and we had a bad fire in the bomb bay (it looked like a big blow torch), so we decided to bail out.

I saw only two other chutes as I floated down and could see smoke rising out of the target area. After a short time I couldn't see any smoke as I was drifting fast away from the area. I saw a church on a hilltop below me and soon the church was higher than me. I landed next to a vineyard where a man and boy stood. They came over to me and tried to converse - anyway, the old man's eyes lit up when he finally understood. "Ah, Americanski" he said. He also indicated that Germans were 10 minutes away and for me to wait right there for Partisans. A few minutes later a group of young people arrived carrying rifles and pistols - both boys

The attic of Mme. Boullette's home. C. Hammock hid here for three months.

Trie-Chateau, France. Jim Armstrong, M. et Mme. Boullette

Paula is second from the left in this picture. Hammock met her while evading capture.

and girls. They led me for a couple of hours, stopping occasionally at a farmhouse for hard cider and bread.

Eventually we arrived at a house sitting on a hilltop where two more crew members had already arrived. One was ball turret gunner, Lucian Zamorski from Chicago, and tail gunner Vernon Sebesta from Kansas. We were questioned by their leader, who asked about things only an American would know (baseball, movie stars, etc.). The next day we started walking (we were near Ptuj) and for two weeks we traveled mostly at night and for an hour or two at a time before changing guides for a new group of guides.

Every day or two we would pick up someone new that was evading the Germans. Once we picked up a South African pilot who was shot down while stafing a train, and we also helped several British soldiers (Scotch, New Zealanders, and English) that had escaped from a prison camp in Austria.

We had some exciting times where we crossed highways, rivers, etc. After about two weeks we were sitting in a farmhouse and two heads passed a window, one was Navigator Richard Rushmore and the other First Pilot George Kulp. Dick had been wounded in the shoulder just before bailout, but the wound was healing - a piece of flak eventually worked up to the surface and we picked it out.

Anyway, we kept traveling by foot and at one point we passed through the enemy front lines and could travel by day. We finally ended up at the Adriatic port of Zara and at British cruiser tied up at the dock. The Germans had been driven out two weeks before.

The British Navy treated us well, (officers and enlisted men were separated), and the next day a British destroyer picked us up and took us to Bari, Italy. Thirty-eight days.

A couple of weeks later another crewman (name unknown to me) returned to the 301st. He had been picked up by the Partisans, but they took him in the opposite direction to the Russian lines, then to Cairo, then back to Italy.

The rest of the crew were captured by Germans: Archie Aitcheson, radio; Gail Waites, engineer; Percy Maden, gunner; Gene Wright, gunner.

I lost my silver ID bracelet in Yugoslavia and a few weeks later it was returned to me by another fellow who had evaded with the Partisans.

After a week in the hospital (dysentery from drinking "water" instead of natural drink - cider) I lost 25 pounds. Zamorski contracted spinal meningitis and spent several weeks in the hospital.

Another week was spent in rest camp on the Isle of Capri and then in January, I was back on flying status. Shot down on my fifth mission, I flew 21 more before the end of hostilities in Europe.

DARING ESCAPE FROM FRANCE! THE HOWARD HARRIS STORY

Second Lieutenant Howard M. Harris and the rest of his 10-man crew of the flying fortress *Forever Yours* were forced to bail out after a bombing mission on the Renault factory near Paris on September 3, 1943. The Renault raid was the third in which the 25-year-old bombardier had taken part.

Forever Yours went down in flames over occupied territory. Young Harris had been taught to wait as long as possible before pulling his rip-cord to try to escape notice from the ground. Even so, he said he heard machine gun bullets whistling by as he was making his decent. Later he discovered holes made by the bullets in his parachute.

The airman landed in a woods and immediately sought cover to hide from the Nazi soldiers searching for him. The soldiers looked for Harris for about two hours and one time passed so close to him, he later remarked that they could have heard his heart pounding if they had not been talking so much.

Harris remained in hiding for three days, making his way cautiously away from his landing spot before approaching anyone. The smattering of French he had purposely learned in case of such an emergency paid off and helped him out of some tight spots.

The young airman faced many obstacles in the three months and one week it took for him to escape to safety. One constant problem was lack of food. Food was very scarce and he later commented that "horse and cat meat made a welcome dish as rabbit."

Meantime, the lieutenant's young bride, Jeannette Burley Harris, was notified that her husband was missing in action by the War Department on September 15, 1943. The two had married just two months before he entered the service in March 1942. A few days after the Missing In Action notification, Mrs. Harris received a message from her husband's squadron commander that the ship and all crew members had "gone down in a blaze of glory." She refused to accept that as fact, however, and remained confident that her young husband would return, safe and sound.

A friend from the same squadron sent Mrs. Harris a message November 16. It read, "Be of good cheer. Howard all right." Just before Christmas, the government sent official notification that Lt. Harris was indeed safe and sound and had returned to duty. That same day, Lt. Harris, himself, sent a cablegram as well.

Lt. Harris was awarded the Purple Heart for slight wounds received in the Paris raid, as well as the Air Medal for bravery and meritorious service.

The source for this story submitted by Howard M. Harris is the Lake Shore News, January 13, 1944.

EVASION STORY OF ROBERT W. HAWKINSON (CAPTAIN, U. S. A. A. F.)

On August 2, 1944 I was on the deck strafing an enemy vehicle near Rouen, France when my aircraft, a P-51, was severely damaged by anti-aircraft fire. I pulled up to about 800 feet and bailed out. I hit hard and, after unbuckling my chute and getting up to run, found I had broken my ankle. I appealed for help from a man and two girls standing nearby but they gave no response and simply stood there watching me.

Seeking cover, I crawled on my hands and knees through a hedge surrounding a pasture. On the field side I continued to crawl toward a wooded area about 60 yards ahead but froze when I heard German voices in the lane on the opposite side of the hedge. Two Germans on bicycles stopped almost

Gilbert Merriene, principal helper and first contact, 1944.

(L to R): Mlle Rolande Dehayes, Mme Alexandrine Hebert.

(L to R): Mme. R. Hebert, Jean Claude Hebert, Jean Jaques Hebert, Mlle Rolande Dehayes. Hawkinson traveled to the farm of Mme Alexandrine Hebert in the farm cart.

Family get-together. Fathers of young children in German forced labor camps. Helpers all in back row, Left, M. Merriene; second from left, Mme Alexandrine Hebert third from right, Mme R. Hebert; second from right, Gilbert Merriene; far right, Rene' Dehayes.

opposite me and, after pointing to my burning aircraft across the field, continued on their way.

As I continued to crawl toward the wooded area I heard more voices, both French and German, of people coming down the lane. Realizing that I must quickly hide, I backed into a space between a large tree and a bush that was part of the hedgerow. On the opposite side of the tree was a narrow opening through which the military and civilians passed in order to go across the field toward my plane wreckage.

My cover was sparse, in fact I was holding a branch down in front of me. As the French and Germans returned they queued up awaiting their turn to slip through the opening and back on the lane. From my hiding place I could see German boots not more than four or five feet away. Later, four Germans came across the field. One relieved himself against the tree behind which I was hiding.

Fortunately, I was not discovered and spent the night in the field. Early next morning a young lad named Gilbert Merriene rode by on a draft horse (it was later that I learned his and other helpers' names). I called to him and he, with very evident excitement, came to my side. Using the language phrase book from my escape kit, I asked if he could get me civilian clothes and hide me, to which he responded affirmatively and left. Some time later another lad, Rene' Dehayes, appeared with the clothing. After changing he directed me to the wooded area I had been trying to reach the day before.

That night the two lads returned with their uncle, Monsieur Merriene, mayor of Vieux Manoir, a nearby vil-

lage. They carried me to a farm which was operated by another member of the family. I was bedded down in the barn and given some jellied bread and milk, my first food and drink since breakfast the day before.

Early the next morning I was put in the bottom of a one-horse farm cart and covered with hay. The cart, driven by M. Merriene, stopped at one point in our journey, and I could hear German voices. After what sounded like an exchange of pleasantries the cart moved on, and after some time we arrived at a remote crossroads called Cauricourt and the small farm of Madame Alexandrine Hebert. I was installed in the hayloft of the barn, given some food and provided with a pillow, blanket and a "thundermug." M. Merriene looked through the items in my escape kit and took two photos of me in civilian clothes which had been taken in England prior to going on operations. A few days later Gilbert returned with an identity card that had an official seal impressed through part of the photo.

My ankle, by this time, was swollen and black and blue with yellowish streaks running up the calf of my left. It throbbed with pain and movement brought further discomfort. My helpers, most likely for security reasons, did not seek medical assistance, and I, respecting their situation, did not ask for any. Travel was out of the question so my only option was to remain where I was until the Allied ground forces, who had broken out of the Normandy beachhead a week earlier, overran the area.

Mme. Hebert left early each morning for her job in a

nearby village and returned each evening, six days a week. Before leaving each day she brought me food and emptied my thundermug. Upon returning each evening she brought me food and drink but her visits were very fleeting.

About mid-August retreating Germans began straggling through the area following backroads and country lanes, most likely to avoid Allied fighter strafing attacks. They came singly, in two's and three's and occasionally in large groups. Few carried arms and fewer still were in full uniform. My helpers, concerned about the many Germans coming on the property seeking food and possibly some soft hay to sleep on, decided to move me into the house. By this time I was somewhat mobile, moving around the three-room house on a homemade crutch. I was able to observe the Germans and on several occasions they came to the front door, knocked and receiving no answer, left.

One Sunday afternoon, when Mme. Hebert was home, a group of four soldiers came to the door seeking food. I hustled into my bedroom and stayed there while she cooked up some potatoes and vegetables. They were loud and boisterous and after they left I experienced a mild case of the shakes.

On another day a good looking young German, probably in his mid-teens, knocked on the door as I observed him through the curtains. Receiving no answer he tried the doorknob. Finding that locked he went around the back and tried that door. Having no success he then went to the vegetable garden, picked some produce and left.

Most Germans I observed were polite and somewhat docile, probably because they were in retreat. One exception was a large group led by an officer who threatened people on a farm across the road. The soldiers were armed, in full field uniform and had some equipment piled on a large flatbed wagon pulled by a lone horse. The officer shook his fist at the people and shouted at them repeatedly but the group finally moved on with no harm being done. (I later learned they wanted horses which the French had hidden in the woods but would not admit to).

One day in late August a spearhead of a Polish armored division attached to the Canadian First Army, rumbled through. I talked to a tanker who suggested I lay low as there were still many Germans around and his own support units were a day or two behind.

I was finally picked up by a Canadian Army medical unit.

LAST DAY ON YOLO SHAN
By William B. Hayes

When I first arrived on Yolo Shan, the Chinese general in charge gave me some extra soldiers to help us move the equipment up the mountain and to build a bamboo shelter to work out of and to sleep in. The shelter was about 10x12 feet and had a lean-to attached for the generator. The three Chinese with me used the lean-to to sleep in and to cook our meals. The shelter consisted of bamboo mats held up by bamboo poles and plastered with mud to keep the wind and rain out. The roof was thatch and the two small windows were covered with oiled paper. The door consisted of another bamboo mat that could be rolled up or let down. I slept on the dirt floor on a bamboo mat that was either rolled up in the day or hung outside.

While the shelter was being built, the extra soldiers strung a line from our location to the tunnel where the Chinese headquarters was located, and a field telephone on each end let me communicate with an English speaking Chinese at the headquarters.

Normally I did not transmit from this location except for emergencies, but rather we moved the transmitter and the generator to one of the several locations that we had prepared. The other sites were located where I could see some of the surrounding areas and consisted of nothing more than several slit trenches and antennas that were left in place. These sites were located just over the brow of the hill or on the far side of a ridge from where the Japanese artillery was located at that time.

There was a piece of a randomly fired shell that went through the upper part of the shelter, blowing mud and dust all over. The Chinese soldiers found it and brought it in. The piece was about one-eighth of an inch thick, approximately eight or nine inches long and varied in width from an inch to around four inches. I was not transmitting at that time and no other shells came in our vicinity.

The Japanese would regularly fire artillery shells randomly throughout the day and at an increased rate during the night as an annoyance factor to disturb our sleep and to work on our nerves. On clear nights the shelling was sometimes replaced by enemy bombers. The bombers would come in one at a time at low level, and they would randomly drop a single bomb every few minutes and fire their machine guns off and on at the ground. When one bomber would leave, it would be replaced by another. This would continue throughout the night. The Chinese never fired at these planes, or any others, as they thought that the planes were trying to locate our positions.

A plane that I think was a Stukka Dive Bomber (I had never seen one but had heard of them) dive bombed near the man-made underground tunnels where the Chinese headquarters was located. Headquarters was located at the end of a small and relatively narrow valley, and I was located about a half mile above farther down the valley. I was high enough to have a clear view as I watched the bi-plane approach at a high altitude and go into its dive. At the same time the pilot unlocked, or turned on, the sirens on the wings. There were several sirens all pitched differently, and the sound of those sirens as they increased in intensity set my teeth on edge. I found myself wanting to scream and drown them out. Just before the plane pulled out of the dive, the pilot shut off the sirens and dropped his bombs. There was a brief period of relative silence, just long enough to let you start to relax before the bombs exploded. They were the percussion type and even at the distance I was, they made the loudest noise that I have ever heard.

One of my Chinese soldiers later communicated to me that some of the Chinese who were caught outside of the cave were deaf and others mentally unbalanced.

As there was no refrigeration, it was necessary, every afternoon, to send one of my soldiers down in the valley to pick up our meat and vegetable rations. We had a good supply of rice on hand and water was available nearby.

On the afternoon of my last day on Yolo Shan, the soldier that went for our rations came back with the news that the main Chinese force had departed during the night. I got on the field telephone and after some time, I found out that it

General Chennault had Capt. John Birch hand pick his men to serve at the "Special Stations." Birch wanted men with communication skills, personal stamina and the "right" mental attitude. In addition, the men were to be impervious to privation, possess a knowledge of Chinese customs and be able to live with the Chinese troops in the field if necessary. Men pictured are: Standing, (L to R): unknown, Sgt. Lassiterm, Sgt. Hayes, Sgt. Kane, Sgt. Eikenberry, Lt. Lu; Seated: unknown, Capt. John Birch, Capt. Su Tu, Lt. Drummond.

was true and that the Chinese who were still on Yolo Shan would attempt to escape to Japanese encirclement that night as soon as it was dark.

A couple of pilots understood how critical our forward position was and made a risky gasoline drop. Their names were Captain Theodore Adams and Colonel Phil Loufbourrow. I would have run out in a few hours if they hadn't made the drop. As it turned out, it was the Japanese and not the lack of fuel, that determined when I had to go off the air.

I didn't get all of the 40 gallons of gasoline that was dropped. The cable attaching the tank to the parachute did snap as reported, when the parachute opened.

The tank with the cushioning tires broke down when it hit near the corner of a small flooded rice paddy. Most of the gasoline spread over the water, but some gasoline mixed with water remained in the broken tank.

A group of Chinese and I salvaged all we could by putting the mixture in all the available containers we could locate. We even "skimmed" some of the mixture from the top of the water.

All of the time I could picture the gasoline fumes flowing downhill and I was hoping no one downwind had a fire burning or would light a cigarette.

We carried the gasoline and water mixture to higher ground near the radio station and filtered it through a chamois to get the water out. We must have finished with four or five gallons of gasoline which lasted until I had to

leave. In fact, it was later that day that the Japanese were all over the place and one of their patrols approached the station location. I heard the Chinese that were assigned to me as guards exchanging gunfire with the patrol, and I went out and joined them. Some of the patrol got away and I knew then that it was time to leave.

I blew up the radio station and left the generator running with the oil plug removed until it froze up. After dark we pulled out, and I scattered the M-209 cypher device over the next few miles. After playing "hide and seek" for the next week I arrived at Pao Ching and flew in to Kweilin on the 26th. I think that they called the small plane I flew back in the *Bo Peep* and I can tell you that this one "lost sheep" was glad to be back.

ESCAPE AND EVASION!
By John F. Hickman

(True story of his capture by the Germans, his escape and his eventual entry into Switzerland for a leisurely summer in 1944.)

I went operational with the 107th Tactical Reconnaissance Squadron, 6th Group in the fall of 1943. On my 19th mission in May, 1944, my P51 was shot down directly over the defense perimeter of one of the German V-1 bomb-

John F. Hickman, 1st Lt. US Air Corps.

launching sites in Pas de Calais province. I was taken prisoner by a German patrol, escorted to their headquarters for a few days, then moved north and eventually to Lille where I was held in a wretched prison for two days.

From Lille I was escorted by a German sergeant and private to a railroad station. The two German soldiers, the tall genial sergeant and the weedy little private, and I were assigned to a comfortable compartment in the middle of a railroad car. I learned very early that this was a German troop train carrying some 500 German troops going on leave, and by mid-afternoon, they would be in Metz and well on their way home.

My first real break occurred in mid-afternoon when the train engine broke down, and we sat for four hours in Charleville, near the French-Belgian border. I knew this would delay our crossing the border into Germany until dark, and I was positively jubilant as the hours sped by. I sat and watched and made frequent trips to the restroom, taking my little bag of goodies with me each time.

Finally, about 11:00 p.m. I got my chance. The big chap was sound asleep and the little private got himself comfortable, placing his pistol and holster between the two of them.

I had learned to judge the speed of the train by the clicking of its wheels, and when it seemed that the train was traveling at a reasonable speed, I got up from the seat with my little bag in hand, saw the now-sleeping private's pistol and picked it up and put it in my belt, opened the door and moved down the aisle to the steps, and jumped out into the night at just the right time. The train kept moving, and I was free!

I wandered around the countryside a bit, and finally sacked out in an old hay stack. The next morning I approached a farm house and managed to get some breakfast and food to take along on my travel (from a very anxious farm owner) and started on to Verdun.

At a second stop I encountered a Frenchman and his son from Verdun who said they would be glad to help me! The Frenchman, Rene Messenger, and his son, Robert, arranged a rendezvous beyond a German check-point, and so I arrived at Rene's house in Verdun without incident.

Rene assigned me his bedroom, and he in turn moved into their parlor. On the 11th day of my stay, Rene received word I'd be moving on, and a few days later I was picked up by a lady from the Underground and taken to the local railroad station. I was to know this remarkable lady as Madame Raymonde. We wandered around a bit, and at another station we were joined by a tall, taciturn young man who was also escaping. We were to remain companions until we slipped over the border into Switzerland with a group of approximately 30 people. Once across the border, I was never to see my young friend nor my guide again, and I later learned that she had been executed by the Germans on her return to France.

Switzerland! We Americans, British and Italian escapees were kept a month in a quarantine camp, a wise precaution taken by the Swiss. After that we were housed in very nice hotels in Glion, a village on a ledge a few hundred feet above Montreaux. Rent and food were furnished by our respective embassies plus a substantial monthly allowance. Once out of quarantine, life in Switzerland was perfect...no uniform, no responsibilities, just one fun day after another! There was the knowledge that our buddies were trading heavy blows to the Germans in France, and we were asking the question, "Shouldn't we be helping?"

From the very start of my stay in Switzerland, I was plotting to get out and back to my squadron. My family, now aware of my whereabouts, urged me to "stay put." However, in July and August, the war had turned our way, and so Gordon Frazier decided to escape back to France! We moved into a Montreaux hotel for a night, then to the beachhead in southern France where I managed to talk an operations officer into preparing orders to fly to Naples. By this time, I had about 15 Americans (refugees from Glion) put on the orders, and shortly we caught a flight to Rome then Naples.

At Naples Gordon and I parted, and I teamed up with Joe Cose, a sergeant with the American embassy in Switzerland. He was able to get us a troop transport to an out-of-the-way refueling stop in North Africa. There pure luck came my way again! The dispatch officer was Richard Frost, a long-time English friend. He arranged dropping enough cargo off the next flight out to Casablanca so we could board the plane.

At Casablanca we wasted no time booking to England, and in a couple of days were on our way. We landed at Land's End and got another flight to London the next day. There I was outfitted and went to Middle Wallop where I'd been transferred from North Africa.

I found out by chance where my squadron, the 107th, was located and made arrangements to get there by the postal delivery plane, an A-46. So, I was back . . . just four months and six days after being shot down! Despite a warm welcome from the squadron and an eagerness for me to rejoin them, the Intelligence officer informed me that since I'd been a P.O.W., for even a few days, I was not eligible to enter combat operations in the same theatre.

After a few days it was back to England and home, but not for discharge. I had joined up for the duration, and because of a little luck had survived it. I'd stay in until the war was over . . . so out to Phoenix as an instructor!

NAVIGATOR'S STORY
By 2d Lt. William A. Hoffman III

As a navigator of B-17s, this was my sixth mission with the 326th Squadron, 92nd Bomb Group, 8th Air Force based at Podington, England. The date was February 8, 1944. Our target was Frankfort, Germany. Over northern France, a mixed group of ME-109s and FW-190s attacked our group from 1:00 with disastrous results to our squadron. Both the squadron leader and our ship, the second element leader, were knocked out of formation with heavy damage to several of our engines. We descended to an altitude of about 2000 feet, and the pilot ordered us to bail out. The bombardier was either dead or seriously wounded. The co-pilot and I opened his parachute and threw him out. The co-pilot went out next and then it was my turn. By this time, we were about at 1,000 feet. My parachute opened and I swung three times and hit the ground. My hands were so frozen, that I had difficulty getting out of the chute and harness.

I ran into nearby woods, a small copse about 100 yards thick. Upon reaching the far edge, a farmer working in a field shouted at me and motioned for me to approach. He asked if I needed a doctor. When I said no, he had his companion, a small boy, take me to a farm house about a half mile away. When we entered, the old lady of the house poured me a glass of what I thought was white wine. It proved to be Calvados! My face was covered with blood from the shrapnel and Calvados was her response to the medical situation.

The Germans had watched our descent and were searching for us, but the French hid me well. At one point, I was hidden in a pit under a pile of brush, and German soldiers were having a conversation above me.

The French Resistance moved me to the town of Crevecoeur-Le-Grand and to the home of the LeFrancs. German officers were billeted next door. It was their wont to shoot pigeons on the theory one of them might be a carrier pigeon. The pigeons ended up on the LeFranc's table. Food was so strictly rationed that this helped immensely. That the Germans were supplying my food was the cause of much merriment. Our two families have kept in touch through the years.

My next stop was Beauvais and then on to Paris by train. On the way into Paris, we were delayed at Creil because American planes were bombing the marshaling yards.

The last part of the journey took six of us American airmen and a French escort by train to Rennes. I had been given papers that identified me as Pierre Henri Kerharro and I was dressed as a farm worker. German soldiers had set up a checkpoint at the Rennes station and just four of us and the escort made it through. Because the last two men had been caught, we tore through streets, alleys and back yards putting distance between us and that station before going to a "safe house" for the night. The next day, using inter-urban trains, we arrived at the coastal town of Plouha in Brittany.

On the evening of the 23rd of March, the family with whom I was staying was listening to the news on the BBC. The granddaughter whispered, "Ce soir". They had been listening for a signal from London that indicated a British boat would be in to pick us up. Thirty-two British and American airmen and some spies were assembled in Plouha that night. We met at rendezvous house "La maison d'Alphonse." There was a mined field to go through before descending a high cliff to the rocky beach. Dorys from British Motor Boat 503 came in to take us out. By morning we were safely back in England. All that remains of the shrapnel is the small piece embedded in my ring finger.

I shall always be grateful to the courageous men and women of the French Resistance who came to my rescue.

BAIL-OUT OVER KOBLENZ!
By Laurie S. Horner, 838th BS, 487th BG

Sgt. Horner, tail gunner on B-17 out of Lavenham, England, bailed out near Koblenz, Germany, September 12, 1944. The group was on a mission to bomb oil installations near Magdeburg, Germany. En route the plane lost one engine (mechanical failure) near Hamburg, Germany. The plane left the group formation, dropped their bombs in an effort to keep up. Failing in this the pilot decided to fly on to the target rally point to rejoin the group. On arrival at R.P. another engine failed. With two engines out they proceeded ahead of the group on the return route to England. Near Koblenz and west of the Rhine River, a third engine failed necessitating a bail out order.

The crew, except for the pilot who stayed at the controls, gathered in the waist, bailing out one at a time. Thus, upon landing they were scattered too far apart to join up and each proceeded to evade alone.

Horner landed in a dense forest, the parachute caught the top of several tall pines, and with the chute shrouds fully extended, he was dangling 20 to 30 feet above the ground. Swinging to an adjacent tree, he released the parachute harness and climbed down, forced to leave the chute exposed due to entanglement in the trees. Hurriedly he left the landing area walking west towards the Allied lines in Belgium. After several sightings of German troops plus seeing large amounts of Allied chaff hanging from the trees, he assumed there were AA Batteries in the area thus, decided it best to hide during the day and travel at night using the North Star as directional reference. Daytime concealment was taken under low ground hanging pine branches or drainage ditches in the fields along the way.

On one occasion just at daybreak, he was forced to hide in a roadside ditch as a German convoy passed the path of his crossing. The morning of September 17, after traveling five nights and hiding four days, he saw a young boy entering the field adjoining his hiding place in the woods. After watching the boy to be certain he was alone, Horner called the boy into the woods. Having not eaten in five days, he used sign language to convey to the boy his hunger. The boy crossed the field, returned with his lunch, a cheese sandwich, which he shared with Horner. With the use of drawings on the lunch bag, Horner conveyed he was a downed flier who had been bombing Germany. Not knowing the lad's nationality nor where his loyalties lay, Horner queried him by drawing swastikas and saying Hitler's name. The boy facially expressed a disdain for both.

The boy responded correctly when asked regarding the

direction of the German troops (Der Bache) by pointing to the east and pointing west for the Allies or Americans, both names he understood in English. The boy agreed to lead Horner to the Americans if he would help him with field chores. After completing the work the boy led him in a westerly direction searching for American troops that he had seen earlier that morning. (Horner marvels at the fact they conversed using sign language, drawings, very limited German and English, yet they were able to communicate.) As they walked, evidence of American troop presence was found with the sighting of tire tracks and discarded "C" ration boxes. Later they came upon American troops belonging to the 102nd Recon outfit on a mission behind the German lines. Horner was greeted with the working end of an MI rifle. Then it dawned on him that he was wearing flying clothes which very few if any Army GI's had ever seen.

After interrogation by the officer in charge, Horner satisfactorily identified himself as an American airman. The boy who had guided Horner was identified as a German national by the American troops. He accepted only a few cigarettes for his service and went on his way.

Horner was returned to Belgium by the 102nd Recon and turned over to 5th Corps. MPs. He learned that his co-pilot had evaded capture and had passed through 5th Corp area earlier. The 5th Corp officers also informed him that his pilot, Lt. Walter Preston, had been killed bailing out too low over Belgium. Preston was buried in St. Vith by civilians. Amazingly, the plane with only one engine and Lt. Preston aboard flew across the lines into Belgium. Had the crew stayed aboard it no doubt would have crashed in Germany.

Horner was assigned to guard prisoners for several days and when they transported the P.O.W.s into France, Horner went along with the convoy, serving as a guard. Upon reaching the "Red Ball" highway (the road to Paris) he was relieved of the rifle, duty and transportation. He was on his own again and told to hitchhike to Paris, which he did, by thumbing rides with American truck convoys returning from the front for supplies.

Several days and some 200 miles later, he arrived in Paris reporting to the S-2 Intelligence Corp. After debriefing he was flown to London for further interrogation and assignment. He was joined in London by five others of his crew who had evaded. They confirmed Preston's death and informed him that their navigator and radioman had been captured by the Germans.

Horner returned to the 487th and gave several talks to new replacement crews concerning evasion tactics he had used. He returned to the States in October 1944 and learned for the first time of the birth of his daughter, Patricia. He was graduated from Instructor's School, Laredo, Texas, taught aerial gunnery, Las Vegas, Nevada, and Kingman, Arizona Air Bases. He was discharged from the service in October 1945.

THE KEN HOUGARD STORY

On May 8, 1944, an 8th Air Force B-17 was shot down over German-occupied France. Of the ten-man crew of the ship, six were killed, three were captured by the Germans, and one man managed to escape. That man was T/Sgt. Kenneth Hougard.

Hougard lived for two months dressed as a French peasant and had only one close call with enemy troops. That

T/Sgt. Kenneth Hougard being interrogated by Gen. Dwight D. Eisenhower.

incident occurred when the young airman was stopped along the road by Germans asking directions. He slipped and answered in English but quickly realized the danger of his mistake. He turned and walked away from the Germans giving no regard to orders to halt. For some reason, they did not shoot.

Liberation came to Hougard on July 4, 1944 as Allied troops advanced swiftly across the Cherbourg peninsula. He was taken to the supreme commander, General Dwight D. Eisenhower and General Omar Bradley for interrogation. The meeting was photographed by a signal corps photographer, and Hougard later received a copy of the print.

Hougard would meet Eisenhower again when the general came to Portland campaigning for the presidency.

This story submitted by Kenneth Hougard is taken from the Union Pacific Bulletin, November, 1952.

A MONTH IN THE MOUNTAINS
By J. K. Hurst

On October 20, 1943, the 8th Air Force dispatched the 390th Bomb Group of B-17s to destroy a railyard in Germany. After dropping our bombs we were returning through Holland when the Luftwaffe shot us out of the sky. There were three fatalities, the ball turret gunner landed with the aircraft, six of us bailed out, and I was the fortunate evader.

From October until the middle of December, I made my way to the village of Perpignan in southern France. We hid in a small farmhouse waiting for a nearby river to recede in order to ford the stream. There were five of us that left one evening to ford the swift river, and the next day we hid out on the river bank to be joined by ten Americans.

We had two Catalon guides to help us cross the Pyrenees. We traversed many vineyards where the old growth would tear the flesh from our shins. Our first loss was a traveler whose feet and legs would not permit him to travel further. He turned himself in at a monastery, and we were told the monks turned him over to the Germans. We had an older traveler who had a valise. He was repeatedly warned to keep up but continued to fall behind until one night a guide shoved him off the icy cliff. What was in the valise? There were now 13 of us.

The next morning before daylight we encountered a German patrol. Immediately blood hounds were brought in and the ten Americans were captured. The remaining three of us waded into a mountain stream and about noon came to the crest of the mountain. A rock makes a good pillow. Now there were only three of us, and we made rapid progress and soon were in Spain.

Our guides left us, and after two freezing nights, a good Spaniard came to take us to his home. We arrived in the early hours of the morning and the good senora prepared a steaming pot of cafe y leche. We were awakened late the next afternoon and served a sumptuous feast.

The following morning we walked to the railroad station and took a train to Barcelona. We arrived at the British consulate and met our Catalon guides awaiting their reward. Now for the delight of delights - a bath - the first in over a month.

E AND E REPORT NO. 795
EVASION IN FRANCE
Submitted by Capt. Jack M. Ilfrey,
79th Fighter Squadron, 20th Fighter Group

Headquarters
European Theater of Operations
P/W and X Detachment, Military Intelligence Service
20 June 1944
Target: Bridge S of Angers
MIA: 13 June 1944
Arrived in UK 17 June 1944

On 13 June 1944 I led my squadron down to attack a train in the vicinity of Angers. My P-38 was hit during the first pass. The cockpit filled with smoke, and as I pulled up to 1200 feet I saw the right engine blazing. I went out over the supercharger on the right side of the plane veered off to the left. I pulled the ripcord and landed almost at the same moment in the backyard of a farmhouse.

Unbuckling my chute and leaving it on the ground I ran around the house and up to the French family standing in the yard watching me. I didn't want to hide there because my plane was burning in the next field, and it was obvious that the Frenchmen didn't want me to stop. I asked the direction north and ran along hedgerows following a small country lane about four kilometers before stopping to rest in a ditch. I still was wearing my summer flying suit, helmet, goggles, flying boots and GI shoes.

During this 20 minute rest I took off my coveralls, insignia, and tie, took the things out of my aid box, ate a bar of candy, looked over my maps and set out north on a dirt road. It was 2230 hours. Now I was wearing my gray sweater, dark green trousers and GI shoes. My shirt was open at the neck and I had no cap.

I had been walking for ten minutes in the dusk when a young Frenchman rode up behind me on a bicycle and asked me in broken English if I was the American who had crashed. I admitted my identity and asked where the Germans were. He had just come from my plane. Two or three Germans had reached the plane a few minutes after the crash and were searching the neighborhood for me. He estimated the Allied lines to be about 200 km north and assured me there were plenty of Germans about. I asked if I could buy his bicycle. He wanted to sell it, but he thought he had better ask his family. He gave me his beret and took me to his home.

The family greeted me cordially and said I could stay the night. They didn't know about the fighting area to the north, but they thought my idea of cycling to the lines was a good one. I asked the head of the family to write a note, as if he were a doctor, stating that I was deaf and dumb and on my way to visit my parents. I carried the note but never found any use for it. There was some argument in the family about selling the bicycle. Several members thought it would endanger them if I were caught and if the Germans used pressured to learn where I had gotten the bicycle. The head of the family overruled this objection, and I paid all the money from my escape purse and L5 (5 pounds sterling) from my pocket for it.

I compared my maps with a Michelin road map, memorizing the route that I meant to follow because I did not want to carry anything British or American with me. I planned to follow highway 1n 162 almost all the way to Caen. Before going to bed that night I left all my escape aids and purse, my crash bracelet, watch and fountain pen, my maps and GI shoes - in short everything that would identify me - behind as souvenirs. I had not taken dog tags on my mission with me so now I had no means of identification if captured.

I started early the next morning so I would not be seen leaving the house. I was dressed in beret, old French slippers, a kind of Dutch trousers that buttoned up the sides, a green shirt and dark blue coat. The family were pleased with my disguise and assured me that the Germans paid no attention to French cyclists. I was given food in an old musette bag. I pedaled without incident to the main road (NI62) and turned north.

About mid-morning I was passed by a small German convoy of three trucks and two staff cars which I in turn passed ten minutes later when it had stopped because of Allied aircraft in the vicinity. On down the road I came to a single parked staff car and was stopped by a German soldier. I was ready to play deaf and dumb, but he spoke in German gesturing to ask if I had just passed three trucks and two staff cars. I answered, "Oui" and cycled on. Soon after this the convoy passed me again, and I was never far behind them all the way into Laval. North of this town I stopped to rest and eat lunch.

In the afternoon about halfway to Mayenne, a German soldier called me to halt. He wanted my bicycle and meant to have it. I began protesting by holding on to the bike and pointing down the road saying mama and papa (in French), and he seemed to get the idea. At just this moment a German truck came along and he hitched a ride on it, or I would have probably lost my bicycle.

I continued on through Mayenne and stopped at a farmhouse where I saw a man alone in the yard. I asked him in French for water and got it. The man began asking questions but I pointed to my ears and said "sourd" (deaf).

I pedaled without stopping to within 10 km of Domfront. I stopped again for water at an isolated farmhouse. Because it was getting dark, and I wanted to get off the road before the curfew, I told them I was an American and asked if they would hide me. I got the water, but they refused to let me sleep there because the neighborhood was full of Germans. Not far from their home I found a small barn off the highway and slept in it that night.

It was daylight when I awakened. I pedaled all morning and into the afternoon without stopping except for a short rest and without speaking to anyone. I was seeing more Germans on the roads and signs of evacuees from the fighting areas, but no one paid me any attention. By mid-afternoon I was thirsty and hungry enough to look for help. I examined the houses carefully and chose one where I would not easily be seen approaching and where a woman was working alone in the yard.

She gave me water and began asking questions while I drank it. I started to tell her I was deaf, but I changed my mind because of her friendly attitude. I admitted to being an American and asked for food. She was not frightened and asked me into the house (I had decided it was best always to leave quickly when anyone showed signs of nervousness at hearing I was an American). I left the woman as soon as I had eaten, cycled through Conde and found a barn before dark.

The next morning the front tire on my bicycle was flat. I had pushed it out to the highway and stopped a man whose cycle had a pump. I managed to borrow his pump without having to speak. However, before I was finished he started talking to me, and I discovered he could speak some English. He was friendly so I told him my story and asked what he thought of my chances. He was not too encouraging but thought them fair. We traveled together until he had to turn off. I could hear the guns now, though they were 20 miles away.

At Thury I turned northwest, away from Caen, and zigzagged over country roads to Fontenay. This took about two hours, and I arrived around 0930 hours. I started north on a road out of Fontenay and had ridden about 15 minutes when I was stopped by two Germans who were carrying a soldier whose leg had been shot off.

They paid no attention to my mama and papa gag, but commandeered the bicycle at once. I walked on north following the same road and two km further ran into a group of Germans just as I was walking out of a wooded area into fields.

They grabbed me and made me get into their trenches. I was not searched or questioned. Allied patrols were on the other side of the fields. Each time I made a move to leave they stopped me with an emphatic "Nichts."

I sat in the trench two hours with British shells passing over us into the woods. Finally one of the German soldiers was wounded in the stomach by a piece of shell. He was put in a wheelbarrow and I was ordered to take him back to the dressing station. I had noticed this field station when I passed it, and they drew crosses in the sand in addition to motioning what I was to do. The German was still conscious and made me stop occasionally so that he could rest.

Finally I dumped him with the medical people and was given chocolate and cigarettes. Then they motioned for me to go back toward Fontenay.

At Fontenay I followed a road leading west to Tilly and St. Pierre. On the outskirts of Tilly I went up to a farmer who was milking a cow and asked him how I could get to British or American lines. I could tell about where they were from the gunfire and from the Allied aircraft that occasionally flew in low over the lines to draw fire and then popped back

again. The Frenchman told me to follow a small dirt road north out of St. Pierre.

After following this road for 15 or 20 minutes, I began to see British helmets over the tops of hedges. I walked toward them and soon heard someone yell for somebody to get that French civilian out of the way. A British sergeant grabbed me from behind a hedge and when I told him I was an American flier, he radioed for permission to take me back to a forward headquarters. After that I was interrogated at British HQ and brought back to my base in U.K.

A cool and skillful job all the way through. The lesson it teaches is that in the confusion of a general engagement, when troops and transport are moving, there is an excellent chance to dodge controls and to bluff one's way in the tight spots. Enemy troops have their minds full of more pressing concerns than the examination of every ragged civilian on the off chance that he may be an evader.

Evader took an unnecessary risk in disposing of his dog tags, although even dog tags might not have convinced nervous and excited troops in case of his apprehension. A safer, if slower, route would have been that to Spain.

HELPED BY TITO'S PARTISANS

By Dee R. Jones, Jr.

On 30 May 1944, our crew had been briefed for a mission to the Wallendorf Airdrome at Wiener Neustadt, Austria. The Airdrome was a two mission credit sortie and would have been my 44th mission in just five months of combat flying. German fighters hit our formation before we got to the TP, and flak was heavy over the target area. Our B-24 was the lead of the high right formation which was a usual position for our crew.

Over the target area we lost an engine because of flak and after dropping our bombs we "high-tailed" it off the target/flak area where German fighters hit us again!

Our fighter escort P-51s were waiting for us and went after the attacking German fighters. It was on such a fighter attack that a P-51 raked us with .50 caliber machine gun fire. The plexiglas top turret cover was shattered and projectiles tore through the back of the turret seat and the material of my flight jacket.

A second engine was disabled by flak and the tail gunner had been killed by an exploding 20mm shell that exploded inside the turret. Control cables to the tail surfaces had been severed by either 20mm shells or flak, and this prompted the pilot, Lt. Bruner, to have the bailout signal sounded and he told us to bail out!

The plane was about 17,000 feet and was indicating 200 mph airspeed. It was around noon when I rolled out the bomb bay, something caught my right arm and the chute was popped open inside the bomb bay. When the opened chute hit the slipstream, nine panels popped open (tore loose). This action busted ribs on my left side. I was in pain as I dropped faster than normal. I landed in heavy brush area that cushioned the fall. The area was on the edge of cultivated fields.

I headed for a group of farm buildings that I had seen as I came down in the chute. There were several people standing around a well near what appeared to be farm buildings.

Dee R. Jones nearing retirement in 1963.

One adult spoke English and told me where I should turn myself in to the German authorities to receive medical help. A group of youngsters had gathered, and they indicated that I should join them and they would take me to a doctor.

I was taken to a residence fairly close to this area, but on the way the group of us took cover on the edge of a forested area while a German patrol went by. In the midst of this patrol was the radio operator of our crew. I learned much later that the radio operator was in a German prison camp.

At the house I was taken to, a man checked me over and they used a piece of my parachute to wrap around my upper body to facilitate my moving about. It was at this residence that I was joined by the navigator and bombardier that was on the plane with me. The navigator (Lt. Harry Parr) and I had been together on the same crew since crew training in Arizona.

This was the start of the first of many adventures before we got to an area where a C-47 flew in to pick us up with others and returned to Foggia, Italy. This journey was handled by the Partisans who were mainly loyal to Marshall Tito.

We walked by night and holed up during the daytime. We were taken to a Partisan headquarters at Chazma. We stayed there for a while and were even included in the interrogation of German officers (captives) by the Partisans.

We also received briefings at Chazma informing us of the internal strife of the Yugoslav people, their fight against the Germans, Mahailovich, and Pavolich Ustashi, their alignment with Russian troops, as well as the United States to free their country from the German occupation.

The United States had OSI agents that coordinated aid to the Partisans in the form of food, money and military assistance. In turn, the Partisans and the people of Yugoslavia assisted in helping "downed" air crew members to return to their home bases. The desire to free their country was evident by the young people that were under arms, both male and female. We saw no infants nor pregnant women which I think speaks for their dedication to "Country."

I had gotten yellow from jaundice (orange eyeballs) caused by the jump so I couldn't eat or keep food down. I lost weight and weighed 100 pounds when I returned to Allied control.

We were taken through German controlled areas and were fired upon several times before reaching an area in southern Yugoslavia where we were flown back to Italy.

THE BUS TO BORDEAUX

By Norman P. Kempton

I was shot down on 4 January 1944 approximately 25 miles northwest of Bordeaux, France. I parachuted into a swamp area where I hid until the following morning. I was helped by a French farmer who gave me civilian clothes. He was evidently not a member of the organized Resistance. He directed me to take the bus to Bordeaux, which I did.

I got off the bus in Bordeaux, walked through the city and walked for the next ten days to the southeast toward Toulouse, France. During the 10 days I obtained food and shelter from French farmers, slept in stables, haystacks, and, sometimes a bed.

After approximately ten days I made contact with the French Organized Resistance near Mantauban, France. I stayed with a French farm family named Ernest La Place for approximately four weeks. I was then transported by auto and train to the foothills of the Pyrenees Mountains. There, in the company of two other American airmen, ten Frenchmen, and two Basque guides, I walked across the Pyrenees. The trip took about ten days, walking at night only.

I reached Isaba, Spain on 23 February 1944. During the next few weeks we were in the care of the U.S. Military Attache Office and the Spanish Air Force. We were transported to Madrid, Spain, then to Gibraltar, then flown back to England.

This is very briefly my evasion experience. I was helped by many French whose names were never mentioned. I will be eternally grateful for their assistance. I was very fortunate and extremely lucky to evade capture.

PERSONAL ESCAPE STORY

By A. D. (Dell) Kneale, Jr.

After ditching in the North Sea on our fifth mission, we were returned to duty and flew on the Regensburg raid which took us to North Africa. On August 25, 1943, our eighth mission was to return to U.K. by way of Bordeaux. We lost an engine over France and dropped out of the formation. Having lost the formation, fighters inflicted further damage. We had turned toward Spain, but when we began to lose altitude so fast that we could not have cleared the Pyrenees, we bailed out. The entire crew was able to get out. However, two were badly shot-up and when taken to a hospital they were captured. One man was badly burned in high-tension lines and was captured.

I broke my leg upon landing in the middle of a plowed field. I was immediately put in hiding. We bailed out at noon, and that same night a doctor looked at my leg. It was then that I was told that what I thought was a sprained ankle was a broken leg. The doctor told me he would be back in four days. In that time I was moved twice, and I was sure I never would see him again. On the fourth night, here he came with gauze and plaster of Paris. He set the leg with a cast from knee to ankle. In a few days I could hobble around.

I was soon moved again and this time the seven of us who were free were together in a large country home that seemed to be an area headquarters for the Resistance.

After some weeks there, I was awakened in the middle of the night to tell the others goodbye, as they were on their way to the Pyrenees. Later that same night, I was taken to the home of the chemist in a small town. The next morning he took the cast off my leg. (I never saw the doctor again. I found later he had done an excellent job.) I lived with the chemist, his wife and daughter while I got some strength back in my leg. In the time I was there, the chemist and I walked every night and at the last we were walking until dawn.

Again at night, I was taken to Foix near the Pyrenees. At daylight the next day, we started walking. By this time I had stopped worrying about my wife not knowing I was alive, as I was sure someone of the crew had let her know. They surely were back in the U.K. if not the U.S. by now.

I was in a party of 35 with two guides to lead us through the Pyrenees. There was a woman in the party who told me and two other Americans in the party to stick with her when we crossed the border, and she would get us to safety in Barcelona. Through this help we were able to get to Gibraltar in a week or so without incident.

After being hospitalized for a few days, I was released one evening to take a night flight to U.K. When I walked into Operations, who should be there but the six crew members I thought were long since home. They had not been as lucky as I. They had spent 27 days in a Spanish prison for "illegal entry" into Spain. We all flew back together that night to England - after 67 days. *(Kneale, Jr. was with the 551st Bomb Group, 385th Bomb Group, 8th Air Force, ETO. He flew as Navigator in the B-17 Old Shillelagh and Old Shillelagh II.)*

DUTCH UNDERGROUND LEADS RAY KUBLY TO SAFETY!

Ray Kubly enlisted in the Air Force Oct. 7, 1942, just four months after having graduated from high school. He was assigned to bombardier navigator school in San Angelo, Texas. He was promoted to second lieutenant navigator in April 1944 and sent to England as part of a replacement crew.

On his ninth mission, he and his fellow members of the crew bailed out of their B-17 bomber over Holland and were captured by the Germans. After their plane had dropped its bombs on an oil refinery in Merseburg, Germany, it was heavily damaged by flak. Kubly's pilot managed to get the plane within a few miles of Allied lines, but fire engulfed it, and the crew was forced to evacuated over a German occupied section of Holland. Two crew members were killed by sharpshooters; the rest were captured.

Kubly was shot while parachuting and was taken to a hospital in Utrecht. Food at the hospital consisted of mainly soup made from cabbage or potato peelings and hard bread. Crew members not shot were taken to POW camps. The hospital was staffed mainly by the Dutch and some were extremely sympathetic to Americans. Kubly was given information on the Dutch Underground and on Oct. 29, 1944, he and five other patients escaped by crawling through the hospital's heating ducts.

The heat in the ducts was very extreme, and the weather outside was winter cold. Kubly, wet with perspiration from the heat, was quickly chilled to the bone once outside. He became very sick with high fever and a very sore throat. In fact, he thought he was going to die.

Fortunately, help would come in the form of a member of the Underground with some medical training. Kubly had severe tonsillitis, and the man used pliers to crush his inflamed tonsils.

Kubly spent about two weeks in hiding in Utrecht, until he and his Underground companion, Jack Murrell, made connections with the Underground.

One night in November of 1944, about 15 people on the Underground line sought to get through the German lines. The men on the line were dressed in British military uniforms so that if they were caught, they'd only be treated as POWs. Civilians caught would be surely shot for treason.

The night was dark and each man practically held on to the belt of the person in front of him. Kubly and Murrell were in back when someone yelled, "Germans!" The two ran amid blasts of grenades, gunfire and the barks of German police dogs. Kubly and Murrell were the only two survivors.

They ran the remainder of the night and at one point were so thirsty, they tried to lick the morning dew off the leaves of trees. They were finally reconnected with the Underground about a day and a half later through a Dutch farmer who did not even realize America was at war.

The next several months were spent in dangerous efforts to evade German capture. There were some close calls.

On March 12, 1945, Kubly and several other men rowed across the Rhine River to the Canadian front line. Eventually, Kubly became a lecturer in England on escape and evasion tactics to Air Force squadrons.

WITH THE BLOODY 100TH
By James Law

James Law was a co-pilot in the "Bloody 100th Bombardment Group" and one of ten crewmen shot down at 18,000 feet over war-torn France. The Group was on its fifth mission together. They left from New Ipswich, England to raid a chemical plant in Ludwigshafen, flying the B-17 "Flying Fortresses".

The Group dropped their bombs and headed back to the base. While over France, they were attacked by a squadron of German Focke-Wulf 190s. The plane caught fire, and the crew was forced to bail out.

Law remembers that the plane was hit in the oxygen

Standing: Sgt. Conrad Stumpfig, Asst. Engineer; Lt. Clyde Manion, Bombardier; Lt. Saul Hershkowitz, Navigator; Lt. Francis Smith, Pilot; Lt. James Law, Co-Pilot; S/Sgt. Swede Swenson, Radio Operator; Seated: Sgt. Bill Wertz, Tail Gunner; Sgt. Al Little, Ball Turret Gunner; Sgt. John Runcel, Armorer and Gunner; S/Sgt. Jack Amery, Aerial Engineer.

system and "our flares were hit." All ten crewmen had to parachute out quickly. All ten men survived, although three of them, including Law, were captured and put in POW camps.

Law was hidden by the French Underground for close to four months. He was captured by the Gestapo on March 24, 1944 and was shuffled between three POW camps, including the famous French Prison near Paris. Some of his time was spent in solitary confinement.

His family did not know if Law was dead or alive for about a year. His parents, Mr. and Mrs. Walter S. Law, stayed in contact with the families of the other missing crew members searching for information about missing loved ones. Eventually, all ten crew members returned safely to the U.S.

Several months after Law's plane was shot down, the Air Force began supplying escorts to fighter planes heading for bombing sites. Up until then the distance between airfields used by bombers and the actual bombing sites was too far for escorting.

The "Bloody 100th" trained in Rapid City, South Dakota before arriving in England to replace one of 20 other crews that had been shot down during bombing missions. According to Law, the famous group was hit hard and "we never had any fighter coverage".

U.S. crews flew daylight missions and English crews made the night attacks, thus increasing the risks for American pilots.

Law, co-pilot of the plane, was reunited with buddy, John Amery, the plane's engineer. The two would like to eventually get together with the entire ten members of the flight crew.

WITH THE POLISH UNDERGROUND ARMY
By Alfred Lea

Lieutenant Alfred Lea and his crew were in the 452nd Bomb Group of the 45th Combat Bombardment Wing, stationed at Deopham Green, England. They were to participate in Operation "Frantic II." This operation was part of a 2,500 plane armada targeted for Berlin. On 21 June 1944, they flew over Warsaw about noon where they picked up a lone German plane tracking the group. About 20 miles later, from underneath the clouds the Germans came up firing. They hit the inboard left engine causing it to catch fire and go into a flat spin.

The crew bailed out over Poland, and all but three were rescued by the partisans. The partisans brought Lea and Joseph Baker to the 34th Infantry Regiment of the Polish Underground Army.

The regiment consisted of approximately 200 men, led by a commander, code named "Zenon". They had been fighting the Germans since Poland's surrender.

Each member of the regiment had a code name, fearing reprisals against their families should their true identities be discovered. The man who served as interpreter had been - and still is - a movie director. His code name was "Dreadnaught," and he and the Americans became fast friends.

A radio had been dropped to them by the RAF with which they could communicate with London in coded messages. They had a bicycle with a generator mounted on it. The sprocket could be shifted to enable the rider to power the generator. If there was anything important to communicate with London, they would send radio messages after dark. That night, word was sent that the seven were under the protection of the Underground. They were Pilot Louis Hernandez, Co-pilot Thomas J. Madden, Bombardier Joseph C. Baker, Navigator Alfred R. Lea, Engineer Anthony Hutchinson, P-51 Mechanic/Waist Gunner Robert L. Gilbert, and Waist Gunner Herschell L. Wise. The other three had been taken prisoner by the Nazis and were presumed to be alive: Radio Operator Jack P. White, Tail Gunner Arnold Shumate, and Ball Turret Gunner William Cabaniss.

According to Lea, when the unit had a military action or maneuver, they didn't look like a bunch of ragtag people. They weren't frightened of the Germans. A systematic method of sentinels and signals was maintained well in advance and to the rear of their caravan. They moved about without fear, since they knew the whereabouts of German troops at all times.

Lea was given the code name Mueller after a Gestapo officer. He was told he looked like a Gestapo guy.

He and the other crewmen were well protected by Commander Zenon and his army of freedom fighters. The Americans soon came to admire Zenon as a born leader and a formidable warrior. He considered himself personally responsible for their safety since the day the men parachuted from their doomed B-17. Says Lea, "That night in the farmhouse, our first night in Poland, Zenon spoke to us as we lay in our straw beds. With Dreadnaught as interpreter, he urged us not to worry, promising that we would be safe. He gave us his pledge that we would be captured by Germans only after every Pole in the Underground army unit assigned to that district was killed."

During their experiences with the Polish Home Army, Al and the crew developed quite a camaraderie with the Commander and Dreadnaught, the interpreter. "The language barrier was really something," says Lea. "Our engineer, Anthony Hutchinson, was from Georgia, and had a real heavy southern accent. When Hutch would say something, Dreadnaught would ask us to interpret it for him! We taught him a lot of slang, like 'the poop from the group', and 'the thing from the Wing.' The one that really blew his mind was 'the decision from the division.' He could not pronounce that to save his life! He didn't acquire his English from school, rather from English theatrical people. It was real English, too, not this hodgepodge we use."

The Polish freedom fighters and their supporters proved to be quite a resourceful group. Given the fact that their methods of acquiring supplies were not the same as those enjoyed by the larger armies, they had to be frugal and quick-witted. The Polish women had carefully retrieved the parachute and Mae West belonging to Louis Hernandez, the pilot of the fallen B-17. It was later discovered that the women meticulously went over these items, cutting yards of silk from which to make clothing and other necessities. They even unraveled some of the fabric to make thread and surgical sutures.

Medical supplies were scarce, but the Poles' ingenuity

was a constant source of amazement to Lea and his crew. Of particular interest to them was the Poles' success in the hospitalization of infirm comrades. Says Lea, "Men who were sick or wounded would suddenly disappear. Days later, they would arrive in good shape after being hospitalized. We never asked questions about how they managed this, but it was certainly a miracle of organization."

The survival instincts of the group of freedom fighters were perhaps best personified by a boy whose code name was "Szef" - "Chief." That name, as well as being put in charge of the Americans, was bestowed on him by Zenon. One morning, the lad saved the Americans' lives by leading them from an intense battle into the safety of a forest hiding place. During the fighting, Szef disappeared. The proud, weary young soldier returned the next morning, carrying a large box of ammunition. From his shoulders hung several belts of machine gun cartridges. While its crew slept, Szef, a 14-year-old-boy, had singlehandedly raided a German supply truck.

An example of the partisans' determination was displayed by another of their young men, a lad of approximately 19 years of age. He found a Spanish machine gun for which no ammunition was available. The young fellow sat for hours, filing down the brass casings of other cartridges to fit into the breach. After completing about 20 rounds, he decided to test fire the weapon, but Zenon stopped him. "That kid would have done anything," says Lea. "He was just going to stand there and pull the damn trigger!" Zenon's assessment of the situation proved to be well founded. He had the young man tie the weapon to a stump and wrap a string around the trigger. The youth then hid behind a tree and pulled the string. After about three rounds, one jammed in the breach and the gun exploded.

During the week after, the partisans held the Fourth of July parade for the Americans; the unit remained concealed in the forest, setting traps for the Germans and gathering more supplies. On 12 July, the seven young crewmen received a visit by three very important men, a Polish general, his aide and a colonel. "We think it was General Bor," said Hernandez, "but we're not sure. He was always addressed as 'General.' All three were dressed in civilian clothes and carried falsified identification papers. They said that they had been stopped by the Germans three times while en route to our hideout. The general, tall, slender with graying hair, inquired about our welfare and promised to have us sent to the Russian lines as soon as it was possible. He also gave us German made shaving lotion, toothpaste, toothbrushes and razor blades. We had a few American dollar bills, so the seven of us autographed one bill with our names and numbers and presented it to the general. We made him a member of the 'Short Snorter Club.' The general reciprocated with bills of Polish occupation currency printed by the partisans."

During the next nine days, the group traveled through several small towns toward the Russian lines. Every day, they could see German planes fly overhead. Many of these flew quite low. Says Lea, "The Germans were flying JU-52s with red crosses on the sides. The Poles called them 'meat wagons,' because they would bring back wounded from the Russian Front. It was a well known fact, however, that they would carry fresh troops and supplies to the front."

The partisans had developed quite an effective tactic to

combat these low-flying planes. The transports were referred to by the Underground as the "Morning Express", since they normally operated just after dawn.

Within the Resistance unit, there were several men who had been in the Polish cavalry, and they possessed what Lea refers to as "the most beautifully trained horses I've ever seen in my life." Lea continues, "Lookouts would be strategically posted so that they would know from which way the planes were coming. These cavalrymen would ride out and hide in hedgerows or under trees and wait for them to fly over. Then they would come out of hiding and ride out right under them, firing at the planes with machine pistols. The JU-52s quite often flew real low, and the partisans would literally "saw a hole in the cockpit" with automatic weapons. Usually the planes would crash. In the 40 or so days that we fought with the Poles, we saw them shoot down four of them."

By this time, the force of partisans had grown to over 300 men. The unit was being joined by fighting men of many nationalities, including Poles, Hungarians, Romanians, Czechs, Germans that hated Hitler and Russians that hated Stalin. The Russians were rapidly advancing during that period, and casualty rates on both sides of the conflict were increasing dramatically.

For the next two weeks, the partisans and evadees fought side-by-side in their attempt to reach the Russian lines.

Soviet relief arrived late in the afternoon of 27 July. Al Lea explains, "The Russian commander, a colonel, came to see us Americans. Zenon, who spoke Russian, introduced us, after which the colonel promised to notify his HQ and facilitate our return as soon as possible."

The next day, a Russian major requested that the Americans, Zenon, Dreadnaught and the Aide de Camp to General Bor accompany him to the Soviet Headquarters. "The Russian HQ was only a few miles away," says Lea. "There, the oddest transaction took place. Zenon didn't trust the Russians, so he made the Soviet colonel fill out a receipt for 'seven American airmen,' which he said he would deliver to the Polish Underground HQ in Warsaw. This receipt was signed by the Russian colonel and by us. The original was kept by Zenon and the colonel got a duplicate. They had this Russian enlisted man with a typewriter with 32 characters on it, trying to type our names in Russian. It took guts, but they stood up to the Russians and made them put down our correct names and serial numbers before they would release us!"

It turned out that the Russian contingent was the major Red Army that was moving on the Germans. Their commanding general, Marshall Zukhov, was there. "We didn't get to meet him," says Lea, "But he came around to look us over. Apparently, the word got around that there were Americans there. We recognized him from pictures."

Their good friend Dreadnaught stayed with the Americans for the next few days. Early on the morning of 30 July, he sadly told them that he had to leave. "We tried to tell him how much we owed him," said Lea, "but he merely replied, "It was my duty. We fight for the same end, Comrades, all." We were to fly from a secret air base in Poland to an American base in Russia. We saluted Dreadnaught, shook hands and left. We saw him standing there. He looked dejected. I knew we were!"

Within the next few days, Lea, Hernandez and Hutchinson returned to their base at Deopham Green. The debriefing with Allied Intelligence took six hours. Their detailed account amazed the Intelligence officers, who said that the experiences of the seven men that floated from a crippled B-17 to the farmlands of Poland on 21 June 1944 were "beyond parallel in the European Theatre." They were the first Americans in history known to have fought with the Polish Underground Army.

They concluded the narrative of their adventure by saying, "If we worked all our lives for the Poles, regardless of the dangers and hazards involved, we should never be able to repay what they did for us."

This story submitted by Alfred Lea is excerpted from CAF Dispatch, Jan.-Feb., 1985 and March-April, 1985.

JOHN MAIORCA'S EVASION

In the early afternoon of a sunny day, November 5, 1943, John Maiorca's B-17 Flying Fortress was hit by anti-aircraft flak over Germany. They tried to return to Britain, but were hit by a German fighter over Belgium. Two of the plane's 10-man crew were killed.

The ship took a dive, and the pilot ordered all to bail out. Maiorca, a member of the 8th Air Force, 388th Bomb Group, decided to free fall to see what it would be like. At about 4,000 feet he tried to pull the rip cord and much to his horror found it wasn't there. He had never parachuted before, and finally found the cord on his left shoulder.

It was a soft landing on flat farm land. He rolled up his parachute and life jacket, hid them and ran. None of his fellow crewmen were in sight. (His faded yellow life preserver was returned to him on a visit 45 years later by a man who had watched).

Maiorca headed towards France, hoping to get help from the Underground. He declined one man's offer to help him board a train to the French border when he learned the man would be shot if caught helping an American.

The young airman dressed in civilian clothes and began a 27-mile walk. After passing through the city of Gent, rain soaked and shivering, Maiorca decided to throw himself to the mercy of the Belgium people.

He began to knock on doors and ask for help. He was turned down a half-dozen times, but no one turned him in. Finally, a man named Modest Vandenbrouck, nicknamed Al Capone because of black-market dealings, accompanied him by train to Waregem and members of the Resistance.

A lot of questions were asked. At first Maiorca would give only his name, rank and serial number. He decided later to trust his new friends and give up more information for help.

For two weeks the airman alternated between the homes of Marcel Windels and Modest Vandenbrouck, with window shades drawn. Windels and others helped Maiorca begin a slow ride on the Resistance's Underground railroad, carrying false papers identifying him as a deaf mute. He traveled by train to Nazi-occupied Paris and Bordeaux, by bike and foot south, walked across a neck-high stream at night into Spain, and found freedom in British Gibraltar.

Maiorca had been told during this time that his family

back in America knew he was safe. Later, however, his wife, Betty told him of being notified of her young husband's missing in action. Even worse, a local newspaper printed his obituary! She refused to believe their horrible news. After all, she had a newborn child.

When Betty Maiorca finally received a telegram from her husband on Jan. 4, 1944, she said, "Oh, God," and passed out.

Maiorca later received a letter from Paul Windels who was the 13-year-old son of Marcel Windels at the time of evasion. The letter resulted in a grand reunion.

The source for this story submitted by John Maiorca is The Hartford Courant.

THE AMAZING UNDERGROUND

By Larry Major

(Excerpt of letter written by Larry Major - 3/1/45)

I guess you can remember the day that I went out (December 1st). Don't believe any of us wanted to fly that day. Well things went O.K. that morning (we were a spare crew). We got to the Channel just keeping up with the formation when the pilot informed us that we were going to go on the mission. Guess we got almost to the target (which was Solingen) when the oxygen system went haywire. Right then and there we turned back and hit the deck; the bombs went out (salvoed) right after then we left the formation. Where they hit, I don't know. Hope they hit something.

Then the fun started. We got jumped by fighters, first by 109s and later 190s. The clouds took care of us. Finally a 210 jumped us from the tail, and he sure did mess things up. The tail-gunner, Hatch was his name, got it from two 20mms. The guy's alive and back home now, but he sure took a beating. Lost his left leg, small finger on left hand, and he has a nice scar over his left eye. I helped him out of the tail and put him in the waist until we gave him first aid. When I went back to the tail to take over, it sure did look good. Blood all over, two big holes that I could have crawled through and the tail guns just hanging - both knocked out. The 210 was still out there, and that's when I said to myself, "Well, it looks like this is it."

The guy must have used up all his ammo because he never opened up from the time I got in the tail until we finally lost him in the clouds. That's one time I really sweated.

After that we didn't have any trouble until we hit the coast, and then it started all over. The coast defenses opened up with the smallest gun to the largest, and believe it or not, the tail gunner gets hit again with a slug in the same leg, but near the ankle. We get out into the sea and start throwing everything out that we can. Practically all the radio equipment was knocked out except the Laison and even the radio compass plus a lot of the controls and the pilot's compass. What a mess. We're lost and flying for a couple of hours over the water's edge expecting any moment for the pilot to say, "We're going to ditch", which he didn't do. After about 2 1/2 hours of water, we see land (which we thought to be England), but it turned out to be France. Coastal defenses again.

All this time the pilot is madder than a beehive, and the navigator is practically ——— in his pants. He was scared stiff the whole day. We finally crash land the big bird (no gas left) in a cow pasture. Let the tail gunner lay some 300 feet

from the plane with Frenchmen all over the place. Kelker and I took off together like dirty shirts. He was the only guy on the crew that I knew.

That night we got up enough nerve to stop at a farmhouse and got something to eat and drink. We didn't know one word of French, but we go along OK. We moved three times that night from one place to another and finally we hit the Underground. What an organization that was. About the seventh day, we meet up with the bombardier and navigator and from then on we traveled together. Paris was the first stop, but only for a few hours. On the 13th of December we got to the Swiss border. By the 16th we were in Bern and at the American Legation. Sad looking sacks.

From then on we lived the life of Riley. (Wine, women, and song). The four of us were the first of our group to get to Switzerland the way we did.

THEY WERE WAITING TO HELP US

By Virgil R. Marco

Looking out the tail compartment I could see a group of B-17s to my left and above our squadron. Many years later I discovered that it must have been the 92nd Bomb Group as they lost four of five planes which I saw go down. We were flying in the rear position usually reserved for new crews. This was my third mission.

While researching what happened on this Monday, April 24, 1944, I learned that our squadron, 366 of the 305th Bomb Group was part of an armada of 750 heavy bombers of the 40th and 41st Wings headed for various targets near Munich, Germany. Ours was a twin engine aircraft repair depot at Oberpfaffenhopen, 15 miles south of Munich.

When approaching our target, 20 or 30 ME-109s attacked us at 1:00 high, hitting our number one engine. Without enough power to keep up, we continued flying over the target, dropped our bombs and began drifting back and below the rest of our group. Our escorting P-47 fighters arrived after the battle and informed us that we would have to fly home the best way possible without their protection. They had to stay with the main group.

The bad news made the nearby Swiss Alps appear inviting. One of my crew suggested that we go to Switzerland. This brought an immediate reply from Capt. Lincoln that we were going to make every effort to reach our home base, Chelveston, England. In the meantime, not far away, there were 14 damaged B-17s on their way to Switzerland. One was not successful as it exploded over Baltenseil, Switzerland. With one engine out, we began to drift further behind the main group, becoming easy prey for the Luftwaffe and enemy flak.

Descending from 20,000 feet altitude to about 5,000 feet, the Swiss Alps faded away. We were now headed home. Just in front of us, a city appeared. The city was protected from low flying aircraft by large balloons anchored in the sky by steel cables. As we flew over the city above the balloons, antiaircraft guns began firing. Flak clouds were popping up all around us until Captain Lincoln took evasive action flying lower and lower until we had flown over the city and out of range of the flak guns.

(L to R): Virgil Marco, Gene Snodgrass and Bill Bergman at Chauny, France, September 1944.

We were now flying at an altitude of 1,400 feet I could see the people in the fields below stop working and look up as we flew low overhead. At 17:00 hours an enemy FW-190 sneaked up on the rear of our plane and began firing its guns. Bullets tore through the plane damaging the intercom system, eliminating further instructions from Captain Lincoln. The navigator, Phil Campbell, left the plane by parachute along with the waist gunner, Bill Bergman. Then a few minutes later the FW-190 opened fire again, producing more holes in the crippled plane. The other waist gunner, Gene Snodgrass, myself and the ball turret gunner, James Mayfield, bailed out in that order.

The plane was full of holes and on fire as Capt. Lincoln guided it down to a successful crash landing in a cow pasture near Leuze, France, close to the French-Belgium border. Four of the five remaining aboard the plane scrambled out quickly to find that the rest of the crew had bailed out except the radio operator, I.W. Denemy, who had been killed by the FW-190's bullets.

An hour after the crash landing, a Frenchman named Julian Mahoudeaux, who had observed the incident, arrived to offer help. The survivors were my pilot, Bill Lincoln, co-pilot, Al Pagnotta, bombardier, Milt Goldfeder, and top turret gunner, Joe Rhodes. Julian hid the fliers in the nearby woods, Foret de St. Michel, which became their home for the next 13 days.

In the meantime, Phil Campbell had bailed out over the village of Mont St. Jean near Aubenton, France and hid in the woods until a French boy named Raymond Honotea helped him by bringing food and civilian clothes. Phil stayed in this vicinity until April 29 when he was taken to Auge.

Bill Bergman had landed near Aubenton also where he found help from two sisters who hid him in their home for the next three weeks.

Gene Snodgrass's chute caught in a tree near the plowed field where I landed. We met in a ravine to plan our next move, when a French boy named Pierre Bonnet approached us and motioned us to follow him. We walked across a field to a large forest where we hid until midnight when Pierre returned with food and civilian clothes.

Gene and I learned later from the Underground that James Mayfield's chute didn't open, and he died in a German hospital.

Dressed in our civilian clothes, we walked with Pierre for an hour until we arrived at a Catholic priest's home in Aubenton. The priest gave us a good road map with some towns circled where we could find help at the Catholic church. He showed us the road to take out of Aubenton, and we walked the rest of the night. At sunrise we reached Rozoy, the first circled town on the map. We received help from a farmer and his family and the Catholic priest of Rozoy. After spending a day, night and another day in Rozoy, we continued our journey to the last circled town on the map, Guignicourt, walking at night and sleeping in the woods during the day. After several days we reached Guignicourt on Sunday, April 30, 1944.

Gene and I saw our first German soldier walking out of a building across our path and then pouring a bowl of water out in the street gutter. He walked back in to the building without suspecting that we were American fliers. Walking faster we followed the local people in the church just in time for church services. After the congregation left, we asked the priest for help. He hid us in the church belfry the rest of the day.

That evening the mayor's daughter had us follow her home near the church. We became the guest of the mayor of Guignicourt until the next morning. The mayor's name was Chevalier. The next morning, May 1, the mayor drove us in his car to Bouconville, where we were hidden in the home of M.L. Bronicke, an Underground agent.

Here we met Ronald Scott, a British flier. His bomber was shot down three weeks earlier. Ron told us that we would be transported to Paris and then to the English Channel where we would be picked up by an Allied PT boat and returned to England. Unfortunately the escape route to the English Channel was discovered by the Germans eliminating an early escape to freedom.

After a week, Ronald Scott left by motorcycle with an Underground agent named Bob. A week later Bob returned to Gene and me and took us to Chauny, France, where we lived with the Tavernier family: mama, papa and daughters, Denis and Genevieve. By the way of the Underground agents, Bill Bergman joined us about a week later.

During this time, the four survivors of the crash landing were moved by Julian Mahoudeaux to Rocroi on May 8. Then they traveled to Revin, six miles northwest of Rocroi where they spent five days with Rober Charton, Chief of the Resistance in that section. On May 16, they were sent to the hiding place of the Maquis of Revin. While in the secret hideout, they learned that Rober Charton's home had been blown up by the Gestapo.

On June 6, D-Day, Gene, Bill and I were taken to a farm near Chauny where we met 50 American and British fliers who had been hiding in Chauny. Some were shot down a few days earlier and some over a year ago.

After a few days in the country, we were returned to Chauny to stay with the Tavernier family. We experienced many air raids by American and Allied medium and fighter bombers. The target was the marshalling yards, not far away from the Tavernier home.

On June 10, while Bill Lincoln, Al Pagnotta, Milt Goldfeder and Joe Rhodes were hiding in the woods with the Maquis of about 300, they were attacked by the Gestapo, made up of 2,000 SS and 1,000 Vichy troops. When the battle was over, three days later, most of the Maquis had been killed. A few Maquis and the four fliers miraculously escaped alive. As a result of this incident, the commandant of the SS, Colonel Grauboski, ordered the shooting of 200 French as reprisal. Al Pagnotta and some Maquis found two Belgians hanging by their feet with their heads underground.

On June 16, Joe Rhodes and P. Clard, a B-24 gunner, left the Maquis for Sedan, Belgium by train. A truck driver gave them a ride to Miecourt, the base of another unit. At Miecourt they were liberated by the advancing American troops, September 3.

On June 23, Bill and Milt also left the Maquis walking to several villages where they received help. After staying with various French and Belgian helpers, Bill and Milt were liberated by the 5th Armored Division of the American 1st Army on September 3. Bill knew all the top brass in the division as he had served with this unit prior to transferring to pilot training with the Army Air Force. The reunion resulted in preferred treatment and prompt transport back to London.

On June 27, the Underground moved Phil Campbell from Auge to the home of Madame Josephene Omeatak in Laigny. Her husband was a French P.O.W.

On July 10, Al Pagnotta left the Maquis traveling to Oignies, Belgium where he was helped by Madame Lucy Francois, Madame and Doctor Collet and Francois Jacques. On September 3, Al walked to Covin where he found the American 87th Field Artillery. He was then sent to the 9th Infantry Headquarters and to the 7th Corp Headquarters. Al spent several days there on a detail guarding German P.O.W.s. On September 10, Al was flown from Paris to London.

On August 15, the Resistance moved Phil Campbell to St. Prevue, France where another French helper named Xavier Babled shared his home with him. Phil learned on the morning of August 30 that the American 1st Army had liberated Sissonne. He then walked to Sissonne and freedom. By September 2, Phil was in London giving his account of his evasion to the Military Intelligence Service.

Gene, Bill and I were liberated by the American 1st Army on September 2, 1944. During the second week of September, 1944, seven of my crew were reunited at the Jules Club in London discussing our past experiences. We were very fortunate that the French and Belgians were waiting to help us.

WE TOOK THE SECRET HIGHWAY!

By Paul McConnell

On the Fourth of July 1943, Second Lieutenant Paul McConnell, navigator on a B-17 Army Air Force bomber, was flying over Normandy on his first mission, a raid on the German Focke-Wulfe airplane plant in LeMans, Occupied France. Approaching target, the B-17 was attacked by four Focke-Wulfe fighters. On the first pass, Paul's ball turret gunner was killed, several other crew members were wounded and two of the four engines were damaged. The B-17 managed to shake off the Focke-Wulfes and was limping toward the sea for a crash landing with its load of bombs, when it was jumped by nine Messerchmitts. Only two of them were left in the air when that dogfight ended, but the B-17 was on fire and one tail stabilizer was smashed. Paul and five mates bailed out; the others were either dead in the plane or died when it crashed and exploded.

Paul parachuted into a barnyard in the farm country of the Orne valley about 20 miles from a village called Domfront to begin a year of adventures in the French Resistance that reads like the script of a TV spy thriller.

NIGHT OF MISERY

When Paul landed, the first man he saw was M. Bouvet, a gamekeeper and woodman. He spoke no English and Paul spoke little French, but Bouvet led him into the forest and out of sight. Here Paul spent one of the most miserable nights of his life. Hunted by Nazis with dogs, he covered himself with damp leaves, fought off the mice, spiders and gnats, and listened to rifle shots until morning. Then he started walking.

By this time he had been without food or drink for nearly 36 hours and was almost dead of thirst. When he came to a couple of woodmen working in a clearing, even at the risk of capture, he approached them and asked in sign language for a drink. They gave him water and took him to another man in a sort of field office, who spoke English and who questioned Paul pretty sharply, then gave him food and wine.

Finding a grounded American air officer was exciting news to these patriotic French people. Although they knew they were taking chances, the neighbors round-about put their heads together on schemes to hide Paul and help him escape from occupied territory. They rounded up an outfit of French civilian clothes for him and took him to the Bourgoins' cottage nearby. Mme. Bourgoin put him in her spare room where Paul, now at the end of his rope, promptly fell sound asleep.

Mme. Bourgoin phoned Le Grand Pepin who in turn got in touch with M. Rougeyron, a community leader in those parts, and the three friends decided to move Paul to permanent shelter in the Rougeyron's chalet in Domfront, about eight miles away.

A RIDE FOR LIFE

Le Grand Pepin had an English motorcycle which he had liberated from the Nazis. With Paul insecurely perched behind him on the single seat he started for Domfront. Approaching a Nazi roadblock which he knew he had to pass, he slowed down until he was almost there, then gunned the throttle and shot by before the amazed soldiers could shoulder their rifles. Paul almost lost his seat, but he saved his life.

For the following weeks, Paul moved back and forth between the chalet, a small house high up on the hillside overlooking Domfront, and the "grande maison" (big house) in Domfront. The grande maison stood side-by-side with a twin grande maison where the Nazi commandant had his headquarters, and many times Paul, dressed as a French civilian, would wave greetings to the soldiers on guard.

Meanwhile, Paul improved his French and learned to act like a French countryman, the part he was to play for almost a year after. Meanwhile, too, he had long talks with his friends, and convinced them to organize the Resistance unit that was to help so many downed airmen to save their lives and join the Resistance.

The story of Paul's operations in the Paris Underground is too long to be told here. Briefly, after several months, the organization was discovered and smashed by SS raids. Paul himself escaped and helped to rebuild the group; but by then the Nazis had put a price of 80,000 francs on his head (he was worth only 20,000 when he landed in Normandy), and it became too risky for him to stay in Paris. He escaped into Spain and finally came back to the U.S. by way of Scotland.
Secret Highway Out

Back in Domfront the Resistance group worked with great success for years. In Paul's case it took two months to prepare his escape, providing him with phony identification and inventing ways to dodge Nazi surveillance on roads and trains; but when the Domfront Resistance got operating at full efficiency, it was only a matter of days to find grounded airmen, hide them, find clothes and papers for them, and arrange their escape.

But in the end, some of the Domfront Resistance leaders were found out, caught and shipped off to the infamous prison camp at Buchenwald where they suffered starvation and ill treatment until the war ended, and they returned to Normandy.

A TIME IN FRANCE

By William A. McCormick, Jr.

I was assigned to duty with the 371st Fighter Group, 405th Fighter Squadron, Army Air Base, Richmond, VA on 8 September 1943, and took my combat training with this Group at Camp Springs, Washington, D.C. I was promoted from 1st Lt. to Capt. on 26 November 1943. The 371st Fighter Group was transferred on 27 February 1944 to England for duty with the Ninth Air Force.

On 10 February 1944 I had been appointed assistant operations officer of the 405th Fighter Squadron. Soon after operations against the enemy were begun by my squadron, on or about 27 March 1944, I was appointed flight leader of "A" Flight. I served in this capacity until 27 August 1944 when I was shot down behind enemy lines on my 77th combat mission.

On 27 August 1944 I was leading the 405th Fighter Squadron on a dive bombing mission to cut rail lines in the area around Besancon, France. After having completed this mission and returning to the base, I located approximately one squadron of FW190s and two or three JU 88s parked around a German held airdrome near Dijon, France. Due to the fact that my flight was the only one in the squadron that had sufficient gas to make an attack, I took it down and attacked the airdrome. I destroyed one JU 88 and one FW190. During the attack my plane was hit in the gas tank and immediately caught fire.

At the time I was flying on the deck, so I pulled up at once

Capt. William A. McCormick, Jr., 29 August 1944, at the home of Mr. and Mrs. George Coudor in France. Mr. Coudor was a French officer in World War I.

and bailed out at less than 1000 feet. I received burns on my right knee, right hand and face. The Germans fired at me as I descended to the ground.

As sound as I touched the ground, I ran rapidly toward a spot of woods I had selected while I was in the air. As I was nearing exhaustion I met a French boy who motioned for me to follow him. He led me to his home and his parents (presumably) hid me in a hayloft in a small outbuilding. During the four hours following, German detachments searched the premises several times.

After the Germans left the vicinity, I was furnished French peasant clothes and was given food. Late that afternoon I was turned over to members of the French Underground, and we traveled by bicycle and auto, on little used roads, to a small French town, St. Jean De Dosne. Arriving there in the afternoon on 28 August 1944, I was to remain in this home until plans could be made to slip me through the German lines. In the early morning on or about 1 September 1944, I was transported to a cafe. There I met Lt. Breton, French officer of the F.F.I., who was in charge of the F.F.I. in that immediate area. (I enclose a copy of a letter that I received from Lt. Breton recently, which I verify except that I think he was slightly confused as to some of the dates.)

Lt. Breton took me with him on a truck loaded with foodstuff and a number of untrained members of the F.F.I. I understood that the destination of the truck was to a newly organized F.F.I. camp. After traveling most of the day and getting within almost eight miles of our destination, as I learned later, the truck skidded off the road, into a ravine, and came to rest against a large tree. Two of the men were killed instantly and several others were injured, and Lt. Breton was pinned inside of the cab of the truck. To my amazement I found that I had been left alone with Lt. Breton and I had great difficulty and exerted much strength and energy in pulling him free from the cab of the truck. Lt. Breton was severely injured and apparently was suffering great pain, while I, myself, was only slightly injured.

Assisting him as much as I could, Lt. Breton and myself made our way in the rain about two miles down the mountain to a village. From there we were transported to an F.F.I. camp and Lt. Breton was taken to a hospital.

I remained at this camp until 4 September 1944. From there I made my way to a town near by and caught a ride with a French officer to Grenable, France. From a light plane airstrip there, I was taken by U.S. plane to a strip at Ramutulle, France. From there I was sent by U.S. transport plane to U.S. Headquarters Army Air Forces, Mediterranean Theatre of Operations, located in Italy. On 6 September 1944 I received an order sending me to U.S. Special Reception Center 63, Brook Street, London West 1.

In London I was given orders to return to my group in France, to assemble my personal effects and report back to London for shipment to the United States. When I contacted my squadron approximately three weeks after I had been shot down, I found that my group had suffered heavy casualties while I was away. My squadron commander and squadron operations officer had been reassigned and their positions filled by the flight leaders of "B" and "D" flights.

The officers who were my Group Commander (371st Fighter Group), my Squadron Commander (405th Fighter Squadron) and my Squadron Operations Officer at the time I was shot down (27 August 1944) have survived the war to the best of my knowledge. They were: Colonel Bingham T. Kleine, 371st Fighter Group Commander; Major Harvey L. Case, 405th Fighter Squadron Commander; Major Philip E. Bacon, Jr., 405th Fighter Squadron Operations Officer. Flight Leader of "D" Flight at that time (27 August 1944) was Captain Gavin C. Robertson, Jr.

McGLYNN'S ODYSSEY

By John A. McGlynn, 2nd Lieutenant, U.S.A.A.F.

My escape story starts Feb. 14, 1944, the first day of Allied daytime bombing of Berlin. Captain Clark and I were alerted the evening before to be present for an early morning briefing. At the briefing, 5:00 double daylight savings time, we, along with two alternate pilots, learned that our mission was to photograph Berlin. I was to fly ahead of the bombers and Clark behind, with the alternates in position at altitude over central Germany to react to coded orders if needed.

Take-off was at 8:00 a.m. on a beautiful, clear morning. I attained altitude of 37,000 feet over south Denmark and took a pre-planned, non-direct course to Berlin. The vertical cameras were set at eight second intervals. There was no wind, so the setting was the same for both directions for four passes over the city at approximately four mile parallels. (At 37,000 feet above terrain, our pictures overlapped 50 percent, so a damaged exposure here and there would still make a readable collage.) The city of Berlin looked as peaceful as Eden - no anti-aircraft fire or ground fire and no fighters.

On the way home to England, nothing unusual occurred until I approached the Rhine. I could see our bombers heading for Berlin at about 24,000 feet. All at once, I noticed several bursts of anti-aircraft fire, below and to the left. The Germans were shooting at the bombers, not me, but their zenith fuse exploded at approximately my altitude. I had been told by experienced R.A.F. pilots that the Germans never shot twice in the same place. I dove toward the last burst and got a direct hit. Obviously, the son of a gun had shot twice in the same spot, hitting my wing or engine and blowing the plane to pieces.

Fortunately, I got out and clear of the plane wreckage before passing out from lack of oxygen. I don't know if I pulled the rip cord then or some 20,000 feet lower. At least, when enough oxygen was available to clear my mind, I realized I was hanging over the Rhine River in an absolute silence you cannot imagine.

Because the wind at lower altitudes was from the east, I drifted across the broad river and landed on the west bank on icy mud. A second echelon anti-aircraft battery of Germans was there, but they were as scared as I was. One old guy motioned with a carbine to get into an empty freight car, which I did with alacrity. The Germans were so fascinated by the B-24s and B-17s overhead that they forgot about me.

I cut up my chute, saving some to keep warm. I took the stuff from my escape kit: silk maps of Europe, a needle full of morphine, a packet of benzedrine pills, some chunks of chocolate, a small dictionary English to German-French-Danish-Dutch, and some money from all of these countries. There was also, of all things, a machete to open coconuts. I left the machete, along with the quilted British flight suit I was wearing.

I started to walk west. Oddly enough, nobody paid any attention to an American pilot wearing a leather flight jacket. It seemed like half the people I saw in the Rhineland part of Germany were wearing discarded or captured pieces of military clothing. Toward evening and some 15 or 20 miles to the west, I found a semi-abandoned farm and hid in a barn.

I had not felt any hunger or thirst until then, but I thought it wise to eat a chunk of hard chocolate, along with some snow from the north side of the building. In my nervousness, I also made the mistake of swallowing about five benzedrine tablets. (I found out later the recommended dosage was one-half tablet.) The result was the damndest high this one man has ever had. For 36 hours I couldn't sit down, shut an eye, or sleep standing up. I just kept walking toward sundown, acting the idiot, mumbling incoherently whenever I met anyone. The Germans, and to some extent, the French seemed to accept a nut at face value, apparently thinking that, at that time, any mumbling idiot was a bombed-out slave laborer, a shell-shocked veteran or a deserter from some army.

I traveled in the daytime and laid up in barns or culverts at night. The Germans enforced a strict curfew and at night were prone to shoot first and ask questions later, but did not seem to bother much in daylight. At any rate, after seven or eight days of this odyssey, on very short rations, I arrived in the vicinity of Paris. I managed by hiding in French barns with the cows, drinking milk direct from the teat. I also ate one raw chicken. It was not young, but it was delicious. I walked most of the way, but caught some rides in French farm vehicles and even got an 80 or 90 mile ride in a German supply truck.

In the town of Antony, a far suburb of Paris, it became evident to me that I needed help. I not only was playing the part of a mumbling idiot; I looked and smelled like one, too. I decided to approach an antique shop, thinking that the Germans had plundered France of untold millions worth of art and antiquities and these people might have an extra hatred for "La Boche."

I entered the shop, still playing the jabbering idiot. By pointing out words in the dictionary, I tried to say I was an American airman in need of help. Mme. Braun, the lady who ran the shop, (may she have a box seat in Heaven), hid me in a closet full of Louis XIV uniforms. She let me know she could speak some English, that I was being watched and she would get someone to interview me. She told me they would have to determine if I was what I claimed or possibly a German agent provocateur, trying to get information on the French Underground. She clearly implied that if they decided I was the latter, I would be a very dead Nazi in a very short time.

After what seemed like an eternity, the closet door opened and a decrepit little man was locked in with me. I learned later that the old gent was a mover and shaker in the French Underground, as well as an employee of British Intelligence since before World War I. His questions were astute, and I doubt that any German agent could have passed his interrogation. Following this inquisition, he vouched for me. From then on, I was in the care of the French Underground.

That night I slept in a bed and had a lavish meal of tripe and artichokes. At the time, I thought that Mme. Braun had awfully strange taste in food. I later realized that was all they had and that I had probably consumed a half week's ration for the family. I must say, I still would prefer raw chicken to tripe. Although the Germans controlled the rations and they were very limited, we did seem to have an ample supply of vin de hote and Cognac.

Mme. Braun provided me with French clothing, as did the people in the Paris Underground later. I found it awkward to wear the typical French dress, particularly the beret and baggy pants.

Within a day or two, a mysterious young man appeared and took my picture and fingerprints. Within a few hours I became "Jean Pierre Millet," a former hotel employee from Berz-Conque. I was identified as deaf and dumb, the result of war wounds in 1940. The film, paper and passport booklet had all been stolen from the Gestapo. (I still have my carte-d'identite, rather an interesting document.)

From Antony, I was sent to Paris in the care of the Paris branch of the Underground. For nearly two months, I lived and hid mostly at 24 Rue Sebastopol with a Paris gendarme, Georges Prevot, and his sister and brother-in-law, Georges and Genevieve Planche. My hosts and guardians lived in an apartment in a four-story building having approximately 20 apartments. When word got out that Georges Prevot was hiding an American airman, little packages of food would be delivered surreptitiously. As a result, I really ate fairly well in Paris, in contrast to England where I had been stationed.

No. 24 Rue Sebastopol is only 10 or 12 blocks from the Cathedral of Notre Dame. I spent many days there. If my hosts thought the Gestapo might search their apartment house when they were at work, I would spend the day in or around Notre Dame. There was an unspoken agreement that the Germans would not violate Notre Dame or Sacre Cour.

I had another reason to go to Notre Dame. The fourth confessional on the right was occupied by a British Intelligence agent in clerical dress who coordinated the movement of M.I.A.s with the French Underground. Needless to say, I went to confession quite often.

I spent almost two months in Paris. Even then, it was not all hardship: my host, the gendarme, had considerable freedom of movement, in spite of the fact that he technically was an employee of the German occupying forces. He could take me anywhere, as long as I played the deaf-mute. Prevot would simply assure any German questioner that I was under arrest or that he was my guardian.

While hiding in Paris, I often watched the German soldiers who were in complete occupation of the city. Every morning at 11:00, a picked company of about one hundred SS troops would march, with muffled drums but without a word, to the Arc de Triomphe and to the Tomb of the French Unknown Soldiers. At precisely 11:00, the German soldiers would salute, do an about face and march off up Les Champs Elysees with never a command given. The French would hiss at them, but the Germans could do nothing about that.

Eventually, the Underground had an escape plan for approximately 17 or 18 people like me, including some 13 or 14 downed American airmen and four British escaped prisoners. The plan was to rendezvous in Brittany near Rennes on a given dark night. We were to be taken off the coast by small boats from the Royal Navy, then transferred either to a submarine or to a large gunboat and then to England.

I left Paris by train. A ticket and escort were provided. The escort was unknown to me, but I was assured that he was on the train, and I was under his eye. When I arrived at the Rennes train station, a nondescript young fellow tapped me on the shoulder and indicated that I should follow him. I did, at a distance. After walking around back streets for some time, he entered the back of a rather nice house. I followed. The house was headquarters of a large cell of the French Underground, and was directly across the main street from General Irwin Rommel's headquarters. The French seemed to love such bravado.

I met one particularly interesting character in Rennes, a beautiful girl who lived in the house where I stayed and was very active in the Underground. My guide told me she made a specialty of seducing young German officers and then murdering them. She was apparently very good at it. She reportedly had buried three in the yard in the compost pit, and still had their uniforms. I had my picture taken wearing one of the German uniforms. I understood that her husband or lover had been tortured by the Gestapo, but I still found her hatred of the Germans almost unbelievable.

After hiding in an out-building of the Underground headquarters for two or three days, I was moved to the rocky coast of Brittany, transported in an old truck with a German Army insignia. The night was as dark as the mouth of Hell, moonless and foggy. On such nights, the Germans stayed close to guard posts, scared of being waylaid by vengeful Frenchmen. We were supposed to make our descent to the coast at a time between the regular German patrols.

Unfortunately, however, one of my Underground guardians and I were caught in a guard sweep along the coast and we had no choice but to do away with the patrolling German soldier. We tripped him from his bicycle with a piano wire as he was riding past and threw him over the adjacent cliff. I had nothing against the man, but if my keeper had been caught, he would have been shot immediately. As it was a choice between ourselves and him, it was our duty.

After climbing over rocks as big as houses and down a precipitous cliff to the water, I found some 16 or 17 others hiding in the dark. About one-half hour later, though it seemed much longer, a whispered command was passed for the first ten to get into the water by a certain large rock. I was in the second group. A few minutes later, after an exchange of light signals between our guides on shore and a British whaleboat in the surf, the first group was taken off.

The second group then took its place in the water. Our whaleboat was supposed to come in a few minutes. About 15 minutes later, a colored rocket went up some miles off shore. I found out later that the rocket was a signal from our rescue gunboat that it might have been detected and had to leave without returning for us. So much for that escape.

We went back up the cliffs and spent the rest of the night and the following day hiding in the rubble of several war-damaged buildings. The next night we were transported back to Rennes by various modes of transport, no more than two men at a time. By then, there were only six in the group, one former British P.O.W. having disappeared. We were scattered around to various safe houses for a day or two, then contacted by our various Underground guardians. We were put separately on the same train, headed for a little French town near the Spanish border. A couple of Basque members of the Underground were on the same train, but not in contact.

When we arrived in the North Pyrenees, our guides motioned us to follow. There were only five of us now, one American having disappeared along the way. It was a wise policy of the Underground that none of us would know anything about them and as little as possible about our fellow M.I.A.s. If caught and questioned by the Gestapo, you couldn't tell what you didn't know.

The next morning, after a big breakfast of fish, we began a 24-hour hike over a smugglers' pass into Spain. At the end of our hike, our guide took us to the nearest good-sized town and turned us over to the chief of police who promptly threw us in a rickety old stone jail. We thought we had been betrayed, but found to our relief that both our Basque guide and the chief were long-time employees of British Intelligence. The next morning, after being threatened with a firing squad or hanging or some such delightful end, we were given a decent breakfast of dried fish, figs and wine. Our jailor shook each one of our hands, left the door wide open and pointed down the street. Then he disappeared. The message was clear.

There were now only four of us. The last British P.O.W., who was very sick, had disappeared the night before. Because the whole town seemed friendly, I have no doubt he was in good hands. Our ubiquitous Basque met us, took us to a farm outside town.

That night, again as dark as the devil, we wound up on a steep rocky slope on the south coast of the Bay of Biscay. Here, the four remaining members of the group and our guardian angels joined a fishing boat with a crew of two, which then put out mysteriously through the surf. About two miles out, our captain hove-to and waited. Within a few minutes, a signal lamp flashed in the distance. Our captain answered with another hand-held signal lamp and then moved our boat close to the source of the signal. It turned out to be a British coastal submarine waiting on the surface. We were taken aboard and traveled all night submerged. I was extremely seasick and filthy to boot.

The next forenoon we surfaced in sight of Plymouth Harbor. On landing we were met by a colonel from the 8th Air Force Adjutant General's Office. I, as the only commissioned officer (the other three were enlisted bomber crew members), was technically in command of the group. We traveled to London by train. After being properly identified, we were released for a few days on the town and for a reunion with our squadron people, in my case the 13th Photo Recon at Oxford, the only high altitude photo reconnaissance group in England.

Unlike Odysseus, I didn't find it necessary to slay a gaggle of my wife's suitors upon my return home. Nonetheless, I did have a feeling of kinship with the old Greek upon his return to Ithaca, since my own ultimate destination was Ithaca, Wisconsin, home of my bride-to-be. Thus ended my odyssey.

ONE-DAY BOMBING MISSION LASTS THREE MONTHS! THE H. C. WOODRUM STORY
By Terrance Miller

Thousands of Americans can tell you what it was like on the beaches of Normandy on D-Day 1944, but very few can tell you what it was like in Paris that same day. One person who can is Henry Woodrum.

Woodrum began what he thought was a routine bombing mission over France on May 28, 1944. The one-day mission stretched to three months and when he finally returned, he was credited with the destruction of a mass of German tanks and later honored by the French government for being in Paris when it was liberated.

"May 28 was not unusual," he recalls. "We were supposed to be on leave, but another crew became ill and we were called up to fly their mission. We left the 9th Air Force airfield outside London and made landfall near Cannes. Flying into a 40-knot headwind, we paralleled the Seine River to Paris and our target, a series of railroad bridges northeast of the city.

"Just after 'bombs away' we got hit off the left nose, which wiped out the controls. I ordered the crew to bail out, remembering what a briefing officer had said before we left,

"If shot down, avoid Paris at all costs." The plane was shot down to about 4,000 feet when I bailed out, my first experience at leaving a plane in mid-air, and the wind blew me west where I landed on the roof of a house."

ENEMY NEAR

"I could see the German troops a block away," Woodrum says. "Four truckloads of them coming to pick up my crew. I slid over the edge of the roof and went around the house and into a yard next door. The briefing officer had also told us that when shot down, do the most obvious things to avoid detection. Because it was too hot for the regular Air Force winter flying suit, and not warm enough for the summer uniforms, I was wearing a mixture consisting of green shirt and slacks with no insignia and a pair of coveralls. Because of this, I was able to avoid detection and I picked up a paint can lying near the house and walked down the street with a group of Frenchmen."

"I wandered around and picked out a house. I was lucky. They steered me toward some people known to be Resistance." The family owned a cafe and bar and Woodrum stayed with them four days.

On June 2 he was taken to a sixth-floor apartment in Versailles where he stayed three weeks. It was during this time that the Allies landed on the Normandy coast and the Gestapo began looking for an American flier known as Henry Woodrum.

"From the apartment in Versailles I could see the Eiffel Tower in the distance and east of the house was the Villa Coublay Aerodrome. I could sit and watch German troops pass in the street below headed for a railroad marshaling area," he said.

"The first I knew of D-Day was when I heard the German airplanes warming up at the aerodrome. The planes took off and an hour later came back all shot up. One crashed northwest of us and another made it to the end of the field. While they were landing a woman next door ran out on her balcony and yelled 'Debarquement! Debarquement!' This was how we found out it was the day of the invasion."

The downed flier would have probably stayed in Versailles except for an encounter with a British agent and a brush with the Gestapo. Woodrum had met the Britisher, who had married a Belgian-French woman before the war. He had been allowed by the Germans to remain free but had to report to them every day. He also headed a group of Frenchmen who radioed messages to the Allies. The apartment in which Woodrum was staying was owned by the station master of the Versailles Railroad. Noticing a large number of German tanks passing in the streets, he asked his host where they were going. When he found they were headed for the railroad yard he got word to the British agent.

"He had a group of Frenchmen with bicycles who would pedal out into the country, have a flat tire and then transmit messages to England using a generator disguised as a tire pump. When London got word the British began bombing the area. The tanks were destroyed."

Following the raid the Germans suspected that a spy was in their midst, rounded up all foreign nationals including the British agent. During interrogations by the Germans, someone mentioned Woodrum's name and he was forced to flee.

HANDCUFFED

He was taken by automobile to a hideout in the forests of Fontainebleau. To pass through two German checkpoints, he was handcuffed and manacled with a Frenchman on either side of him. As they passed through the checkpoints, they told the guards he was a convicted French murderer.

Woodrum returned to Paris on Bastille Day, July 14, 1944 and remained in the city until the Allies arrived.

"I picked up five other Americans between the forest and the city, and we were billeted in three houses," he said. "After a few days we became very blase. We had bicycles, and we rode them openly into Paris."

He barely escaped detection on one occasion during a visit to the French Naval Museum. While looking at a painting he was surrounded by German soldiers who also expressed an interest in the picture. Unable to say anything, he moved along with the Germans from picture to picture, unsure as to how he should leave without being suspected. The seven-year-old son of the family with whom he was staying saved the day. He tugged at Woodrum's sleeve and motioned him to leave, saying to the Germans that his father was mute.

Woodrum has returned to France several times since the war. In 1965 he went back as the guest of the French government on the anniversary of the liberation of Paris. They invited him because he was one of the few Americans inside the city when it was freed. The boy who saved him from the Germans has grown up now, but Woodrum still corresponds with him and his family, who visited in 1966 as Woodrum's guests.

As far as he can determine, he is the only American to be shot down over Paris in the daytime and escape. Of the six men who were shot down with him, two were killed by the Germans and four survived.

THE ESCAPE AND EVASION STORY
By Ralph D. McKee

The 305th Bomb Group turned over the initial point and headed down the bomb run. It was the Fourth of July, 1943. The target was a German airfield on the outskirts of Nantes, France.

The navigator's job was finished for the moment. I unslung the 50 caliber machine gun which was mounted over my worktable and scanned the blue sky. Only a handful of ME-109s had come up to challenge the bombers, and they were not aggressive today.

In the plexiglass nose, the bombardier was hunched over the bombsight, centering the target in the crosshairs. A few powderpuffs of exploding flak were out in front of the formation. The pilot had our flight neatly tucked in the formation. The bomb bay doors were open now. In a minute, tons of bombs would rain down on the target. The bright summer sky would be darkened by a hail of death and destruction.

Only seconds remained until bombs away. The formation seemed to hang motionless; waiting expectantly. Suddenly the Flying Fortress shuddered, faltered and fell back in the formation ever so slightly. A piece of flak must have hit a turbo-supercharger, causing one of the engines to lose power. Up in the cockpit, Bill Wetzel and Chuck Cockrell, the pilot and co-pilot, were increasing power on the remaining good engines.

"Bombs away." "Bomb bay doors coming closed." The formation began a gentle turn to the westerly heading that would take us out over the Bay of Biscay and home.

Our Fortress continued to fall behind the formation and lose altitude. One of the other engines must be damaged. The situation wasn't good but I had been in worse spots and we had made it back. Many Fortresses had limped home with one or even two engines shot out.

Suddenly we were not alone. The German fighters had been waiting for a straggler. Now they came in for the kill. Tracers raced toward us. Shells tore the Fortress's skin. The Fortress vibrated from the recoil as the gunners fought back savagely. The fighters attacked again and again. One of the gunners shouted jubilantly, "I got one. He's on fire." But the fighters had killed the Fortress. One engine was burning fiercely, and there was a fire in the vicinity of the bomb bay.

The pilot sounded the bail-out signal on the emergency alarm system. I didn't weigh his decision. The Fortress couldn't hold together more than a few minutes. I rechecked the parachute chest pack. It was then that I first noticed cuts on one hand caused by an exploding enemy shell. Just off the left wing, one of the victorious fighters was flying with his landing gear in the down position, surveying his prize. Unfastening the oxygen mask, I crawled back to the escape hatch. The hatch door was already jettisoned. With my right hand on the rip cord, I tumbled out.

As I fell free of the airplane, my back hit something. Then I was falling face up staring at the flames from the wings and bomb bay that licked back past the tail. I was losing consciousness. Pull the rip cord! No, wait until you're clear of the flames! Pull . . .

I was first conscious of a gentle swishing sound as the air rushed around the nylon canopy of the parachute. The D-ring, attached to the rip cord, was still clutched in my right hand. In the distance, I could hear the faint drone of the Fortress returning home. It was difficult to face reality. A few minutes ago I had been part of a smoothly functioning bomber crew, able to make decisions and command power. Now, I had been projected into a cold, hostile environment and I was at the mercy of nature and the enemy. For some unknown reason, I thought of the meal I was going to miss back at the base. Today the mess was serving steak and ice cream. It had been months since we had food like that.

There was a total absence of odors and sounds except for air rustling around the parachute. Underneath, there was a neat patchwork of fields, pastures, roads, and fence rows. I felt alone and powerless as I swung gently, back and forth under a few yards of nylon.

Trees and houses could be distinguished now, and I could smell the ripening grain fields and grassy pastures. I thought of our farm back in Oklahoma where the wheat would be standing in shocks, waiting to be threshed. It seemed impossible that this peaceful, orderly countryside belonged to an enemy conqueror and that I was a hunted animal.

The earth was rushing up faster now. I was going to land in a small field which was surrounded by tall poplar trees. My feet slammed against the ground and I rolled backwards on one shoulder. The parachute settled to the ground and collapsed gently. My back hurt and I was tired, so I lay back to rest.

My mind cleared and I remembered the briefings on the techniques for evading capture. I had to hide my flying gear and travel as far as possible, as quickly as I could. German patrols had undoubtedly spotted the area where I landed.

While I was contemplating these moves, there was a rustling in one of the hedgerows and a voice was calling "Camarade." Two boys about 15 years old came through the hedge. I was relieved to see that they were not wearing uniforms. As the boys approached, I sat up with difficulty, and got to my feet. Fierce pains had shot through my back when I got up from the ground, but they eased a little when I was standing. I knew only a few words of French, but I could understand that they wanted to help me.

One of the boys helped me remove the parachute harness and Mae West life preserver. He indicated that I should follow the other boy, while he hid the flying gear. I followed him across the field and crawled through the hedge.

Two bicycles were lying by the side of the road. The two boys must have been following my parachute as it drifted down.

We mounted the bicycles and started pedaling down the narrow road. Pain was racking my back, and I wasn't sure I could ride any distance. With the extra spurt of energy and determination that is available in emergencies, I was able to stay about 20 feet behind my cycling companion. We rode through a small village where several German soldiers were lounging in the street. They glanced at us but took no special notice. Why hadn't they recognized me as an escaping American flier? I was wearing flying coveralls and a flight jacket which had a brightly colored squadron insignia sewed on the left breast. I had been foolhardy to tempt fate in this manner. I would have to be more cautious.

After pedaling for about 20 minutes, we turned off the road and entered a farmyard. A dog ran after us and barked. As we dismounted, the farmer came out of the house. The farmer and the youth talked excitedly, and then hurried me to the barn. I climbed up the ladder after them; into the hayloft. The three of us sat down on the floor and I suddenly felt very tired.

I tried to thank my new-found friends. They were more interested in how our airplane had been shot down. By using gestures, I was able to convey the story to them. I had a package of cigarettes in my shirt pocket, which I passed around. There was a long conversation between the Frenchmen about American cigarettes as they inhaled deeply. Later in the afternoon, the farmer went to the house. When he returned he was carrying a small loaf of dark brown bread, a bottle of wine and glasses.

I washed the bread down with wine. We finished the bottle as dusk fell. Later my friends climbed down the ladder and I lay down. I was soon sleeping soundly on the soft fragrant hay.

Dawn was breaking and a rooster was crowing when I awoke. I was covered with a U.S. Army blanket. The farmer appeared, carrying fried ham and an omelet in an iron skillet, and a bowl of hot milk. I tried to sit up and found that I couldn't. By rolling over on my stomach, I was able to push my body up, get on my knees and finally sit.

When I had finished eating, he showed me the words "U.S. Army" on the bottom of the skillet. He had fought with the United States soldiers in World War I.

The farmer indicated that German patrols would be searching the countryside for me. He led me to a briar thicket some distance from the barn. I crawled into the thicket and waited for the day to pass. About 10:00 a truck drove into the farmyard, and I could hear voices. The truck left in about 15 minutes. That evening I learned that the truck was driven by German soldiers. The farmer had no knowledge of any American and the soldiers had left after a cursory search.

I spent the next two days in the thicket during the day and returned to the barn at night. A number of Frenchmen came during the evenings to see the American and discuss my plight. They paused frequently to curse les Allemands and pour more wine to toast the coming German defeat. The French, apparently, disliked water and never drank it when wine was available. Their wine was light and tasted good and seemed to be plentiful. Late in the second night, it was decided that I should be moved the next day. It was dangerous to stay too long in one place.

The next morning I was placed in a wagon and a small load of hay was thrown over me. A horse pulled the wagon out of the farmyard and we jostled over roads and through a field. When the wagon stopped and the hay was pulled back, I saw that we were on the edge of a marsh which was covered with tall grass.

The farmer and I found a dry spot and he gave me some bread and cheese and a bottle of wine which he had brought along. He had tears in his eyes as he indicated that he would like to help me more, but the Germans would kill his family if I was found on his farm. He said that friends would come for me that night.

Time passed slowly as I sat in the grass with nothing to read and little to do. I examined my escape kit again and again, surveying the possible routes of escape on the map. There were only two possibilities: make my way to the coast and hope to get passage on a neutral ship, or walk south and cross the Pyrenees into Spain.

I wasn't too far from the bay, but the coastal areas would be heavily patrolled and I might be unable to find a neutral ship whose crew would help me. That course seemed to offer too many obstacles, especially since I was clothed in a cotton khaki uniform and flying suit. The Pyrenees were approximately 250 miles away as the crow flies. Add fifty miles for the road distance and the total would be 300 miles. That would take at least 15 nights of walking since the nights were short.

While I was pondering these thoughts, I was startled by a distant burst of machine gun fire. Across the flat valley I could make out a number of barrack type buildings. Apparently, it was a German Army camp.

After the sun set, I was visited by two young men. They brought food, a bottle of wine, and a bottle of cognac. They had been trying to contact the organization but had not been successful. I should not despair, though, because they would surely be successful tomorrow.

The night was warm and sleeping on a bed of marsh grass wasn't too uncomfortable. I arose with the sun the next day and began another day of doing nothing.

About noon, I had another visitor. He was a priest who spoke excellent English. We talked at length about England, the United States and the war. Several of the men who had befriended me were members of his church and had sought his help. He did not have contact with the organization and knew of no way to make contact. Further help by the friendly

Frenchmen would only result in endangering their lives and their families' lives. I had to agree, that without organized help, the risk to them was not worth the doubtful outcome. The priest gave me his blessing and departed. I wondered if there was another place on earth where men would have risked death, if caught, by helping me as much as they had.

My fate was now in my own hands. I weighed the problems that confronted me. I would have to walk at least 300 miles and then cross the border. My back still caused me constant pain, and it might become worse. I would have to travel at night and avoid the towns and villages. Guards and patrols would have to be avoided. I would have to forage for food, but it was mid-summer and fruit and vegetables should be available. I decided to spend one more night in the marsh, plan my route the next day, and start traveling the following night.

As night fell, clouds blanketed the sky and a cool rain began falling. My clothes became soaked and sleep was sporadic. The bottle of cognac made the wet night more bearable. Toward morning the rain stopped and I slept.

With the first light of dawn, I awoke suddenly at the sound of voices. It was the two young men who had visited me the first night in the marsh. They feared that I might have left and started my journey. They were very excited. My troubles were over. This evening two men would arrive with three bicycles and I would be taken to the city.

That evening two men in their middle thirties arrived carrying a bundle of clothing. I discarded my flying clothes and uniform, after removing the wings and silver lieutenant bars, and dressed in civilian clothes. My new friends showed me how to wear the beret.

We must have ridden 12 or 15 miles before the city came into view. My friends were in good spirits and had joked and laughed a lot during the trip.

It was necessary to cross a river before entering the town. This was Saturday night and there was a large number of people crossing the bridge on foot and on bicycles. The German guard at the far end of the bridge was not checking identification papers and took no notice of us as we rode by.

We rode up an alley, parked the bicycles in the backyard and entered a modest but comfortable house. I learned that we were in Jean's house and his companion was Felix. Jean introduced me to his wife, a charming Frenchwoman.

Jean produced a bottle of wine and glasses. We drank wine and talked far into the night, despite my limited French vocabulary. That night I slept in a wonderfully soft bed for the first time in a week.

Jean woke me late the next morning and said he had another guest coming for dinner. He produced a razor, toothbrush and hot water for a bath.

I felt clean and fresh for the first time in a week as I entered the parlor. Jean's guest startled me; I could hardly believe my eyes. Bill Wetzel, my pilot, was sitting in this very room.

Bill and I had a great deal to talk about as we recounted the events of the past Sunday. With Jean and Felix filling in details, we learned that the rest of our crew had fallen into German hands the first day.

Bill had a long, narrow wound on one cheek which was starting to heal. A German soldier had shot and grazed him as he was descending in the parachute. On one occasion during the week he had narrowly escaped being captured when a German patrol searched the farm where he was being hid.

Life at Jean's house settled into a routine. Listening to the BBC news program in the evening was a luxury we hadn't expected. Bill and I spent the daytime hours in an upstairs bedroom, being very quiet. The household continued to function normally to avoid arousing suspicion. A small number of Frenchmen were apparently still sympathetic to the German cause. They and the Germans represented a threat that had to be reckoned with in planning every action.

In the evenings Jean, Felix and their friends would discuss hopes and plans for our escape, while we all drank wine. They were investigating two possible plans for our escape. One plan was to arrange for a small boat to pick us up at some isolated part of the coast. This plan was soon discarded when they learned that the Germans had recently strengthened the coastal defenses and patrols. The other plan was to have an Allied airplane fly in below the radar defenses, land at a prearranged field or pasture and then return to England. The Frenchmen were very optimistic about this latter plan. When they learned, some four or five days later, that it was impossible to arrange for an airplane, they were downcast. It would now be necessary to plan for the long journey south.

Several times we took long walks in the evening. It was a relief to get outside, even if some risk was involved. One evening we visited a doctor at his home. The doctor examined my back, which still pained me most of the time. He couldn't determine the exact injuries without an X-ray picture, but his examination indicated that I had suffered a fractured vertebrae. The doctor had several bottles of vintage champagne which the Germans had not liberated. We drank a number of toasts to the defeat of les Allemands.

It was decided that the number of people going to and from Jean's house might arouse suspicion. Arrangements were made for us to stay at two other homes for four or five days until the plans were completed for our journey.

The plans were completed, and we returned to Jean's house for final preparations. Identification papers had been expertly forged. We would ride a night train to Paris where the final plans for escape would be made. Our companion and guide would be a young Frenchman. We were to play the part of deaf mutes and our guide would do the necessary talking.

Bidding farewell to friends like these was difficult, even though I was experiencing the exhilaration of finally beginning the journey to freedom. Jean had presented me with one of his best pipes when he learned that I enjoyed pipe smoking. Before leaving, his wife gave me a small medal of St. Christopher, saying that he would guide me on a safe journey. I was not familiar with the roles of the various saints, but I was grateful for her prayers and concern for my safety.

I decided to give her my navigator wings. I still had my identification tags and rank insignia to prove my identity if I was captured. A pair of silver wings seemed to be a very small gift for a group of people who had risked death, under the very noses of the Germans, to aid me.

The train ride to Paris was uneventful. We flashed our passes as we pushed through the station gate in a large crowd. The German guard motioned us on, mechanically.

Bill and I were taken to a modern apartment house not far from the center of Paris. Here we spent the balance of the night and the next day and night. Our host's library contained several American classics which we read eagerly.

The following day we were moved to another apartment to begin the final preparations. That afternoon two more American fliers were brought to the apartment. We learned that they were from a neighboring bomb group back in England.

An elderly woman who lived in the apartment amused us and caused us some concern. From her rocking chair on the balcony of the third floor apartment, she spat at the German soldiers as they walked past and cursed them not too loudly.

A distinguished looking, middle-aged man gave us a briefing for the final leg of our journey to Spain. We would ride a fast express train to the southern terminus, travel by bus to a town near the frontier and cross the border the following night. Each of us had a bundle consisting of bread, food and a few clothes held together by a knotted kerchief. Again, we were to play the part of deaf mutes and our guide would be speaking for us. Our guide was making his final trip as an escort and would accompany us on into Spain. From Spain, he would go on to North Africa and join General de Gaulle's Free French Forces.

Our guide purchased tickets at the station office, and we walked through the gates without showing our identification passes. Within an hour I was to learn why an inspection had not been made.

The train was crowded, and we found that all the seats were taken. Our little group was left with no alternative but to travel standing in the narrow aisle. We were rapidly joined by a number of other travelers talking positions in the aisle. This wasn't going to be a comfortable ride, but perhaps we would be less conspicuous among all the standing passengers.

The train got under way. I found that a conscious effort was necessary to act the part of a deaf mute in this crowded railway coach. The clanking of the wheels on the rails sounded like music. Each minute was speeding us on toward freedom.

I was brought sharply back to reality. The conductor was coming down the coach collecting tickets. Immediately behind him were two uniformed Gestapo officers checking identification passes. My heart beat faster and there were butterflies in my stomach.

Was my forged identification card good enough? Would my disguise pass? The beret didn't cover much of my blond hair and ruddy face, which was definitely not French. Would four deaf mutes in one party arouse suspicion?

The Gestapo men worked down the coach. I produced my pass and waited. The officer looked at my face, studied the card momentarily, and moved on to one of my companions. Everything in the coach was in order, and they moved on to the next coach. I felt a deep appreciation for the bold and detailed plan that was being executed.

The night wore on. My back pained and I couldn't sit or lie down for relief. I half-dozed while leaning against the side of the coach. The need for sleep faded with the light of dawn.

All the passengers' identification cards were checked again by the Gestapo men. I felt and looked more like the rest of the weary travelers now. Again, the identification papers passed inspection.

At mid-morning we left the train at Mont de Marsan, after riding about 11 hours. I discovered that our party had grown to two guides and about nine evadees. Two of the evadees, I found later, were Polish fliers who had escaped from a German prison camp.

Our guides inquired about the bus schedule and bought tickets. We ate in a small cafe and lounged in a city park until the bus arrived.

A local official inspected identification passes after we had boarded the bus. We stood again on the crowded bus until a number of passengers were discharged several hours later. The bus was old and made slow progress on the road. In addition, it seemed to stop at every village and crossroad.

In the evening several conversations ensued between our guides and the bus driver. I could sense that our guides were becoming apprehensive.

About 9:00 the bus stopped in a village and the driver went into a lighted building. As he stepped inside the building, our guides whispered and motioned for us to alight and follow them, quickly.

We tumbled out of the bus, grabbing our bundles as we left. Like frightened deer, we jumped over a stone fence and fled down a hill, across a creek and up another hill. I learned later that during the evening we had entered the border zone where special passes were required. The bus driver had become suspicious of the explanation our guides had given him. When he stopped the bus in the village, it was almost certain that he had gone to summon the gendarmes.

After skirting back around the village, we headed south, walking and trotting at a fast pace. There was no moon, and we were getting into a hilly country. About midnight we came upon a road and followed it to an intersection. The guides were finally able to determine our location from the signpost, and we proceeded down the road.

Just before dawn, we found a secluded grove of trees, thick with underbrush, not too far off the road. We were now in an area that was undoubtedly patrolled by the Germans. Travel in the daytime was out of the question, so we settled down for the day in the grove.

When we had made our hurried exit from the bus, we had been joined by a man and a woman, presumably husband and wife. They claimed they were escaping from the Germans. There was no way of verifying their story, so we had to keep them in the party. The guides were dubious about their story, but the risk of having them report us was too great.

The fatigue from traveling two nights and a day without sleep was asserting itself. Most of us fell asleep on the ground without even eating a piece of bread.

One of the guides had walked down to a village in the morning. He returned shortly after noon with the news that he had hired a truck to haul us on part of the night's journey. We would now be able to regain some of the time that was lost when the bus ride was ended prematurely.

The mountain ranges rose to the south. Somewhere beyond those mountains was freedom, but there was still a hard march ahead of us. My feet were hurting from the last night's march. I had been wearing a pair of fleece lined, English flying boots which were warm and comfortable but would not have passed for French footwear. The boots had been discarded for a pair of black slippers with pointed toes which were about one size too small. I wished I had heeded the group commander's advise and worn a pair of rugged, comfortable, service shoes. I slept again in the hot afternoon sunshine.

After dusk the truck arrived. All of our party, except one guide, sat on the floor with a huge tarpaulin thrown over our bodies. The truck stopped at the end of a two-hour drive, and we crawled out and began the march. There were no roads now and we walked on trails. There was no moon, and the only light was provided by the stars. The trail became steeper. The long uphill climbs were punctuated by short downhill walks as we ascended the mountain range. Each step became a greater task than the last. The guides were up and down the line whispering loudly "allez, allez." I heard that word a thousand times that night and the next morning.

When mountain streams were found, we drank from them and washed our faces. Rest stops were infrequent, and we pushed onward and upward at a steady pace. Shortly after dawn we arrived at a mountain farmhouse. The farmer did not seem surprised to see us and showed us the hay mow. The house and barn were in one building. The farm animals were stabled and penned in the bottom floor, while the living quarters and hay mow occupied the top floor. I fell asleep on the hay as the sun rose over the mountains.

Most of us were awake by mid-afternoon. Tonight we would cross the border. There was much conversation and speculation on what we would do after we crossed into Spain. The guides thought there would be no difficulty in contacting the nearest British consulate and securing help.

The farmer's wife had prepared a large kettle of meat stew. It was nourishing, though not tasty, but we ate it ravenously. Food had not been plentiful during the past two days.

After sunset we left the house. We pushed forward eagerly on a steep but well-worn trail. The trail soon diminished to a narrow rocky path. Only a sure-footed goat could negotiate such a path. As we climbed higher, the mountain seemed to become a solid rock. In the dim starlight, I could often see steep precipices below the path.

At midnight, the guides estimated that we were within three or four kilometers of the border. Extreme caution was now required. Weeks of work and planning could be lost in a single minute. We stopped often to listen and peer into the darkness.

We crossed what appeared to be the highest ridge of the mountains and continued down the rocky path. The guides were confident that we were now across the border, but we should push on deeper into Spain before daylight. In this rugged country it would be easy for the Germans to range into Spanish territory and capture us yet.

The path became better and now ran alongside a swift mountain stream. Thus far we had eluded both the Germans and Spanish border guards. The toil and suspense of the last three nights seemed like a dream that had never been true.

Down the trail we could see smoke rising from a chimney. One of the guides went ahead to investigate. He returned, and we walked down to a Basque mountaineer's house.

The Basque family sold us a little food and wine. The wine was in a skin bag and required skill to direct the small liquid stream into the mouth. Our stomachs and spirits were warmed by the wine.

The guides had learned that we were now well into Spain. We had made it! Freedom was ours! We would push on to the nearest village and ask an official to contact the nearest consulate for us.

We were in a gay, carefree mood as we walked down through the foothills.

Late in the forenoon we were walking on a good, though narrow, road. Suddenly two uniformed Spaniards, carrying rifles, sprung out from behind some bushes. They were members of the Giardia Civile. The guards demanded that we show our passport papers. Since we had none, they would escort us to the next village. There, the formalities of papers could be taken care of. With one guard leading the way and one following, our party walked on to the village. There, we were placed in a large jail cell and the doors were locked until an official could be summoned.

No one in authority seemed to be in the village. We could not have permission to telephone the consulate. We sat on the rough benches or slept on the stone floor the rest of the day and that night.

The man and woman who had joined us when we jumped the bus back in France, secluded themselves in one corner of the cell. We speculated on what their exact status was. One of the guides was now convinced that they were spies who had been planted by the Germans to expose the Underground route. I never learned the answer to that riddle.

During the night, I began to experience the discomfort of stomach cramps and dysentery. I had apparently gotten the dysentery bacteria by drinking water from the mountain streams.

The next morning we were herded out of the cell and loaded on an old bus. Two guards accompanied us. We learned that the bus was taking us to Pomplona.

After a hot, dusty ride the bus stopped in front of a complex of buildings surrounded by a high wall. It was the first week of August. Pomplona seemed to be a lazy, relaxed city in the hot noon-day sun. The guards marched us inside the compound. It was the most modern and imposing building I had seen in Spain. Here was a modern, secure prison.

We were herded into a room where prison officials went through the formalities of registering and searching us. The officials did not seem impressed by the fact that I was a United States citizen. The three other Americans and I were assigned to the same cell. It measured about 14 by 20 feet. There was one small barred window and a door of iron bars. The furnishings consisted of four rough, straw mattresses, a wash basin, and a non-flush toilet in one corner.

I became well acquainted with the corner where the toilet was located. My dysentery became worse each day. There was no toilet tissue or paper and I resorted to tearing pieces of cloth from my shirt as a substitute. When I finally left the prison, not much of the shirt remained.

The next morning we were escorted to the prison barber shop. There our heads were clipped close and we were shaved by trusty barbers. I began to think that my stay there was going to be longer than a few days.

Later we were summoned before the prison commandant and his staff. There was more questioning concerning our units and why we had entered Spain. We declined to answer questions and gave only our name, rank and service numbers. We requested the commandant to notify American or British authorities that we were in his prison.

When I had been searched, on entering the prison, a hacksaw blade, which was molded in a piece of black rubber, had been taken from me. The commandant wanted to know what it was. I told him I had no idea what it was. He was still

puzzling this object when I left his office.

Most of the cells in the prison were filled. The inmates were mostly Spaniards whose crime had been having been on the losing side when the Spanish Civil War ended. Trusties ladled our food from a kettle down the cell block from door-to-door. A guard would unlock the door and our wooden bowls and spoons would be handed in. The food was always the same - a watery, barley soup with some olive oil floating on top and a piece of bread. Sometimes the soup contained potatoes but I never found a piece of meat in it.

Part of the prison routine consisted of a half hour in the courtyard each day. We looked forward to this time when we could exercise in the sun and talk to our French friends. Once each week, prisoners were allowed to bathe under crude, cold water showers. Each prisoner also received a shave and haircut once a week.

One day a Red Cross official arrived to interview new prisoners. He wanted to know a great deal about us but again, we gave name, rank and service number only. We asked him to contact the United States authorities for us.

The days and nights in the cell became more monotonous. There were no reading materials or playing cards. There was nothing to do but talk or look at the walls. Sometimes I looked through the barred window trying to figure a way to escape. But, escape from this well-designed institution appeared to be hopeless. Tobacco and cigarettes were scarce and the luxury of a smoke several times each day became a ritual. By saving the short cigarette butts, I was able to accumulate a pipe full of rather terrible tasting tobacco every two or three days.

We had been in prison about a week, when an American official arrived. He interviewed each of us and recorded details of our conversation. He said arrangements would have to be made for our release and three or four days would be necessary to make them. Before leaving, he gave us some American cigarettes and advised us not to attempt to escape from the prison.

Several days later a prison official came to our cell and informed us that we were leaving the prison. The formalities of being released required some time in the prison office. Before I left, the prison commandant showed me the piece of molded black rubber that had been taken from me. The rubber had been stripped back and the hacksaw blade was bared. The commandant seemed extremely pleased to have finally discovered what the object was.

Our escort was a handsome, engaging Spanish Air Force major. He drove us to the resort town of Zaragosa in an official automobile. During the ride, I wondered how many thousand political prisoners might be serving sentences in other prisons in Spain. Many of the prisoners were still young. They couldn't have been more than boys when they were fighting in the civil war.

What would become of the young Frenchmen who had escaped into Spain with us? They had left France with the dream of fighting for their country. Would they ever realize that dream?

The Spanish major registered us in an old resort hotel. We were required to stay within the town until further arrangements were completed. The hotel dining room served good food, and I looked forward eagerly to mealtime. My weight was now about 20 pounds below normal, and I was weakened by the dysentery. The hotel had a number of baths which were fed by warm mineral springs. I spent hours in the baths reading and relaxing. The mineral water seemed to have a beneficial effect on the sores that were caused by bites from the bugs that had inhabited the prison mattresses.

Several days later the Spanish major returned and drove us to Alahama. There would be several more days, he said, until we could leave Spain.

We had finished registering at the hotel when we were approached by a young man with a shaved head. He introduced himself as Lieutenant John Dunbar. John helped us get outfitted with clothes from a cache in the hotel. We spent enjoyable hours sipping beer and talking during the next few days. He had escaped from France with no organized help - a feat in itself - and had often gone for days without food and water.

The story of our trip out of Spain and our return to England is told in Dunbar's exciting book, *Escape Through The Pyrenees*, and will not be repeated in detail. In brief, from Alahama, we were driven to Madrid where papers were arranged for us to leave the country. From Madrid, we traveled by automobile to Gibraltar where we were delivered to the United States military authorities. Several days later we flew to Marrakech and after a delay of several more days, we were flown back to England.

After returning to England, I attended a Royal Air Force Intelligence school and later gave several lectures on my experiences to newly arrived bomber crews.

While attending the school, I learned that an unofficial emblem existed for airmen who completed their last mission on foot. Some former escapee had devised the emblem, which consisted of a small silver boot with wings attached. It was symbolic of a mission I would never forget.

When I returned to my bomb group for a visit, there were many unfamiliar faces. Losses had been heavy during the summer of 1943. Perhaps some of my friends, if they were fortunate enough to evade capture, were now starting the adventure which I had completed.

The elapse of years has faded my memory of some of the exact dates and places of the events that occurred. My memory will always remain bright, however, for the group of Frenchmen who risked death to help me.

The courage and fortitude of that group of Frenchmen - and other groups like them - symbolized the spirit and determination of a freedom-loving people in resisting oppression.

JAN SMIT—"DOOFSTOM"
By Claude C. Murray, Col., CAF
and Don Norton, Col., CAF

I had left about nine o'clock in the morning, and one of my buddies in the squadron, Lt. Robert Hall, a guy that slept right next to me, had targets in the same area. We took off at the same time, headed in the same direction; he was flying about a mile off my wing, and we were in radio contact. You weren't supposed to do much talking on the radio, but he gave me a call and said, "Bat Crap" (our real call sign was 'Baylo'—I was Baylo 28) "you're off course."

"No, Bat Crap, I'm not off course."

That was the only conversation I recall that we had—until he call in "Bogies." "There's Bogies at four o'clock"—meaning that enemy aircraft were somewhere coming up from that direction.

Lt. Claude C. Murray, Jr., from Cheney, WA was flying out of Mount Farm, England for the 7th Photo Recon. Group. Oct. 6, 1944, while on a lone photo-recon. mission over Germany, he was hit by an Me-262. He was able to turn-over his P-38 and bailed out into the Zuider Zee in Holland. He eventually made contact with the Dutch Underground and evaded the Germans for seven months until his liberation on May 5, 1945.

The minute he called in the Bogie, I was hit. Smack!

I didn't see the guy coming or going. Lt. Hall later reported that we had been attacked by German jets.

But he had hit me, and I didn't know where. All I knew was that there had been a huge, huge impact — a big jolt. I knew that something had happened, and it turned out that it was my right engine, which eventually caught fire.

In your training, you are trained and trained in various procedures, which come second nature to you. Everything to the firewall! Drop the belly tanks! But I forgot to switch from the reserve tanks (the belly tanks) to the main tanks. And all of a sudden, both my engines were windmilling, because they weren't getting any fuel.

Realizing that, I switched to main and got my port engine started again, but I couldn't start my starboard engine, the one that was hit. So I figured I would go back home.

I guessed I was down to 6,000 to 8,000 feet, and could fly very nicely on one engine. I would go back.

Pretty quick, I'm getting smoke in the cockpit. Boy, if there's anything that scares you, it's fire and smoke in an airplane! I'd been calling "Mayday, Mayday" on the radio. I was over the Zuider Zee. I'd gone into Germany, and probably had come back over Arnhem, turning back toward England.

I popped the canopy, and when I did, off went my helmet, my goggles, and my oxygen mask — because I didn't have my helmet buckled. That didn't make any difference, because I couldn't talk to anybody anyway. We had an IFF (Identification, Friend or Foe) system in the airplane, which is wired. You break the wire and push the switch, and there will be an automatic signal that identifies you as friend or foe. So if anybody was on that IFF channel, and I had been in their vicinity, they would know that I was an Allied aircraft.

This is where the counterrotating propellers come in. When the right engine stopped, I held in hard left rudder, in order to keep the airplane going straight and level. I didn't trim it. What you're supposed to do is trim the airplane, get into a slight climb, slow it down to around 120 mph, slip out the side, and go down between the two tail booms and underneath the horizontal stabilizer.

That's how the book said to do it, but there had been a few people decapitated trying to do that.

I was still holding the rudder in, and I stuck my elbow out over the side, and God, I thought the wind was going to tear my arm off! I said to myself, "How on earth can I get out of this thing?" I was sitting on a seat-type dinghy, I had a backpack type parachute (and these are strapped together down below), I had a Mae West over me, which is also strapped to the dinghy — how would I slip out of this thing, with all that wind going by me, without getting hung up? Some people had that experience too.

"I think you've had it," I thought to myself; and I let go of everything. I took my foot off the rudder and started to pray.

The airplane, with the port engine propeller going one way, flipped over and split-s'ed, and I fell out. The next thing I knew, I was coming down in a parachute. You're supposed to hang on to the D-ring for good luck — the ring that opens the parachute.

"Have I got the D-ring! Where's the D-ring!" I don't know. Obviously I had pulled it, but I don't remember doing it. Maybe I had blacked out a little, or something. Anyway, I was coming down in the parachute, and I didn't realize what had happened. Obviously I hadn't trimmed the airplane up so it would fly straight and level on the one engine, and therefore it simply flipped over, due to torque.

I was coming down and below was the damned water. Here your training comes in again. You are supposed to unbuckle your chest buckle, and the two buckles on your legs, and slide out of the parachute just before you hit the water, so you don't get tangled up in the chute harness.

I couldn't get out of one of the buckles. So I was in the water, bobbing up and down. I finally got rid of the parachute. I inflated the Mae West. It is connected by a little strap to the dinghy, which is floating in the water. You reach down to the dinghy, find the CO-2 cylinder, and inflate the dinghy. Now you climb into it.

When I got in the dinghy, I looked for the equipment that's supposed to be in it — paddles, something to make a sail out of, a sea anchor, a bail-out bucket, a whistle, sea dye (green). There was nothing except the sea anchor and bail-out bucket.

The sea anchor is something you string out in back of the dinghy—something small on the front end, and fanning into a sort of a funnel shape. The sea anchor keeps you going with the waves, instead of against them.

I don't know what the water temperature was when I went down, but it was damned cold. And of course all I could do was sit there, though there was a flap you could pull over yourself. I couldn't do anything but just sit there and float!

I wondered where I was, where I was going, what was going to happen. I figured I would be captured.

This happened about 1300 hours — about one o'clock in the afternoon. I couldn't see very much, although I was only about a mile or so off shore. I don't remember seeing the shore when I was coming down; I was too worried about how I was going to get out of that parachute when I fell into the water. All I know is that I got in the dinghy, and I was floating there.

It was getting dark, but it must have been a clear night, because all of a sudden I saw on the horizon what looked like the low form of a boat, maybe what a submarine would look like. I started to paddle with my hands and I came into shore. I floated into a little island, which turned out to be the "Fortress Pampus" — an old Dutch fortress, about two and one-half acres in size. It's only about a mile from shore.

Jan Van Etten, a young Dutch Underground Resistance member, prepares to transport Lt. Claude Murray (alias Jan Smit) on the first leg of his journey back to England after evading the Germans in the vicinity of Muiden, Naarden and Weesp, Netherlands. They departed on May 8, 1945.

"Jan Smit" listens on a crystal set to some German propaganda probably being broadcast by "Lord Haw-Haw." This photo was taken of Lt. Murray during his six week stay in hiding at the home of Mevrouw Dietz, in Naarden.

I was tired by now, after thirteen hours in a boat, and all I wanted to do was sleep. I crawled out of the dinghy and deflated it, then lay down underneath some bushes and went to sleep.

At dawn, the next morning, I started my escape and evasion tactics. I started walking and crawling around, to see if there were any enemy troops around. You're supposed to reconnoiter; to see if there are any enemy troops; to see if you can stay away from them.

When I stood up, I saw a sign: "Verboten." I knew what that meant: you are "forbidden" to be there. I discovered some chambers down inside the fortress; as I walked down the cement steps, I found all kinds of rooms. This fortress was used to protect the harbor, but it had been stripped of all guns and other uses. It had been used by troops many years ago, but the Germans didn't want anyone out there now. The Dutch in the little nearby village knew they couldn't come out there. But of course I didn't know that at the time.

I had an escape kit, a little plastic box about four inches by six inches, and an inch and a half thick. Inside the box were a couple of tiny compasses, halazone to purify water, something to keep you awake, concentrated chocolate, vitamins, some chewing gum, some matches, a razor, a fishhook, a plastic bag for collecting water, and so forth. In addition, I had a little fiber bag about the same size as the escape kit, which contained the famous little silk maps. So I was able to figure out where I was.

I went down inside the fortress and built a fire to try to dry out a bit. I was still pretty soggy, but I ruined my GI shoes, because I put them too close to the fire and left them sitting there; they became as hard as rocks. But I still had my fleece-lined flight boots on.

I went back up on top and said to myself, "Okay, it's about nine o'clock in the morning." Then I saw fishing boats, about a mile away, so I waved my hands and started whistling. I tore the flap off my dinghy and hooked it onto a stick and waved it, trying to get somebody to come out. I was getting hungry. I wanted a cigarette. I wanted to talk to somebody. I wanted to get captured. How could I possibly evade? I was sitting out there on an island and no one was going to come out and get me.

I started to accumulate trash and wood, gathered it together, went right to the top of the Pampus and said to myself, "At twelve o'clock noon I'm going to set this stuff on fire. I'm going to build the damndest bonfire anyone ever saw."

So I built the fire, but nothing happened. The fishermen saw the fire, I know, because I later talked to a Dutch policeman, and he saw it. But they didn't dare go out there, because of the very stringent rules of their Nazi occupiers.

That was decision number one. For decision number two, I said that at three o'clock, if I hadn't talked to anybody, I would get back in that dinghy (even though I'd sworn I would never do it — I didn't want to get wet again). But I had to get to shore. I could see what I thought were some smokestacks, so I figured maybe there were some factories on shore. And maybe if I got to shore by four or five o'clock, I could start walking. Maybe nobody will notice me. I had a flight suit on, but so what?

So at three o'clock I blew up the dinghy (don't ask me how I did it), got into it with a couple of pieces of wood I could sort of paddle with, and paddled for about fifteen minutes to half

an hour. Then came three kids in a fishing boat: Jan Dobber, his brother and a friend. They came alongside of me, got me into the boat, deflated the dinghy, and hid it under some fishing nets. I think my flight jacket was a B-10, which has an Air Force insignia. So I said, "I'm an American." They didn't speak any English, and I couldn't speak any Dutch.

A German patrol boat came by, and the boys hid me under the nets. They knew what they were doing. When it left, they rowed the boat into shore and pulled up beside a dike, on the water side. Over the dike was a village. One of the kids said he was going to "Haul his fodder" ("Haal zyn vader"). It sounded to me like he was going to go get his father.

I said to him, "Fine, go ahead."

My next escape and evasion tactic was to never stay in the same place. If somebody is going to help you, go back a ways, so you can watch the spot where they're coming back to, to see if they're bringing some soldiers. I told Dobber that we should get back in the boat, and row around a while. I don't know how I told him that, maybe with hand signals or something.

We got back in the boat, and soon I saw the kid coming with a man. "Okay, let's go back to shore," I said. It didn't look like the Gestapo to me.

They'd told the father what had transpired, I suppose. He looked me over and said, "Wacht even" — "Wait a minute."

He went back to the village on his bicycle and returned with Joh Rozendaal, the leader of the Underground organization in the little village of Muiden. That was my fourth stroke of luck.

Joh Rozendaal asked, "Kan je fietsen?" — "Okay, can you ride a bike?"

"I guess so. I used to be a paper boy." Now I couldn't understand what he was saying, but I figured out what they were talking about. We got on bikes and rode a few blocks to a house where I was given some farm clothes to put on over my flight suit. They took my escape kit and maps.

They went on ahead, and when it got dark, we all went into the village. I came into a house, and there sitting around a dining table, under a light, was all the stuff from my escape kit laying there. And here were a bunch of young guys, members of the Rozendaal Resistance Group, sitting around a table, and also a Dutch minister — Dominee Douma — who spoke English. They wanted to know my story.

They were sure I was a "Kraut", trying to get into their organization or something. They didn't know who I was and I didn't know who they were.

But they fed me and cleaned me up.

The next day, one of the Underground leaders came in, Daan Spoor. He had been an officer in the Dutch Army, but had gone Underground. He had become what was called an "onderduiker" (meaning "to dive under and change identity"). Spoor traveled all the time. He never slept in the same house twice. He never went home because the Germans were on his trail.

He spoke excellent English, and he had a written examination for me. They wanted to determine if I was who I said I was and if I were "legitimate." I'd given them my name, rank, and serial number but they wanted to know the name of my flight surgeon. I told them, because I figured that if I was going to get them to trust me, I was going to have to trust them. And I did. I was on the defense, and they were on the offense.

Questions like "What is a 'meat' wagon?", an ambulance. "What is a 'flying prostitute'?" That's a B-26 bomber, because with its little tiny wings, it had "no visible means of support." "What do the Boston Red Sox do?" And other things like that, to see if I could answer very elementary American questions.

A day or two later, Daan Spoor came back, and in the meantime was in contact with British Intelligence. They had confirmed who I was, but my group never found out I was alive. They said I was MIA.

"Okay," Daan said, "you are who you say you are, so we have orders that you are not to try to escape or get back, and we are dedicated to help you evade capture. We will hide and protect you, but we can't help you escape."

They took my picture, put it on the "persoons bewijs" (personal permit), put my fingerprint on it, and my name became Jan Pieter Smit - a "doofstom" (deaf and dumb) salesman from the province Edam. The story was that during Operation Market Garden, with all the bombing, there were a helluva lot of refugees, some of them shell-shocked, that got out of there. And there were a lot! The Underground was busy trying to find places for these people to live and hide, and a lot of them were Jewish.

I had civilian clothes and they took my dogtags and uniform. This was a very ticklish thing, because if you're captured and have dogtags, they are evidence that you're an American, not a spy. If you don't have dogtags, they can shoot you on the spot.

Another time, Daan asked me if I could ride a bike for about ten kilometers. "Sure," I told them.

The next day, Jan Van Etten, a young Dutch guy about my age (now a resident of Edmonton, Alberta, Canada) came to see me. He had a bike, and I had a bike. We rode to the town of Naarden, not very far from Muiden.

We got on the bicycles, and he said, "Now I'm going to be about ten yards ahead of you. If I get stopped, you stop and turn around."

There we were, me in my civilian clothes, riding a bicycle down the streets. We got to Naarden, and went to the house of Vrouw Dietz, a widow. She had a nice home, and two sons: Jaap and Peter. Peter was maybe sixteen years old, and Jaap fourteen. They had a Jewish boy hiding out there, Ted Cohen. Vrouw Dietz got extra food stamps for permitting the Underground to house the "onderduikers." Incidentally, they could all speak English, including Ted Cohen. Whenever they wanted to talk to me, they spoke English; whenever they wanted to talk about me, they spoke Dutch. That was par for the course.

We got acquainted. Ted and I slept up on the second floor, and I supposed the others slept on the main floor. I wasn't allowed to go anyplace, not even out in the yard, except one night when they let me walk around in the back a little bit.

This was getting very discouraging. Every now and then, Daan Spoor would come to visit me in Naarden. Earlier on he had brought a pint of bourbon. On his visits, we would each have a jigger of that bourbon. Oh boy, was that ever good! Because it relaxed me. I was tense; I was under stress.

One day a Catholic priest came to the house, looking for a place to house refugees, but he had nothing to do with the Daan Spoor group. Vrouw Dietz said to him, "By the way, I've got an American pilot here."

"Do you want me to talk to him?" he asked.

"Yes", she said.

So we talked, and he found out the situation. "Do you want me to investigate the possibility of your leaving here? To get back to your lines?"

"I certainly do. Is there any chance?"

"I think there is. I think maybe I can figure out a plan for your departure."

He told me to get some dirty old farm clothes, a shovel, a potato bag and a bicycle. "We'll ride this bicycle down to a town, where you'll be picked up in Red Cross ambulance. The ambulance will then take you across the bridges."

There were three rivers: the Waal, the Maas, and the Rhine — three places to cross to get to the area of Belgium that had been liberated. I guess the Red Cross had some leeway with the Germans, because this was going to be the system.

By the way, you had to have your dogtags and uniform on under your old clothes.

We sent word back to Muiden to bring my dogtags and flight suit. Well, Mother Rozendaal (as I've come to call her) came on her bicycle and had the uniform with her, but she didn't tell us. She came in the house and talked to Vrouw Dietz and tried to talk to me. Then she left without leaving the uniform with me.

The next day, Daan Spoor came. "I hear you've got an escape plan rigged up. You know, you haven't got a fifty-fifty chance of making it out, and we don't want you to try it. We've got another place for you."

He escorted me out of Naarden and back to Muiden and got me a place on a farm at Weesp, only about a kilometer from Muiden.

I was on the farm of Gys Regtuyt, a great big strapping Dutch farmer, age 27 at the time (I was 22). The deal had been made with Gys that I would stay there, and he being one of the Dutch patriots and a member of the Underground group, it was fine. He had a wife, a baby and a little boy by the name of Eppie, who was probably four years old.

It was a dairy farm, and I was going to get outside a bit. I had my klompen (wooden shoes) and work clothes. The first evening there, Gys took me around the farm. He was very proud of it. The cow stalls were connected onto the house, and the cows were kept inside in the winter. Gys talked to me in Dutch, because none of his family spoke English.

Twice each day the Underground received secret code messages from the British over the BBC news. So we would sit and listen to the eight o'clock news. Then Gys would come home back from the village with his cigarettes. Again, this was relaxing. What the hell! We didn't have any cigarettes there, and when somebody was able to get a package, I'll tell you they were definitely like a drug. Inhale a cigarette after not having had one for a while, and man, you're flying high. So it was a real treat when Gys would go into town and pull off something like that.

The Dutch treated me with kid gloves. They didn't want anything to happen to me. I was a hero — an Ally; I was winning the war for them; I was a symbol for them. They never let me go anywhere I would be confronted by a German. In other words, whenever a German came down the road, the Dutch knew it and I was hiding. We had a hiding place out by the river, a cave. If I was out in the fields, that's where I would go; if I was in the house, I'd hit the attic and go into the hole in the floor. The Dutch didn't want to take a chance — they couldn't afford to take a chance.

There was a weekly ritual. Every Monday, Gys Regtuyt had a woman come to help his wife do housework. Bear in mind that the family didn't have any electricity, except for the radio. So they couldn't do any ironing, or any kind of normal housework.

Well, this woman was kind of "iffy". They suspected her of fraternizing with Germans. So when she came, I had to get out of there. In the evening, Jan Van Etten, the man who had escorted me on bicycle to Naarden, would come out to the farm from Muiden and I would follow him to Muiden on bicycle. I would sit there all day long and talk to the Rozendaals and the kids, as best I could with the language difference, using a word book much of the time. Every now and then someone who spoke English would come along. That gave me a little bit of diversion.

In the evening, Jan would come again and escort me back to the farm at Weesp. I didn't know at the time that he was armed. He lives in Edmonton, Alberta, Canada, now, and I met with him in Vancouver, B.C., in 1990, for the first time in forty-five years. That's when I found out that he'd had a gun all that time. A tough guy! He had a lot of nerve.

Whenever they figured that it was safe, I worked on the farm. I didn't go a long way from the house. I don't remember what some of the chores were, though I did learn to milk the cows, which we did twice a day by hand. I had my own one-legged stool, and my own piece of rope. You'd get your cow, clean off her udder, tie her tail to her legs, and milk. I couldn't strip a cow very good, though I worked at it.

I was in fact a little overweight, because I wasn't getting enough exercise. I would get up in the morning and have three pieces of bread with cheese and three cups of hot milk. In midmorning, I had a coffee-drink. At noon I had the big meal — a pile of potatoes and a pile of cabbage. That might be it. Then for dessert, we had what was called "pap". I think it was some sort of gruel or porridge, and they would put some kind of syrup on it. I think it was made out of barley. I was eating a lot of starchy food. Then after the noon meal, they'd go to bed for a couple of hours.

It seemed like I'd get up about two o'clock, and everybody would be out working. So I'd go out and mess around, but I didn't work hard. Then in the middle of the afternoon, I'd have a tea-drink; and at night, bread and cheese and milk.

Sometime around March of 1945, the Germans were getting pushed back into Holland, and as they were getting pushed, they were breaking down dikes and flooding areas. Some real German troops started showing up in the Weesp and Muiden area. We got word that the Germans wanted to occupy the Regtuyt farm. So I had to get moved back into Muiden.

The Germans threw straw all over the Regtuyt living room. They bivouacked their soldiers there and put gun emplacements along the river.

I was moved back into Muiden, but I should tell about the weapons dropping. This was the activity of the 801/492nd Bomb Group, who were called the "Carpetbaggers." Their major function was dropping agents behind enemy lines and supplying the Underground organizations all over Europe.

I called my Underground group in Muiden the Rozendaal Resistance Group. They were expecting a weapon drop. This was a big thrill. They felt, right after Operation Market Garden, that there would be another airborne invasion. That's how they thought they were going to get liberated. They wanted guns, ammunition, weapons.

So the night came for the dropping for the Rozendaal group. It would arrive at midnight. All the guys went out to the site with their horses and wagons, to try to intercept the parachutes as they came down. I don't know what it looked like, because they wouldn't let me go. And it was a good thing, because I wouldn't have known what to do — where to run if we'd got caught.

A couple of days later, they did let me go down to the church where they were unloading all the stuff — kegs and boxes of guns, sabotage equipment, sten-guns (a very simple 9 mm sort of a submachine gun, with an iron stock — a very common, rugged kind of gun that anyone could operate), hand grenades. They had all the weapons hidden down at the church, under the floor. Of course they were getting nervous, because the Germans were coming and occupying all the villages around there. They worried that somebody would find the guns, or somebody would tip the Germans off.

Then all of a sudden, the ceasefire came. The Allies had negotiated with the Germans, so that food could be dropped. This was in late April. There's a book written about this operation. The British part was called Operation Manna; the American version was called Chowhound. So it was called Operation Manna-Chowhound. With this deal, bombers could come over at 300 feet altitude right on the deck, over an exact route (they couldn't stray), and drop their food on various sites.

Shortly after that, the Germans capitulated, and north-west Germany, Denmark, Norway, Holland were liberated — shortly before V-E Day. We received the news by radio, and I'll tell you, I was fit to be tied. It was just wonderful. We heard about it the night before.

The next day, the Germans were supposed to lay down their weapons. And of course some of them did, and some of them didn't. But the Underground took over. They knew who all the black marketers were, and who the girls were who had been fraternizing. The Underground went out and picked them up and were walking around, but of course there were Germans all over the place. You didn't know when someone was going to take a shot at you.

But everybody was so happy, they didn't care. This was the 5th of May, their liberation day; the 8th of May was V-E day.

The Underground was well organized. They knew what they wanted to do. There was no shooting, but of course they had their own weapons, hidden all over the countryside. They came out in the open and tried to enforce the ceasefire. The Germans were supposed to be herded into schoolyards and places like that and they cooperated. The Underground cut off the hair of the women fraternizers, put them in cages, and showed them off to the Dutch people. There were probably some trials, but I didn't see any. I'm sure there was some violence at this time, but I didn't see it. There certainly were SS and Gestapo who didn't want to take defeat very well, and it was pretty tough to communicate with troops all over the area.

Pretty soon the 1st Canadian Army came in, but they didn't have much force. They had some weapon carriers just running around the block, to make the Germans think that there were a lot of forces coming in. But there weren't. The Canadians were pretty well spread out too, and they had to come in and take over occupied countries.

I was given my uniform back and put it on. I was a big hero. They carried me around on their shoulders and entertained me. They told everyone that Jan Smit was there. "We've had this pilot here for seven months, and nobody knew it," they said. Well, a few people knew it.

When I was to leave, I got on a motorcycle with a guy, and we rode down to the town of Blaricum. And when I got there, Daan Spoor, one of my benefactors from the area was there. And there I met Gene Maddox, a B-24 pilot, and two other airmen, whose names I can't recall right now. They had been hiding in the same area. We were to leave together.

We didn't know how we were going to leave. We had a little goodbye ceremony and started walking. We hitchhiked. We met some Canadian troops, who took us to a town where we were interrogated. Then we were flown to Paris, where we were interrogated again. It wasn't so important now as it had been while hostilities were still going on. The interrogators had wanted to know who helped you, what the procedure was, how you evaded, was your escape kit right, what do you need, what should we do different? With us, after the cessation of hostilities, it was different, more a matter of identification and of our Helpers, because they wanted to acknowledge them with the Eisenhower Certificate, a recognition for Resistance workers.

After Paris, we were transported to the famous Camp Lucky Strike, at Le Havre. And there, which had been a staging area for a division during the war, about 40,000 POWs and evaders were gathered. The weather was kind of bad. It was muddy. We were all living in tents and eating peanut butter sandwiches. That was when some guys got in touch with their congressmen. So Eisenhower flew over. He stood on the wing of a C-47 and said, "For you, the war is over. The sick and wounded first. Then you guys are going home."

Well, a funny thing happened. Apparently Eighth Air Force headquarters wanted some aerial pictures of Camp Lucky Strike, with all the ex-POWs down there. So my 7th Photo Recon Group over in England was assigned a mission to fly and take photos of the camp. The next day or so, they came over and dropped off the prints. There were four guys there (I didn't know where they were) from our group who had been POWs or evaders, and one guy got a hold of the pilot who brought the prints and said, "For God's sake, get us out of here!"

The next day he came over in a C-47, and somehow all four or five of us got together, from the 7th Photo Recon Group, scratched our names off the roster and flew back to our group. No orders. No nothing. I could be there still, MIA.

I don't know when my group headquarters learned we were alive. When we were interrogated in Paris, that was the first time we could send a telegram to our families. They had only known that we were MIA — no other word.

I went back to my base in England for a week or so. I still knew a few people there, but not very many. I'd only been in my group for two months before I was shot down, and then I'd been gone for about seven months. There were a lot of new faces.

I was without orders, so in order to get into channels again, I had to turn myself in to a general hospital, where they would write me orders, give me a physical, and get me assigned to a deployment group, to go back to the States.

So I went back to the States, and that was it. I was discharged.

In conclusion, I lived under the protection of the Dutch Underground, in hiding from the Nazi occupiers. I lived with them for seven months. They risked their lives to save mine. Without them I would not be here today.

I've seen, in my research with the Air Forces Escape and Evasion Society, a lot of missing air crew reports, by the last person or crew that saw your plane come down. These are on file in Suitland, Maryland, and you can obtain one on any airman who was shot down, if you have the facts. I've got many reports on airmen who were helped by the Partisans and the Chetniks in Yugoslavia. Of course many of these men were liberated while the war was still going on, and there were a lot of problems — the wrong kind of stuff in the escape kit, this compass doesn't work, or that doesn't work, we need a better dinghy or this or that. So Intelligence got a lot of valuable information by interrogating the escapers and evaders. But our interrogations after V-E Day were pretty routine.

BATTLIN' BOBBIE!
THE BILL MILLER STORY

Battlin' Bobbie was the name of the B-17 bomber that William J. Miller (Bill) and the rest of a 10-man crew had manned at Kimbolton Air Base back in 1944 en route to their target, a ball bearing factory in Nantes. It was the *Bobbie's* 23rd mission. Another two missions and the men could relax with no more worries of German flak.

The bomb bay doors swung open over Nantes, the bombardier was right on target. Miller activated the camera that would follow the action from the belly of the ship. The factory below became a mass of smoke and flames. *Battlin' Bobbie's* mission was a success and the ship made a wide turn to head back home. German fighters caught up with her over Redon, France. The plane's wings were ripped open, full of gaping holes. Harry Minor, a fellow crewmen left the plane a couple of minutes before Miller and the two landed 40 minutes apart.

Miller landed in an apple orchard near a ragged Frenchman working there. The young airman quickly hid his parachute and left the orchard. He found a dirt road and had started down it when a guy came up to him and said, "You are an American, aren't you?" When Miller said yes the man told him the Germans were looking for him.

The Frenchman led him to a thick grove of blackberry bushes and told him to stay there, and he would return for him. He told the 25-year-old crewman that he would be whistling the *Marseillaise* so he would be recognized. He came whistling at about seven that evening and brought bread.

Miller had landed on the Brest Peninsula. The Underground took him north up into the Cherbourg Peninsula to St. Malo, a place where a boat could occasionally slip in, load up with downed airmen and sneak back to England. There was no boat, but Miller linked up with a fellow crewman, Harry Minor, at the estate of Madame Pansart.

German troops were thick in the north. Miller and the

other airmen he met managed to dodge them for two weeks while they waited for a boat. No boat came.

The men were told to backtrack. They started south, returned to Ploermel, north of Redon, and linked up with two more men in the French Underground, Georges Joubaud, a baker, and Alex, his brother. Here Miller and the five other airmen boarded a Nazi troop train for Paris.

The Americans each bore phony French names and had fake identity cards describing made-up occupations. Photos were attached to the cards in which each man could be seen wearing the same, wide necktie.

Miller and the other five Americans were instructed to help load produce aboard the Nazi troop train. After setting the boxes down in the dining car, they simply made their way forward, mixing in, unnoticed, with the German troops. They had to travel a nervous 480 miles before swinging down on a platform as the train ground to a halt. Slowly and quietly they walked away from the station and on to a cafe two blocks away.

The men were to meet their contact at the cafe. Miller ordered coffee for them all in his best high school French. Across the room an old man with an odd gray cap, not seeming to pay any particular attention to the group, finished his own coffee and left the cafe. The Americans drank up, paid the tab and followed the old man out. He was the contact and led them to an abandoned house.

Miller's French improved quickly, and he found himself a member of the French Underground. Many lives would be dependent on him. His job was to interrogate the new American airmen being shuffled through the Underground to rendezvous points.

On one occasion two downed American fliers made contact with the Underground in Paris, and Miller talked with them about the United States. He asked one of them where he was shot down. The man answered and then asked him what type of bomber Miller had flown. Miller was getting suspicious and answered, "A P-38." The new American then asked how many men had been in the crew. Miller answered, "Ten."

The P-38 is a one-place fighter. Both "new Americans" were executed. One was hung in the barn, the other was shot.

Another "new American" had infiltrated the Underground and had gone undetected. His English was perfect and he knew a great deal about the U.S. Eighty men, including an Underground leader known as Monsieur Streetcar, were captured and shot in three days early in 1944. Miller and seven others were out of Paris at the time.

While a member of the Underground, Miller met Ernest Bernard in February of 1944. Bernard had been a machinist at the factory where Miller and the *Battlin' Bobbie* had dropped their bombs on Bastille Day, July 14, 1943. Miller had manned the camera capturing the raid in pictures. (He and the rest of the crew viewed the film at Kimbolton). The pictures showed the factory being destroyed and also caught one bomb crazily wavering out of the frame. Bernard retold the story of the factory bombing to his new friend, marveling at how not only the factory was destroyed, but a German training bomber two miles away!

Ernest Bernard hid downed fliers and rabbits in his attic. He had always raised rabbits and with each new litter Germans came for meat. Bernard began taking two or three rabbits from each litter to stash in the attic along with Miller and the other men. Before long the attic was full of rabbits. Bernard was very pleased with himself for putting one over on the Germans.

Miller later stayed in a hotel owned by a Frenchwoman who had lived in Chicago. Her husband had been killed by the Nazis, where German troops were garrisoned. The woman and her housekeeper were the only ones who knew about Miller. The housekeeper knew he liked cigars and often stole them for him from the Germans.

Miller inched toward Spain. Nine months and three days after having been shot down, he hooked up with Lloyd Busboom of Pocatello, Idaho, Ed Neu of Portsmouth, Ohio, and Campbell Brigman of Louisville, Kentucky. They were arrested for entering Spain illegally and immediately jailed. An American official got them released and went with them by train to Gibraltar to hand them to the British. One day later, a day before the invasion of Normandy, Miller and the others were flown back to England.

The source for this story was an interview with William Miller printed in the <u>Rocky</u> <u>Mountain</u> <u>News</u>, June 14, 1969.

FRIENDS IN BELGIUM
By David W. O'Boyle

The Mowers crew was shot down over the little town of Court St. Etienne in central Belgium on Jan. 24, 1944 while aborting a mission into Germany. As navigator of that crew I attempted to tell the crew over the intercom that we were over occupied Belgium before jumping. I landed two miles southeast of Waterloo in that country. The only other chutes I observed on the way down were those of Jerry Dechambre, the bombardier, and Jerry Roderick, co-pilot.

I landed on the top of a partially wooded hill where I was helped by four farm boys to get rid of my parachute and heavy boots. I dashed for a hiding place in the woods and two of these young farm boys followed me and told me they would come back with clothes at nightfall, which they did, and then guided me to a hayloft to spend the night. The next morning at 4:00 a.m. they awoke me, took me into the farm kitchen and gave me ersatz coffee, a handful of black bread and gave me directions south toward France through Charleroi. That day I walked about 30 odd miles to a point south of Charleroi when the skies opened up with a freezing cold rain. I tried to find shelter in a lamb birthing shack, but soon became so cold I gambled on the farmers being friendly and knocked on the door of their cow barn where I could see light around the cracks. They took me in and kept me for about two weeks until they could make contact with the formal Underground.

One night a young woman showed up and said in good English, "You're coming with me," and we walked several miles to her home where I spent one night before being taken to an empty country chalet they owned. After several days there I was taken by streetcar to the home of a gendarme and thence to the home of a baker close to a railroad station. After several days a guide, a young boy, came for me and I was taken on a hair-raising train ride to Brussels. At the time this was very disconcerting since it looked to me like I was backtracking from the direction of France through which I would have to pass to get to Spain.

A French I.D. card prepared for Lt. David O'Boyle for travel through France to escape from occupied Europe in 1944. It was never used because of orders to remain hidden until Allied troops reclaimed the area.

On arrival in Brussels I was taken to an empty apartment furnished with a table and two chairs where I was interrogated by what I now know were members of Comete Line. They decided I was a bona fide American and placed me with one middle-aged and one elderly woman, aunt and niece, in an apartment in Anderlecht at the corner of the Chaussee de Mons and the Avenue Aristede Briande.

During the several months I spent at Avenue Aristede Briande I was introduced to a group of young Belgians known as the Insoumis which means "unsubmitting". Their purpose in life was to sabotage the Germans in every way possible short of doing something serious enough to provoke reprisals. They delighted in having an American officer join them in their forays. In fact I suspected, even then, that we did some things that they would not have done had they not wished to impress me with their bravado. I didn't learn until after the war that the Comete people were outraged at my exposing myself to danger in this manner which annoyed me because I considered it my duty to continue to fight the war rather than hide safely in a closet.

Some of the things we did actually were rather childish, but quite satisfying. We recovered gasoline from B-47 drop tanks found in the countryside after air raids to fill our cigarette lighters and burned newspaper kiosks. We let the air out of the tires of German vehicles, stole bicycles from German couriers and, the most dangerous of all, recorded bomb hits on the local rail yards for transmission back to England. Another favorite ploy was to get out into the countryside and mess up signs on signposts.

It was an interesting place to spend the next four-and-a-half months as the Chaussee de Mons was the direct route from Germany to Paris. While there a German troop convoy stopped on one occasion and I looked out the south window of the apartment and directly below me was General Rommel in his staff car. At the time I thought, "one grenade and that would be the end of him", and, of course, me.

When things got hot at that address, or at least someone thought it was getting dangerous, I was moved to 93 Avenue de l'Opale. This house was also in an interesting location since it was midway between a school used as German barracks and the Belgian National Armory called the Tire Nationale where Edith Cavell of World War I fame was executed by a firing squad. During the war it was a German army headquarters. Every morning and every evening several companies of German soldiers marched by singing their marching dirges as we watched out our front window. In this house was not only another American navigator, Roger Blake of the 96th Bomb Group, but four Jews, and an extended family of an elderly couple, their niece and her two children, nine and 11 years old. Had the house been denounced there would have been a blood bath. Blake and I were told that the American authorities had ordered us to make no further attempts at walking out, to remain where we were and lay as low as possible until liberated. Reluctantly we did so until we were liberated in September by the Irish Guards of the British Tank Corps.

THE SHELBURNE NETWORK
By Ralph Patton, 94BG

"When do you wear epaulets?" barked the interrogator. "Do you wear anklets? What was your last stopping point when you left the USA? Where were you stationed in England?"

"Wait a minute!" shouted a voice from the rear, "You don't have to answer those questions - you're an officer in the U.S. Air Force - give only your name, rank and serial number."

"Shut up," shot back the interrogator. "I'm Captain Harrison of British Military Intelligence. It's my job to get you back to England. Some of you may have a hole in your belly, but you'll get back."

This was serious business and Captain Harrison (alias for Sgt. Major Lucien Dumais of the Canadian Fuseliers Mont Royal) wasn't about to stand on protocol. He had expected 22 men to arrive at the rendezvous point and we were 24. Who were the two who had shown up at this secret rendezvous two kilometers from the French coast on the English Channel? Lt.'s Jack McGough and Ralph Patton, both from the 94th BG. We were the uninvited guests.

We had been hiding in western France since 4 January 1944, when our B-17 had been shot down over Brittany while returning from bombing Bordeaux. After two and a half months, our travels had brought us to this small farmhouse near the village of Plouha. Here we were given a bowl of hot bread and cabbage soup. It wasn't exactly gourmet fare, but under the circumstances, it did hit the spot.

The 24 men who gathered at "La Maison d'Alphonse" that night, 18 March 1944, were a motley-looking group. They were French, English and Canadian, but mostly American. They were dressed in a wide array of civilian clothes and various items of military dress. There were a fortunate few with G.I. shoes, but most wore ill-fitting civilian shoes of every description. They had arrived at this particular farm in western France at this precise hour by virtue of one of the best organized and executed escape operations of World War II. Not one of them had a clue as to who the interrogators were or what made them tick. This was especially true of myself and McGough. We were not sure if we were going back to England, going back to our previous hiding place, or if we were going to Heaven or Hell at the hands of Captain Harrison and the GI issue .45 that looked more like the famous French 75 as it pointed at our nervous bellies.

OPERATION BONAPARTE was the code name given to this "Escape by the Sea" mission of the Resistance network named Shelburne. Two French Canadians from Ottawa and Montreal were parachuted into France by British Military Intelligence to organize and operate an escape network to try to help the hundreds of Allied airmen who had been, and were continuing to be, shot down during the massive Allied air raids on Germany and the occupied countries.

Great numbers of airmen were holed up in Paris and Brittany, thus endangering the lives of hundreds of patriotic Frenchmen who were hiding them. Something had to be done to relieve this pressure.

With Sgt. Major Lucien Dumais in command and Sgt. Ray LaBrosse as radio operator and second in command, the organization of Reseau Shelburne began to take form. Both Dumais and LaBrosse had escaped from France earlier and had volunteered to go back to organize SHELBURNE. Dumais had been captured at the ill-fated Canadian raid on Dieppe in August 1942. He escaped from a German P.O.W. train and made his way to Marseille from where he escaped by way of the famous "Pat O'Leary" escape line. LaBrosse had parachuted into France with Val Williams in February 1943 to organize a sea escape route. Their group was forced to escape to Spain when the leader, Val Williams, was arrested.

Taking advantage of the contacts that LaBrosse (code name "Claude") and Val Williams had made in Brittany in early 1943, Dumais and LaBrosse went to work to build the most successful escape network of World War II. Not one airman was ever lost once he was in the hands of SHELBURNE, nor was an agent or helper of this network ever captured by the Gestapo.

In Paris an organization was set up to interrogate, make false papers, shelter and to pass airmen on to Brittany. This was under the direction of Paul Francois Campinchi, a French lawyer who had worked with LaBrosse and Val Williams on the ill-fated mission earlier in 1943. Marcel Cola, a Ford Motor Company executive in Paris, recruited a nucleus of English-speaking agents to work with him in finding housing in and around Paris and to do preliminary interrogating. One of these agents was Anita Lemonnier, now Mrs. P.K. Hartman, living in New York City.

The transfer of airmen from Paris to Brittany was dangerous work, work that took courage, patience, and great acting ability. One of the greatest of these was Rene LeOiseau, who on numerous occasions, guided a total of 35 airmen from Paris to St. Brieuc and Gunigamp. During one of these transfers, he was petrified to see an American airmen offer a light to a German officer with a Zippo lighter. Fortunately, the officer wasn't sharp enough to realize what was going on.

503d boat, 15th Motor Gun Boat Flotilla, British Royal Navy. Used during Shelburne Operations to bring 94 American Airmen to Dartmouth, England from the northern coast of Western France in early 1944.

Leaders of Reseau Shelburne's Operation Bonaparte meet in Buffalo, NY 1946. (First meeting of AFEES.) (L to R): Col. Raymond Labrosse, radio op. and 2d in command; Anita Lemonnier Hartman, Paris interrogator for Shelburne and Burgundy; Lucien Dumais, officer in charge of Shelburne; Mathurin Branchoux, French Underground Leader in Guingamp.

On arrival at St. Brieuc or Guingamp, the airmen were taken under the wing of the Brittany organization under the direction of Francois Lecornac. Guides like Andre Chareton and Fernand Trocel met the trains and escorted airmen to homes in the area, including their own. Airmen were usually kept in the area of Plouha for three days...timing was important.

Moving them out was part of Francois Kerambrun's responsibility. Owner of a garage in the town of Guingamp, Francois carried supplies for the Germans by day and carried airmen by night. His truck was the main mode of transportation to the last rendezvous, the House of Alphonse.

La Maison d'Alphonse was a primitive Breton dwelling belonging to a sailor named Jean Giguel who lived there with his wife and newborn baby. This tiny stone place was about 3/4 of a mile from the cliff and the beach where the airmen would meet the small boats from the British Corvette 503.

Unknown to the 24 airmen in the Maison d'Alphonse, that moonless night of 18 March 1944, the BBC had broadcast a code message at 7:30 and 9:30 that evening. "Bonjour tout le monde a la maison d'Alphonse". It meant that the high-speed diesel gunboat of the Royal Navy was ready to leave Dartmouth and all was set. Corvette 503 worked her way between German patrol boats and anchored two miles off Bonaparte Beach prepared to pick up her cargo of grounded airmen on signal.

The two uninvited guests to the escape party, McGough and myself, had managed to satisfy Capt. Harrison that they were not spies by stumbling and fumbling through a series of questions that a true spy would have answered promptly and intelligently - and probably would have been shot for it. We were assured that we were on our way back to England. This came about when it was learned that we had been scheduled to depart on the mission set up for two nights later. Some eager beaver decided to move us

out of hiding in Guingamp for this earlier mission.

In the short space of three hours, 24 subdued airmen had been brought from a radius of 50 kilometers to this small farmhouse less than two kilometers from the coast. As it approached midnight a curt, business-like Capt. Harrison issued his last instruction. "This is the most dangerous part of your escape, do exactly as you are told. When you leave here, follow the man in front of you very closely, don't deviate one step left or right. When you get to the cliff, sit down and dig your heels and hands in tightly. Don't slip or you might take the whole line down with you. Above all, keep your damned mouth shut."

We apprehensive fugitives headed out into the dark unknown. Patrols, mines, coastal defenses and weak hearts were a few of the hazards between La Maison d'Alphonse and Bonaparte Beach. Pierre had the mines located. LeCornec and his men had the patrols spotted and timed. Job Mainguy, a former sea captain, had the German coastal defenses well located. Since we airmen were the "cream of the crop", all hearts were strong enough to take the strain.

Numbering 35 now, the escape party reached the beach without incident. Capt. Harrison, from a spot halfway up the cliff, sent his morse code letter "B" to the corvette anchored offshore. The signal was flashed every two minutes with a masked flashlight. Below the signaler was a blue light, hidden in a cove off of the beach, to direct the small boats to the exact spot on the shore.

The minutes seemed like hours as the party on shore waited for the boats. Impatience stimulated low-throated conversation. "Where the Hell are they? Can they find this slight indentation in the coast?" The talk came to an abrupt halt when the sky lit up as in daylight. This was followed instantly by the loud roar of a giant coastal defense cannon. The surprising salvo was followed by a second and a third, then silence again. Thoughts raced, "Have the Krauts sunk the boat? How will we ever get back up the cliff? What do we do now?" More signals to sea, more impatience, more nervous conversation, more waiting. Finally, at 3:00 a.m., five plywood skiffs rowed in on the gentle swell. In five minutes all of the airmen were aboard and headed out to meet the corvette anchored off shore, out of reach of German searchlights.

Capt. Harrison and his courageous band of French patriots waved adieu to the men that they risked their lives to help. Then they turned to climb back up the cliff to begin planning for the next mission, two days later.

The men and women of OPERATION BONAPARTE made eight trips to the beach to deliver 128 airmen and seven agents to British gunboats for passage to England.

In addition, the SHELBURNE network, under the Canadians, Dumais and LaBrosse, sent 98 men to Spain and arranged for the safety of the 74 in the group that was rescued from the Forest of Freteval in August 1944. Three hundred and sixty-five airmen owe their early freedom to SHELBURNE.

RETURN TO ITALY
THE BILL PETTY STORY

William (Bill) Petty was a nose gunner and assistant engineer on a B-24 bomber stationed at 15th Air Force Field near Bari, Italy. On the afternoon of January 20, 1945 his plane was returning from a bombing mission over Lienz, Austria, when it was hit by enemy flak and downed near Caporetto, Italy.

All ten crew members bailed out. Four were captured by the Germans at Caporetto. The remaining six were able to evade capture.

Three men, including Petty, who was a technical sergeant, the plane's waist gunner and its radio operator escaped detection and began walking in waist-deep snow for two days, trying to get to the top of the mountain above Caporetto.

They were 300 miles behind enemy lines. It was cold and they were hungry.

The second day of the ordeal, a Sunday, Petty heard church bells ringing in Caporetto. The sound made the young airman realize just how lonesome he was feeling. "I prayed to the Lord then and there to help us get back home," Petty explained.

The three men saw a concrete house as they neared the top of the mountain and were discovered by two Yugoslav spies watching the railroad and highway movements of German troops. The spies aimed their automatic rifles at Petty and the other two men and the three quickly raised their hands and shouted, "Americanos, Americanos." The Yugoslavs then welcomed them and fed them cooked potatoes, the only food they had.

Secret agents took the airmen to a small village. The villagers were very curious about them as they had been told by the Russians that all Americans were monsters. Here they were fed and cared for and allowed to sleep with the cows.

The next day, further into the mountain, they came to the home of Mrs. Faletic Giovannia, an elderly lady who had a married daughter and three children living with her. Here they spent five days. They slept in the barn and all got body lice. The three were rescued later by the British and American underground. After three weeks in hiding, they walked to Zagreb. They were flown out of Zagreb to their base in Bari, 72 days after having being shot down.

Petty and his wife, Geraldine toured Europe in 1969. He was determined to return to the place where he had found help and to find Mrs. Giovannia. It was not an easy trip. To get to the Giovannia farm, the couple had to cross the Yugoslav border and travel over a narrow, perilous road.

The place looked much the same. Someone brought Mrs. Giovannia to the front yard and after a bit she came to understand just who the people in her yard were. She embraced Petty and they had an emotionally charged reunion. The language barrier did not hinder the most important aspects of the reunion, love and compassion between human beings.

*The source for this story submitted by William Petty is the *Carthage Courier*, 1969.

This photo was taken by a military photographer on Sept. 17, 1944 near Kotselyevo, Yugoslavia, just north of Valyevo. The pilot landed on a short clearing with a considerable downward slope. He had to "ground-loop" his ship in order to avoid disaster in the trees ahead. Thus, his right wing is buried in the trees. On this "flight to freedom," with the chatter of machine guns in the background, 21 American airmen evaded Nazi concentration camps. The Radio-Op was not so fortunate. His parachute landed on a highway and he was quickly captured by German soldiers. He became a POW for the duration and barely survived. Other members of the crew evacuated on this flight were: Co-Pilot, Wm. B. Crawford; Bombardier, Waldo (Mike) Koo; Engineer, Rudolph C. Schmidt; Asst. Radio Operator, Gerald E. Wagner; Tail Gunner, Leland Porter; Ball Gunner, Howard A. Ford and Nose Gunner, Curtis Diles. Pilot, Wm. L. Rogers, was too badly injured to make the flight. He survived and was evacuated on a flight some weeks later. The C-47 pictured was part of an Air Rescue Unit flying out of Italy. (Courtesy of Curtis Diles)

Identification Papers

Downed American airmen could not have successfully avoided capture without false identifcation papers provided to them by members of the Underground. For obvious reasons, many of the evadees posed as deaf/mute salesmen; this occupation allowed them the freedom of movement necessary to get back to Allied lines and avoid capture by the Germans. Because they were mute, this plan also offered some protection against their incriminating native tongue. Pictured here are examples of those papers carried by the evadees.

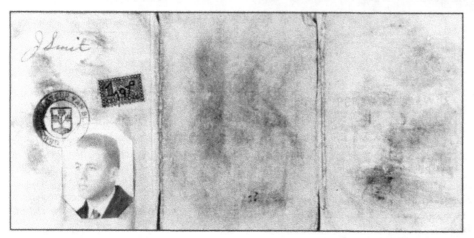

Above left, A French identification card issued to Gus Bubenzer during his evasion. Above right, Front side of a Czechoslovakian passport used by Col. Silas Crase, who posed as a deaf-mute. Above, Passive resistance as practiced by the French Underground during the German occupation. Note lower left hand corner. Left, Front side of a "Persoonsbewijs" (Dutch Identity Card) issued to Lt. Murray that changed his name to "Jan Smit," a deaf/dumb salesman. He carried this card for seven months, while evading the Germans in Holland. He is still known as "Jan" by his many Dutch friends.

The Men Who Flew

"Hubba Hubba" in Spspka Crnja, Yugoslavia. Second from the left is Ziva Popov. The man in the center with the fur cap is Djuro Knezevic. At the extreme right is Doid K. Raab. (Courtesy of Doid K. Raab)

2nd Lt. Asley Ivey, March 1945. He is wearing the uniform of the First Canadian Army. He was the navigator on B-17G "Straighten Up and Fly Right."

Flight crew with their B-17G "The Fox". Standing (L to R): Pilot, Lt. John R. Martin (The Fox); Co-pilot, Lt. Charles Halfen; Navigator, Lt. Carl Carden; Bombardier, Lt. Dean W. Tate; T/Sgt. Bishop. Kneeling (L to R): S/Sgt. Kelly, S/Sgt. Slick, S/Sgt. Taylor, T/Sgt. McCaffrey, S/Sgt. Johnson. Picture taken at Kimbolten, October 1943. (Courtesy of Dean Tate)

History of AFEES

The nucleus for AFEES was formed in Buffalo, New York when 35 American airmen who had been spirited out of France by a Resistance group know as Reseau Shelburne met with the Canadian leaders of this operation in 1964.

Lucien Dumais and Raymond LaBrosse were sent into France in late 1943 by British Military Intelligence to organize an escape line for Allied airmen who were in hiding throughout Western Europe after having been shot down. Operation Bonaparte of Reseau Shelburne turned out to be the most successful escape operation of World War II. Not one agent was lost and 135 Allied Flyers and agents were successfully evacuated by sea to England. Ninety-four of those evacuated were American airmen.

Thirty-five of these former American airmen met in Buffalo, N.Y. in June 1964 to personally thank Dumais and LaBrosse and two former members of the French part of the network, Anita Hartman, interrogator from Paris, and Mathurin Branchoux, district leader of the Underground in Guingamp, western France. This first meeting was truly an outstanding success, and those present unanimously voted to form a society of evaders and to continue periodic meetings. Ralph Patton was elected President and William H. Spinning was elected Vice President.

In September of 1967 14 Helpers from Western Europe were entertained for a day in Niagara Falls, New York, topped off by a memorable banquet at the Niagara Falls Air Force Base. This group was brought to Canada by the Royal Air Forces Escaping Society (Canadian Branch) who graciously agreed to bring them to the USA so that AFEES could honor them.

In 1969 more than 100 Canadians and Americans visited Holland, Belgium, France and England, where the group was royally received by Helpers, the Crown Prince of Holland, the King and Queen of Belgium, the French Foreign Minister, the Mayor of Paris, and the Queen of England.

In 1974 AFEES hosted 71 members of the Belgium Comete Line for ten days in Detroit, Washington, D.C. and New York City.

In 1975 a delegation of AFEES members dedicated a bronze plaque to the members of Reseau Shelburne in Plouha, western France.

In 1976 AFEES hosted 50 members of the French Reseau Shelburne in Detroit, Pittsburgh, Washington, D.C. and New York.

In 1978 AFEES hosted 35 members of the Dutch Resistance in Pittsburgh, Washington, D.C. and New York.

Visits to Western Europe were organized in 1981, 1985, and 1990.

During the 1985 visit, a total of approximately 400 helpers were hosted by AFEES and given certificates and pins. They gathered in seven different cities in Holland, Belgium, and France. Recognition was not a one way affair, the group of 55 Evaders and wives was warmly received and toasted by groups of helpers at every stop. Doors were opened to sights the regular visitor never sees.

Between 10 and 50 Helpers have been the guests of AFEES at each of our annual meetings from 1981 to 1992.

The slogan of AFEES is "We will never forget". Since its founding in 1964 AFEES members have proven this slogan on numerous occasions by the presentation of citations and Helper pins to several hundred Helpers.

AFEES Officers and Directors

Ralph K. Patton Chairman of the Board	Paul E. Kenney Treasurer	Clyde J. Martin Director	Richard M. Smith Director	R.E.T. Smith, ESQ. Legal Counsel
Clayton C. David President	Harry A. Dolph Communications Editor	Gilbert Millar Director	Edward J. Spevak Director	
Gerald R. Dechambre Vice President	James J. Goebel, Jr. Director	David Shoss Director	Leslie A. G. Atkinson Representative in France	

Reunions

"We meet again" at the Canadian Embassy in Rotterdam, 1969. Claude Murray, former P-38 pilot and evader, is reunited with his benefactor, Joh. Rozendaal, leader of the resistance group in Muiden, the Netherlands. Rozendaal and his wife are known to Murray as Father and Mother Rozendaal. They likewise consider him a son and member of their family.

Lt. Murray (third from left) returns to Holland in 1969 to find and visit some of his Dutch rescuers. Shown here are Jan Dobber (center), who as a 14 year-old fisherman picked Murray out of the Zuider Zee and brought him to the Dutch Underground. Reitje, Dobber's daughter, is on the left.

1st Lt. Ike K. Killingsworth (Col., USAF, Ret.) soon after descent on Aug. 27, 1944 with Mayor Pierre LeBrun and Mme. Bellhouse, (in between with hat) an English jockey living in Alligny-Cosne. Dr. Laval is behind the man with the gun.

Clayton David with helpers George Guillon, Jean and "Claire" Arhex and wife Scotty David at a reunion in Paris in October of 1990. George and his parents housed Clayton and Ken for one night in their home south of Paris and got them back on a train. They were the only Evaders to stay there. Jean and "Claire" had other responsibilities with the Maquis in Southern France, but when Clayton and Ken came along, they took on an additional task. They delivered Clayton and Ken to a mountain guide who took them to the top of the Pyrenees and pointed the way down into Spain.

Air Forces
Escape and Evasion Veterans

With the Maquis in France. Top, (L to R): Herman Seidel, Travis Ross, Carl T. Nall, Wm. Gaboireu. Bottom (L to R): Richard Weiss, Michael Negro, Wm. Masasko, Kenneth Walley.

All Biographies were typeset as submitted. The Publisher is not responsible for errors or omissions.

LOUIS H. ABBOTT, Capt. U.S.A.F. (ret.), was born Dec. 14, 1920, in Asbury Park, NJ. He joined the U.S. Army Air Corps on June 17, 1942.

Abbott took navigation training at Selman Field, LA and was commissioned Oct. 16, 1943. He had combat training at Pyote, TX and Dyersburg, TN.

He flew with 418th Sqdn., 100th BG, 8th A.F., Thorpe Abbotts, England. He led wing formation on shuttle mission to Russia and Italy from June 21-July 5, 1944. He also flew with 413th Sqdn., 96th BG and 335th Sqdn., 95th BG.

Completed 31 missions, and hit over Leipzig, Germany July 20, 1944. Crash landed in Holland. Evaded with Underground in Brussels, Belgium until Sept. 9, 1944. Returned to U.S. Sept. 14, 1944. Served as budget and fiscal officer until released from active duty Oct. 13, 1945.

Civilian employment: public accountant, accounting manager (Xerox Corp.), El Segundo, CA. Retired May 1, 1984.

Married Bette Brown, Aug. 8, 1945. Children: Robert and Jeffrey. Grandchildren: John and Mariel. Currently resides in Burbank, CA.

DAVID GASTON ALFORD, Col. U.S.A.F. (ret.), was born May 29, 1917 in Rising Star, TX. Attended Rising Star High School, 1934; earned a B.S. degree from Daniel Baker College, 1939 and his M.B.A. from East Texas State College in 1959.

Enlisted in the Army Air Corps in December of 1939 and attended flying school at Randolph and Kelly Fields, San Antonio, TX. Commissioned 1940. Pilot flying B-17s with 92nd and 91st BG in England. Shot down Feb. 4, 1944 on 20th mission to Frankfort, Germany. Crash landed in Holland and evaded with help of Underground and finally was liberated by 1st Army in Belgium in September of 1944.

Flew B-29s in Korea; 35 missions. Served in different assignments in U.S. and overseas. Retired in December of 1965.

Employed by City of Wichita Falls, TX as safety director immediately upon retirement from Air Force. Later served as criminal justice coordinator for Nortex Planning Commission, Wichita Falls, TX until April of 1981.

Married to Dorothy Burkett Alford and have two children: Michael Alford of Framingham, MA (served as Army helicopter pilot in Vietnam) and Patricia Lanier of Shawnee, OK. Have a stepdaughter, Dee Phillips, of Jupiter, FL. Grandchildren: Chad Lanier, age 17; Lea Alford, age eight; and Lori Lanier, age six. Reside in San Antonio, TX.

LESTER E. ANDERSEN, was born March 27, 1922 in Wadena County, MN. Joined the service in April of 1943 and had basic training in Fresno, CA, engineering for B-24 Bombers in Biloxi, MS. Gunnery school at Brownsville, TX. Crew training and assembly were at Westover Field, MA. Flew to Africa then Italy in August of 1944 with the 461st BG, 765th Sqdn. as top turret gunner and flight engineer.

On his 11th mission was shot down over Munich, Germany Oct. 4, 1944 and escaped through Austria to Yugoslavia. Built dirt runway in Semic, Yugoslavia, radioed Bari, Italy and was picked up by DC3.

After a short stay at Bari Hospital, returned to fly; plane was badly damaged after his 15th mission. Crash landed in Yugoslavia and after a short stay in the hospital returned to flying. On his 25th mission his badly damaged plane crashed at home base. After another short stay at the hospital, returned to complete 50 missions.

Returned to the U.S. in June 1945. Discharged and married Margaret Scolari in August of 1945. Became the parents of a girl and two boys. Presently have four grandchildren. Moved to Springfield, MA in 1950 and opened a construction company. Retired in 1985. His two sons presently manage the company.

FRANCIS E. ANDERSON, was born March 20, 1924 in New Smyrna Beach, FL. Graduated from New Smyrna High School in 1941. Enlisted in U.S. Army Air Corps in October of 1942.

Took basic training at St. Petersburg, FL, then A.C. mechanics school at Gulfport, MS November 1942-March 1943. Aerial gunnery school at Harlingen, TX March-June 1943. Salt Lake City to Ephrata, WA. Assigned to 401st BG as flight engineer B-17s. O.T.U. at Cut Bank, MT. Group

departed in October 1943 via Scott Field, Syracuse, Bangor, Grander to Prestwick, Scotland. Crew transferred to 351st BG, 8th Air Force in November of 1943.

Shot down Dec. 31, 1943 over Cognac, France. Evaded to Spain and returned to U.S. in March of 1944.

Discharged in November of 1945 and retired from A.F. Reserve as master sergeant in 1970.

Employed as locomotive engineer for Florida East Coast Railway for 40 years. Retired in November of 1987. Resides in Edgewater, FL.

ROBERT O. ANDERSON, 1st Lt. U.S.A.F. (ret.), was born March 29, 1920 in Round Lake, NY. Joined A.A.C. April 16, 1942. Flew as B-17 navigator with 410th Sqdn., 94th BG, 8th A.F., WWII.

Shot down near Bordeaux, France Jan. 5, 1944. Walked alone over substantial portion of distance to Pyrenees before locating French Underground and escaping to Spain. Returned to England April 27, 1944.

Completed active military service Oct. 22, 1945 after Intelligence assignments instructing air crews in evasion/escape techniques, followed by teaching aerial navigation.

Returned to France with wife in 1965 and 1971 on successful personal missions to retrace escape route, find and thank persons who had helped him, locate crash site and visit village cemetery where eight crew members had been buried. Was Exxon Corp. executive until Jan. 1, 1980 retirement.

Married Nov. 4, 1944. Children: Kevin and Kirstie. Grandchildren: Jamie and Brett. Resides with wife, Marjorie, in Mendham, NJ.

JAMES A. ANGELUCCI, a graduate of Vineland High School in New Jersey, class of 1940, entered the Air Force on Jan. 28, 1942. He and Robert Brown bailed out at 4 a.m., on Mission 159, Nov. 25, 1944 on the fifth mission of the "Nic" (Nichols, 736) crew returning from a night raid on a Munich, Germany Marshalling Yard. He attributes not being captured initially because at 4 a.m. it was still dark.

"Brownie" and Angelucci, a tail-gunner on a liberator bomber, were M.I.A. from Nov. 22, 1944 to Feb. 13, 1945. They bailed out over northern Italy near the Austrian border and had to stay and walk in the crest of the deep snow-covered Alps as roads were heavily patrolled by enemy troops. Angelucci said he "begged, borrowed and at times had to steal" in order to survive and evaded capture many times. They walked for 81 days through the Carnic Alps and into Yugoslavia where they had to cross the Yugoslavian battle line to the coast where they were picked up by a British destroyer escort.

When the destroyer put out to sea, they became entrapped in an enemy mine field, but finally backed out safely and made it across the Adriatic to Bari, Italy.

Angelucci now resides in Jensen Beach, FL. A brother, First Lt. Augustus J. Angelucci served in Germany.

EDWARD W. APPEL, was born April 14, 1917 in Onamia, MN and was raised on a farm in Redfield, SD. Joined Army Air Corps July 29, 1940 as a private. Was promoted through the ranks to staff sergeant, then entered Aviation Cadets Aug. 4, 1942 and graduated May 20, 1943 as second lieutenant, class of 43E West Coast Training Center, Stockton Field, CA, where had previously been crew chief and flight chief as enlisted man.

Trained as a pilot in B-25s, B-17s and B-24s. Flew B-24 Bomber to 8th A.F. via South America, Africa and on up to England. Flew combat against Germany in B-24s from February 1944 to Sept. 5, 1944 when shot down on 30th and last mission while bombing railroad yards at Karlsruhe. After about three months of evasion behind the lines, finally escaped first part of December of 1944.

Went back to England to 8th and volunteered for P-47 fighters with the 56th Fighter Group. Flew fighters escorting bombers, dive bombing and strafing until again being shot down strafing Muldorf Airfield, east of Munich on April 16, 1945. Again escaped after nearly being caught by German soldiers several times and made it back through to our lines. Got back to Paris and the war was over.

Returned to the U.S. aboard an L.S.T. composed entirely of ex-POWs and evaders in May of 1945. Left the service in December of 1946, but stayed in the Reserves. Retired as a lieutenant colonel.

Received two Distinguished Flying Crosses, five Air Medals, four European Campaign Stars, the Purple Heart and several other ribbons.

Married April 10, 1950 to home-town girl, Crystal Crook, and had five children (all grown now) and 10 grandchildren. In civilian life was in fuel, oil and gas business and retired from that in April of 1984.

Still flying a rag wing Oironca which he restored in 1983.

JAMES E. ARMSTRONG, Lt. Col. U.S.A.F. (ret.), was born Aug. 3, 1922 in Bradenton, FL. Joined Army Air Corps, MacDill Field Jan. 21, 1942.

Took pilot training in southeast, Class 42K. Received wings and commission at Columbus, MS. Trained in B-17, Henricks Field, FL; crew training in northwest. Flew B-17 to England, May 1943. Assigned to 546th Sqdn., 384th BG, Grafton-Underwood.

Flew missions Heroya, Norway; Paris; in Germany: Hamburg, Gelsenkirchen, Frankfort, Scheinfurt, and Stuttgart. On latter mission, Sept. 6, 1943, shot down in Normandy. Walked almost to Paris and there was aided by French Resistance. After aborted escape attempts from Quimper in Brittainy and the Pyrenees, evasion came Jan. 21, 1944 from Douarnenez, Brittainy to Falmouth, England by a fishing boat.

Returned to U.S. Assigned to gunnery school in Fort Myers, FL for duration.

Now retired pastor. Married Juanita DesChamps, Aug. 15, 1948. Children: Alice, James, Jean. Five grandchildren. Currently resides in Thomasville, GA.

ROBERT (BOB) AUGUSTUS, of Cape Coral, FL, was born March 17, 1923 in Cleveland, OH. He joined the Army Air Corps in February of 1942 and was stationed at Maxwell Field, Kelly, Buckingham, Arcadia, Scotts Bluff, Casper, Boise, England. He was a B-24 pilot and flew six-and-a-half missions before he was shot down on April 12, 1944 on the way to bomb a fighter field at Zwickau, Germany.

Augustus was discharged in October of 1945. He married in 1944, divorced and remarried in 1959. He has two daughters, six grandchildren and two great-grandchildren. He retired in August of 1978 as marketing manager of Ohio Bell.

ROYCE F. AUSTIN, went into the Army with the 75th Div. (as a medical aidman) to Ft. Leonard Wood, MO. Stayed with them until May 1943 then transferred to pilots training to Amarillo A.F. Base, TX. His whole barracks was transferred to Laredo, TX for gunnery training then on to phase training in Peterson Field, CO on to Omaha, NE to pick up their own B-24 to fly on to North Africa (Marakesh) then on to Spinazzola, Italy, where he started flying training missions.

On July 8, 1944, on their first mission (kept asking what this flak looked like) this veteran crew with 42 missions already under their belts said you'll see soon and they did. All hell broke loose. Austin counted about 10 B-24s going down and approximately 60 chutes going down. They got hit over target (Vienna, Austria), at 18,000 ft. around noon on July 8, 1944. Tito's Partisans helped them evade and make contact to be picked up. After about three weeks they were picked up and sent to Bari, Italy.

Austin spent nearly a month in the hospital with a fractured leg. His original crew found out they were in the hospital and came to see them on their down days.

He asked to be sent back to his squadron. He told them he would stow away on a plane if they didn't put him back on crew. He had to go see Col. Babb and he said that he wasn't caught and they didn't know that he was over there being as he had escaped. Col. Babb finally let him go back to a crew upon his discharge from the hospital. He was placed on a crew who had lost their nose gunner on a mission. He flew 31 more missions with his new crew, until their misfortune on a direct hit over Blechammer, Germany on Dec. 2, 1944 (oil refineries and marshalling yards).

After evading for several days he was taken prisoner and put in a stockade in Premiscel, Poland. He was questioned for six days as they did not believe he was "Americanski". They moved him to L'Wow, Poland and then to Poltava Russia.

They traveled to Siberia, Tehran, Iran, Tunis and back to Italy. He was back in his base on Christmas Day and was first in line and guest with Col. Price that day for Christmas dinner. He was grounded and shipped back to the States in February 1945. He went to Miami, FL and was sent to Washington, D.C. for interogation for six days. Part of the parachute that he saved was turned into a wedding dress by his wife in March 18, 1945. Married to Imogene "Thomas" Austin for 46 years. Son: Dale A. Austin; daughters Dianne L. Shattuck and Janet L. Duhaime; six grandchildren, two girls and four boys and one great-grandson.

He stayed in the Air Force until Nov. 30, 1964 (22 years). He was selected as "U.S.A.F. Outstanding Airman" 1957.

From 1945-46 was recruiting officer in home town of Burlington, VT, transferred to Ft. Slocum, NY into the M.P.s Security and was teaching in the OSI Training School as small arms instructor. In 1949, he was transferred to the Armed Services Police Dept. Washington, D.C. to form a cadre of all services. Retired Nov. 30, 1964 Larson A.F.B., Moses Lake, WA. When he got out of the service he was studying to become an undertaker but the man sold his business. He then applied for a job as chief of police in Maine and got it. Resigned to run for county sheriff but didn't make it (incumbent too strong).

He then went into business for himself as a general contractor, had trouble collecting checks so he quit. Then he went into the business of sand blasting and a bicycle shop and started selling monuments and engraving in cemeteries (it was said that this was a dying business).

Retired now and enjoys a leisure life of camping with a 40 ft. Holiday Rambler 7th Wheel and Ford crew cab.

F.M. BAILEY, Capt. (ret.), was born Dec. 11, 1921 (Milton Farrell Bailey) in Safford, AZ.

Had civilian flight training in Mines Field, CA in 1938. Enlisted military pilot 1939 to 1941. Assigned Half-Mast Field, Las Vegas, NV flying A-T6s to train gunners in Army Air Corps. Changed to Army Air Force in the winter of 1941 and rating was changed to ROMG and was assigned to multi-engine B-24 in 1942.

Served in Halverson Provisional Group (HALPRO) British Command, Middle East forces. In September of 1942 was with the American 9th Air Force Command in the Middle East Forces organized. Assigned 98th Group B-24 MEF February 1943. Assigned to 376th Group B-24 MEF. Total missions to this date were 60.

Returned to Z of I in September 1943. Picked up crew and B-17. Returned to England joining the 398th BG. Total missions out of England 8th Air Force were 27.

Shot down four times: once in 1942; twice in 1943 and once in 1944. In enemy territory in 1942 and 1944 and in the water off of Malta in 1943.

Combat credits: Distinguished Service Cross, Silver Star, Distinguished Flying Cross with Oak Leaf Cluster, Purple Heart with Oak Leaf Cluster, Air Medals with 16 Oak Leaf Clusters. Eight enemy air craft shot down. Seven major battles including Ploesti raider.

Retired Reserve Officer, Provost Dept. 1985.

JAMES L. BAKER, Ph.D., was born May 2, 1927 in New York, NY. Joined the military March 22, 1945. Served in the U.S. Navy Reserve, with active duty in WWII (1945-46), and in the Korean War (1950-52), aerial gunner (ABM), NORVA; USS Charger (CVE-30); USS Lake Champlain (CV-39).

Also served in the U.S. Army Reserve (1958-

80), retired captain, U.S. Army Special Forces (Airborne), Military Intelligence and Unconventional Warfare officer. U.S. security clearances: (Top Secret) Central Intelligence Agency; U.S. Department of Justice; U.S. Information Agency; and U.S. Army Military Intelligence.

Served in North Africa, England and Italy. WWII: Slc (CAC); Korean War: flight engineer 1st class; captain U.S. Army S.F. (ABN). Also served in Southeast Asia/Far East for about 13 years; six in Vietnam (Jan. 1966-July 1971) until medically evacuated July 28, 1971.

During that time, one of their missions was to rescue allied POWs. One of their very successful rescues was a Viet Cong POW camp located in a mangrove swamp in Vinh Binh Province (the Delta-IV Corps). The raid was a complete surprise to the enemy, and they freed all POWs (allied officers), with no losses or wounds. He commanded the operation, and his Seal advisor led the PRU company in the surprise raid behind the lines. He got the Silver Star for him on that.

Most memorable experience: secret mission behind Yugo "divided forces (Communist)" as crew member for rescue of two escapees (scientists) from U.S.S.R. and Yugo Communist Forces in the fall of 1945 as TDY crew to Special OPs Squadron.

Awarded Joint Service Commendation Medal with V Device; U.S.C.G Commendation and Special OPs; awards/medals from U.S.A., Poland, Vietnam, France, etc. Also received Orders of Chivalry, i.e., Order of Polonica Restituta; Kt. T.; OSJ; Knights of the Holy Sepulchre of Jerusalem, etc.

Education: Ph.D. (1980) International Political Science; B.S. (1957), Business Administration/Economics; Special Agent Basic Training, U.S. Dept. of Justice, BNDD; Officers Advance Course, U.S. Army Intelligence Center and School; Field Case Officer, Covert Intelligence, C.I.A.; Southeast Asia Studies, U.S. Foreign Service Inst., Dept. of State and Command and Staff, CAP National Staff College, Air University.

Married to June Marguerite, nee Goldsworthy, of Essex, England Retired captain, U.S.A. Special Forces (Airborne); Commissioner, International Friendship Commissioner, city of Chula Vista, CA. Retired U.S.A.F./Aux. Senior Pilot (Lt. Col.), 1985; U.S.C.G. Aux. Vsl. Examiner, etc.

LEON G. BALLARD, U.S.A.F., was born Nov. 23, 1914 in Boone County, MO. Enlisted in Army Air Corps Oct. 13, 1942 and was discharged Oct. 23, 1945 as technical sergeant.

Attended about all the major airplane mechanics schools in the States and was a qualified B-17 crew chief. Got shunted off into aerial gunnery school and became an aerial engineer gunner. Flew tailgun on B-17G Number 42-31831 named *Banshee*.

Went overseas with the 463rd BG (H) and became part of the 15th Air Force. Flew his first two missions out of Tunis, Tunisia, then moved to Celone Field, Foggia, Italy.

Was shot down on his seventh mission, April 6, 1944, northeast of Zagreb, Yugoslavia. Returned to his home base through the courtesy of Tito's Partisans.

Spent the rest of his military career in a training command as an engineer instructor on B-17s at Ardmore, OK.

Retired as sales manager of Universal Foods

Corp. Jan. 1, 1977. Has a son and daughter. He and his wife Irene live just one-half mile from where he was born.

JOHN F. BARNACLE, S/Sgt., was born March 30, 1919 in Winthrop, MA. Enlisted U.S. Army on Dec. 24, 1940; active duty Jan. 16, 1941, stationed at Camp Edwards, Cape Cod, MA with the 26th (Yankee) Div., 101st Field Arty. Later transferred to U.S. Army Air Corps, Columbia Army Air Base, SC. Attended gunnery school at Myrtle Beach, SC and trained on B-25 medium bombers.

Volunteered for heavy bomber aircraft duty and was sent to advanced gunnery school at Salt Lake City, UT. In July 1943, while stationed at Clovis, NM, was assigned as an original member of the 450th BG Cadre and then was sent to Alamogordo, NM for group combat training.

After arriving in December of 1943, flew combat bombing missions with the 450th BG, 720th Bomb Sqdn., 15th Air Force, stationed at Manduria, Italy. Served as the armorer-gunner (ball turret gunner) on a B-24 Liberator Bomber.

On March 17, 1944, on 19th mission, Barnacle bailed out of his disabled aircraft while flying over Yugoslavia. Being declared MIA for approximately 30 days, he was subsequently rescued by Marshal Tito's Partisan soldiers who helped him to escape and evade capture.

He retired in 1980 from Redstone Arsenal, AL after 32 years of government service. He was employed as a budget analyst with the Dept. of the Army (Civil Service). He and his wife, Camilla, still reside in Huntsville, AL.

EUGENE E. BENNETT, Maj. (ret.), joined the Air Corps as Air Cadet at age 19 in July of 1942. Received wings and 2nd lieutenant commission in November of 1943. Joined the 56th Fighter Group, 62nd Sqdn., 8th Air Force in England in April of 1944.

On May 4, 1944, on combat mission number seven, destroyed one FW 190 in the vicinity of Nordhausen, Germany. Credited with 1c2 aircraft. Because of no enemy aircraft to be found, was ordered to begin bombing and strafing ground targets.

Parachuted on June 7, 1944 from P-47 at 7:30 a.m. near Argentan, France, about 100 miles west of Paris. Was strafing German tanks when they returned the fire by cutting the engine oil lines. Was hidden in French farms by the Resistance and took part in their activity until Aug. 6 when Patton's boys went by on their way to Berlin. Was MIA for 60 days as an evader.

Promoted to first lieutenant in September of 1944. In October returned to the U.S.A. to become instructor of French pilots learning to fly the P-47 in combat. In August 1945 was released from the service, but signed to the active reserve.

In May 1948, took part in organizing the 137th Fighter Squadron of the NYANG at White Plains, NY. Was extended federal recognition in three positions: flight commander of "B" flight, aircraft maintenance officer and automotive maintenance officer. Promoted to captain May 1950. In June 1951 promoted to operations officer and was called from civilian job to organize the 137th for Korea but orders were canceled.

In January 1952 was promoted to squadron and base commander at Westchester County Airport. Orders for promotion to lieutenant colonel by state of New York were denied by Nat. Guard Bureau in 1952, but in June 1954 was promoted to major and in April 1956 was promoted as commander of the 105th Fighter G. Resigned from U.S.A.F. and Air Guard with 20 years service in July of 1962.

GEORGE F. BENNETT, was born June 3, 1924 in Wheeling, WV. Joined Army Dec. 4, 1942. Radio operator/gunner on B-17, 379 BG, 527 BS. Shot down Feb. 8, 1944 en route to Frankfort, Germany. Evaded capture, escaped 500 miles into Spain with aid of the French Underground.

Graduated U.S.A.F. pilot school class 49C. Flew 51 missions as B-29 pilot in the Korean War. One year tour in Vietnam added 17 missions in several different aircraft.

Retired as colonel Aug. 1, 1973, wing commander, 44th SMWg. (SAC) Ellsworth, A.F.B., SD. Secretary of Public Safety of South Dakota on Gov. Kneip's cabinet for two years.

Awarded Legion of Merit with Cluster, Bronze Star, Meritorious Service Medal, Air Medal with five Oak Leaf Clusters, Air Force Commendation Medal with two Oak Leaf Clusters, Purple Heart and RVN Medal of Honor.

Married Iris Glenn from Waco, TX on Sept. 30, 1949 at Barksdale A.F.B., LA. Proud of son, daughter and six grandchildren.

ELMO H. (BUD) BERGLIND, Lt. Col. (ret.), was born Jan. 14, 1921 in Anoka County, MN. Joined the National Guard in Bellingham, WA when he was 16 years old.

He became an Aviation Cadet in April 1942, graduating with class 43F at Luke Field, AZ. He was assigned to the newly activated 363rd Fighter Group, Hamilton Field, CA.

From England he flew P-51s and on March 18, 1944 he bailed out over Europe after his plane was hit by enemy ground fire. He escaped over the Pyrenees Mountains, arriving in Spain one day prior to the Normandy invasion.

Returned to the U.S. as a fighter aircraft instructor until July 1945, when he went to the Pacific, flying P-51s with the 21st FG from Saipan and Iwo Jima.

Separated from the U.S.A.A.F. in February of 1946 but was recalled during the Berlin Air Lift and remained as a career Air Force officer until retirement in October of 1965 with 20 years active, 25 total years service.

He and his wife, Dorothy reside in Bellingham, WA.

GORDON H. BICKLEY, was born Sept. 26, 1921 in Detroit, MI. Joined U.S. Army Air Corps as Aviation Cadet Sept. 8, 1942.

Cadet training was at Kelly Field, San Antonio, TX and Stanford, TX. Assigned to A.A.F.G.S. Las Vegas, NV; then to CIS, Fort Meyers, FL. After completion was assigned to BG at Drew Field, Tampa, FL. Joined crew as ball turret gunner on B-17s, in February of 1944.

Arrived E.T.O. May 1, 1944. Assigned to 452 BG, 729 Sqdn., 8th Air Force. On Bickley's 18th mission, July 8th, plane was severely damaged by flak over Rouen, France. After bailing out, he evaded capture and was hidden by several French families until area was taken over by Canadian ground forces.

After returning to U.S. he was assigned to A.A.F.C.S.F.G., Laredo, TX, then to K.A.A.F. Kingman, AR as gunnery instructor. Discharged Sept. 3, 1945.

Married Donna Carswell June 16, 1943. They have four children and five grandchildren and reside in Redford, MI. Bickley retired in December of 1983 after careers in industrial advertising, sales promotion and auto parts manufacturing.

CHARLES R. BLACKWELL, was born Dec. 22, 1921 in Sedalia, MO. Joined Army April 3, 1942 and trained on the west coast. Flew B-17, B-29, C-45, C-46, C-47, L-5 and L-16.

Shot down over OCC France June 14, 1944 on mission 29. MIA for 10 weeks, five crew members POW, 457th BG, 750th Sqdn. Assisted by French Resistance and very nice little old lady in Blonville, France. Released from active duty in September of 1945.

Recalled to active duty in May 1951, Scott Field, IL. Was auto maintenance officer in Fairchild,

AL; instructor L-16, L-5 in San Marcos, TX. Then sent to Randolph Field, TX (B-29 Pipeline). Released from active duty in December of 1952 at Forbes A.B., KS.

Was structural DES. McDonnell AB St. Louis. Helped on F-4, F-111, F-15, Hornet.

Received Air Medal with four Oak Leaf Clusters, Distinguished Flying Cross with Oak Leaf Cluster, E.T.O., etc.

Worked for Caterpillar in Peoria, IL for short time. Worked for FMC in Cedar Rapids for short time. Retired ABT six years. Do woodwork. Enjoy old cars. Have missed taking lots of fishing trips. Married Rose Lepak in Oklahoma in 1945. Have four daughters, six grandchildren, one great-grandson.

ROGER J. BLAKE, was born March 21, 1918 in Chicago, IL. Married Dec. 28, 1945 to Georgianna Blake. No children.

Graduated in November of 1943, Monroe, LA as a navigator. Shot down while member of the 92nd BG on March 23, 1944, at or near Breda in northern Holland on a mission to Muenster.

Flew 19 combat missions and evaded successfully to Sept. 7, 1944. Hid out in Brussels mainly, until liberated by the Irish Guard. Following discharge, completed law school at University of Michigan, and was called to active duty again during the Korean conflict, and was mainly a staff judge advocate in Korea and at March AFB.

His most exciting mission was when, after he had been evading approximately six weeks and was in very poor physical condition, he was in the northern portion of Brussels and Belgium in the neighborhood of the large railroad yards, hiding out with a salesman of birth-control devices and his lovely wife. They all left, he was alone in the apartment, and told him under no circumstances answer the door and stay quiet. There were beautiful wooden floors in the apartment and in the hallway and suddenly, to his horror, around 1:00 in mid-May, he heard the floor creaking outside the apartment door. He immediately went to lie face down on the floor near the door and watched the doorknob. He stayed there watching the doorknob turn slowly every now and then and force being exerted on the door and the floor creaking outside as the would-be "Pandora" kept trying the door. He said he believes someone knew he was there and he stayed watching the doorknob for about an hour-and-a-half. He heard the floor creak down and the front door of the apartment close.

He thought of becoming a prisoner of the Gestapo and the torture of every person who had helped him. He got his few possessions (a razor blade, razor, some chocolate bars and a map) and left through the back door and hid out to the park near the streetcar stop where he knew the wife of his helper would return home soon. He slowly went up to her and told her of his experiences. She told him to stay in the park and she would check the place out. She checked with friends and found that the Gestapo had been there looking for him. He went back to a bar in Brussels and called the Cafe Albert at Rue de Conciliation and Rue de Justice and contacted the organization again.

It was the highlight of my suspenseful evasion because after he got to the park he was shaking like a leaf and could not stop from trembling violently. Never had he been so frightened even on experiences of passing through controls and road-blocks and bombing.

ROBERT W. BLAKENEY,
was born June 19, 1923 in Newton, MA. Enlisted U.S.A.F. Sept. 1, 1942. Rank achieved: technical sergeant. Served in North Africa, Italy and Bengasi. Discharged Nov. 5, 1945.

Waist gunner, B-24, 44th BG, 67th Sqdn. Shot down Aug. 16, 1943 on Foggia, Italy mission. Survived crash landing in Reggio di Calabria. Escaped German prison in Sulmona, Italy; 25 days behind enemy lines; then Canadian 5th Army.

Awarded Silver Star, Air Medal, Distinguished Unit Citation, P.O.W. Medal and Good Conduct Medal.

Married Eileen Derocher April 14, 1945. Children: Steve and Cindy. Grandsons: Ian, Brett and Robert. Graduate of Boston College (1949) and Boston College Law School (1952). Retired after 37 years as a trial attorney. Now active in volunteer and church work.

CONRAD M. BLALOCK,
was born Dec. 1, 1918 in Cooleemee, NC. Joined the service in November 1938. Was in 120th Infantry, Company G, North Carolina National Guard. Based at Fort Jackson, SC and U.S. Air Force Langley Field, VA. Achieved rank of major.

Was MIA in France in 1944. Awarded two Air Medals. Married Sadie June in 1945. One daughter, one son.

Retired after 30+ years as a technical writer for AT&T.

ROBERT (BOB) G. BORST,
was born Nov. 1, 1922 in Delhi, NY. Graduated high school and joined U.S.A.A.F. in February of 1943. Had basic training in Miami Beach, FL; air gunnery school in Tyndall Field, Panama City, FL; and received air gunners wings upon completion of training.

Went to bombardier navigator school in San Angelo, TX, November 1943-March 1944 and graduated with class 44-4 and received rank of 2nd Lt. Had heavy bomber training at Gowen Field, Boise, ID March 1944-May 1944.

Assigned to 8th A.A.F., 466th BG, 787 Sqdn. at Attlebridge, England in mid-June 1944.

Shot down by German fighter planes over northern Holland on Aug. 15, 1944 on 13th combat mission bombing German airfield at Vechta, Germany. Shot down on return after bombing. Parachuted into a farm field and was contacted by Dutch Underground who hid him in several places for eight months.

Liberated on April 13, 1945 by Canadian Army Forces. Turned over to U.S. Forces within a few days.

Returned to U.S. June 1945. Promoted to first lieutenant in June 1945. Discharged October 1945.

Retired July 1986 from private business as customer service manager for Electro-therm, Inc., Laurel, MD.

Received Air Medal with one Oak Leaf Cluster; Victory Medal; and Good Conduct Medal.

Married to Eileen and have four children, four grandchildren and one great-granddaughter.

EUGENE B. BOWARD,
was born March 2, 1921 in Leitersburg, MD. Joined military Sept. 3, 1942. Photo-gunner on daylight and night-intruder missions in A-20 light bomber, 86th Sqdn., 47th BG., 12th A.F., from bases in Italy, Corsica, and southern France.

Shot down on 51st mission over Apennine Mountains of northern Italy at 1:30 a.m. Nov. 12, 1944 while participating in night-intruder (single aircraft) mission to destroy German pontoon bridge across the Po River. Parachuted, joined Italian Partisans, and evaded southward through the U.S. 5th Army front lines on Nov. 20, 1944 in company with two other crew members (Lt. Dowdell and S/Sgt. Schultz), Partisans, escaped P.O.W.s, other Allied evadees and six or eight German soldier defectors. Discharged Oct. 25, 1945.

Civilian engineer with U.S. Army. Retired in 1986. Lives with wife, Sue, in Springfield, VA. Son: 1st Lt. Gary D., U.S. Army.

ARDEN ANDY BRENDEN,
was born Jan. 8, 1922 in Starbuck, MN. Enlisted Oct. 14, 1942. Was in Air Force 407th Bomb Sqdn. A.A.F. Went to mechanic school in Amarillo, TX, gunnery school in New York and engineer school in Boeing

Factory, Seattle, WA. Achieved rank of staff sergeant.

Was shot down on first mission over Chalones, France. Landed in field near a wooded area. There was a church nearby where a wedding was being performed. Landing interrupted the wedding as everyone stopped to watch the parachute landing. Was helped by French families until he reached French Underground. Underground helped him get over the Pyrenees Mountains. Entered Lerida, Spain May 15, 1944. Discharged Oct. 14, 1944.

Was awarded the Purple Heart, Good Conduct, E.T.O. two Battle Stars.

Married Pauline on Oct. 20, 1945 at Alexandria, MN. Have four sons and four grandchildren.

Was field rep. for Marquette Cement for nine years. Owned and operated Culligan Soft Water business at Canton, SD for 18 years. Retired after 18 years as administrative officer for Farmers Home Adm. Currently an A.A.R.P. instructor in 55/Alive. Live in Mesa, AZ six months during winter and in Huron, SD the other six months.

WALTER BRESSLER,
was born Feb. 20, 1923 in Unionville, PA. Joined the Air Force in 1942 and trained as a mechanic in various schools in U.S. Started flying in 1943 a mechanic gunner on B-24. Went to England as a replacement to the 8th A.F., joined with the 448th BG, 713th Sqdn.

Flew seven missions. Bailed out April 1, 1944 and landed in northern France. Escaped over the Pyrenees Mountains with help of French Underground. Entered Spain, got help from U.S. government, returned back to England then back to U.S. Discharged December 1945 as a staff sergeant.

Received Air Medal and Purple Heart.

Married Ruth April 17, 1948. Had three children, (two boys, one girl) and five grandchildren.

Retired June 1986 as a mechanic from local utility company. Live in Centre Hall, PA.

HERBERT BRILL,
was born Feb. 27, 1920 in Hoboken, NJ. As a navigator on a B-17, flying out of Podington, England, on a so-called "milk run" to a German-occupied airfield near Cognac, France, they crash landed a little after

noon in southwestern France on Dec. 31, 1943.

After two days of walking eastward, away from the coast, across fields and roads with the engineer, covering approximately 60 kilometers, made contact with the Maquis (the French Resistance). Stayed with the Maquis (Group "Section Speciale de Sabotage"), living, working and fighting with them against the enemy for nine months, returning to England in September 1944.

Received French Resistance medals as volunteer and also Combatant from the French government for working and participation in battles in the Dordogne and Charente regions.

Married Millicent Pokrass in June 1948. Has three sons and four grandchildren. Worked for PepsiCo International for over 35 years, 25 outside U.S. Currently reside in Corona del Mar, CA.

GEORGE JOSEPH BROOKS, was born Feb. 14, 1924 in Salina, KS. Graduated Silver Lake High School in Kansas in 1942.

Enlisted A.A.C. Cadets September 1942. Reported classification and pre-flight, San Antonio, TX March 1943. Graduated Foster Field, TX class 44A Jan. 7, 1944.

Trained in AT-6 gunnery and transition in P-40 at Marietta, GA. Trained in P-51 Mustang at Bartow, FL. Joined 363rd FG, 382nd Fighter Sqdn., France July 1944.

Shot down Aug. 13, 1944 over Normandy. Evacuated in England hospital two weeks, returned to disbanded 363rd FG. Joined 9th Weather Reconnaissance Sqdn. November 1944 flying P-51 Mustang until war's end.

Married in 1947. Has five children and four grandchildren. Retired U.S.P.O. postal clerk. Resides in Topeka, KS.

DEWEY C. BROWN, JR., S.N. 0673704, was born March 6, 1920 in Mathis, TX. Joined the Army Air Corps as an Aviation Cadet Jan. 29, 1942 in San Antonio TX.

Pilot training was in Sikeston, MO, Randolph Field, and he received his wings at Lubbock, TX Feb. 15, 1943. He flew as a co-pilot on B-17s with 544th Sqdn., 384th BG, 8th Air Force from Grafton-

Underwood, England, WWII. His plane was the *Merrie Hell*.

On his 13th mission on Aug. 17, 1943, his plane was hit during the bombing run over the ball bearing factory in Schweinfurt, Germany. They crashed landed in occupied France near Rheims. Four of his crew of ten evaded capture. Brown and another crewman traveled through occupied France over the Pyrenees into Spain.

He spent the last two years of the war instructing B-17 combat crews at Dyersburg, TN.

He was awarded the Air Medal with two Oak Leaf Clusters. Discharged on Nov. 4, 1945.

He and his wife live in Corpus Christi, TX and are involved in the life insurance business.

GUS E. BUBENZER, was born in Rome, IN, Oct. 7, 1923. Entered military service in March 1943 in Anderson, IN. Served in 640th Bomb Sqdn., 409th BG, 9th Air Force, as engineer gunner on an A-20 aircraft.

Was shot down over France on 20th mission on May 27, 1944. Evaded with the help of five French families and was liberated Sept. 1, 1944.

Returned to U.S. and served the duration as a hydraulic instructor at Keesler Field, MS.

Discharged with technical sergeant rating in September 1945.

Married LaVera Young, Nov. 1, 1942. Has one son, Guane E. Bubenzer, daughter-in-law, Tara (Nichols) Bubenzer and four grandchildren: Kimberly, Michael, Joy and Kevin.

Retired from General Motors as a machinist in 1982. Currently resident of Anderson, IN.

JOHN R. BUCKNER, was born Feb. 2, 1924 in Atlanta, GA. Enlisted U.S.A.A.F. Nov. 14, 1942. Basic at Miami Beach, FL; armament school, Buckley Field, Denver, CO; gunnery school, Harlingen, TX; heavy bombardment, Salt Lake City, UT; crew assignment and first phrase training Pyote, TX; phrase II training, Halls, A.A.F. Dyersburg, TN.

The crew flew their new B-17F *Pistol Packing Mama* from Grand Island, NE to Presque Island, Maine, Gander Newfoundland on to Preswick, Scotland.

Assigned to 8th A.A.F., 388th BG, 560th Sqdn. Station 136, Knettishall, England

After being hit with flak and losing two engines over Gelsenkirchen, Germany Nov. 5, 1943, they lost the third engine at about 8000 ft. They crash landed in Holland trying for a ditch in the English Channel/North Sea. Captured at crash site while attending the wounded, by German army troops.

While being taken by train to Amsterdam, they attacked the German guards near Delft, Holland. Five of the crew escaped, four made contact with Dutch Underground.

Buckner evaded until recapture Feb. 26, 1944 in Paris, France. Under Gestapo control for eight weeks in prison near Paris. Taken to Frankfort on the Main by Gestapo on a train. Interned 21 days, solitary confinement. Became P.O.W. May 6, 1944, under Luftwaffe control. Sent to Stalag Luft IV near Kiefheide in Pomeranian sector of northern Germany until first of February, 1945. In (40 & 8) box cars, spent eight days/nights in overcrowded conditions with deplorable sanitary conditions. Arrived Nurnburg Stalag 13D Feb. 9, 1945. Forced marched to Moosburg Stalag 7A. Liberated April 29, 1945 by Patton's Third Army. No regrets.

Retired Union Camp Corp. Savannah, GA plant after 36 years. Member of Hardeeville Baptist Church, fire chief Hardeeville Vol. Fire Dept. 25 yrs. Appointed by Gov. Richard Riley to South Carolina Fire Comm. Serving third four-year term. Past master Hardeeville Lodge #348. Past president of Lions Club. Member of 8th A.F. Historical Soc. Life member 388th BG Assn. A.F.E.E.S., Ex-POW, Stalag Luft IV and D.A.V.

Married to Betty and have married daughter, one granddaughter and one great-granddaughter. Live in Hardeeville, SC.

DAVID L. BUTCHER, T/Sgt. was born March 11, 1918 in Oak Park, IL. Joined the Air Corps Aug. 21, 1940.

Took gunner training at Las Vegas aerial gunner school and went to Salt Lake City Armament School. He flew in AT6s and B-17Es. Received Purple Heart and Medaille De La France Liberee.

He flew in combat with the 545th Sqdn. of the 384th BG at Grafton-Underwood England in WWII. He was in the Free French Resistance with the Hercules, Socristan, Budenaster Resean and escaped through the Pyrenees Mountains. He came out of the Air Corps Aug. 22, 1945.

He returned to the States and became a carpenter for 36 years. Married Gertrude W. Langhart April 16, 1943 and had four children, 11 grandchildren and five great-grandchildren. Lives in Fergurson, MO.

THOMAS W. CANNON, JR., Lt. Col. (ret.), was born July 4, 1922 in Memphis, TN. Joined the

U.S. Army as an Aviation Cadet Feb. 18, 1942. Completed fighter pilot training at Lake Charles, LA, Dec. 7, 1942.

He flew combat in P-51s with the 354th Pioneer Mustang Fighter G. in England and France. Other tactical aircraft flown were: P-40, P-47, P-61, F-82 and B-25.

Shot down over France July 14, 1944. Retired from active duty as a staff civil engineer.

In 1966, he went to Turkey as a civil engineer until 1973, then Spain until 1974. In 1975, he went to Saudia Arabia as a consultant for ITT. From 1976 to 1979, he was engineering and construction project manager in Taif, SA. He's now retired.

Married in Bad Wiessee, Germany to Pataricia A. Erk of Cleveland, OH on Feb. 25, 1947. They reside in Colorado Springs, CO.

FLOYD M. CARL, M/Sgt. (ret.), was born Feb. 24, 1923 in Mount Jewett, PA. Joined the Army Air Force on Nov. 7, 1942. Took gunnery training at Fort Meyers, FL. Went overseas with 8th Air Force in 1943.

Shot down over Stuttgart, Germany on Sept. 6, 1943. Evaded through France. Picked up by boat, crossed English Channel and arrived in England Dec. 7, 1943.

Returned to U.S. Discharged from service and went to college for two years. Joined service and went to Panel Engineer School, Chanute Field, IL.

Flew in B-29s, B-50s, C-97, C-124s, KB-50s. Flew as panel engineer in SAC, MATS, TAC, Proving Ground Command and Weather Sqdn. in Guam.

Currently resides in San Antonio, TX with wife, Doris.

THORNTON LEE CARLOUGH, P.O.W., M.I.A., graduated as a second lieutenant pilot, class 43J at George Field, IL Nov. 3, 1943. Was in 1st Replacement Crew, 460th BG, Spinazzola.

Returning from Bucharest, April 15, 1944, crossed Danube with two engines out and eased B-24 into a 180 to avoid mountains and bailed. Landed inside Bulgarian border with two other crew members. Held by Bulgarians. Together with

gunner escaped into Yugoslavia. (Other member was shipped to Stalag 111).

Seized by a small band of Chetnick guerrillas. Traveling over goat paths, high narrow ledges with precipitous drops, and sheer rock faces, interrupted by a skirmish between the Chetniks and Ustachi, reunited with the seven crew members that landed in Yugoslavia. Furnished with sten guns and Chetnik guides, the nine covered over 200 miles indescribable terrain avoiding many German patrols. After four weeks, connected with a B-17 crew downed in January. All trekked to reach British Underground Unit Force 399 CMF, British Intelligence, ordered by London to diverge from Mihailovich. On orders of Gen. Armstrong (British) Lts. Al Romans (pilot of B-17) and Carlough were furnished with horses and instructed to select the best of five suggested landing sites. The strip at Pranjne was chosen, some plum trees removed. On May 29, hundreds of Chetnik, led by Mihailovich himself, surrounded the field to protect the people who were deserting them, from approaching Germans. Smoldering kerosene lamps lined the strip and an R.A.F. ship made an incredible blacked out landing to evacuate them all to Bari.

After seven weeks in occupied territory, returned to combat flying June 3rd. Received Cluster on Purple Heart July 15th on fourth trip over Ploesti. Returned stateside in October. Instrument school Bryan, TX, instrument instructor Napier Field, AL until separated in August of 1945.

Resides in East Hartford, CT.

CHARLES V. CARLSON, was born in Minneapolis, MN on Nov. 16, 1917. Joined the Aviation Cadet Program in March of 1942. He graduated from the San Angelo Bombardiers School with the class of 43-6.

Joined Robert Grimes' crew at Moses Lake, WA. They were some of the first crews to train at the air field.

In England the crew was assigned to the 96th BG (H). On Oct. 20, 1943 on a mission to Duren, Germany, the plane, *Shack Rabbit III*, was shot down. Carlson was blown out of the plane by an explosion. His face and hands were burnt. On

landing with the parachute, he broke a bone in his foot. With help from many brave Belgians and French he evaded and returned to England in 1944.

Carlson finished the war as a bombardier instructor in B-29s.

Called up with an ANG(MINN) and then served in Korea in 1952-53.

He taught science in the Morris Public Schools for 27 years and retired in 1980.

JOHN PHILIP M. CARLSON, was born April 16, 1915 in Shickley, NE. Entered Aviation Cadet Program in August 1942 at Santa Ana, CA and completed training at Hondo, TX. Assigned as a navigator to the 460th BG. Operational training at Clovis, NM; Kearns, UT; and Savannah, GA.

Flew combat missions from Italy in B-24s and was shot down May 18, 1944, in Yugoslavia returning from a bombing mission over Ploesti, Rumania. Evaded capture with aid of the Chetniks and returned to base August 10, 1944.

Reassigned as an aviation psychologist with the Air Force Redistribution Command at Atlantic City, NJ. When separated from active duty in 1945, held the rank of captain.

Awards included the Distinguished Flying Cross, Air Medal with Oak Leak Cluster and Distinguished Unit Citation. Retired from the Air Force Reserve in the rank of lieutenant colonel.

Married Maryjo Suverkrup Oct. 14, 1950 and they reside in Fairfax County, VA.

Now retired from a career in the federal government and the practice of law remains active on a part time basis in government liaison matters.

LAWRENCE R. CASEY, born Oct. 23, 1920 in Marengo, IA. Entered Army Air Corps on Nov. 3, 1943, second lieutenant. Retired May 31, 1963, lieutenant colonel.

Was a P-47 pilot, stationed at Duxford, England; shot down over Elbeuf, France, June 11, five days after D-Day, flying fighter escort. The Pierre-Rose family (daughters Ferdinand, Yvette and Jeanette and Mme. F. Pierre-Rose) provided cover for him at their country home, Chalet du Franc Boisier, Tourville la Campagne, until he was liberated by American troops on August 25th.

Retired in San Antonio, TX where he was resident manager of the El Tropicano Hotel.

Died after a brief illness in San Antonio on Oct. 7, 1988. Survived by wife, Betty Waid Casey and son, Larry Garth Casey.

JAMES C. CATER, Maj. (ret.), was born July 4, 1922 in Chicago, IL. Joined the Army Air Corps as an Aviation Cadet on May 5, 1942. Took pilot training at Southeast training command bases, graduating with class 43F in June of 1944. Completed B-17 transition training at Lockborne A.A.B.,

Columbus, OH in August 1943. Combat crew training at Pyote, TX. Served with the 91st BG as a B-17 pilot at Bassingbourne, England

Shot down on 21st mission over Avord, France on April 28, 1944. Escaped and evaded through France and returned to England in July of 1944.

Returned to U.S. and served in various bases and positions until the Korean Conflict. Flew 56 missions as a B-29 aircraft commander.

Left the Air Force in 1956 to employment as an airline pilot. Then became a regional airline vice president and operations director.

Presently the president of a transportation management corporation specializing in municipal transit systems.

There are three children and seven grandchildren. He and his wife, Frances, reside in Poughkeepsie, NY.

H. PHILLIP CAUSER, was born April 11, 1916 in Weymouth, MA. S.E. Training Com. class 43C. Spent six months training Dutch pilots in Jackson, MS. Assigned to 356th FG, Martlesham Heath, England

Shot down by enemy ground fire strafing enemy airfield alone. Picked up and fought with the F.F.I. (Maquis) for 30 days plus, liberating towns, blowing bridges, and harassing the enemy in general. Picked up and flown out in R.A.F. Dakota in the middle of the night.

Stateside assignment Craig Field, Selma, AL, training the first group of officers from the French Military Academy. Attended A.F. School of Aeronautical Engineering at Chanute Field, Rantoul, IL.

As reserve, flew F-86s with 50th Fighter Interceptor, Otis A.F.B., MA.

Wrote book, *M.I.A. (Missing in Action).* Founded Phillips Manufacturers, sold in 1980s. Now owner and president of New England Manufacturing Co. At 75, still flies his Grumman AAIA for business and pleasure.

MARTIN CECH, T/Sgt., born Nov. 14, 1920 in Akron, OH. First enlisted in federal service on Dec. 15, 1937 at Fort Screven, GA and was assigned to Fort Moultrie, SC for processing and

subsequent assignment to Hawaii, where he received basic training and duty in field artillery. He returned to Fort Benning, GA in October of 1940, where he was discharged on Dec. 14, 1940. He reenlisted Jan. 7, 1942 at Fort Hayes, OH and was assigned to the Army Air Corps with duty in the chemical warfare branch.

In December of 1943, while assigned in England, he volunteered for and was assigned to B-17 gunnery duty. On March 6, 1944, after dropping bombs on Berlin, they headed for the coast and had engine trouble and left the formation. They were attacked by three or four 109s. Over Holland the intercom was knocked out, the waist door was blown off and Cech got a back full of shrapnel. He saw one of the crew members come running through the waist and motioned to bail out, so he did what he was told to do. The safety strap was still across the door opening and he lifted the strap and pushed himself out.

He landed in a fresh plowed field and hid in a small woods until dark. He could see Germans looking without luck. He slept in a haystack that night and got to a farmers house. The next morning and he got him in touch with the Underground. Worked actively with the underground until liberation by the Canadians in 1945. Sent to Belgium for interrogation and was then returned to U.S. to Camp Atterbury, IN. Discharged July 26, 1945.

Reenlisted July 30, 1948 at Cleveland Municipal Airport, OH. Served at several bases stateside and in England, Germany, Korea and Japan. Assigned to 6143D Air Base G. (PACAF) in San Francisco, CA in March of 1960 and remained until retirement (technical sergeant) Jan. 31, 1962 after 20 years of active federal service.

Worked 17 years for U.S. Postal Service, retiring in 1978. Married 1963 and divorced 1989. Five daughters and five grandchildren. Feels great and lives in Venice, CA.

JOHN J. CHAPMAN, was born Sept. 22, 1922 in New York City, NY. Inducted Oct. 24, 1942. Was in Infantry, Air Force, Transp. Corps.

Military locations were: Yaphank, NY; Nashville, TN; Miami Beach, FL; Santa Ana, CA;

Kirtland Field, NM; (bombardier training) Walla Walla, WA; Dalhart, TX; Tampa, FL; (overseas) Tunisia, N. Africa; Aerignola, Italy, Foggia (Lucera), Italy; Barksdale Field, LA; Sheppard Field, Wichita Falls, TX; Lakeland, FL; Midland, TX; Ft. Eustice, VA; 670th Med. Port, Manila, P. Is., then to States for separation.

Missions with 301st BG, 32nd Sqdn. Rimini, Klagenfurt, Anzio, Rome, Toulon, Cassino, and shot down March 17, 1944 over Wiener Neustadt, Austria. Caught flak in the starboard engine, waist and tail. Left formation and pilot headed down for safety of clouds below as three Me109 fighters mauled them. Attack left them with two engines gone, three crew wounded and fire on the flight deck. Mortally wounded the *Queen* headed for the Adriatic and home. The third engine quit and the crew was forced to bail out over enemy territory.

That afternoon the 32nd Sqdn. of the 301st BG lost a B-17 and her combat crew.

Received Air Medal and Presidential Unit Citation. Discharged June 19, 1947.

Most memorable experiences: first combat mission and first parachute jump.

Married wife Garnett. No children. Retired in May 1985 from Sears Roebuck and Co. after 37 years service.

WALTER E. CHAPMAN, SR., was born Feb. 16, 1921 in Lexington, KY. Entered service in July 1942, U.S.A.A.F. Aviation Cadet. Graduated class 43-10, Midland, TX as a bombardier, rank second lieutenant. Discharged in July 1945, with rank of first lieutenant.

Served overseas with 484th BG, 826th BS, 15th A.F. Credited with 24 combat missions on B-24 type aircraft from May 5, 1944 to June 13, 1944, when shot down by German Me109. Parachuted out of aircraft over Italy and with assistance of Italian and Yugoslavian partisans evaded capture until August of 1944. Two crewmen killed in action, four taken prisoner of war and Chapman, along with three other members of the crew evaded capture with help of Tito's Partisans.

Retired industrial engineer with 32 years of service with International Harvester Co.

EVERETT L. CHILDS, Lt. Col. (ret.) was born Oct. 26, 1918 in Manchester, IA. Joined U.S.A.F. April 7, 1941.

Received navigation training at Monroe, LA, class of 43-4. Assigned to 8th A.A.F., Grafton-Underwood, 384th BG, 547th Sqdn.

Shot down from B-17 on second Schwienfurt mission, Oct. 14, 1943, near Bar- le-Duc, France. Captured near Spanish border May 16, 1944. Escaped from train July 10, 1944, near Bar le Duc. Traveled through lines Aug. 20, 1944 at Orleons. Released from active duty June 3, 1946.

Worked at Rocky Flats, CO as chemist. Retired Aug. 1, 1989 as principal engineer. Has written a story of escape, *A Year to Remember*.

Lives in Boulder, CO. Married to Helen Frantzen, Jan. 4, 1945. Children: Craig E., Kathleen K., and Susan L. (deceased).

FORREST S. CLARK, was born July 6, 1921 in Newark, NJ. Graduated from Rutgers University with an M.A. in English.

Joined U.S. Air Corps in October of 1942. U.K., Norfolk, England, 8th Air Force, 44 BG on B-24. Achieved rank of technical sergeant. Discharged Oct. 9, 1945.

Clark was on a bombing mission to Lechfeld, Germany, April 13, 1944 when his B-24 was crippled by enemy fire, lost considerable fuel and was forced to make an emergency landing in Switzerland. They had bombed the target for the date. The crew was interned by Swiss authorities at Adelboden, Wengen and Davos, Switzerland, internee camps under guard.

In late December of 1944, he managed to escape with the aid of the U.S. Legation in Bern and the French Resistance. They crossed into France near Geneva and went through Annecy, in the Haut Savoy Province. He got to Lyons, France before Christmas 1944 and returned to his base in England. Clark did not remember who helped him escape. In his group were internees and former prisoners of war.

Married Ruth Buck Clark and have two children and two grandchildren. Was a journalist, Gannett Group, until retirement in August of 1986. Resides in Kissimmee, FL.

GEORGE F. CLARK, was born March 17, 1921 in Ames, IA. Joined the Army Sept 10, 1942. Trained at Camp Crowder, MO, Buckley - Lowery Fields, CO, Harlingen - Laredo, TX, Salt Lake City, UT.

S/Sgt. Clark flew with the 389th BG, 567th Sqdn. Hethal, England, tailgunner B-24J.

On his 19th combat mission, July 25, 1944, over St.-Lo, France, plane was shot down by flak. Captured by SS troops when landing in chute. Next several days transferred by foot and truck to different locations. Loaded on a train August 5 and on August 8, he and six others escaped from moving train east of Chateau Thierry, France. He and fellow crew member walked and found a French farmer who helped and hid them until American Army was near. Made it back to Yank lines August 28.

Sent back to England, then to States, where finished service at Sioux City A.B., IA., as a gunnery instructor. Discharged Oct. 4, 1945.

Received Purple Heart and Air Medal with two Oak Leaf Clusters.

Married in June 1945 and had four children. Farmed until his death Aug. 16, 1978.

JACK F. CLIFFORD, 1st Lt. (ret.), was born Feb. 17, 1920 in Indianapolis, IN. Joined Army Air Corps Feb. 5, 1942. Was a navigator in B-24. Flew with 373rd and 425th Sqdn., 308th BG, 14th A.F.

Hit by fighters on first bombing mission over Hong Kong on July 17, 1943 and bailed out on way back to base near Yangki, China and on 97th mission on May 20, 1944 hit by destroyers in South China Sea and bailed out over enemy-held territory. Helped to avoid capture by Maryknoll missionaries, Father James F. O'Day and Father Jo-

seph Boggard, who dressed crew in coolie outfits and hid them in sampan to pass through Japanese territory to mission house in Kaying.

After war, graduated from Harvard Law School and presently practices law in Chicago, IL.

CHARLES WILLIAM COMPTON, JR., 1st Lt., born Nov. 10, 1917 in Irvington, NJ. Joined the Army Air Corps Dec. 8, 1941.

Bombardier and navigation training in the Gulf Coast training command. Combat training, Moses Lake, WA and Kearney, NE. Flew in B-17s with 100th BG, 8th Air Force, Norwich, England. As bombardier on *Laden Maden*, shot down near Epernay, France, returning from third mission over Ludwigshafen, Germany, Dec. 30, 1943. Evaded with help of French Underground over Pyrenees into Spain via Gibraltar to England.

Returned to U.S. May 2, 1944 to instruct in Gulf Coast training command. Separated from active duty Oct. 26, 1945. Served in Reserves and was recalled to serve in Korean War. Resigned Reserves 1951. Member Caterpillar Club and A.F.E.E.S.

Married Lucille Lord March 6, 1943; four children, nine grandchildren. Deceased May 6, 1990.

ROBERT D. COUTURE, 1st Lt., U.S.A.A.C., born Feb. 1, 1924 in Rice Lake, WI. Joined Army June 3, 1942.

Received pilot training at West Coast training command bases; combat training, Bartow, FL. Flew C-19s, P-40 and P-51. Released from active duty Nov. 3, 1945.

Flew with 354th Sqdn., 8th A.F., Steeple Morden, England in WWII. Shot down on mission over Nogent-le-Rotrou, France June 7, 1944. Crash landed near Vicheres and was hidden on a farm by Mr. and Mrs. Marcel Rousseau. He was hidden by the French Underground and later taken to Forest Freteval, near Cloyes.

Liberated with 151 other allies of Fretval, by the 5th Armored Div. of Patton's 3rd Army on Aug. 13, 1944.

His last year in service was spent as P-51 instructor at Venice, FL. He married Priscilla

Greenwold on Oct. 14, 1945. Discharged Nov. 3, 1945. Spent 32 years in management positions in the trucking industry until retiring.

SILAS M. CRASE, D.M.D., M.P.H., A.B., F.A.C.D.; Col. (ret.), was born Jan. 30, 1925. As a 97th BG, 414th Sqdn., 15th A.F. S/Sgt. ball turret gunner, flew 11 combat missions from Foggia, Italy. Bailed out Aug. 27, 1944 after bombing Blechhammar oil refineries, Germany. Evaded out of Germany into Czechoslovakia. Joined and worked with Slovakia Partisans in Zilina/Vella Byctcia area.

With "Russian Liberation", the Russians urged that he be shipped to Moscow for repatriation. Evaded the "Russian Allies" after about three weeks. With a deaf-mute passport traveled across war wrecked Czechoslovakia and checked in with the American ambassador in Prague. Then transferred to the U.S. Army in Pilsen June 15, 1945.

Worked with Kentucky and Ohio state health departments. Retired in January of 1985 from U.S. Army Dental Corps with a total of 30 years.

Married Anna Marie Auton. Children: Deborah Ann and Michael and five grandchildren. Retired in Fort Pierce, FL.

WILLIAM LEE CUPP, was born Sept. 23, 1923 in Davenport, IA. Active duty in U.S. Army Air Corps Jan. 18, 1943-Nov. 7, 1945.

Sergeant and B-24 ball turret gunner in the 861st Sqdn., 493rd BG, 8th A.F. On June 14, 1944, on a raid against an air base near Laon, France, the plane crashed in Belgium. Six crewmen found sanctuary there. In July, with fellow crewman Robert Donahue, and aided by citizens along the route, walked toward Allied lines. Captured near Paris on Aug. 29.

After discharge in November, 1945, attended the universities of Iowa and North Carolina and taught sociology in the S.U.N.Y. Upstate Medical Center, Butler University, St. Olaf College, and Kearney State College, Nebraska. With wife Elizabeth (Penny), now resides in Northfield, MN.

HOWARD J. CURRAN, was born March 27, 1918 in Pratt, KS. Enlisted in the Army Air Forces

87

at Ft. Riley, KS on July 15, 1941. Accepted for Aviation Cadets and entered pilot training in August 1942 in southeast training command.

Graduated and commissioned with class 1943-E, single engine advance, Spence Field, at Moultri, GA on May 28, 1943. Completed fighter pilot training (R.T.U.) in P-39s at Venice, FL. Assigned to the 510th Fighter Sqdn., 405th FG at Walterboro, South Carolina on Nov. 1, 1943. The 405th FG sailed from New York City on Feb. 27, 1944 on the "RMS Mauretania" and docked at Liverpool, England on March 6, 1944.

The 405th FG traveled by rail to its assigned airfield at Christchurch on the south coast of England. After being equipped with new P-47 fighters, the 405th FG was assigned to the 9th A.F. and moved to France on July 11, 1944. Primary mission was to give support to Allied Forces and U.S. Third Army. Group moved Sept. 10, 1944 to A-64 near St. Dizier, France.

Shot down while flying 95th mission in his P-47 Thunderbolt named *Kansas Tornado* over enemy occupied France east of the Moselle River near Pont-A-Mousson, France Sept. 12, 1944. Bailed out and evaded capture for six days thanks to help of French civilian named Francois Lertex and other Frenchmen. Capt. Curran was liberated by troops of the 35th Infantry Div. then returned to the U.S. Remained on active duty after the war. Two years in Panama Canal Zone flying P-80s, Lockheed's "Shooting Star", the first U.S.A.F. operational jet fighter. In August 1948 the 36th FG moved from Canal Zone to Europe to support the Berlin Air Lift, based in Furstenfeldbruck, West Germany. 1949-50 was with 1st FG at March A.F.B., CA, flying F-86s.

Volunteered for Korea in July 1950. Flew 105 missions with 16th Fighter Sqdn., 51st FG. 1952-57 assigned to U.S.A.F. flight test acceptance pilot in New York testing F-84 type jet fighters. Reassigned to Europe testing F-84, F-86, and F-100.

Married Jacqueline Siourd of Orbec, France, in 1959, whose home was not far from the fighter strip he flew out of in 1944.

Retired from U.S.A.F. in 1961, rank major. Flew a total of 200 combat missions and received Purple Heart, Distinguished Flying Cross with three Clusters and Air Medal with 24 Clusters. Retired from U.S. Postal Service in Tacoma, WA April 1, 1983.

ELDON H. DAHL, Lt. Col. (ret.), was born Jan. 13, 1918 in Rhame, ND. Enlisted as a cadet in the U.S. Army Air Corps, pilot training class 42-I in California. Flew with the 416th Sqdn., 99th BG out of Algeria and Tunisia.

Bailed out of a B-17 on his 41st combat mission on a raid to Foggia airdromes on Aug. 25,

1943. Escaped from the Germans and returned to American lines near Cassino, Italy Nov. 13, 1943. Spent several months with Military Intelligence, briefing combat crews in the U.S. on escape and evasion. Retired from Air Force Reserves Jan. 13, 1978.

Flew: B-17, B-24, B-25, B-26, C-47, and AT-11. Decorations: Air Medal with seven Oak Leaf Clusters, Purple Heart, European Campaign Ribbon with three Bronze Battle Stars, Presidential Unit Citation and Prisoner of War Medal.

Member of Air Force Assn., Retired Officers Assn., 99th BG Hist. Soc., Air Force Escape and Evasion Soc. and is a Red Cross volunteer.

Dahl is president of Dahl Funeral Chapels, a Montana corporation.

At Las Vegas Air Force Base, in addition to flying duties, he was squadron Air Force personnel management officer, assistant to the director of supply and maintenance. He was the training officer of the Air Reserve Unit at Montana State University for several years.

He and his wife, Virginia, live in Bozeman, MT. They have three daughters, one son and four grandchildren.

CLAYTON C. DAVID, Lt. Col. (ret.), was born July 19, 1919 in Topeka, KS. Joined Army Dec. 1, 1941 and eventually served in U.S. Army Air Corps, U.S. Air Force.

Took pilot training at Gulf Coast training command bases; combat training, Pyote, TX and Dyersburg, TN. Flew B-17, C-47, P-51, P-47, P-63, trainers. Released from active duty Dec. 11, 1945. Retired from Reserves July 19, 1979.

Flew with 358th Sqdn., 303rd BG, 8th A.F., Molesworth, England, WWII. Shot down as copilot on mission's return over Holland, Jan. 11, 1944. Evaded through Holland, Belgium, France into Spain. Returned to England May 25, 1944.

Returned to U.S. and worked with Intelligence; then assigned to Great Falls, MT and Long Beach, California, (for ferrying planes).

Married to Lenora M. (Scotty) Scott Feb. 11, 1945 and has two children, Lynn A. and James S. David and one grandchild, Jonathan David.

Was district field superintendent of Pet Inc. and associate professor at West Virginia Northern Community College. Retired for last time Aug. 1, 1985. Currently resides in Hannibal, MO.

CURTIS L. DEATRICK, Capt. U.S.M.C. (ret.), was born Oct. 6, 1924 in Gettysburg, PA. Joined Army Air Corps in February 1943, trained in B-26 aircraft and specialized in electronic countermeasures and pathfinders.

Flew 65 WWII combat missions as T/Sgt. out of England, France and Belgium with 496th Sqdn., 344 BG, 9th A.F. Was shot down Sept. 30, 1944,

captured and escaped and evaded from Germany. Discharged in July 1945.

Reenlisted in U.S.M.C. September 1946; serving in 1st, 2nd, and 3rd Marine Air Wings flying as Naval flight officer in various night-fighter, intercept and electronic warfare aircraft. Served tours in Korea, Japan and other Asian bases launching electronic reconnaissance missions.

Awarded Silver Star, Distinguished Flying Cross, 13 Air Medals, Purple Heart and seven Battle Stars.

Retired with 100% service-connected disability April 1, 1966. Added degrees in Communications; specialized in free-lance investigative journalism. Currently writing a WWII European Air War Book titled *Ultimate Challenges*.

ALBERT H. DEBACKER, SR., 1st Lt., was born Oct. 18, 1920 in Topeka, KS. Joined Army Air Corps May 28, 1942. Pilot training at Gulf Coast Training Command. Operational training P-51 Hillsborough, FL. Flew 46 missions in E.T.O., 8th A.F., in P-51s. Mostly long range bomber escort and strafing.

Shot down while strafing Aug. 1, 1944. Suffered severe head injury and knee injury. Had temporary amnesia with no recollection of the events of that day until he recovered consciousness at about 3 o'clock in the afternoon in a French farmyard.

Made contact with Maquis. Was moved from place-to-place by them and crossed American lines in about two-and-a-half weeks.

Awarded Distinguished Flying Cross and Air Medal with Clusters.

Now retired after spending 37 years in the printing trade. Married Betty Sommers Oct. 9, 1943. They have six sons and one daughter.

FREDERICK DeMATTEIS, 1st Lt., was born April 24, 1923 in Brooklyn, NY. Joined the service Feb. 3, 1943. Trained at Texas A&M University, pre-flight at Ellington Field, TX, gunnery at Laredo, TX and bombardier at Midland, TX. Flew B-24s, 15th A.F., 464th BG, 778th Bomb Sqdn.

Was shot up by flak upon returning from a bombing mission to Regenburg, Germany and crash landed in the Po Valley of northern Italy Feb. 5, 1945. Picked up immediately by the Italian Partisans and hid throughout the area for 59 days. On day after Easter, 1945, a C-47 with fighter escort picked up crew and returned them to Bari, Italy. Sent home to U.S.A. two weeks after return to southern Italy.

Returned to Midland, TX for bombardiers instructor training, then on to Langley Field, VA as an instructor until discharged Oct. 12, 1945.

Received Purple Heart, Good Conduct Medal and Presidential Unit Citation with three Clusters.

Currently Chairman of the Board, DeMatteis Organizations, builders/developers, in Uniondale, NY.

Married to Nancy Marconi on Jan. 5, 1947 and has four children and six grandchildren. Lives in Old Westbury, NY.

CURTIS DILES,
was born July 15, 1925 in Portsmouth, OH. Inducted Sept. 10, 1943, Ft. Thomas, at Covington, KY. Completed basic training at Amarillo A.A.F. base Dec. 10, 1943, air-to-air gunnery at Harlingen, TX March 15, 1944 and combat crew training at Davis Monthan, A.A.F. base at Tuscon, AZ.

Boarded USS troop ship, *Santa Rosa*, June 30, 1944 for E.T.O. Debarked Naples, Italy July 15, 1944 and assigned to 15th A.A.F., 455th BG, 740th Sqdn. Completed first bombing mission at Bucharest Aug. 31, 1944.

Shot down Sept. 8, 1944 over German occupied territory, Belgrade, Yugoslavia. Protected by Serbian (Chetnic) soldiers under the command of Gen. Draza Mihailovich. Spent nine days hiding and running to avoid becoming P.O.W.

Picked up Sept. 17, 1944 by "Air Rescue" C-47 with P-51 fighter cover and returned to base. Last bombing mission was Jan. 8, 1944, Linz, Austria. Tour completed. Flew waist and nose gunner positions.

Returned to U.S. March 15, 1945. Assigned to San Antonio Aviation Cadet Center for pre-flight training. Sept. 2, 1945, end of war, pilot training program ended. Separated from service Oct. 10, 1945, rank of staff sergeant, at Wright Field, Dayton, OH.

Awarded Purple Heart and Air Medal with three Oak Leaf Clusters.   Married Inez L. Pruitt Sept. 25, 1948. Has one son, three daughters and eight grandchildren. Employed 1946-73 by NAPA engine rebuilder and 1974-89 at Dayton, OH manufacturing laser gaging systems. Retired Sept. 30, 1989.

Enjoy gardening, travel, computers and the study of WWII Air War.

JOSEPH R. DIXEY,
Col. (ret.), was born March 28, 1922 in Philadelphia, PA. Joined the military March 15, 1942. Took pilot training,

Southeast training command and graduated class 43-D. Joined 8th A.F., 351st BG (B-17) December 1943.

Shot down June 14, 1944 over Le Bourget, France on 24th mission. Worked and lived with French Freedom Fighters until late August 1944. Returned to England when American ground forces reached Paris.

Left military service November 1945. Flew with Reserve unit until recalled in March 1951. Flew Airlift (C-97) during Korean War and served one year in Vietnam flying gunships and Fac's.

Had two years in air weather service flying B-29s on weather and typhoon reconnaissance. Spent 21 years in SAC and accumulated over 10,000 hours while flying B-36, B-47, B-52 and KC-135. Retired Aug. 31, 1975.

Married Jane O'Neill Sept. 30, 1944 and has four children and ten grandchildren. Oldest son Col. U.S.A. (ret.). Son-in-law is captain in U.S.N. still on active duty.

Currently living in Satellite Beach, FL.

IRA JAMES (TOM) DOBBIE,
was born March 9, 1925 in Washington, D.C. Joined the Army March 1943.

Took basic training in Greensboro, NC, Air Student, University of Pittsburgh, Armament School, Denver, CO, gunnery, Laredo, TX, overseas training Dyersburg, TN, where he joined the crew. Shipped to Lincoln, NB and was given a brand new B-17G. Flew the B-17 to Steparoni, Italy. Served as right waist gunner on the *Bachelor's Baby* 483rd BG, 840th Bomb Sqdn., 15th U.S.A.A.F.

On mission nine, forced to parachute into Yugoslavia Dec. 28, 1944. With help of Partisan Forces, escaped and evaded to return to Italy. Three months later, on mission 23, crash landed in Austria. Was a P.O.W. in hospital at Veldon, Austria until liberated at the end of the war. Grade of S/Sgt.

Following discharge, returned to Pittsburgh, PA to complete education. Met Jeanne Birdsong at Pitt in 1946, married in 1949. Joined Capital Airlines, later to merge with United Airlines, in 1952. Retired from United Airlines in 1982. He has two daughters, three sons and nine grandchildren.

HARRY A. DOLPH,
of Pasadena, TX, was in the 8th A.F., 786th BS, 466th BG. Staff Sergeant Dolph enlisted in the Air Corps using the alias Harry A. Clark, (for reasons explained in his book, *Evadee*). He bailed out at 25,200 ft. over Havelte, Holland and free fell for 35 seconds. While in his chute he was attacked by a German Me109. His MIA date was Aug. 15, 1944. He was wounded but recovered. Some of the parachute shroud lines were cut away and the chute was full of holes. Wounded, he was removed from the woods by

Pieter van den Hurk and two others on bicycles, then taken to the town of Meppel, where he recovered at the de Grote home nursed by Mimi (then de Jong, Pieter's fiancee). During the time of his stay in Holland he participated in the Resistance activities receiving air drops of weapons, explosives, etc. Then, he instructed in weapons and explosives use, and participated in Resistance actions. For several months there was a S/Sgt. James Molton of Albany, Oregon with him.

They had a harrowing experience on the island of Engelsmanplatt while waiting to be picked up by submarine. Finally they had to return, walking through the North Sea for four kilometers, often in water over their heads. He almost drowned. Most of the time during his evasion was spent in the province of Friesland. He was liberated by a force of Royal Canadian Dragoons, given rifle and participated in their advance, including being allowed to assist in the use of the howitzer to destroy a German armored column. They remained with the Canadians for four days until they were able to provide a jeep to enable him to make his way to Allied hands in Brussels (British) and then to Namur, where he reported to U.S. Forces for the first time. His free date was April 15, 1945. He finally arrived at Camp Lucky Strike in Le Havre, France and sailed for home on the S.S. George Washington about May 5, 1945, arriving U.S.A. on May 15, 1945 to return home. He wrote a book, *The Evader*, about his experience.

JAMES N. DOWDELL,
Lt. Col. (ret.), was born Aug. 6, 1919 in Johnstown, PA. Entered U.S. Army Air Corps Oct. 2, 1941.

Was bombardier/navigator on A-20 bombing mission (daylight and night intruder) from air bases in Italy, Corsica and France with 86th Sqdn., 47th BG of 12th A.F.

Shot down on 27th mission over northern Italy on Nov. 12, 1944, while participating in single aircraft mission to destroy German bridge across Po River. Parachuted, and evaded along with S/Sgts. Boward and Schultz. Received Purple Heart.

Remained with Air Force as career officer with service as navigator on A/B-26 and other aircraft.

Retired in 1965 in grade of lieutenant colonel (physical disability).

Married Marguerite Lydia Roux (Lt. Col. U.S.A.F. ret.), on Feb. 13, 1960 at Braintree, Sussex, England.

WILLIAM W. (BILL) DRISKO, was born in Bartlesville, OK March 15, 1925. Joined Aviation Cadets in March 1943. Received Pilot's Wings Jan. 7, 1944. P-51 training at Bartow, FL. Arrived in England at Bodney Airdrome on June 5, 1944. Assigned to 487th Fighter Sqdn., 352nd FG. Flew escort and strafing missions until June 25.

Got in front of an Me109 that shot off the right wing so bailed out. Had some difficulty getting out of plane with only half of a wing. Picked up by French Underground and hid from Germans until September. Liberated in Paris.

Assigned in States to various fighter units flying P-51, P-40, L-5, B-25, T-6 and BT-13s.

Relieved from active duty October 1945. Graduated from Oklahoma State University Jan. 1949. Worked for Phillips Petroleum Co. in sales and was recalled to Korean Conflict at Great Falls, MT, flying C-54. Sent to Korea December 1951, staying until December 1952, flying C-47, T-6, and C-54. Relieved from active duty in December 1952. Returned to Phillips Petroleum Co. for 21 years. Worked as special accounts supervisor for Echrich Meats Co. for eight years.

Retired in 1987. Stayed in A.F. Reserves 20 years. Retired as major in March 1970. Retired for pay March 15, 1985.

Married with three sons and two grandchildren.

WILLIAM C. DuBOSE, was born March 27, 1924 in San Francisco, CA. Joined Army Air Force in November 1942 and was stationed at many bases and locations. Was P-38 pilot. Achieved rank of first lieutenant.

Received Air Medal, Purple Heart and E.T.O. Ribbon.

Married to Deanna. Children: David, Desiree, Steve and Ken.

Planned to retire in November 1991 after 36 years with 3M in sales and marketing of aerospace products.

BOB EIDENMILLER, was born Feb. 8, 1924 in Hopedale, IL. Entered Army Air Corps March 20, 1943. Took basic training at Clearwater, FL, radio school at Scott Field, IL, gunnery at Harlingen, TX and phase training at Tonopah, NV.

He was a B-24 tail gunner on a replacement crew in the 456th BG near Cerignola, Italy. The crew crash landed Aug. 27, 1944 after a Blechammer, Germany raid and bailed out over central Yugoslavia Dec. 2, 1944, following a second trip to Blechammer.

Yugoslav Partisans provided escort to the British mission near Split, Vis Island, and then to 15th A.A.F. Headquarters at Bari, Italy.

Eidenmiller has been in agriculture since service discharge and is still an active farmer. He married Ramona Fitzpatrick Aug. 1, 1949.

Has worked ten years in the Adult Education Center at a local junior college in the G.E.D. and literacy programs as a volunteer.

FRANK W. ENROUGHTY, was born Dec. 15, 1918 in Henrico County, VA. The 29th Inf. Div. activated Feb. 3, 1941, Ft. Meade, NY. O.C.S. August 1942, commissioned December 1942. Assigned to 26th Inf. Div. Charleston, SC. Transferred to Air Corp in 1943. Pilot training in grade, Albany, GA; Greenwood, MS, class of 44D. Flew to England in August 1944, assigned to 452dn BG, 730th Sqdn. Flew 17 missions. Shot down on the 18th mission over the target March 21, 1945.

Returned to States in May 1945 and on June 1, 1945 he married Rebecca Allen. They have two boys and three grandchildren and live near Richmond, VA.

Worked for the Virginia A.B.C. Enforcement Div. for 37 years and retired in 1983 as assistant director of enforcement. During the 37 years he flew a Super Cub looking for illegal distilleries. He now farms part time.

Awarded Air Medal and Purple Heart. He retired from the A.F.R. a major.

JERRY ESHUIS, was born March 4, 1922 in Ireton, IA. Joined the military Sept. 8, 1942. Served in the European and Sout Pacific theaters, rank staff sergeant, 8th Air Force with 95th H-BG, 336th Sqdn. as ball turret gunner on B-17.

Bailed out over occupied France on Dec. 30, 1943, 17th mission, on mission to Ludwigshafen, Germany. Wounded but evaded capture.

Returned to service February 1944 and flew 21 missions (April 1945-Oct. 1945), as tail gunner on B-29 with 20th A.F. in South Pacific. Retired from service in October of 1945.

Dairy farmer until 1974. Parts manager for farm implement company from 1974-88. Retired

and resides with wife Alberta in Lynden, WA. Three married children: Carol, Cliff and Cynthia.

JAMES C. ESTEP, JR., was born Feb. 29, 1924 in Coal Grove, OH. Inducted Jan. 12, 1943. Basic training in Miami Beach, FL, A&E school Amarillo, TX, gunnery school Kingman, AZ, crew assignment Salt Lake City, UT. Overseas training Pyote, TX, North to England January 1944, 381st BG, 532nd Sqdn. Missions March 4, 6, 8, 1944.

Shot down over Holland and evaded to Liege Belgium. Captured May 27, 1944. Sent to Stalag Luft IV. Marched across Germany. Liberated by U.S. April 27, 1945. Discharged Nov. 2, 1945.

Spent six years in Ohio Air National Guard. Attained rank of master sergeant. Worked at U.S.A.F.B. 28 years.

Married his school sweetheart 45 years. One daughter, one son and four grandchildren.

IVAN WAYNE EVELAND, was born May 18, 1916 in Missoula, MT. Private (Reserve) 1936 and Flying Cadet 1939. Commissioned May 1940 at Kelly Field.

Pre-war service: Barksdale, Ft. Benning, and Manchester, NH. November 1941 accepted captaincy Pan American Airways, Africa. Flew jungle routes (Bathhurst to Lagos) and interior routes (Accra, Khartoum to Cairo) until July 1942, except for temporary loan to 10th A.F. in India to evacuate Burma and pioneer the Hump route to China.

Assigned B-17s July 1942. Became squadron commander at Ainsworth, NB January 1943. Appointed commander 614th Sqdn., 401st BG April 1943.

Shot down over France December 1943. Escaped to Spain over Pyrenees after evading capture (about three months).

Released from active duty 1946. Formed 9095th Volunteer Reserve Group in Montana and became CO thereof. Promoted to colonel 1950.

Citations: B.S.M. (with "V"), Purple Heart, Air Medal.

Became insurance agent, member Million Dollar Round Table, served as president of Montana Life Underwriters.

Married Dawn Farrar in 1942, widowed 1970. Married Lois Barnett in 1974; daughter Nicole Eveland Keller, (step-son) Charles E. Barnett. Enjoy fishing, reading and writing. Live in Helena, MT.

EUGENE E. FARROW, was born Feb. 12, 1919 in Winnebago, WI. Enlisted and entered the Army Air Corp Dec. 18, 1941. Went to A.M. school in Newark, NJ and Buffalo, NY. Assigned to 16th Sqdn., 27th BG (L) in Hattiesburg, MS on A-20s as ground crew. Entered gunnery school in Harlingen, TX and finally was attached to the 463rd BG (H), 772nd Sqdn. on B-17s at McDill

Field, FL. Flew from Florida to Trinidad then Brazil across the Atlantic to Africa, to Marrakech to Tunisia and then to the base in Foggio, Italy.

As top turret engineer gunner, he flew 20 missions and was shot down over Weiner-Newstadt May 10, 1944. Seven of the crew were captured and spent the remainder of the war as P.O.W.s. The pilot, Jim Lackey, co-pilot, Joe Luckey and Farrow were picked up by Marshal Tito's Partisans. They moved southward, a lot of it at night, and about three months later they arrived at a small field where an English Dakota (DC-3) picked them up and ferried them back to Italy.

He retired in 1977 after over 30 years as a small town postmaster. He and his wife Marjorie have six children, eleven grandchildren and still live in Winnebago, WI.

Farrow is a volunteer docent at the E.A.A. Museum in Oshkosh, WI. This museum has a new addition called the Eagle Hangar. It is a collection of WWII aircraft and artifacts.

RICHARD J. FAULKNER, was born Oct. 8, 1924. Enlisted in Air Corps Dec. 11, 1942. Airplane and engine school Seymour Johnson, NC, went to Fort Meyers for gunnery school then joined Paul Martin crew at Pyote, TX. Assigned as ball turret gunner on B-17 with 8th A.F., 100th BG, 350th Sqdn. March 9, 1944.

On first mission over France on March 18, 1944, was in a mid-air collision and plane broke in half. Faulkner bailed out of the ball turret and was the only survivor. Picked up by a farmer, hidden in a barn, then worked through the underground. April 16, 1944 was picked up off the coast of France by British M.O.T. boat, along with Ken Williams, a P-47 pilot. German E Boats spotted them and gave chase, shooting three holes in their boat and killing one gunner. Faulkner was asked to take his place. Then the British Spitfires came and chased the E Boats off, and he returned to England. Discharged from service Oct. 27, 1945.

Retired from New York State Electric & Gas Corp. in 1986.

Lives in Skaneateles with wife, Jane and has three children: Robert, Donald and Ann.

LEE FEGETTE, T./Sgt., was born July 30, 1918 in Oglesby, TX. Joined Army January 1941.

Took basic training at Camp Bowie, Brownwood, TX and transferred to Army Air Force in Scott Field, IL. Was attached to 303rd BG. Flew with 8th A.F., Molesworth, England, WWII. He was radio operator on B-17, *Wulfe Hound*.

Flew three missions over submarine pens and railroad yards and was shot down 60 miles southeast of Paris. Evaded through France and Spain and returned to England May 1943.

Sent back to Washington, D.C. on temporary

duty with the War Department. Requested to go back to England in 1944. Flew 30 more missions. Discharged in San Antonio, TX June 1945.

Retired from Texas Power & Light (now T. U. Electric) Aug. 1, 1983. He was married to Dorothy Hudgins on Sept. 6, 1947. Children: Gerald and Cerise. Currently resides in Dallas, TX.

LOUIS FEINGOLD, was born July 11, 1919 in Brooklyn, NY. Drafted January 1941 into the Infantry, transferred to the Air Corps, June 1942. Completed navigation training, Mather Field, Sacramento, CA, June 1943.

Flew 20 combat missions in B-17s in E.T.O. Shot down Dec. 30, 1943, 60 miles north of Paris. Was immediately aided by the French Underground who hid him and helped him escape along their Shelbourne Line. Arrived by boat in England, through Operation Bonaparte, on Feb. 27, 1944. Returned to U.S. and served as navigational instructor until discharge as a lieutenant.

Following discharge was self-employed as a garment contractor in New York where he remained until December 1990. He is now semi-retired. Married Leah in 1954; they have four children.

VICTOR J. (VIC) FERRARI, Col. (ret.) S.N.33057A, born Feb. 24, 1916. Enlisted as an Aviation Cadet Jan.12, 1942 at Maxwell A.F.B., AL. Education: Bloomsburg State, B.S., University of Southern California, M.S.

Commissioned second lieutenant Big Springs A.A.F.B.S. class 43-1. Navigation training, Hondo

U.S.A.A.F. NS 43-7. Navigator crew member 392nd BG 578 Sqdn., 8th A.F.

Shot down over Holland Nov. 13, 1943, returning from mission to Bremen. Aided by Dutch-Paris Underground. Returned to London May 1944. Reassigned to navigation schools at Monroe, LA and Ellington, A.F.B., TX.

Remained on active duty 30 year tour. Retired August 1971. Duty at Mather A.F.B., Saudi Arabia, assistant to the dean to U.S.A.F. Academy, A.F.R.O.T.C., Notre Dame U. Vice commandant AFIT.

Second career with U.S.A.A., San Antonio, TX. Retired June 1988. Assignments: chief of staff, president U.S.A.A. Federal Savings Bank. Now a consultant to U.S.A.A., Educational Affairs.

Decorations: Air Medal, Presidential Unit Citation, Legion of Merit.

CHARLES A. FISHER, was born July 11, 1922 in Conemaugh, PA. Joined Air Force Jan. 12, 1942. Discharged rank of technical sergeant Oct. 31, 1945. Basic training Jefferson Barracks, MO; airplane mechanic school, Chanute Field, IL; bell aircraft specialist school, Niagara Falls, NY; aerial gunnery training Las Vegas, NV.

Assigned to B-17 crew as engineer gunner at Walla Walla, WA. Served in combat with 384th BG, 544th Sqdn. Stationed at Grafton-Underwood, England.

Returning from third mission on Sept. 6, 1943, target Stuttgart, Germany, Fisher's plane crash landed 50 miles northeast of Paris. Frenchmen hid him and Jim Wagner, ball turret gunner, in a haystack for four days until the French Underground could be contacted. The French Underground smuggled them into Paris, to southern France, over the Pyrenees through Andorra to Seo De Urgel, Spain.

After return to U.S.A., assigned to overseas training unit, Gulfport, MS. Married Norene Olson June 22, 1945, has two sons, Alan and Robert. Retired after 35 years with Bell of Pennsylvania. Resides in Jeannette, PA and spends winter months in Lake Placid, FL.

RICHARD M. FORTNER, was born July 6, 1923 in Keystone, OK.

Joined U.S. Air Corps July 18, 1941. Member of 97th BG, 414th BS, 15th A.F. Stationed at Jefferson Bks., MO, Lowry A.B., CO, McCarran A.B., NV, Alexandria, LA, Amendola, Italy. Achieved rank of master sergeant.

Bailed out over Albania after 13 missions. Escaped capture for two weeks. Completed 30 missions. Retired from Air Force 1964 with 21 years service.

Graduated Belmont College, Nashville, TN in 1971.

Awarded Purple Heart, Air Medal with two Clusters.

Married Edna Waline Edwards (died in 1990). Has two sons in Washington and Massachusetts.

Retired as Baptist minister and prison counselor 1988. Moving to Soldiers' Airmen's Home, Washington, D.C.

PAUL E. GARDINER, Col. (ret.), was born in Cherokee, OK on May 24, 1918. Attended Southwestern State College in Weatherford and the University of Oklahoma in Norman, graduating from there in January 1941. Joining Aviation Cadet Class 41-I, he got his primary training at Tulare, basic at Taft and advanced at Stockton, all in California. Received his wings Dec. 11, 1941.

As a second lieutenant in the Army Air Corps, his first tactical assignment was with the 54th FG, stationed at Paine Field, WA and then at Harding Field, LA. Met Marie Louise Kroger in 1942 and married her in Tampa, FL that December, after being transferred to the 20th FG, Spartanburg, SC and the 337th Replacement Training Unit, Sarasota, FL.

Became group operations officer when the 405th FG was activated in 1943 when the group moved to Walterboro, SC. In January 1944, as one of the advance party of the 405th, flew his first combat mission with 56th FG at Boxted, England. Promoted to major and assigned as commander of the 509th Fighter Sqdn.

Major Gardiner was shot down June 18, 1944 by flak while leading his squadron in an attack on an ammunition dump near St. Lo, France. He bailed out of his burning P-47 at an estimated 400 ft. and survived the jump with only a dislocated shoulder, broken ribs and a leg wound.

After spending three days and nights hiding in a hedgerow, while Germans were searching for him, he slipped away very early the fourth morning and walked to a communal farm in La Sauvagre, near Cerisy la Salle, France, about seven kilometers south of the crash site. He stayed in the commune 40 days and nights and was helped by three French families and two refugees from Paris. Gardiner was given civilian clothes and hid in a hayloft for five weeks. He was able to escape

during the sixth week to an orchard and then an abandoned stone shack, surrounded by anti-aircraft artillery units and shelling. Carpet bombing by American forces finally brought liberation. The major went by jeep with an American captain and sergeant to the Advance CP of the First Army Armored Combat Command. The column was attacked by two Ju-88s at dusk. Six weeks of evasion ended for Gardiner July 31st.

Colonel Gardiner and his wife have three sons, one daughter and two grandchildren.

President, Select Enterprises, Inc.; Director Vision Products, Inc.; vice president for marketing, Spectrum Sound, Inc.; assist. manager; Oklahoma Abstract Co.; jr. executive trainee, Oklahoma Natural Gas Corp; bookkeeper, Farmers Cooperative; county engineer assist.; chairman, East Holiday Park Homeowners Coop. and Crime Prevention Com., Albuquerque Chamber of Commerce; candidate for county commissioner and city councillor.

He received two Legions of Merit, Distinguished Flying Cross, eight Air Medals, Purple Heart, Presidential Unit Citation, Army-Air Force Commendation Medal, Bronze Star, Turkish AF and Chinese Nationalist AF Commendation Medal, VNAF Flying Cross.

OLIN E. GILBERT, was born July 4, 1918 in Collinsville, IL. Joined Army Air Corps, second lieutenant, April 15, 1941. As a career pilot, his service schools include Command and Staff College, A.F. School of Applied Tactics, R.A.F. fighter leader school, air tac school, A.F.F.S. jet fighter course, Armed Forces Staff College, VA, Air War College. He was promoted to colonel in December 1951.

Gilbert flew 118 missions, 424 combat hours in the P-47 and P-51. Among his commands were: 83rd Fighter Sqdn., 78th FG; director of fighters 8th Air Force; base commander and commander 327th FG, Traux, WI, commander 355th Tactical Fighter Wing, George, CA; commander 835th Air Div. McConnell, KS, flying F-105.

Medals awarded are the Silver Star, Legion of Merit, Distinguished Flying Cross with two Oak Leaf Clusters, Air Medal with eight Oak Leaf Clusters, Purple Heart, Army Commendation Medal, A.F.L.S.A. with six Oak Leaf Clusters.

Married Anne Ford, Birmingham, AL, had two sons. Capt. Olin Gilbert, Jr., Vietnam veteran, died in 1968 in an F-106. Gregory Gilbert is an attorney with four children.

Olin Gilbert retired as commander of the 552nd A.E.W.C. Wing (after serving in Vietnam and Thailand) on Nov. 30, 1969.

MARVIN THOMSON GOFF, was born in Angleton, TX on Nov. 2, 1918. Graduated from Angleton High School in 1937.

Enlisted Army Air Corps 1941. Basic training Randolph Field, TX. Aircraft mechanics school, Chanute Field, IL. Mechanic, Mather Field, CA. Accepted as Aviation Cadet. Pre-flight, Kelly Field, TX. Primary, Pine Bluff, AR. Basic, Waco, TX. Washed out pilot training. Married Ida L. Davis and had two children, two grandchildren, one great grandchild. Commissioned second lieutenant bombardier Midland, TX 1943.

Went to Clovis, NM for crew assignment. Assigned Clay Mellor crew and had training at Alamogordo, NM. Flew liberator to England via Natal, Dakar, and Marakesh.

Crew assigned to 713th Sqdn., 448th BG, Seething, England. Bailed out over northeast France on seventh mission, April 1, 1944. Five months with French underground. Picked up in August by advancing American Forces. Returned Midland, TX for navigation course. Attained rank of first lieutenant. Transferred Ellington Field, TX and discharged in late 1945.

Earned Doctor of Veterinary Medicine degree from Texas A&M in 1952 with a private practice in Houston, TX. Then Department of State Foreign Aid Program 1956-67. Served in Thailand, Yugoslavia, Republic of Mali (W. Africa) as advisor in livestock diseases and production. With U.S. Dept. of Agriculture 1967-80. Served as laboratory virologist, laboratory director, Ames, IA. Served as Assoc. Administrator for Veterinary Services, Washington, D.C. Retired to Angleton, TX 1980.

MILTON M. GOLDFEDER, was born Aug. 16, 1921 in Brooklyn, NY. Took bombardier training at Victorville, CA. Graduated Oct. 23, 1943. Received additional training at Dalhart, TX with the crew piloted by Capt. Joseph W. Lincoln.

Assigned to Chelveston, England with the 366th Sqdn., 305th BG, 8th A.A.F. Flew four missions; shot out of formation over Oberpfaffenhopen, Germany. Crashed near Leuze, France and evaded capture. Was passed through the Ardens with the French Underground until liberated in early September.

Returned and assigned as an instructor in Victorville, CA and then at Las Vegas, NV. Dis charged as a first lieutenant at Fort Dix, NJ Sept. 15, 1945.

He and his wife, Adele, married in 1945, have three children: Janet, Gene, and Carol and grandchildren. They currently reside in Bethlehem, PA where he is a C.P.A.

WALTER G. GRAF,

WALTER G. GRAF, was born Feb. 17, 1920 in Philadelphia, PA. Graduated Franklin and Marshall College, Lancaster PA. Received his wings at Moore Field, Mission, TX in the class of 44F and P-47 Thunderbolt. Operational training at Abilene, TX. Assigned to the 27th FG, 523rd Fighter Sqdn., 12th Tactical Air Command at Pontedera, Italy in the winter of 1944-45. The 27th was transferred to St. Dizier, France, in February of 1945 to supply tactical air support to the Seventh Army on the drive for the Rhine.

On March 20, 1945, "Coalbox" Red Flight of four Thunderbolts looking for targets of opportunity crossed Speyerdorf, the main Luftwaffe field in the German Palatinate at tree-top level. All four Jugs caught heavy flak and Graf bailed out at minimum altitude when his plane caught fire and exploded. After hiding in the mountains the rest of the day, he walked in a westerly direction at night hoping to make it to France. On the second night he was captured by Wehrmacht artillerymen and taken to German headquarters.

After an unsuccessful attempt at interrogation he was sent en route to a prison camp somewhere deep in Germany. The car in which he and his captors were traveling was caught by American artillery fire and destroyed. Proceeding on foot for two more days, Graf, who could speak German, became acquainted with his guards. On the second night he lured one of the guards aside, clobbered him and took off. He was successful in getting through to the 100th Infantry Div. of the American Seventh Army which had just cracked the Siegfried Line in the area. After a hot meal and some medical attention for a wounded leg, he was returned to base by an Infantry L5. From there he was returned to the States on Project "R".

Today he is employed by the County of Montgomery, PA as chief administrator of farm and forest land to the Board of Assessment. He lives in Fort Washington with his wife Irene. He has one daughter, two sons and three grandchildren.

ROBERT Z. GRIMES,

ROBERT Z. GRIMES, Col. (ret.), was born Nov. 24, 1922 in Portsmouth, VA. Joined the Army Air Corps as an Aviation Cadet March 11, 1942. Took pilot training at Montgomery, AL; Jackson, TN; Greenville, MS; graduating at Blytheville, AR in February 1943.

He flew B-17s and B-24s in WWII and was assigned as first pilot with his crew to the 96th BG in England. He was shot down on his fifth mission

in October 1943 on a raid to Germany and although wounded, managed to parachute into Belgium, where he was helped by friendly Belgians. He managed to evade through France and Spain, returning to England in January 1944.

After the war he was integrated into the Regular Army and then the Regular Air Force when it was formed in 1947. He served as a pilot on the Berlin Airlift in 1949, and served additional tours in Europe in 1951-54 and 1964-67 with the European Command Headquarters and in Vietnam. Assigned to the Joint Chiefs of Staff from 1967-71. Retired in 1972 after 30 years of military service.

Received a B.S. from the University of Maryland and an M.A. in Business from George Washington University. Military schooling included the Air Tactical School, the Command and General Staff College and the Industrial College of the Armed Forces.

Decorations include: Legion of Merit, Meritorious Service Medal, Joint Service Commendation Medal, Air Force Commendation Medal, the Air Medal, Purple Heart and the Berlin Airlift Medal.

After military retirement, he worked as a management consultant and as associate superintendent of schools in the Washington, D.C. area.

Married to the former Mary Helen Moore of Blytheville, AR. They have three daughters, Dale Lee, Mary Susan and Jennifer and two grandsons. The Grimes reside in Fairfax, VA where they have been active in local civic activities.

JOE GROSS,

JOE GROSS, was born Jan. 25, 1922 in Philadelphia, PA. Enlisted military Nov. 7, 1942.

Jan. 5, 1944, T/Sgt. MOS 757 (radio operator gunner) on *Little Girl II* of the 96th BG, 339th Bomb Sqdn. was hit by flak over the target (Bordeaux France aircraft factory) and hit by fighters off the target. Only two planes in the group remained just below Brest on the return. They were losing altitude fast at 4000 ft. and turned inland. They said goodbye and tossed out all guns and cargo, over the Atlantic and turned inland, losing altitude.

Capt. Don Cole, the pilot, ordered everyone out east of Royan. He was wounded and never bailed out. Gross saw the plane go down while in

his chute. Four of the crew were captured and the ball turret gunner, Harold Thorne was wounded. They were joined together by the Maquis (Thomas Scott co-pilot, James Bradley bombardier, Clarence (Bud) Norton gunner and Gross), within two weeks. They lived in a private house in Charente Marantine, helped by the family and Maquis. They were in a room on the second floor in Royan overlooking the main street. Germans billeted in the same house.

In July 1944 they were united with British special commandos to stop the Germans from going north to fight the American troops. They dropped supplies at night via an aircraft dropping out of a British bomber group; Jeeps, bazookas, sten guns, enfields, RDX, grenades, ammo, gasoline, medical supplies, food, etc. They would listen to BBC and wait for the code wording as to when the drop would be made to a designated area with a code they would flash by searchlight to the plane. Some of the British commandos were John Sindoni, Stephenson, Bill Jacobs, (Scotty) Armitage from Scotland, M. Smith, an Englishman, an Irishman named Patty and a few others, mostly English. It seems there were more originally but they had gotten shot up pretty badly.

They proceeded to blow up troop trains and tracks and used the bazookas to stop German troops. They had some skirmishes with German troops who found them in the hills and lost one of their three Jeeps during one of the skirmishes. They buried drums of gasoline and made maps to locate them if they needed them. An American C-47 came in one night and lifted them out. They had come in with Free French Fighters and they turned over their equipment to them. On board the plane was a photographer in an enlisted mans naval uniform. They never saw the pictures he took of them, Aug. 10, 1944.

Discharged Nov. 5, 1945. Now lives in Cherry Hill, NJ.

KENNETH L. HAINES,

KENNETH L. HAINES, Capt., was born March 29, 1920 in Coleman, MI. Joined U.S. Army Air Corps on March 30, 1942. Received navigation training at Hondo, TX; combat training Pyote, TX and Dyersburg, TN. Flew in B-17 with 388th BG, 8th A.F., Knettishall, England, WWII.

Bailed out over Holland Nov. 5, 1943 and was captured by Germans. Escaped after three days. Recaptured 12 hours later, ending up in Stalag Luft I. He was court martialed for beating up guard during escape and was sentenced to 18 months in fortress prison in East Prussia. After being marched away from advancing Russians, was liberated and returned to Allied control May 7, 1945. Released from active duty Dec. 31, 1946.

Retired from the State of Michigan in 1980. He and his wife, June, reside at Roscommon,

MI. They have one son, Bruce, and three grand-daughters: Lisa, Jill and Hilary.

LOUIS L. HALTOM, was born June 14, 1919 in Nacogdoches, TX. Joined the military Sept. 8, 1940 and achieved the rank of lieutenant colonel, U.S.A.F.

Education: College, 1938-40 Stephen F. Austin University (Business Admin.), Nacogdoches, TX; Texas Christian University 1951 (Public Law), Fort Worth, TX; Landman's Assn., 1961 (Minerals Laws), Wichita, KS. Military schools: (1940-41) Air Corps training command, primary basic and advance single engine pilot training, Sebring, FL; (1943) B-29, first pilot check-out training, AMC, Midwestern Procurement Command, Wichita, KS; (1945) single engine jet pilot and maintenance training, San Bernardino, CA, U.S. Army; (1947) food service supervision course, San Francisco, CA; (1951) U.S.A.F. Air University, Craig A.F.B. Selma, AL, personnel management; (1951) U.S.A.F. Strategic Air Command 7th BG, Fort Worth, TX, B-36 (10 engine) first pilot check-out training; (1953) U.S.A.F. Air University, field grade, Command and Staff School; (1958) U.S.A.F. Strategic Air Command KC-135 four engine jet first pilot training; (1961) Petroleum Landman's Assn., Minerals Law, Wichita, KS; (1968) State Department, Internal Defense Course, Washington, D.C.; (1974) Treasury, Secret Service Police Academy, Washington, D.C.; (1978) Civil Service, management analysis course, Washington, D.C.; Dept. of Justice-1981, Freedom of Information/Privacy Act course.

Military experience: (1940-60) -1941-flight instructor, Randolph A.F.B., San Antonio, TX; 1942-43- B-17 aircraft commander, combat 8th A.F., England; 1943-44- B-29 service test pilot and operations officer; 1944-45 - B-29 aircraft commander and combat lead pilot, 20th Bomber Command, Saipan, combat tour; 1945-46 - chief of flight test, AMC San Bernardino, CA; 1946-48 service installations officer in charge of post exchange, service clubs, messes, theater, rest camp and post engineers, Muroc, CA; 1948-50 chief of flight test and operations, Alaska Air Depot, Anchorage, AK; 1950-54 tactical operations and training inspector, inspector general, field maintenance squadron commander, chief of Combat Operations, 7th Bomb Wing SAC, Ft. Worth, TX; 1954-55 executive officer, B-26 BG, Laon, France; 1955-57 headquarters section commander, 12th Air Force Commandant, Ramstein, Germany; 1957-60 chief of Combat Operations, wing logistics officer, deputy for Material, 4123rd Strategic Wing, SAC, Clinton Sherman, OK.

Discharged Dec. 31, 1960.

Worked for the government 1966-71 in numerous assignments. Worked for Petroleum Landman, Wichita, KS 1961-66.

Married to Chi D. Haltom and have two sisters. Retired from Treasury Dept. Jan. 2, 1991. Manage my own properties and wife owns and operates a woman's fashion shop.

Honors and medals: Distinguished Flying Cross with two OLC, Air Medal with three OLC, Commendation Medal with OLC, Purple Heart, European-African Middle Eastern Campaign Medal with two Battle Stars, Asiatic-Pacific Campaign Medal with five Battle Stars, Air Defense Service Medal, American Campaign Medal, National Defense Medal, WWII Victory Medal, Air Force Reserve Medal with Cluster, Air Force Longevity with three OLC, Occupation Medal of Germany, Outstanding Unit Award, Presidential Unit Award with OLC, and Vietnam Civilian Medal.

CLIFFORD HAMMOCK, was born Feb. 21, 1923 in Pitts, GA. Joined Air Force June 10, 1942.

After basic training in Biloxi, MS went to gunnery school in Las Vegas, NV, armament school in Salt Lake City, UT, flight training in Tucson, AZ. Was assigned to 384th BG, 546th Sqdn. as a tail gunner on B-17, *Sad Sack II.*

On 11th mission Sept. 6, 1943, returning from a bombing raid over Stuttgart, Germany, we were hit and were running out of gas. Bailed out near Trie Chateau, France. Had rank of staff sergeant. Received Air Medal with Oak Leaf Cluster.

Was gunnery instructor in Gulf Port, MS until discharge Oct. 28, 1945.

Married Frances Bayard in 1947 in Columbus, GA. Moved to Pensacola, FL in 1951. Owned and operated auto repair business until retiring in February of 1985. We have three children.

JEREMIAH F. HAMMOND, was born Dec. 7, 1921 in Reform, AL. Inducted Aug. 7, 1942, pilot training (single engine) commissioned second lieutenant Nov. 3, 1943 at Eagle Pass, TX, R.T.U. in P-40s. Shipped to North Africa, to Italy and assigned to the 314th FS of 324th FG.

Shot down on 33rd mission. Evaded capture for six days. Returned to the Allied control. Flew 11 more missions and returned to U.S.A. Flew PT 19, BT-13-14-15, AT-6, P-39, P-40, P-47. Remained in the Reserves and retired Dec. 1, 1971 as a lieutenant colonel.

Worked 33 years for the state of Alabama as highway patrolman and investigator. Retired April 1, 1980 as an investigator supervisor.

Married Dec. 24, 1944. Wife, Myra, four children, three girls, one son, and six grandchildren. Resides in Mobile, AL.

Awarded Presidential Unit Citation, Purple Heart, Air Medal with OLC, Air Force Commendation Medal.

Life member A.F.E.E.S.

ALBERT P. HALL, T/Sgt., was born Sept. 23, 1921. Joined the A.A.F. in June 1942. Flew 26 missions with 8th Air Force over Germany and France. Radio operator, B-24 liberator, 489th BG (H), 845th Sqdn., out of Halesworth, England.

Shot down over Munich on 26th mission. Made it to Switzerland. Escaped later through French Underground. Returned to U.S.A. and finished service as gunnery instructor.

Earned Distinguished Flying Cross and five Air Medals.

Worked as a salesman for Westinghouse Electric for 40 years. Retired Oct. 1, 1985.

RALPH HALL, was born May 8, 1920 in Dadeville, AL. Entered service Oct. 1, 1942. Discharged Sept. 18, 1945, Maxwell Field, Montgomery, AL, rank of technical sergeant.

Airplane mechanic, Biloxi, MS, Lockeed, Burbank, CA, gunner, Pyote, TX, Wendover, UT, B-17 flight training, Dyersburg, TN.

Arrived at Rougham, Bury St. Edmond, England with 94th BG, 331st Sqdn., B-17. Shot down on my seventh mission to Bordeaux, France. Evaded until last of August 1944. Arrived in U.S. on Italian liner, Oct. 12, 1944.

Married wife Bernice, July 3, 1941. Children: Beverly, Jerry, Ralph, Jr., Sara and seven grandchildren. Resides in Dadeville, AL.

GENE HANER, was born May 16, 1922 in Ann Arbor, MI. Joined military Oct. 2, 1942. Primary flight training, Ft. Stockton, TX, basic flight training, San Angelo, TX. Graduated Cadet Class 44-C Lubbock, TX.

Commissioned March 12, 1944 as first lieutenant. Was with 301st BG, 353rd Sqdn. Flight instructor, Ellington Field, TX, Italy, SD, NM.

Most memorable experience: flew war-weary B-17 from Italy to Florida, first time ever landed a plane in any state but Texas. Received Air Medal with five Oak Leaf Clusters.

Married 45 years, one daughter, one son and two grandchildren. Partially retired and spend winters in Florida. Resides the remainder of the year in Ann Arbor, MI.

MARINO HANNESSON, was born on Sept. 6, 1915 in Upham, ND. Joined the Army on July 1, 1942 and was assigned to the Army Air Corps. He took basic training and airplane mechanics at Wichita Falls, TX; factory school on B-26s in Baltimore, MD; gunnery school at Buckingham A.F.B., Fort Meyer, FL; overseas training at Barksdale Field, LA.

Left for overseas in June 1943 and flew the north route to England over Labrador, Greenland, Iceland and Scotland. Assigned to 452nd Sqdn., 322nd BG, the first mission was Oct. 8, 1943.

Was on 51st mission on May 7, 1944 when shot down by enemy aircraft. Bailed out and landed in the woods. Was helped by the Belgium Resistance and stayed with them until the U.S. 9th Army came.

Returned to England and was sent to the U.S. Spent the remainder of the time at Biloxi, MS as engine mechanics instructor. Discharged Sept. 5, 1945 as technical sergeant.

Married with two sons and one daughter. Retired as a farm laborer in 1977.

HOWARD M. HARRIS, was born July 28, 1918 in Port Byron, NY. Joined Army March 18, 1942. Changed to U.S. Army Air Corps, July 1942. Graduated April 1st Bombardier Class 43-5, San Angelo, TX. Completed crew training Dalhart, TX. Assigned to B-17s, 349th Sqdn. of 100th BG Norwich, England, Aug. 12, 1943.

Shot down Sept. 3, 1943 near Renault factory near Paris.

Third day was hidden by Vi Comtesse Henri de Sugny. From there Andre and Pauline LeFevre and daughter, Paulette, concealed him and crewmate, Alfred Zeoli for two-and-a-half months in their home in Juvisy, France.

Evaded from Paris to Spain with Alfred Zeoli. Spent 12 days in Spanish prison. Release obtained by the British. Arrived Gibraltar by convoy ship from Seville, Spain.

Graduated pilot training class 45-A Jan. 1, 1945 at La Junta, CO.

Recalled to Korean War 1951. Assigned to 5th Air Force K5.

Retired from Maislin Transport 1983.

Married Jeannette R. Burley Feb. 22, 1942. Children: Gregory H.; one grandson, Clayton M. Resides in Wolcott, NY.

WILLIAM C. HAWKINS, was born July 26, 1922 in Langdale, AL. Graduated from pilot training in S.E. training command in 1943. Married childhood sweetheart Phyllis Foster. Received operational training in P-51s at Bartow, FL and proceeded to England as a fighter pilot with the 4th FG of the 8th Air Force.

On a fighter sweep to the Bordeaux vicinity, encountered numerous FW-190s and lost the battle. Made it back as far as Brest before bailing out. Evaded capture and was hidden by many French families for four months before being smuggled back to England aboard a British boat leaving from Plouha via operations "Bonaparte".

Discharged in Oct. 1945 and returned to Langdale, AL. Graduated from Auburn University as a mechanical engineer and worked with Shell Oil Co. in Houston, TX.

Recalled to active duty when the Korean War broke out. Flew missions as a fighter pilot in Korea and later in Vietnam.

Retired from the Air Force as a lieutenant colonel in 1971 and now lives in Costa Mesa, CA.

ROBERT W. HAWKINSON, Capt., was born Jan. 12, 1920 in Chicago, IL. Was Aviation Cadet March 28, 1942. Discharged Oct. 25, 1945.

Pilot training, Gulf Coast training command. Operational training (P-47) 1st Air Force, Republic Field, Farmingdale, Long Island, NY.

Flew 81 combat missions in E.T.O. in P-47s and P-51s, dive bombing, strafing and bomber escort. Shot down near Rouen, France while strafing on 81st mission. Evaded capture and hidden by French family until area overrun by Allied ground forces.

Following discharge completed schooling and began business career as an engineer with Belden

Corp., Chicago. Rose through ranks to president and C.E.O. Retired after 36 years service with company.

Married Janet Barbara Ristow Dec. 16, 1944. Have three children and seven grandchildren. Resides in Glen Ellyn, IL.

Currently owns and flies a 1941 Stearman open cockpit biplane used as primary trainer in WWII.

WILLIAM B. HAYES, was born Dec. 15, 1917 in Lakewood, OH. Joined U.S. Army Air Corps Oct. 1939. Went to six months communications school at Scott Air Force Base, IL. Was at Pope Field (Fort Bragg), NC on Dec. 7, 1941 and started flying anti-submarine patrol as radio operator in a P-47, over the Atlantic on Dec. 8, 1941.

Sent to India and on to China to serve with Gen. Chennault's American Volunteer Grp. (AVG), as a member of the "China Air Task Force", to learn the AVG un-orthodox methods of operations.

Served with various organizations as radio operator, forward observer, and with a special team selected by Gen. Chennault and headed by Capt. John Birch, as an operator of an intelligence radio station behind Japanese lines near the city of Changsha. During the biggest campaign ever launched by the Japanese in six years of war in China: code name: "ICHI GO", he volunteered to remain at his position, with three Chinese privates, to help move equipment and cook. He was the only American present.

Directed air strikes on Japanese targets and was under artillery, bombing and strafing attacks almost constantly. When the Chinese pulled out one night without notifying him he decided to wait until dark and blow up his equipment and leave, as the Japanese had already taken Hengyang some 200 miles to his south and our fighters and bombers were needed more urgently to defend Ling-ling and Kweilin.

He blew up his equipment and walked out. Moving mostly at night, it was necessary for him and his three Chinese soldiers to live off of the country and the rice they carried as the Chinese had followed a "Burnt Earth" policy. Rejoined his outfit at Kweilin.

Returned to the U.S. and married his wife, Julia. Children: William, Donald, and Edward. Grandchildren: Donald, William, Julia, Patrick, Heather, Charlie and Jon Paul.

Retired from the Air Force October 1965. Graduated from Arkansas State and taught high school physics until he retired from teaching in 1980. Resides in Fayetteville, AK.

LOUIS R. HEAD, M.D., was born April 8, 1924 in Madison, WI. Joined the U.S. Army Air Corps in October 1942. Was second lieutenant with 451st BG (H), 725th Sqdn., Castelliccio, Italy.

On March 16, 1945, B-24 was damaged in raid on synthetic oil refinery on Danube upstream from Vienna, Austria. Crew bailed out near Bittac, Yugoslavia. Evaded Germans in the area for five days before contacting Tito's Partisans and returning to Italy.

Received Air Medal.

Married Emily Dean Johnson on Sept. 15, 1951, seven children.

Stopped chest surgery at age 65, 1988. New career - Representative for the Joint Commission Accreditation Heathcare Organization.

H.L. HEAFNER, JR., was born Oct. 26, 1920 in Greenwood, MS. Inducted in Army Oct. 18, 1942 at Camp Shelby, MS. Discharged Oct. 31, 1945 at Barksdale Field, LA.

Took basic training in Miami Beach, FL; armament school at Lowery Field, Denver, CO; gunnery school at Tyndall Field, FL and Myrtle Beach, SC.

Joined Lt. Catner's crew formed in summer of 1943 in Boise, ID. Trained in B-24s in Casper, WY and Almogarda, NM as a staff sergeant. His ten-man crew were all good friends and had respect for each of the others and the six of us still living still do.

Their plane was named the *Play Boy*. T/Sgt. Pipes wrote a book about the crew called *Play Boy Crew 1944-45*. He was in the 466th BG, 8th Air Force.

Received the Air Medal with one Oak Leaf Cluster and the Purple Heart.

They made ten successful missions and were shot down on our 11th mission by FW 190s on the way back from Berlin on April 29, 1944. The tail gunner and top turret gunner shot down at least three and maybe more of the FW190s.

T/Sgt. Pipes and Heafner escaped and stayed together at various places in Holland until the night Feb. 27/28, 1945. That night they were raided on the farm of deBruin with four other Americans hiding there. They all escaped with most of their Dutch friends but he and Pipes were separated and he didn't see him again until the Canadians (Manitoba Dragons) liberated their section of Holland on April 5, 1945. They were in Paris for a while before coming back to good ole U.S.A.

Heafner got back to Camp Shelby, MS and left there on VE Day with a 60 day free furlough.

He married Mary Louise Thibodeaux on June 20, 1947. They live in Orlando, FL.

WALTER S. HERN, JR., was born June 15, 1921 in White Sulphur Springs, WV. Enlisted in the Army Air Corps July 9, 1940 and was sent to Ft. Slocum, NY for basic training, then to the Panama Canal Zone, France Field and assigned to the 6th BG. Since he was a HAM radio operator prior to service, he was assigned as an aircraft radio operator where he attained the rank of staff sergeant. He was one of 500 selected to attend the Army's West Point Prep School in the Canal Zone. He became one of four finalists competing for two academy openings. Since he came in third, he applied for the Aviation Cadet Program.

Hern went through SAACC in Texas, then to primary, class of 43K. He failed to pass and was assigned to the bombardier-Dr class 44-1. He was commissioned a second lieutenant in January 1944 and assigned to a B-24 crew. After phase training in Tonopah, NV, he was shipped to England and assigned to the 446th BG (Bungay Buckeroos).

On Aug. 26, 1944 his aircraft was badly hit and abandoned near Ossendrecht, Holland. He evaded capture with the help of the Dutch Underground until liberation by Allied troops in November 1944, when he was returned to the States.

After separation from service in September of 1945, he received a BBA degree with management major from the University of Houston, TX. He worked for Shell Oil Company until 1959 when he joined Beckman Instruments in California. He retired as a Beckman division controller in 1985.

He has been married for 47 years and has two grown children and one granddaughter. He and his wife have lived on a golf course in San Juan Capistrano, CA for the past 18 years.

JOHN F. HICKMAN, 1st/Lt., was born Nov. 8, 1917 in the Philippines. Family returned to NE Indiana in 1930. Drafted into Infantry in February 1941. Later accepted for Air Corps flight training, completed 1942. Assigned to 67th Tac. Recon. Grp. in 1943, transferred to England.

Shot down flying P-51 in western France,

May 1944, taken prisoner by Germans, escaped while being taken to Germany. Helped by French Underground to get to Switzerland in late May. In August hitched plane rides from southern France to England, rejoined 107th Sqdn. at Versailles, France, but was sent back to U.S. to training command.

Awarded Air Medal.

In 1985 the account of his caper was published by Ballantine Books, *For God, Country and the Hell of It*.

Earned an M.A. degree from Northwestern University; worked for U.S. Agency for International Development, retired in 1974.

First wife died in 1974. Remarried in 1979. Worked in Eastern Kentucky for Gateway Area Development District. Resides in Clearfield, KY.

HENRY J. HODULIK, was born July 25, 1922 in Irvington, NJ. Joined the military on Feb. 23, 1943 and served with the U.S. Army Air Force. Trained at Scott Field, IL; Las Vegas, NV Air Field; Barksdale Field, Shreveport, LA; and Savannah Air Field, Savannah, GA. Ended up as a radio/gunner on a B-26 Martin Marauder.

Crew flew own plane to England via South America, Ascension Island, North Africa. Flew with the 9th Air Force, 397th BG, 596th Bomb Sqdn.

Bailed out on mission over Normandy, France on May 8, 1944. First day escaping was difficult, "Jerries" everywhere, and he said it was only dumb luck that he evaded capture. Next day he got some help, and from that point on, the many wonderful French helpers kept him out of trouble and saved his life.

Eventually was reunited with his flight engineer through the French Helpers. They had many, many close calls and intrigue, and were liberated by the Canadian Forces Sept. 2, 1944.

Held rank of technical sergeant. Received Air Medal and Purple Heart.

Discharged on Nov. 3, 1945. Married Pauline "Kelly" Kelyman on Sept. 10, 1949. Has five children: Charles, Christine, Ann Marie, Andrew and Matthew and seven grandchildren. Retired in July 1987, and resides in Dunellen, NJ.

WILLIAM A. HOFFMAN III, Lt. Col. (ret.), was born Sept. 3, 1918 in Alexandria, VA. Joined Army Aviation Cadets May 10, 1942. After training at Monroe, LA, commissioned second lieutenant navigator and trained for combat at Kearney, NE. Assigned to 92nd BG, flew B-17s from Podington, England.

On Feb. 8, 1944, during sixth mission, the B-17 was shot down over northern France. Evaded through France to the Brittany coast with the French Resistance and was picked up by British motor gun boat 503 on the night of March 23rd and returned to England. Remained on active duty until Dec. 12, 1949.

After return to civilian status, worked for the Army Map Service as a geodesist retiring March 3, 1979.

Married Ann Bowen of Alexandria. Two children: Kathleen Cassidy and Kurt Hoffman. Four grandchildren: Sabrina, Jennifer and Ryan Cassidy and Keri Ann Hoffman. Presently resides in Palm Harbor, FL.

LAURIE S. HORNER, was born Feb. 26, 1924 in Deemston, PA. Joined Army Air Force April 26, 1943. Completed training courses including radio repair, aerial gunnery and advanced aerial gunnery instructors school. Flew with 8th Air Force, Lavenham, England, 838th BS, 487th BG, WWII.

Bailed out on 11th mission returning from raid on Magdeburg near Koblenz, Germany. Evaded capture crossing front lines into Belgium near St. Vith. Returned to U.S. via Paris, France and London, England.

Taught aerial gunnery Las Vegas, NV and Kingman, AZ Air Force bases until discharge Oct. 20, 1945.

Awards: Air Medal, European Theater, with four Battle Stars, American Theater, Victory and Good Conduct Medals.

Civilian occupation: architect and manager of construction, B.F. Goodrich Tire Co. Married Grace E. Metzler May 29, 1943. Children: Patricia and John. Grandchildren: Laurie, Amy, Stacie and Elizabeth. Retired in September of 1982. Resides in Akron, OH.

KENNETH N. HOUGARD, was born Oct. 21, 1922 in Portland, OR. Inducted Oct. 28, 1942 in Portland, OR. Trained at Fort Lewis, WA; Buckley Field, CO; Fresno, CA; Ephrata, WA; Rapid City, SD. Achieved rank of technical sergeant. Was a tail gunner, B-17 Fortress, 28 missions, 384th BG, 544th Bomb Sqdn, 8th Air Force, Graft Von Underwood, England.

Was shot down by flak, while bombing target on coast of Normandy, France. Six crew members were killed, three were taken prisoner and one evaded (Hougard).

Discharged at Ft. George Wright, Spokane, WA Sept. 16, 1945.

Worked for Union Pacific Railroad for 42 years. Retired Oct. 21, 1982 at the age of 60.

Also ran insurance agency for 20 years. Wife, Elizabeth Hougard. Resides in Portland, OR.

JOHN K. HURST, was born Sept. 20, 1919 in Anderson, TX. Aviation Cadet January 1942. Released in October 1945.

Navigator, 390th BG, 8th Air Force, Framlingham, England. Shot down on seventh bombing mission. Landed in Holland, spent Thanksgiving, 1943, in Brussels. Crossed the Pyrenees, was in the British Embassy in Madrid, New Years Day 1944.

Returned to the States, served in the Air Transport Command and later as an instructor training air crews in Dyersburg, TN.

Married Mary Palm in October 1946 and has four children.

President of Texwood Furniture Corp. in Austin, TX which sold in 1988. Now retired and resides in Austin, TX.

JACK ILFREY, was born July 31, 1920 in Houston, TX. Graduated from high school there and went to Texas A&M where he learned to fly in the first civilian pilot training program in 1939. Had secondary C.P.T.P. University of Houston, 1940, while working for the Hughes Tool Co. at night. Entered Army Air Corps as an Aviation Cadet April 1941. Graduated 1941 I Luke Field, AZ, first wartime class, Dec. 12, 1941. Assigned to the 94th Pursuit Sqdn., 1st Pursuit Grp., flying P-38 D and E's in defense of the southern California coast.

In late Spring 1942 the 1st Fighter Grp. was equipped with new P-38Fs and flew to Dow Field, ME to stage with the 97th BG in preparation for the Bolero Mission, first mass flight of fighter planes to England. All pilots awarded first 8th A.F. Air Medal (those who completed the trip).

On July 4, 1942, the 94th "Hat In The Ring" Ftr. Sqdn. took off on first leg of mission, Presque Isle ME to Goose Bay Labrador. July 6th Goose Bay to Bluie West I. Greenland. July 15th B.W.I. to Reykjavik, Iceland. Six of the 94th's P-38s and two B-17s, low on fuel went down on Greenland's

icecap. All crews were rescued but the eight aircraft are there to this day.

July 26th saw most of the 94th land at Kirton in Lindsey, Lincolnshire, England to be stationed with their Polish 303 Koscuisko Sqdn. On Sept. 1st, the 1st Ftr. Grp. made the first all American pilots and aircraft fighter sweep over northern France for the 8th A.F. Other missions followed.

On Nov. 15th, shortly out of Chivenor, in Lands End area on Operation Torch, the invasion of North Africa, Ilfrey lost a belly tank and had to land in Lisbon, Portugal. He was told he and the plane would be interned, but he conned the Portuguese out of some gas and made an unauthorized takeoff. By the time he got to Gibraltar an international incident had flared up and at the urging of the State Dept. Gen. Eisenhower wanted to send him back to Lisbon but Gen. Doolittle stepped in.

Awarded Commendation letter from chief of staff, U.S. Army, dated Feb. 3, 1943 for being one of the first aces in 12th A.F. Mediterranean Theater; 5th plane shot down day after Christmas 1942. Some historians say he was the first ace in a P-38.

After 208 combat hours, 72 missions, he was relieved from combat duty, returned to the States and instructed in P-38s and P-47s. Went back to E.T.O. in April 1944 and became squadron commadner of the 79th Ftr. Sqdn., 20th Ftr. Grp., flying P-38s. Credited with two Me109s near Berlin. One of the 109s collided with his P-38 and ripped out four-and-a-half to five ft. of his right wing, but he returned to England.

Shot down June 13th after successfully dive bombing a railway bridge over the Loire River near Angers while strafing a train. Evaded and was back in England in four days.

Busted to second lieutenant for infractions of rules, but was left in command of the 79th Sqdn. Probably was the only 2nd Lt. C.O. of a combat fighter sqdn. during the war until began promotional climb back.

After 70 missions, 320 hours of combat flying, he was reassigned to the States where he later became troop commander at McChord AFB. In two tours, he completed a total of 142 missions, 528 combat hours.

Decorations: Silver Star, D.F.C. with five OLC, and Air Medal with 12 OLC. Tally records: eight kills, all air. Presently a retired bank officer after 30 years Alamo Nat. Bank, San Antonio. Historian 20th Ftr. Grp. Assn. Editor "King's Cliffe Remembered" newsletter.

Presently a director of the 8th A.F. Historical Society and the P-38 Nat. Assn. Author of "Happy Jack's Go Buggy".

ASHLEY IVEY, Lt. Col., was born Dec. 13, 1923 in Milledgeville, GA.

Enlisted U.S. Army, July 30, 1942; Infantry OCS, 2nd Lt., May 8, 1943, Fort Benning, GA.

Transferred to U.S. Army Air Corps, Nov. 21, 1943; navigator, May 20, 1944, San Marcos, TX; B-17 crew training, MacDill Field, Tampa, FL.

Flew with 863rd Sqdn., 493 BG, 8th A.F., Station 152, Debach, England, WWII. Shot down on sixth combat mission while navigator of B-17G *Straighten Up and Fly Right*; crash landed in German-occupied Holland (Leimuiden) on Nov. 2, 1944. Evaded until escape to Allied territory, March 18, 1945. Returned to U.S. May 5, 1945. Released from active duty Oct. 26, 1945.

Returned to active duty U.S. Army, Infantry Aug. 13, 1946. Peacetime overseas duty in Okinawa and West Germany. Overseas combat duty: 19 months in Korean War, 12 months in Vietnam War. Last 12 years of service in U.S. Army Military Intelligence. Retired from U.S. Army July 31, 1974. Civilian employment as part-time high school teacher.

Education: A.A. Georgia Military College, 1942; B.A. Kennesaw College, 1983.

Married Marian Ruth Asbell Aug. 31, 1946. Children: Jack William and Janet Ruth. Currently resides in Acworth, GA.

DEE R. JONES, JR., was born Jan. 18, 1923. Enlisted Oct. 27, 1942 in U.S. Army Air Corps. Basic training at Clearwater, FL; aerial gunnery training at Tyndall Field, Panama City, FL, as a sergeant; B-24 mechanic school, Keesler Field, Biloxi, MS; air crew training Davis Monthan Air Base, Tucson, AZ, combat crew training 722nd Bomb Sqdn., 450th BG (H), B-24s Alamagordo, NM.

The bomb group flew their aircraft to North Africa and on to Manduria, Italy. Aircraft was disabled on 44th mission to Wiener Neustadt, Austria. Bailed out and evaded capture. Tail gunner was killed when a 20mm shell exploded in the turret. Four enlisted men and pilot and co-pilot were P.O.W.s. Bombardier, navigator and engineer gunner (T/Sgt. Jones) were evadees and returned to Foggia, Italy.

Awards: Air Medal with one Silver Cluster, Purple Heart and Presidential Unit Citation.

Single/Divorced. Retired from the military in 1964 as a first sergeant (M/Sgt. E-7). Early retirement from Dept. of Defense Police (Lt.) in 1981. In 1991, just tired.

CLYDE S. JUDY, was born Feb. 27, 1921 in Fairmont, WV. Enlisted June 1942. Completed pilot training at West Coast training command, (P-38s and B-17s), then took operational training in B-24s at Mountain Home, ID.

Flew 35 missions in E.T.O. with the 777th Sqdn., 464th BG, 15th A.F. On 25th mission was forced to parachute into the Adriatic Sea near Yugoslavia's island of Korcula. Rescued from the sea and helped to escape the enemy by native islanders. Returned to Italy and completed remaining missions.

After returning to the U.S., became an instructor pilot at Cortland, AL. Later re-assigned to Lowry Field, Denver, CO to different administrative positions. Discharged in April 1946.

Following discharge, graduated from Fairmont State College and began business career in sales and marketing. Served as sales manager for FMC and Allen & Garcia companies. Retired 1983.

Married and have two sons and four grandchildren. Now resides in Fairmont, WV.

PAUL P. KASZA, was born Jan. 14, 1921 in Cleveland, OH. Entered service Nov. 3, 1942. Graduated radio operator mechanic school Chicago, IL May 1943. Graduated aerial gunnery school L.V.A.G.S., Las Vegas, NV July 1943. Assigned to E. Fitzpatrick crew Aug. 1943. Trained on B-24 at Davis Monthan, Tucson, AZ and Blyth, CA. Arrived in England Nov. 1943 assigned to 8th A.F. 801st BG, 406th BS at Alconbury, Watton and Harrington, made rank of technical sergeant.

Flew first carpetbagger mission Feb. 6, 1944. Shot down 1:30 a.m. by German Me110 night fighter on 17th carpetbagger mission May 30, 1944. Evaded (Belgium) May 30, 1944 to Oct. 2, 1944. Returned to the 492nd BG and departed for U.S. Oct. 22, 1944.

Awards: Distinguished Unit Citation, WWII Victory Medal, Air Medal with two OLC, E.T.O. Ribbon with two Bronze Stars, Purple Heart, Good Conduct Medal.

Married, two children. Retired carpenter, 1984. Lives in Seven Hills, OH.

THEODORE R. KELLERS, was born Dec. 8, 1915 in Akron, OH. Inducted Aug. 10, 1942, sent to Fort Hayes then to Keesler Field to study B-24s. Upon completion of course, sent to gunnery school at Harlingen, TX; then to Salt Lake City for assignment. Delayed by illness. Had to be assigned to a crew when he was shipped to Moses Lake, WA.

Although he trained for B-24s, Kellers was scheduled as an engineer with a B-17 crew. The airfield was under construction and they had about three months before they were able to start flying.

At the start of September 1943, they flew to

Maine, then to Gander, then to E.T.O. They were assigned to the 339th Sqdn., 96th BG. On their fifth mission they were not able to keep in the formation and turned back. A flock of Me109s and FWs shot the tail off.

Bailed out and was met by a farmer of the Belgium resistance. Went to Brussels, then Paris, then Toulouse, then to the Pyrenees for a two-day hike. The Spanish guides who left them to get food sold them to the Krauts.

Went back and ended up at Dulag Luft, then Stalag Luft IV, then to Stalag I and from there to Camp Lucky Strike in France and finally home again on June 18, 1945.

Married in 1949, has four children. Retired from B.F. Goodrich on Dec. 31, 1977.

NORMAN P. KEMPTON, was born May 13, 1918 in Morristown, SD. Obtained a private pilot's license in 1939 through the civilian pilot training program at South Dakota School of Mines, Rapid City, SD. Joined the U.S. Army Air Corps Aug. 20, 1940. Graduated from the U.S.A.A.C. Aircraft Mechanics School at Chaunte Field, IL in 1940.

Military pilot training was completed at the Southeast training command class 43C at Maxwell Field, AL, Orangeburg, SC and Columbus, MS. B-17 transition training was at Sebring, FL in 1943.

After crew training, he was assigned to the 8th A.F., 388th BG, stationed near Thedford, England.

Shot down on 10th mission Jan. 4, 1944, near Bordeaux, France. Parachuted and evaded capture for ten days until contact was established with the French Resistance. Walked over the Pyrenees and reached Isaba, Spain on Feb. 23, 1944. Returned to England April 13, 1944 by way of Gibraltar.

Next tour of duty was piloting C-54s with the North Atlantic Div. of the Air Transport Command.

Discharged November 1946. Obtained a B.S. degree from Colorado State University in 1949.

Upon receiving degree, was employed as a research and development engineer at Wright-Patterson A.F.B., OH and later as an aerospace engineer at Patrick A.F.B., FL. Retired after 36 years with the Air Force in December 1979.

Married Pearl L. Sturgeon and they have one

son, Gary L. and one grandson, Wesley Norman.

IKE K. KILLINGSWORTH, Col. (ret.), was born Nov. 29, 1917 in Longview, TX. Joined U.S. Army Air Corps Oct. 23, 1942. Graduated pilots training as second lieutenant in class 43-H Aug. 1943 Aloe Army A.B., TX. Flew PT-19, BT-13, 14, AT-6,7,11, P-40, 47, 51, B-24, 25, 26, 29, C-45, 46, 47, UC-78, L-2,3 and A-24.

Flew 100 combat missions in P-47 Thunderbolt in close ground support with D-Day support and follow on with Patton's Third Army. Assigned to 404th Ftr. Sqdn., 371st Fighter Grp., 9th A.F. and 19 T.A.F. in E.T.O.

Hit by flak while strafing a train near Barbizon, Alligny-Cosne, Nievre, France, near Loire River Aug. 27, 1944. Hit in right eye by debris/shrapnel. Rescued from German gunners by FFI led by Alexandre LeRoy and Robert Boulmier. Placed in basement of Mayor Lebruns' home. A lasting relationship exists with M. Lebruns' daughters and family members of FFI, the present Mayor P. Doudeau and many others. Revisited the site on 40th anniversary of D Day, 1984, and again in 1990. Plan to return in 1994.

Graduate of a number of U.S. intelligence schools, Command and Staff College, Air War College, Nat. War College and Industrial College of the Armed Forces.

Also graduate of Lon Morris College (B.A. and M.A.) and S.M.U. Attended Georgetown University, University of Texas, North Texas State University, Midwestern University, University of North Carolina as post graduate student.

Received Air Medal with 16 OLC, Distinguished Flying Cross, E.T.O. Ribbon, American Defense Ribbon and French Croix de Guerre.

Retired Nov. 29, 1977 and reside in Longview, TX. Sons, Fred, U.S. Navy Reserves Intelligence. and David, Lt. U.S. Navy, M.S.C., assigned U.S.S. Tarawa in Persian Gulf.

ERNEST C. KING, was born Dec. 25, 1918 in Chanute, KS. Enlisted in the U.S. Army Air Corps May 17, 1941. Assigned to 8th Air Force, 381st BG, 535th Bomb Sqdn. Waist gunner on B-17, stationed at Ridgewell, England.

Plane shot down Aug. 17, 1943 on his 16th mission. Evaded the Germans for nine months in Belgium and France. Captured attempting to cross Swiss border. Prisoner of Gestapo for two months and 25 days. Prisoner of war nine months at Stalag Luft IV. On forced march for 80 days covering 460 miles. Liberated April 26, 1945.

In 1946 he married Mary Lou Grady. They have three children: Mary Jo, Janice Lou and Ernest Alan. Before retirement he was parts manager for a new car agency.

Published a book, *Beyond Fantasy* on his life in the military.

He and his wife live on their ranch "Circle K King Ranch" near Erie, KS.

JOSEPH L. KIRKNER, was born Jan. 21, 1924 in Malvern, PA. Joined U.S.A.F. Sept. 20, 1942. Trained in Amarillo, TX; Las Vegas, NV; and Seattle, WA. Formed crew at Redmond, OR, flight engineer-gunner B-17. First replacement crew with 614th Bomb Sqdn., 401st BG, 8th Air Force, England.

Shot down Dec. 31, 1943 on first mission over Bordeaux, France. Four chutes out of plane over Pyrenees Mountains into Spain. Evaded via underground. Returned to England March 1944.

Home to U.S. after treatment and rehabilitation. Taught ground school in Ardmore, OK. Discharged Nov. 10, 1945.

Ordained April 1955. Served two churches as senior minister.

Retired 1988. Currently receiving treatment for injuries at Coatesville Medical Center. Married Eleanor Mae Bell Oct. 20, 1943. Three children: David, Douglas and Dorothy. Seven grandchildren. Now living in Malvern, PA.

THEODORE H. (TED) KLEINMAN, Col. (ret.), was born July 26, 1919 in New York City. Joined U.S.A.F. March 16, 1942. B-17 crew navigator. Married Dorothea Godlove after forced landing and blind date in Eugene, OR. Combat assignment, 349th Sqdn., 100th BG (B-17), England. Partial engine failure and fighter attacks force bailout. Pulled delayed jump into occupied Belgium near Turnhout. Monitored clandestine radio net at Basecles. September 1944, picked up by pseudo "resistance" team.

Taken to Brussels -Luftwaffe Hq., St. Gilles Prison. Marched to train, destination Germany. Found his pilot, Second Lieutenant John W. Brown, aboard. With 41 other Allied airmen escaped in Brussels freight yards after fruitless attempts to move east. In advanced twin-engine pilot training when separated in Oct. 1945.

Volunteered for active duty. Recalled Jan. 26, 1951. B-29 navigation instructor; B-36 lead navigator; KC-135 Jet Tanker development and training team; operations/training officer Headquarters SAC; Vandenberg A.F.B., missile operations.

Retired June 30, 1970. Promoted to father of four and grandfather of seven. Looking forward to next promotion.

A.D. (DELL) KNEALE, JR., was born Dec. 17, 1916 in Tulsa, OK. Enlisted in Oklahoma Air National Guard, 125th Observation Sqdn., Tulsa, in April 1941. Unit was called to active duty in September 1941; applied for and was accepted in Aviation Cadet training in December 1941. Received navigation training at Hondo, TX navigation school.

In January 1943 was assigned to 551st Bomb Sqdn., 385th BG, Great Falls, MT. Flew with this unit in the E.T.O. as navigator on the *Old Shillelagh* and *Old Shillelagh II*. On fifth mission, ditched in the North Sea and was picked up by Air Sea Rescue. On eighth mission, Aug. 25, 1943, shot down over France and broke my leg after bailing out. Evaded capture and walked over Pyrenees.

Arrived back in U.K. after 67 days. Returned to States and taught navigation at Hondo and later radar at Victorville, CA. Separated from service as first lieutenant October 1945.

Awarded Purple Heart and Air Medal with Oak Leaf Cluster.

Now retired after various accounting positions including 23 years with Sun Oil Co., and ending with three years in my own C.P.A. practice.

Married to Geneva and has three children and three grandchildren. Resides in Bella Vista, AR.

RICHARD H. KRECKER, was born Dec. 21, 1922 in Pottsville, PA. Joined service in 1942 in Philadelphia, PA. Basic training Miami Beach, FL; radio school Souix Falls, SD; aerial gunner, Kingman, AZ.

Became member of crew B-17 in Moses Lake, WA; further training in Harvard, NE. Flew as 447th BG from Bangor, ME to Nutscorner, Ireland and on to base Rattles Den, England. Flew 17 missions over Europe.

Shot down on mission to Augsburg, Germany on March 17, 1944. Evaded Germans with help of French Underground. Got through to Spain June 3, 1944 to Gibraltar and back to base. Medical discharge in 1944.

Married Shirley Burns, three children, six grandchildren. Retired as art director of advertising agency after heart attack in 1985.

ROBERT V. KRENGLE, was born July 13, 1921 in Boston, MA. Enlisted Feb. 7, 1942 and graduated bomardier school Dec. 17, 1942.

Assigned to sixth Anti-Sub Sqdn. and patrolled North Atlantic and Bay of Biscayne until November 1943.

Reassigned to 8th Air Force as first lieutenant, 389th BG. They were shot down Dec. 30, 1943 about thirty miles north of Paris, west of Soissons. Was given workman's clothes and ticket to Paris and proceeded there four days later.

Was almost caught in Paris, Bourges and Toulouse. From Carcassonne, Krengle proceeded on foot to Quillan in the foothills of the Pyrenees; and finally made contact with the Resistance. Because of snow, he was not successful until March 30-31 to cross into Spain. After internment, he returned to the 389th BG June 6-7, 1944. Returned to States.

Was instructor B-29s until Japan's surrender and discharged.

Retired 1983 from Houston Health Dept. Resides with wife in Livingston, TX.

ALVIN RAYMOND (RAY) KUBLY,

was born May 22, 1924 on the Kubly farm in Watertown, WI. As a youth, he worked on the farm, was active in 4H work and served as basketball manager for his high school team. After graduating in 1942, he enlisted in the Air Force on Oct. 7, 1942. Graduated as a bombardier-navigator and was assigned to a B-17 Flying Fortress with the 34th BG in the 8th Air Force.

On his ninth mission, an oil refinery target near Meresburg, Germany, the plane was hit by anti-aircraft flak and the crew had to parachute out over Holland. He was shot through the leg while still in the air and when he landed the Germans took him prisoner.

Germans took him to the St. Antonius Hospital in Utrecht, Holland and after 19 days there, he and five other P.O.W.s escaped. The Dutch Underground took care of them. After five months and 23 days, he returned to freedom through the front lines.

After WWII, he returned to the family farm until May 1948. He married Ruth Wegwart Sept. 4, 1948. Graduated from the University of Wisconsin-Madison in 1952 with a B.S. in Soils and Agronomy and worked for Cargill Seeds in Rochester, MN. A son, Roger Ray was born July 19, 1950. Joan Kristine was born June 15, 1952 on Father's Day. Carol Ann was born March 30, 1955 in Tracy, MN. Mary Lee was born Jan. 6, 1960 in Watertown, WI.

Was in Air Force Reserve and in 1968 was promoted to lieutenant colonel. Went to work for the Dairyland Seed Co. in 1961 as only salesman. By 1979 he was vice president of sales with over 100 employees now in the company.

Served on Watertown School Board, president three terms. Also served five years on the CESA Board of Control, three as chairman. In 1987 Lt. Col. Kubly was selected as executive sec./treasurer of the Reserve Officers Assn. and as editor of *Wisconsin Reservist*.

Ray and Ruth Kubly have seven grandchildren.

RICHARD G. LAMIE, 1st. Lt.,

was born Oct. 16, 1921 in Dover, NH. Enlisted June 22, 1943 White Hall, St., NYC. Pilot training Gulf Coast training command, Bonham, Greenville, Ellington, TX, combat training Dalhart, TX in B-17.

Flew with 364th Sqdn., 305th BG, 8th A.F. Chelveston, England. Shot down as co-pilot bailing out over Aalten, Holland on sixth mission. One of first helpers was Martin Lelivelt who was later executed by the Germans for his efforts as a helper. Twenty homes later, liberated in the village of Trooz, Belgium. Separated from service Oct. 19, 1945.

Completed education, worked as science coordinator, Valhalla New York School Dist. Retired.

Married Mary O'Brien (deceased). Three children: Richard, Peter, Susan. Married Marcella Dodd. Resides in Manchester, CT.

JAMES P. LAW, 1st. Lt.,

was born Sept. 14, 1919 in Akron, OH. Joined Army Sept. 1941. Pilot training on west coast. Graduated class of 1943G. Flew with Bloody 100th BG, 8th A.F.

Shot down as co-pilot on B-17 Flying Fortress over Ludwigshafen, Germany Dec. 30, 1943. Escaped with help of French Resistance Forces (Robert and Germaine Frossiart) in Rheims, France. Later moved to Sedan, France where he was hidden by family of Madame Vin. Here he helped Resistance to interrogate shot down airmen whom the French thought could be Gestapo planted to infiltrate French Underground.

Captured in April 1944 by Gestapo when leaving for Paris for Spain over Pyrenees Mountains into Spain. Held in solitary confinement in Fresne Prison, south of Paris, France and Frankfort prison, Frankfort, Germany before being sent to Stalag Luft III in Prussia. Marched to Nurnberg, then to Munich, Germany. Liberated by 14th Armored two days before V-Day.

Married to Helen Erdley of Johnstown, PA with one daughter Nancy, married to Bruce Sickel, Philadelphia, PA.

President and owner of Law's Jewelry Inc. in Johnstown, PA for 32 years.

DUANE J. LAWHEAD,

was born Oct. 14, 1921 in Eaton County, MI. Joined military in September 1942 and was discharged in October 1945. Took his gunnery training at Las Vegas, NV. First phase of combat training at Blyth, CA and second and third at Pyote, TX.

Flew with the 8th A.F., 305th BG, 366th Sqdn. Shot down Sept. 6, 1943 on 20th mission. Evaded and returned to England Dec. 3, 1943.

Promoted to technical sergeant and was instructor, chin turret, at Gulfport Mechanics School at Denver, CO on B-29.

Worked for Navy Civil Service as aircraft sheet metal mechanic and retired after 22 years.

He and his wife, Fay, live in Suwannee, FL on the Gulf. They have five great grandchildren.

VINCENT LAYBE,

was born July 19, 1919 in Clayton, NM. Was in Arizona National Guard 1939, transferred to Air Force in 1941, 99th BG, 348th Bomb Sqdn. Stationed at Scottfield, McDill, Gowen, Sioux City, Tyndell Field, Mitchell, SD, and overseas. Achieved rank of technical sergeant.

His B-17 was severely damaged by flak Sept. 2, 1943 on 19th mission, target Bologna, Italy. Crew bailed out and was captured by the Italians and sent to Camp 54, Sabina, Province of Rome. Escaped and headed for hills. Lived behind enemy lines for 10 months in village near Rome and in Rome, aided by underground. Lived in different places until our forces took Rome in June 1943.

Returned to base in Foggia, Italy, then sent to a hospital in Bari, Italy and finally stateside to a hospital in Washington State. Discharged in 1945. Entered A.S.U., Tempe, AZ. Met and married

Patty Kielgass and had two sons, Michael and Patrick. Lost Patty to cancer in 1988.

Retired after 33 years of teaching science. Enjoy tennis, science projects and astronomy.

Awards: Air Medal, Purple Heart, P.O.W. Medal. Resides in Phoenix, AZ.

ALFRED R. LEA, was born Feb. 5, 1919 in Marshfield, WI. Joined U.S.A.A.F. in 1940, assigned to deferred priority service on U.S.A.A.F. CG4A cargo glider and Navy shipbuilding and base construction programs.

Active duty March 1943; commissioned navigator, San Marcos, TX A.A.F.B., twice-wounded combat navigator, 729th Sqdn., 452nd BG (H), 8th A.F., Deopham Green, England.

Shot down in German-occupied eastern Poland on first England/Russia shuttle raid, crewing B-17G "BTO in ETO" June 21, 1944. Evaded capture, joined 34th Regt., Polish Home Army (AKA), served as combat infantryman, assaulting German SS, Gestapo, Wehrmacht troops and Soviet renegades, plus ambushing truck convoys and trains. M.I.A. status terminated when Soviet tanks and infantry overran 34th Regt. at Biala Podlaska.

Recalled to Korean War, SAC navigator; medical discharge 1952. Served as airshow and tour navigator, Confederate Air Force's B-17G *Texas Raiders* 1973-87.

Architect Emeritus; he and his wife, Dorothea, live in Houston, TX. Sons: Steven, Thomas.

DALE V. LEE, was with the 44th BG, 506th Sqdn. Entered the A.A.F. June 13, 1942. Trained at Kiesler Field, MS; B-24 consolidated, San Diego; gunnery school, Las Vegas; crew training at Tucson, Alamogardo, Clovis.

Picked up new airplane *Southern Comfort - 778* at Lincoln, NE and flew to England, then to Bengagi, North Africa. Raids included Kiel, Germany, low level Polesti (Aug. 1, 1942), Rome, Wiener Neustadt and last raid - Foggia. They were on fire at 30,000 ft. with 150 Nazi fighters on a six ship formation. His crew (H. Austin, A. Fobiny, P. Singer, Fender, J. Jett, D. Lee, R. Whitley, G. Hickerson, T. Purcell, J. Worth) had eight captured

and interned, two lost with the plane.

Medals: two Presidential Citations, Distinguished Flying Cross, three Air Medals, Purple Heart, Winged Boots, and commendation from Gen. H.H. Arnold.

Three months after being shot down, all but one had escaped and they all had a reunion at Long Bar in London - a super crew. This all happened before any invasion of Europe.

Returned to U.S. Was flight engineer instructor at Edwards A.F.B. until discharge in Sept. 1945.

After military service, obtained commercial pilot's, flight England and A&E licenses. Flew flight test for Air Force, also designated acceptance pilot. Flight test at Edwards on 101, F-4, F-3D, F-4D, and F-5D.

Married an Army nurse, Alice. She landed on Omaha Beach shortly after D-Day, served in field, station and general hospitals, one of which was receiving hospital for P.O.W.s. They have five children: Ivan, Kathy, Gary, Dean and Mary.

Operated a successful dairy farm for number of years and sold replacement dairy hefers. In U.S., Canada and Mexico; developed over 200 acres of land for homesites. Currently resides in Everson, WA. Plans to retire at Sun Lakes, AZ and just sit and rock!

JOSEPH WILLIAM LINCOLN, Lt. Col., was born Sept. 25, 1915 in Gifford, PA. Graduated Culver Military Academy 1933, Stanford University 1937, master's 1940.

Married Mildred Painter of Asheville, NC April 25, 1940. Two daughters: Stephanie Biorn (Kris and Betsy), and Pamela Senfield (daughter Stephanie).

Called to active duty in September 1941 with 5th Armored Div. Transferred to pilot training. Graduated Stockton, CA class 43H.

Shot down April 24, 1944 as B-17 pilot with 305th BG returning from Oberpfaffenhopen, (near Munich) Germany. Evaded capture. Spent a month in Maquis of Revin (OSS-FF1) including three-day intense battle with German occupation troops. Liberated by American First Army in September 1944.

Duty in Pentagon next two years. Released from active duty in Jan. 1947.

Retired from U.S.A.F.R. in Sept. 1975.

Quote: "I shall be forever grateful to my helpers in Belgium and France."

ROBERT M. LITTLEFIELD, was born March 19, 1922 in San Francisco. Entered U.S. Army Air Force Jan. 6, 1943. Graduated from pilot training Williams Field, AZ, Nov. 3, 1943. Flew combat with 38th Fighter Sqdn., 55th Fighter Grp., 8th A.F., Wormingford, England in P-38s and P-51Ds.

Shot down by flak, Barentin, France, while strafing a locomotive in a P-51D on 59th combat mission Aug. 13, 1944.

French who helped were: Rene' Renard and family; Marcel and Catherine Hennetier; Henri Couture and sons Daniel and Andre'; Armand, Angele' and Huguette Greux; Mme. Glasson and daughter Janine; Micheline Guilloux and a small boy, Pierre, last name unknown.

Lived with the French in Chateau le Matre', near Pavilly, France. Returned to England through German/English lines Sept. 3, 1944.

Flew fighters throughout an Air Force career, Flew trainers and RP-322, P-40, F-5G, B-25, F-84E, G and F, F-100, F-104, F-5A and numerous support type aircraft.

Retired from the U.S.A.F. in 1966, rank lieutenant colonel. Now lives in Carmel, CA.

GARY L. LOCKS, was born June 26, 1943 in Passaic, NJ. He graduated from Grove City College, PA January 1967. Commissioned a 2nd lieutenant through R.O.T.C., assigned to 17th BW and went TDY to Da Nang in 1968, where he went on an 0-2 mission and was shot down over enemy territory. He escaped after 17 days and returned to kill his nine captors with an Army patrol who found him on the night of his escape. He returned to Wright-Patterson Air Force Base, OH.

In 1972, he married Deborah Long of Beavercreek, OH. He went to Wright State Univerity and finished his Masters program in guidance counseling.

He is in the active Reserves as a lieutenant colonel. He is assigned to Defense Logistics Agency (DLA). His full time job is in civil service on the B1 Bomber program in logistics management at WPAFB, OH.

Locks is a member of the American Defense Preparedness Assn., Society of Logistics Engineers, National Contract Management Assn., American Legion, The Company of Military Historian, V.P. of the Kittyhawk Chapter, Reserve Office Assn., Young Republicans, NRA, and American Ex-Prisoners of War.

WARREN E. (BUD) LORING, was born July 19, 1923 in Brockton, MA. Education: three years of college.

Joined the Army May 20, 1942. Stationed at Williams Field, AZ and in Europe. Graduated class of 43K.

Flew PT-22, BT-13, AT-6, AT-9, RP-322, P-38, P-39, P-63, P-51 and C-47 in WWII, E.T.O, England, with 55th Fighter Grp., 343rd Fighter Sqdn.

Shot down while strafing an enemy airfield on June 30, 1944.

Achieved rank of lieutenant colonel in the Army. Retired June 1, 1968. Joined A.F.E.E.S. in 1980.

Married Helen Jan. 14, 1944 and has three children and four grandchildren. As a civilian, worked for Colonial Gas Company as plant operator. Retired April 1, 1989. Resides in Monument Beach, MA.

JACK O. LUHERS, was born Dec. 12, 1920 in Ontario, OR. Joined the military Dec. 8, 1941. After basic training in Jefferson Barrick, MO, went to radio school at Scott Field, IL, then to Geiger Field, WA. Assigned to 305th BG, 364th Bomb Sqdn. as radio operator/mechanic. Went overseas in September of 1943, plane *Available Jones*.

Shot down on 19th mission April 4, 1943, target Renault Work, Paris, France. Landed in orchard and helped by Frenchmen. Moved to northern France, then back to Paris and Bordeaux and over Pyrenees, prison in Spain, back to England. Gave talk on escape and evasion to new bomb group.

After return to States assigned to Sioux City, IA, and Elk Point, SD on bombing range. Married and has a son and daughter.

Discharged in September 1945, rank of technical sergeant. Retired after 35 years with State Highway Dept. as engineer.

Awarded Distinguished Flying Cross, Air Medal with three Oak Leaf Clusters, Purple Heart and Presidential Unit Citation.

JOHN J. MAIORCA, was born July 10, 1918 in New Britain, CT. Entered military service Oct. 18, 1940. Basic training at Fort Devens, MA. Assigned to 1st Div. and transferred to A.F. April 1, 1942.

Bombardier training at San Angelo, TX. Graduated April 1, 1943. Assigned to B-17 bombers. Trained with crew at Pyote and Dalhart, TX. Joined 8th A.F. 388th BG at Knetishall, England on Aug. 20, 1943.

Memorable raids to Gaynia, Poland and Schwienfurt, Germany. On Oct. 5, 1943 hit by AA fire en route to Gelsenkirchen, Germany. Limped back to Belgium, bailed out under fighter attack. Evaded Belgium, France, Spain. Returned to England Jan. 6, 1944.

Returned to U.S. Assigned as instructor Midland, TX bombardier school. Discharged Aug. 17, 1945.

Currently resides in Manchester, CT with wife. Have two children, boy and girl. Retired

Service Dept. Manager DeCormier Mtr. Sls., Manchester, CT.

LAWRENCE N. MAJOR, was born July 25, 1922 in Port Carbon, Schuylkill, PA. Entered Army Sept. 10, 1942.

Received radio operator and gunnery training before departure for Europe. With the 526th Sqdn., 379th BG and flew two bombing missions on B-17s. Waist gunner on Dec. 1, 1943, his second mission, when shot down and crash landed in France. Escaped through the underground and arrived in Switzerland almost two weeks later. Several members of the crew were P.O.W.s. The bombardier, navigator and radio operator also escaped.

Spent 1944 in Klosters, Switzerland living "the life of Riley". Returned to U.S. in October 1944. Conducted ferrying operations at Reno, NV and Great Falls, MT until after V-J Day.

Awarded four Bronze Stars and the Purple Heart. Separated as technical sergeant on Oct. 18, 1945.

Married Dorothy Bensinger of home town and fathered four children. Died Nov. 16, 1975 of a heart attack.

JOSEPH E. MANOS, M./Sgt., was born Dec. 28, 1923 in Brooklyn, NY. Enlisted Sept. 23, 1942. Retired Sept. 30, 1962.

As a tail gunner with the 331st Bomb Sqdn., 94th BG, 8th A.F., England, was shot down over Le Bourget, France July 14, 1943. Evaded and returned to England Dec. 1, 1943. (A portion of this evasion was described in a book by R.A.F. Grp./Cap. Frank C. Griffiths, titled *Winged Hours*.) Served in Air Force as a gunner, aircraft mechanic, flying crew/chief and a panel flight engineer.

Graduated from flight engineer school in July 1950 and spent four years in SAC flying on KB-29, B-50 and B-36 aircraft. Participated in FOX PETER ONE with 93rd Air Refueling Sqdn., the first mass jet crossing of the Pacific by a fighter wing. Flew weather reconnaissance tracks and typhoon penetrations with the 54th Air Weather Sqdn., Guam, making 13 penetrations in typhoons during the two year assignment.

Flew for six years out of Travis A.F.B. with MATS, in the 84th Air Transport Sqdn. in C-124 and C-133 type aircraft. Upon retirement had 7500 hours as a panel flight engineer.

Worked for Aero-Jet General for two years as a rocket test technician, then 20 years with the Sacramento Municipal Utilities District as a senior meter tester. Retired in December 1985 at age 62.

Married to Dorothy D. Manos May 25, 1952 and has two sons, Joseph Jr. and John. Grandchildren: Jennifer, Talia and Anthony. Hobby in retirement: general aviation. Presently an instrument rated private pilot with over

a thousand hours in light aircraft. Residing in Sacramento, CA.

VIRGIL R. MARCO, was born Jan. 10, 1924 in Dallas, TX. Entered the service Feb. 12, 1943. Received aerial gunner wings at Las Vegas, NV. Served in 8th A.F. as a tail gunner on the Lincoln crew, 366th Bomb Sqdn., 305th BG.

Shot down over France April 24, 1944. Separated from the service on Dec. 10, 1945 at Camp Beale, CA with rank of staff sergeant.

Received B.B.A. degree from Southern Methodist University in January 1949.

Married Bobbie Nell Haynes June 3, 1950. Raised four children. Presently working for Gulf Insurance Company in Irving, TX.

JOHN M. MARR, was born Aug. 13, 1921 in Columbus, IN. Graduated from Columbus High School 1938 and Kentucky Military Institute 1939. Attended Purdue University three years studying mechanical engineering. Enlisted Army Air Corps in 1942 and spent four years in military service.

Trained in Texas, Oklahoma, Kansas and at Dale Mabry Field, Tallahassee, FL. P-40 fighter plane training at Thomasville, GA. P-51 pilot in 8th A.F. based at East Wretham, England.

Shot down over France Jan. 29, 1945, bailed out, hit the airplane tail, spent 20 months salvaging leg. (Revisited France 1985 and located town in whose main street he came down, people who remembered him, and dug up pieces of his airplane that crashed in woods.

Thirty years in motel business in Tallahassee. Retired 1976 to spend more effort promoting constitutional government as a conservative, political activist.

Marr is a Christian worshiping at First Christian Church. He is a member of D.A.V., American Legion, The Reserve Officers Assn., The John Birch Soc. and Rotary.

Family is wife, Norma, Jeff with two sons and Greg with one son and Donah with two daughters and one son.

Commercial pilot, holding a flight instructor's certificate in airplanes and instruments, but doesn't have time to practice it. Has a real estate salesman's certificate. Teaches an occasional C.P.R. course and enjoys that along with yard work, reading, traveling, visiting grandchildren and church work.

ROBERT A. MARTIN,

ROBERT A. MARTIN, 1st Lt., was born May 14, 1916 in Spokane, WA. Volunteered Nov. 1940. Assigned to 17th Infantry, Presidio of Monterey, CA. Transferred to A.A.F. Feb. 1942.

Pilot training King City, Chico and Stockton, CA, where commissioned Oct. 1942, class 42J. Married same day. Flew B-24s, B-26s, A-26s, P-38s and AT-11. Flew bombing approach at bombardier school, Deming, NM.

Combat training Fort Worth, TX; Boise, ID; Sioux City, IA. Stationed Norwich, England with 714th Sqdn., 448th BG, 8th A.F., WWII.

Returning from an aborted mission on March 5, 1944, his B-24 was hit by heavy flak. With one engine left, he landed it in a field near Niort, France. Evaded capture and escaped to Spain.

Awarded Air Medal with OLC, Purple Heart, E.A.M.E. Theatre Ribbon with two Bronze Stars and the Winged Boot. Established contact with all his French benefactors in 1946.

Returned to U.S. under Project R; served in 6th Ferry Grp., ATC, Long Beach, CA delivering planes to Africa, India, Australia and U.S. Discharged Jan. 15, 1946.

Returned to Bakersfield, CA where he became owner of the Q-Ne-Q Drive-In for 10 years. Later became a partner in Kern Battery Mfg. Co. until his retirement in 1982.

Diagnosed with leukemia in 1985; achieved remission, but died in October 1988 after a reoccurrence. Survived by his wife, Jeane, two children and four grandchildren.

FRANCIS C. MARX,

FRANCIS C. MARX, T./Sgt., was born March 1, 1918 in Oppenheim, NY. Entered service Nov. 2, 1942, Scott Field, IL, Laredo, TX, Clovis and Alamogordo, NM. Based: Seething, England, 8th A.F., 713th Sqdn., 448th BG.

Returning from a mission to Ludwigshafen bailed out north of Paris. A Parisian family hid him until he was directed towards neutral Spain. As he walked over the Pyrenees, guides deserted him in a freezing rain and he climbed on while assisting an injured British pilot. Reaching Spain he slept on the floor of jails until rescued by the American Military Attache and became an internee.

Upon return to U.S., he was named N.C.O. in charge of Intelligence, 5th Service Command, St. Louis. Discharged Nov. 13, 1945.

Married Ida Mae Wiener Sept. 29, 1943. Children: Francis C. Jr., Sioux Falls, SD; Dean L., Brussels, Belgium; Michelle Ann Gardiner, Cresskill, NJ. Grandchildren: Brian, Michelle, and Kelly Ann.

Retired accountant/auditor and wife Ida is retired school educator, both Rider College. Residence Tampa, FL.

WILLIAM R. MATTSON,

WILLIAM R. MATTSON, born Dec. 11, 1916 Rockport, MA. Enlisted USAAF 1942. Trained at Keesler Field, Sheppard Field, Willow Run, Laredo and Gowen Field, IA, where he joined a B-24 crew as a flight engineer and top turret gunner with a T/Sgt. rating.

Went overseas in 1943 and was assigned to the 392nd BG, 579th Sdn., 8th AF Wembling, England. Tenth mission was to Frankfort, Germany, Jan. 29, 1944. Was shot down and with the help of the Underground, he evaded capture and escaped over the Pyrenees into Spain arriving in May 944.

During this period was listed as Missing in Action and then as Killed in Action. Was awarded the Air Medal with OLC, Purple Heart plus Theatre Medals. Discharged Oct. 16, 1945 Boise, ID.

He and Ester have been married since 1947 and have two sons. Worked as an industrial designer for GTE. Now retired and lives in Gloucester, MA.

CHARLES J. McCLAIN,

CHARLES J. McCLAIN, was born Sept. 12, 1919. Entered the U.S. Army Oct. 13, 1941 completing basic training in the Corps of Engineers, Ft. Belvoir, VA. Transferred to the Army Air Corps and was commissioned a second lieutenant, May 13, 1943 upon graduation from bombardier training at San Angelo, TX.

Feb. 28, 1944 as a first lieutenant in the 359th Bomb Sqdn., 303rd BG, Molesworth, England was shot down on 13th mission. Three crew members were blown out of the B-17 when it exploded. Was captured by a German squad and three days later escaped. Evaded through France, climbed the Pyrenees Mts. and returned to Allied control on June 6, 1944.

Awarded the Silver Star for gallantry in action, Nov. 26, 1943, while on a bombing mission to Bremen and the Distinguished Flying Cross on Feb. 20, 1944 for extraordinary achievement while serving as lead bombardier for group of B-17s on a mission to Leipzig, Germany. Received Purple Heart for wounds received Feb. 28, 1944.

Married Patricia O'Brien of Corona, NY in 1945. Completed advanced navigation, radar, and bombing training in 1948. Retired as a lieutenant colonel in 1968. Has seven children, 11 grandchildren. Lives in Rockledge, FL.

PAUL H. McCONNELL,

PAUL H. McCONNELL, 1st Lt., was born April 22, 1920 in Fort Wayne, IN. Appointed Aviation Cadet Jan. 13, 1942, Maxwell Field, AL. Trained as navigator Selman Field, Monroe, LA. Graduated Jan. 13. 1943.

Combat training Blythe, CA and assigned to 533rd Bomb Sqdn., 381st BG, 8th A.F., B-17s original 381st group training, Pyote, TX, Pueblo, CO, Salina, KS. Navigated new B-17 from Salina, KS to Ayr, Scotland. 381st became operational in Ridgewell, England June 8, 1943.

Shot down July 4, 1943 in raid on Le Mans, France (first raid) by enemy fighters. Evaded capture with aid of French Underground in Normandy, Paris, Brittany. Escaped into Spain Jan. 13, 1944. Released from active duty December 1945.

Awarded E.T.O. and Presidential Unit Citation.

Active in corporate marketing 1945-74, Horton Mfg. Co., Monsanto Chemical Corp., RealKill, Inc., U.S. Borax & Chemical Corp. 1974 to present: employee benefits, investments, Connecticut Mutual Life Ins. Co.

Married, two sons, one daughter, four grandchildren. Resides Santa Ynez, CA.

WILLIAM ALBERT McCORMICK, JR.,

WILLIAM ALBERT McCORMICK, JR., was born March 27, 1921 in Lumberton, NC. Joined the service Aug. 15, 1941 at Fort Bragg, NC. Was Aviation Cadet, U.S. Army Air Corps.

Pilot training at Gulf Coast training command, instructor pilot, Foster Field, TX. Army Air Base, Richmond, VA, Camp Springs, England, France, S. Johnson Field, NC, Freising, Germany, Grenier Field, NH, Roswell Air Field, NM. Discharged rank of major Dec. 31, 1947.

Memorable experiences: flying two missions over the beaches at Normandy, France June 6, 1944. Flight of four indog fight at the edge of Paris, France with eight Me109s. Being shot down over a German air field at Dijon, France.

Awarded: Distinguished Flying Cross, Air Medal with 12 Oak Leaf Clusters, Purple Heart, American Theater, European Theater with three Stars, American Defense Medal, Army of Occupation (Germany).

Married Mary Gladys Bracey July 23, 1942. Have three children and one grandchild. Retired tobacco farmer. Live in Rowland, NC.

HOMER E. McDANAL, Lt. Col. , joined Army Air Corps as an Aviation Cadet Sept. 1, 1942. Pilot training Southeast training command, Tuscaloosa, AL, Newport, AR, Blythville, AR.

Took B-17 training in Sebring, FL; B-17 crew training at Ephrata, WA and Remond, OR. Flew B-17s, B-25s, A-20s, AT-6s, AT-9s, AT-10s, PT-17s, BT-13s. Released from active duty in December of 1945. Retired from Reserves in September 1973.

Flew with 614th Sqdn., 401st BG, 8th A.F., Deenethorpe, England, WWII.

Shot down over Bordeaux, France, Dec. 31, 1943. With the help of the French Underground, evaded through southern France and walked over the Pyrenees into Spain.

After returning to U.S. in the spring of 1944, I ferried airplanes with Air Transport Command, Long Beach, CA until war's end.

Graduate of the University of Denver with a B.S. Degree in Business Administration, class of 1939.

After the war, owned and operated a wholesale optical laboratory in Denver, CO.

Married Betty Ashton in July 1941. She died in 1968. Then married Janet Lierk. Have two sons, a daughter and two grandchildren.

FRANK G. McDONALD, was born July 15, 1917 in Beaumont, TX. Called to active duty with Troop "B", 124th Cavalry, Texas National Guard 1940 Fort Brown, Brownsville, TX. Took short discharge to join Army Air Corps, Lowry Army Air Field, March 1941, armament instructor. Flight training July 1942 to March 1943. Assigned to Gowen Field, Boise, ID B-17. Converted to B-24 as pilot and combat crew training in Casper, WY.

Arrived in England Oct. 1943. Volunteered

for secret "Carpetbagger" missions delivering munitions and supplies to Resistance groups in occupied Europe, flying low altitude individual missions at night.

On fifth mission, a short "milk run" just across the Channel to St. Quentin/Laon in the Pas De Calais area, failed to find their man, a Frenchmen with a flashlight in an open field, and got lost. They decided to come out on the deck, 200 ft., to surprise the enemy anti-aircraft guns and successfully penetrated Ack-Ack until we passed over Doullens near the coast. Intense Ack-Ack fire set aircraft on fire and one and three engines went out. McDonald noticed a relatively smooth field to his left and turned towards it, clipping the tops of some trees hidden in a ravine, but managed to set the burning aircraft down in one piece. All survived the landing but one, engineer Norman Gellerman.

Operated a flying school in Fort Worth, TX. Married Sybil Brown and fathered four children. Recalled to active duty in 1951 assigned to SAC with B-36, B-52 and AGM-28B. Retired after 27 years as a lieutenant colonel in 1965.

Earned M.A. Degree and taught industrial science subjects at Colorado State University. Teach flying in sailplanes and build experimental certificated aircraft. Also active life member of the Daedalian Fraternity of Military Pilots.

JAMES D. McELROY, was born April 28, 1919 in Farwell, TX. Joined Army Air Force on April 6, 1942. Flew with 339th Sqdn., 96th BG, 8th Air Force at Snetterton Heath, England, as navigator.

Shot down on Oct. 20, 1943 on mission to Duren, Germany. Walked alone from Belgium to Paris. Helper contacted underground and evaded over Pyrenees to Spain. Returned to England via Gibraltar on Nov. 16, 1943.

Returned to the U.S. and was instructor at Navigation Training School, Ellington Field, TX until leaving service Oct. 2, 1945.

Graduated from the University of Southern California in Industrial Engineering. Spent a career with Monroe Systems for Business as branch manager of sales and services. Retired in 1982.

Married to Linnette Cain Dec. 25, 1942. Two daughters, Diann and Nancy. Four grandchildren: Kristin, Timmy, Elizabeth and Sammy.

JOHN A. McGLYNN, 2nd. Lt., was born July 26, 1919 in Cazenovia, WI. Enlisted Nov. 11, 1940. After training as a cook and baker and as a radio operator, accepted into flying school, Western training command of the Army Air Force.

After being commissioned and receiving tactical training, ultimately stationed with the 13th Reconnaissance Sqdn., High Altitude Reconnaissance, at Mount Farm, Oxford, England

in Aug. 1943. Piloted P-38 Lightening carrying five cameras: two verticals, two obliques and one horizon to horizon. Flew 15 high altitude reconnaissance missions over France, Germany, Italy and Africa between Aug. 1943 and Feb. 1944. Received Air Medal and Distinguished Flying Cross.

On Feb. 14, 1944, the day of first daylight bombing of Berlin, plane was shot down over the Rhine while returning from photo reconnaissance flight over Berlin. Landed on west bank of the Rhine; made his way to Paris where he stayed for several weeks under the protection of French Underground. After unsuccessful escape attempt near Rennes, Brittany, trekked over the North Pyrenees. Escaped with help of Spanish Basques, to a British submarine waiting off the south coast of the Bay of Biscay on April 29, 1944.

After returning to U.S., assigned as a pilot instructor in Selma and Montgomery, AL from May 1944 until discharge June 30, 1945.

Married Anna Marie Schauf May 13, 1944. Ran family farm and worked as a rural mail carrier for 31 years until retirement in 1982. He and his wife raised 10 children and now have 17 grandchildren. Continues to reside on family homestead near Cazenovia, WI.

RALPH D. McKEE, P.E., C.M., Lt. Col., was born Sept. 19, 1921 near Southard, OK. Joined the U.S. Army Air Corps on Feb. 22, 1942. Graduated from the Air Corps Navigation School, Mather Field, CA on Sept. 5, 1942. Flew with 366th Sqdn., 305th BG, 8th A.F., Chelveston, England, B-17, WWII.

Shot down near Nantes, France on July 4, 1943. Evaded capture, escaped into Spain and was interned briefly at Pomplona. Returned to England in Sept. 1943.

Performed B-29 navigation duties in the 370th Sqdn., 307th BG during the Korean War, and a variety of air training and research and development assignments until retiring from active duty Sept. 1, 1965. Since then has performed a number of engineering assignments supporting the Apollo and Shuttle programs at the Kennedy Space Center.

Children: Dianne B. Rhodes, Ralph D. McKee, Jr., Helen M. Duncan. Grandchild: Shannon E. Rhodes. Resides in Merritt Island, Florida.

LLOYD E. McMICHAEL,
1st. Lt., was born Dec. 3, 1924 in Austin, MN. Entered A.F. June 19, 1943, Cadet Santa Ana, CA; Hondo, TX. Graduated April 22, 1944. B-17 crew formed at Avon Park, FL; July 20, 1944 to 486th BG, 8th A.F., Sudbury, England.

Flew six-and-a-half missions in "Baby Shoes II." Arrived on south shore of Westerschelde in south Holland by chute Sept. 7, 1944. Avoided Germans by hiding in Dieleman barn. Biked to Van Wesemael farm during the night to meet three crewmates. Rescued by Polish 1st Armored Div. Returned to U.S. and flew with ATC until Dec. 31, 1945, ferried B-25s to India.

Married Dorothy J. Beckel, June 6, 1946, three children: Kevin, Steven, and William and four grandchildren. Graduated University of Minnesota in 1949, C.P.A. in 1953.

Returned to Netherlands to find helpers in 1984. Dieleman family in Walsoorden, Netherlands and Van Wesemael family in Hengstdyke, Netherlands. Returned home with much love, my boots, gloves, parachute ring, part of chute and escape kit map.

SAMUEL MELANCON,
S. Sgt., was born Feb. 2, 1916 in Donaldsonville, LA. Joined the military Oct. 10, 1941.

On 36th mission, Feb. 22, 1944 was shot down over the Netherlands above enemy territory. He was knocked unconscious and Norman Bell pulled him out of the tail gun section. He put on Melancon's chute pack and pushed him out of the waist window. He landed in Breda, Holland.

Major Thornton was the pilot and they were leading a flight. After days of walking, received help and was taken to a convent near Antwerp, where a doctor treated him for frozen feet. Later helped by the "White Brigade" who took him to Mr. Albert Van Campenhout's home where he remained for six months until liberation.

After returning to New Orleans, kept in touch with benefactors by corresponding and returned to Belgium several times. Passed away May 21, 1990.

JOHN I. MERRITT, JR.,
was born April 15, 1920 in Garden City, NY. Entered the Army 10 days after class graduated from Princeton University in June 1942 as a second lieutenant in the field artillery via R.O.T.C.

While stationed at Camp Hood, near Waco, TX, met Jonnie McBay on a blind date and they were married June 4, 1943. Was transferred three weeks later to the Gulf Coast training command and began flight training as a student officer in class 44B. He and Jonnie went to Cuero, TX for primary, then back to Waco for basic and Brooks Field, San Antonio for advanced. Assigned to B-24 transition at Tarrant Field in Fort Worth and then to March Field to train with combat crew. From there sent to 15th A.F. in Cerignola, Italy, 741st Sqdn., 455th BG.

On Oct. 7, 1944 we were hit by flak immediately after dropping bombs on railroad yards outside Vienna and lost two engines. Flew an hour losing altitude and tried unsuccessfully to get back to Italy. Our navigator, Carl Rudolph, located a Partisan held piece of Yugoslavia and I ordered the crew to bail out. Two hours later all except tail gunner (captured by Germans) were brought together by Partisans to a farm house outside Koprivnica, from which we started a hike the next morning to Zara on the Dalmatian Coast. Sailed across the Adriatic 49 days later to Ancona in a Royal Navy launch and were picked up by the 15th A.F. and flown to Bari in a C-47.

Flight instructor at Blackland Army Air Field in Waco before separation in July 1945 with rank of first lieutenant. Awarded Air Medal and Distinguished Flying Cross.

Settled in New Jersey with son and daughter. Worked my way to C.E.O. of Bellemead Development Corp., a real estate development firm operating in New Jersey, Connecticut, Pennsylvania, Michigan, Illinois, Maryland, Virginia and Florida. Retired in May 1985, but stay involved on limited basis.

Son, Jim, is a writer and his latest book, "Goodbye, Liberty Belle" is being published by Wright State University Press and is about our adventures in Yugoslavia in 1944 and traveling back in 1986 to meet people who picked up our crew.

ROBERT W. METLEN,
was born Aug. 6, 1922 on a sheep ranch outside Townsend, MT. Joined U.S. Army at Pocatello, ID Oct. 1942 and was assigned to the Air Corp training as radio operator and mechanic at Scott Field and attended gunnery school at Laredo, TX.

Joined crew at Moses Lake, WA. Trained there and Spokane, WA. The crew went overseas via Pendleton, OR, Grand Island, NE and Bangor, ME to Scotland. Assigned to 96th BG, 339th Sqdn., stationed at Snetterton Heath near Norwich, England.

Completed five missions. On sixth mission, Oct. 20, 1943, in a B-17 borrowed from another squadron, en route to Duren, the turbocharger began to fail. At 24,500 ft. the rest of the squadron went to 29,500 ft. leaving them with an escort of German fighters. The pilot told the crew to bail out as they lost the tail section. Bailed out at about 20,000 ft. and free fell for a while. Pulled the red cord hard and nothing happened. Pulled it a second time much harder and it opened. Metlen swung twice and landed in a potato

field flat on my back. The retainer prongs had been bent close to a right angle instead of 30 degrees. Landed near Ath, Belgium. Six of the 10 crew members made it out.

The underground passed him from Belgium, through France to Spain (locomotion by car, bicycle, train and foot). He was back in England by Dec. 19, 1943. Sent stateside for more training and was on a B-32 on his way to the Pacific when the war ended.

Discharged in December 1945 as technical sergeant. Awarded Bronze Star and Oak Leaf Cluster at Mountain Home Air Base.

Earned degree in Range and Forestry at the University of Idaho, Moscow, ID. Worked as a forest ranger (U.S.) until retired in 1977. Farming ever since.

Married Ruth Walden in 1947. They have three sons and seven grandchildren.

EDGAR W. MICHAELS,
was born July 20, 1923 in Pittsburgh, PA. Military service February 1943 to September 1945, rank first lieutenant.

M.O.S. aerial navigator B-24 with 8th Air Force. Trained at Ellington Field, TX; San Marcos, TX; Harlingen, TX and Pueblo, CO. E.T.O., Shipoham, England with 44th BG, 506th Sqdn. Was M.I.A. in occupied France.

Awards: Air Force Medal, Purple Heart, E.T.O.

Instructor (navigation) March A.F.B., Riverside, CA 1945.

Presently C.E.O./Chairman Hinkel-Hofmann Co., Pittsburgh, PA.

PHILIP M. MIHOLICH,
Capt., was born May 20, 1917 in New York City, NY. Went to Bridgeport Engineering School and joined 242nd Coast Artillery National Guard for extra money. Inducted into service in Aug. 1940. Transferred to U.S.A.F. early 1942 and sent to Kelly Field, San Antonio, TX for pre-flight and testing. Passed for pilot training in Gulf Coast area; primary, Vernon, TX, basic, Waco, TX, advanced, Victoria, TX, class 43C; fighter training P-40s, Sarasota, FL.

Flew to Africa and Cairo to join 57th Fighter Grp., 65th Sqdn. Flew P-40s in Africa, Sicily and Italy up to Foggia. Flew P-47s then, dive bombing and close support for English along Foggia front, also close support along Yugoslavia coast line.

Shot down in Yugoslavia by Trogir area Jan. 1944. Jumped and landed in Adriatic. Got together with Partisan fishermen on coast who took him inland to Commandant Miesta Trogir at a Partisan Headquarters. Spent a couple of months with them, then came back through underground to island of Vis, then to Italy and his old group.

Flew with 65th Sqdn. until in Corsica, then sent home as escapee-evadee. Stationed in Selma, AL at Craig Field instructing French students and West Point grads to fly fighter ships (P-40s) and combat maneuvers as a flight team. Transferred to McClellan Field, Sacramento, CA. Asked for discharge Jan. 1947.

Awards: Purple Heart, Air Medal, Presidential Unit Citation with eight Bronze Stars and American Campaign Medal.

EDWARD C. MILLER,
was born April 25, 1920 in Brooklyn, NY. Entered active duty May 2, 1942. Took pilot training in the Southeast training command and received his pilot's wings June 30, 1943.

Flew the following types aircraft: P-40, P-47, B-25, B-26, A-26, B-17, B-24, and C-47.

While serving in the 8th A.F., 93rd BG, 328th Bomb Sqdn., his B-24 was shot down by flak on a mission to Ludwigshafen, Germany on Jan. 7, 1944. Evaded through Germany and France and crossed the Pyrenees into Spain. Finally flew from Gibraltar back to England and returned to base on June 5, 1944.

Released from active duty Jan. 26, 1946 as captain.

Worked for the Spury Corp. in New York in quality engineering for 43 years before retiring. Reside in Sedona, AZ.

WILLIAM J. MILLER, was born Nov. 19, 1916 in Pittsburgh, PA. Joined military April 30, 1942.

After basic training in Biloxi, MS went to armament school at Buckley Field, Denver, CO; gunnery school in Wendover, UT; and then to Boise, ID, assigned to 379th Grp., 525th Sqdn., as waist gunner on B-17, *Battlin' Bobbie*.

On 23rd mission, Sept. 16, 1943, plane was shot down near Rennes, France, on way from Kimbolton Field, England to target in Nantes. Landed in apple orchard, immediately helped by two Frenchmen and then by many more moving from Rennes to Paris to Luchan, over the Pyrenees into Bosost, Spain on May 19, 1944.

After return to U.S. was assigned to Lowry Field, Denver, CO. Married Lilly on March 24, 1945. Discharged in September 1945.

Worked in construction, taught carpentry apprentice classes and, for 25 years, worked for the City and County of Denver. Retired July 1, 1982 as director, City Building Inspection Dept.

MILTON J. MILLS, was born April 22, 1923 in Kenova, WV. Drafted into military Jan. 25, 1943. After basic training at Goldsboro, NC, radio school at Salt Lake City, UT and flight training at Pyote and Dalhart, TX, assigned to 379th Grp., 527th Sqdn. as radio operator gunner on B-17 "Judy", Kimbolton Field, England.

On T/Sgt. Mills, second mission Dec. 30,

1943, after bombing raid on Ludwigshafen, Germany, his plane was shot down near Paris, France. Bailed out and landed in open field. Aided by French Resistance in Gouveux, Amiens, Paris and Pau, France, crossed Pyrenees into Spain April 21, 1944.

After return to U.S., assigned to A.A.F.B. at Yuma, AZ. Married before going overseas to Evelyn L. Pygman Aug. 16, 1943.

Discharged from A.A.F. Regional Hospital, Santa Ana, CA Nov. 29, 1944. Worked as merchant ten years and employed by Ohio River Co. for 33 years. Retired Aug. 9, 1985.

GEORGE C. MONG, Lt. Col., was born Oct. 6, 1923 in Oil City, PA. Enlisted at Buffalo, NY Aug. 29, 1942.

Received pilot training at Southeast training command, graduated class 43K, Moody Field, GA. B-17 phase training, Rapid City A.A. Field, SD. Flew B-17s, C-47s, B-25s, P-38s, SA-16s, T-29, C-131, C-54, C-118.

Released from active duty in October 1945. Recalled in May 1953. Retired Nov. 1, 1970 with a total of 28 years military service.

Shot down July 13, 1944 on raid to Munich, Germany. Bailed out near Ciegy-En-Vofis, France. Aided by French Underground, returned with American Tank Unit of 3rd Army in September 1944.

Served in England, Alaska, Korea, Japan, Southeast Asia. Resides in Sebastian, FL and Warren, PA.

ERNEST T. MORIARTY, was born Feb. 21, 1922 in Winchendon, MA. Graduated Murdock High, Winchendon in June 1939.

Enlisted U.S. Army Air Corps June 26, 1941, Boston, MA. Basic training 34th BG, 18th Bomb Sqdn., Westover Field, Chicopee, MA. Group to Pendleton, OR after war started.

Transferred to Perry Institute, Yakima, WA. Graduated as engine mechanic May 27, 1942. Assigned to 306th BG, 368th Sqdn. at Wendover Field, UT.

Overseas on the Queen Elizabeth, reaching Thurleigh, England on Sept. 6, 1942.

Volunteered for gunner course at Bovington, England. Flew first mission on Jan. 3, 1943 to St. Nazaire, France. Flew first German mission to Wilhelmshaven Jan. 27, 1943.

Shot down in occupied France on March 8, 1943 on ninth mission. Otto Buddenbaum, pilot K.I.A. Some on crew badly wounded. All P.O.W.s. Evaded and escaped on fishing boat with 16 Frenchmen and one French woman. Landed in England April 1, 1943.

Returned by Pentagon to States for lecture tour. Returned to England July 13, 1944. Assigned to 96th BG, 337th Sqdn. Crashed on railroad tracks on 19th mission on Nov. 21, 1944. Crew in hospital. Finished last six to complete tour of 25 as spare engineer. Made a round-robin to Russio, Italy and then returned to England.

Returned to States Feb. 1, 1945. Discharged June 6, 1945.

Married second time with two daughters. Son and daughter from first marriage and three grandsons. Daughter died at age 18.

Author "One Day Into Twenty-Three", self-published with wife, Maggie.

PAUL F. MORITZ, was born June 1, 1922 in Bronx, NY. Enlisted June 30, 1942. Discharged Oct. 19, 1945. Reenlisted March 1951. Discharged November 1952. Served in Active Reserve until June 1980.

S/Sgt. Moritz, 15th A.F., 455th BG, 742nd Sqdn. flew B-24 "Ready Teddy". On a mission to Munich on Sept. 12, 1944 lost two engines over the target and headed for southern France. Forced down by Swiss fighters, landed and interned in Adleboden, Switzerland.

On Sept. 22, Moritz and 8th A.F. Sergeant David Whitman left on foot for Lausanne, where they contacted a British Major Field House who put them in touch with a member of the French Underground. They were caught crossing the wire south of Geneva and put in the Lausanne prison.

On Sept. 26, while being transferred under guard to a Swiss concentration camp, they managed to jump off the train and spent the night walking back to Lausanne. With the help of the F.F.I. they arrived in France Oct. 1 and became the first Americans in Annemasse (or so they were told).

Resides in Sheffield, MA.

JAY MUELLER,
was a bombardier, 15th Air Force, 5th Wing, 483rd BG (H), 815th Bomb Sqdn., Stysarone, Italy, APO 520.

On July 9, 1944, after a strike at Ploesti his crew was downed near Mostar, Yugoslavia, on their 42nd mission. Chetnik soldiers and civilians made our evasion possible. After 33 days seven of us were airlifted by the ATC to Bari, Italy.

Memorable was a night in Rudo, Yugoslavia, when Chetnik and Partisan forces fought a fierce battle and destroyed that picture postcard little city.

After R&R in Capri, finished his remaining eight missions with other 815th Bomb Sqdn. crews. Separated from the U.S.A.A.F. at Davis-Monthan Field in September 1945, where he was a B-29 bombardier instructor.

Now an attorney in Orlando, FL.

CLAUDE C. MURRAY, JR.,
was born Dec. 30, 1921 in Spokane, WA. Enlisted U.S.A.A.C. in November 1942, graduated class 43J, Williams Field, AZ.

Combat assignment was to the 8th A.F., 7th Photo Reconnaissance Group, Mount Farm, England, Aug. 1944 as a replacement pilot. After three successful missions, he was "hit" by an Me262 on Oct. 6, 1944 while on a lone trip to Hamm, Germany. Learned the hard way to bail out of a Lockheed Lightening via the "split-ess" maneuver and falling out.

Luck began with a 13-hour experience in a dinghy in the cold Zuider Zee, Netherlands. Picked out of sea by young fisherman, Jan Dobber, and two companions, who proceeded to take him ashore and ultimately to contact with the Dutch Resistance leader in the village of Muiden, Joh. Rozendaal. The Resistance received orders that Murray was to remain there and not attempt escape. Although unknown to him at the time, hundreds of other airmen were also evading the Nazi while posing as deaf and dumb Hollanders. Liberated May 5, 1945 and returned to base in England

via Camp Lucky Strike and a C-47.

Although most three-and-a-half mission evaders received no medals and no decorations, Murray is an accredited and documented member of the following honorary organizations: Caterpillar Club (Irvin Great Britain), Caterpillar Club (Switlik Parachute Co.), Sea Squatters Club (Walter Kidde & Co. NY), and the Goldfish Club (London, England). Murray "walked out" of Holland along with three bomb group evaders.

Post-war was a director of the 8th A.F. Historical Soc., director of the Air Forces Escape and Evasion Soc., director and secretary of the P-38 National Assn. In 1979 he founded the 7th Photo Recon. Grp. Assn. and for eight years he served the 7PRG as treasurer, corresponding secretary, computer manager, newsletter editor, PX manager and advisor to the association presidents. Became widely known among members of 8A.F.H.S., A.F.E.E.S. and the 7PRG as "Gadfly" and for his many innovations.

Married to Shirley and father of three sons: Jeffrey, Steven, and Thomas. Resides in Sun City, AZ.

CARL T. NALL,
Lt. Col., was born Feb. 14, 1921 in Concho County, TX. Joined U.S. Army Air Corp Aviation Cadet Program April 6, 1942. Received wings and commission at Blackland Base, Waco, TX; combat training at Tucson and Blythe, CA. Flew B-24s, C-47s, single and multi-engine trainers. Released from active duty Nov. 9, 1945. Retired from Reserves Feb. 14, 1981.

Ferried B-24 via South America and Africa to combat assignment with 389th BG, 8th A.F., Wymondham, England.

Shot down on March 5, 1944 on mission to southern France. Heroic aid by the French Maquis Underground helped him and seven other crew members to evade over Pyrenees to Spain. Returned to England on D-Day.

Returned to U.S. serving at Bryan, TX, Smyrno, TN, Albuquerque, NM, Pecos, TX and Love Field, Dallas, TX. Separated at Randolph Field, TX. Returned to civil service position at Naval Air Station Corpus Christi, TX. Retired Feb. 1976 after serving as deputy comptroller and accounting officer. Second career in data processing. Last retirement December 1983.

Married Clara M. Potter July 31, 1943. Children: Carl Than, Jr.; Judith Clare and Randall Potter. Grandchildren: Nicky and Than Niles. Currently reside in Missouri City, TX.

KENNETH E. NEFF,
was born May 23, 1918 in Paden City, WV. Joined Army Air Corps Aug. 29, 1940. Discharged Oct. 19, 1945. Reenlisted Oct. 24, 1948. Retired U.S.A.F., master sergeant, May 31, 1966.

During WWII, flew as a B-17 ball turret gunner with the 92nd BG. Shot down April 29, 1944 and spent four-and-a-half months with the French Underground.

During the Korean War, again flew with the 92nd BG but on the B-29. Went from bottom of the plane to the top C.F.C. gunner. Since went down on 17th mission on a B-17, didn't fly 29th mission on the B-29, just 28A-28B then number 30.

Gave up flying in 1951 and spent 12 years training crew members in the art of "survival".

Married Mildred "Midge" Dvoracek Aug. 4, 1945. Two sons, Randy and Jerry and their families reside in Fresno, CA. Enjoy five lively grandchildren.

Lived in Atwater, CA for the past 28 years. Volunteer tour guide at Castle Air Museum.

ROBERT E. NELSON,
was born April 8, 1917 in Gresham, OR. Educated in Oregon, earning a B.S. from Oregon State University. Entered U.S.A.A.C. as cadet Jan. 12, 1942.

Commissioned second lieutenant and pilot and married July 26, 1942 in Stockton, CA. Cadet training at Visalia, Bakersfield and Stockton, CA. Four engine training in Washington, Kansas, Texas and New Mexico. Assigned to 532nd Sqdn., 381st BG, Pyote, TX Feb. 19, 1943 as pilot and then as squadron operations officer. Group arrived in United Kingdom joining the 8th A.F. in June 1943, stationed at Ridgewell Station 167.

On Aug. 17, 1943, while flying as deputy group commanding officer of the 381st BG (target: Schweinfurt-Regenburg, Germany) his aircraft was destroyed on the way so they hit the silks about five mile SW of Koblenz. He and M/Sgt. Raymond Genz of Minnesota evaded capture in Germany and arrived in occupied Luxemburg 13 days later, and were offered hiding by some brave Luxemburgers. They successfully started them on the way south through occupied France, Andorra into Spain and they eventually arrived at Gibraltar, then England Oct. 31, 1943. They were sworn to secrecy nine different times to keep escape routes open and not to jeopardize people involved.

Told that they were the first U.S. Airmen to evade and escape out of Germany, therefore, were assigned temporary duty with A-2, section of 8th A.F. to visit all the American air stations in England giving their experiences to fellow airmen for confidence.

After returning to the States, was assigned temporary duty at Headquarters War Dept., Washington, D.C., assigned to Military Intelligence Service for furtherance of escape and evasion tactics, etc.

Then served at Roswell A.F.B., later training Headquarters Ft. Worth as member of Liaison Team to coordinate training with Bomber Command.

Discharged in December 1945 and stayed on as Air Force Reservist to retire at rank of lieutenant colonel.

Resides in Medford, OR, as a partner in a lumber wholesale company where they owned a company aircraft. Now enjoys semi-retirement.

EDWARD F. NEU, was born Sept. 15, 1916 in New Boston, OH. Entered military July 1942. Graduated A.A.F. navigation school August 1943. Assigned with crew to 8th A.F., 92nd BG, Podington, England.

Plane crash landed in occupied France Dec. 31, 1943. Neu and Co-Pilot L.C. Busboom were found by French Underground several days later, taken to southern France, hid in an old stone stable in the mountains until May 1944. They were led across the mountains (three days and nights of walking(arriving at Bosost, Spain about May 19. After two or three weeks they were taken to Gibraltar and back to England and later back to the States.

Lt. Neu was separated in November 1945, returned to his job in the civil engineering department of the N&W Ry Co. where he retired as resident engineer of the Scioto Div. in June 1977.

Married Marie Sturgill Oct. 4, 1941. Resides in Portsmouth, OH.

JACK E. NOSSER, was born Sept. 14, 1920 in Johannesburg, CA. Served in the U.S. Navy 1938-41. Joined the Army Air Corps March 1942. Pre-flight at Santa Ana. Bombardier training at Kirtland Field, class of 43-2. Gunnery school at Las Vegas.

Joined the 570th Sqdn., 390th BG at Geiger Field, WA. Shot down on 13th mission Oct. 10, 1943 at Munster, Germany. Crash landed in Germany, evaded into Holland and there was betrayed by Dutch civilians. Sent to South Camp, Stalag Luft III. On the blizzard march to Stalag 7A, Moosburg. Escaped Moosburg, April 1945 and reached American Forces north of the Danube. Recalled to active duty in July of 1951. Assigned to 64th Bomb Sqdn., 43rd Bomb Wing at Davis-Monthan.

Separated March of 1953 as first lieutenant. Bombed from AT-11, B-17, B-25, B-29 and B-50s.

Retired from the Southern California Gas Co. in 1983. Married Mary Ellen Drage in 1946. Reside in Panorma Village, Hemet, CA.

DAVID W. O'BOYLE, was born Nov. 13, 1920 in Framingham, MA. Joined 181st Infantry, 26th Div., Massachusetts National Guard 1937, at age 16. Enlisted in Air Corps in April 1942 as prospective Aviation Cadet. Pre-flight training as pilot came next at San Antonio Aviation Training Center. Transferred to primary flight training at Parks Air College near St. Louis, MO.

At completion of primary with class 43D, several members, including O'Boyle, whose primary qualification was for navigation training were ordered to the navigation training center at Ellington Field in Houston, TX for accelerated navigation school due to high combat losses of navigators. Graduated Hondo Advanced Navigation School Aug. 5, 1943 as second lieutenant and assigned to Mowers crew in third phase training at Dalhart, TX. Left for overseas Nov. 11, 1943, eventually joining 95th BG (H), mid-November 1943.

Shot down over Belgium Jan. 24, 1944 on ninth mission. Evaded capture until liberated in September 1944.

Returned to U.S. late September 1944, assigned Ellington Field, Houston, TX for postgraduate navigation training and subsequently assigned as navigation instructor in Del Rio, TX. After one year and promotion to first lieutenant, transferred to Dow Field, Bangor, Maine until relieved of active duty in September 1945. Transferred to active reserve and eventually to Massachusetts Air National Guard until mid-1955.

Awarded Air Medal and Purple Heart.

Married. Post-war career was in sales, Massachusetts sales manager for Sonatone Hearing Aid Co., Kansas City sales manager for Geo. A. Breon Pharmaceutical Co., western sales manager in Denver for the Upson Co., sales manager at Clinton Aviation 1961-68. Self-employed as Cessna, Bellanca and Grumman aircraft dealer through 1978. Owner and operator of Proficiency Pilot Training Center 1978-86 training corporate pilots in operation of corporate jets such as LearJet, Falcon and Queenaire. Retired. Resides in Denver, CO.

BENJAMIN L. O'DELL, Capt., was born Aug. 30, 1921 in Cumberland Gap, TN. From Reserve, called to active duty April 1943. Basic training Keesler Field, MS, college training detachment U.T. Knoxville, TN, primary and advanced navigation training Selman Field, LA, combat training Pyote, TX.

Flew with 359th Sqdn., 303rd BG, 8th A.F., Molesworth, England. Navigated 8th A.F. lead plane (B-17) over target at Merseberg, Germany on 30th mission Jan. 10, 1945. Navigator on lead plane to Cologne, Germany, took a direct hit from flak. Bailed out in Belgium, Battle of Bulge area. Aided by F.F.I.

Returned to States March 1945. Released from active duty to reserve September 1945.

Graduated University of Tennessee 1950. Recalled to active duty for Korean War January 1951. Served at Kelly Field, TX.

On C-97 set world record time non-stop Hickhan Field, HI to Kelly Field, TX April 1951. Served as group navigator, 374th Troop Carrier Group at Tachikawa, Japan. Also manpower management officer at 374th Troop Carrier Wing. Released from active duty September 1952.

Married Ruth Rogers (deceased) and has a daughter, Linda Pierce. Grandchildren: Jennifer, Heidi Lynn, Jerry Michael. Retired executive, dairy industry. Resides in Johnson City, TN.

JOHN H. OLIPHINT, was born Dec. 8, 1921 in Hemphill, TX. Joined U.S. Army Air Corps Dec. 1941 to be a flying sergeant. Graduated second lieutenant pilot class 43C, Victoria, TX.

Flew military prop and jet fighters, bombers, cargo, V.I.P, reconnaissance, trainers, seaplanes, civilian, foreign my own and anything else he could get his hands on for 27 years.

Active in three wars. Awarded Command Pilot Wings, Silver Star, three Distinguished Flying Crosses, eight Air Medals, Purple Heart, Bronze Star, Commendation, P.O.W., numerous theatres, foreign and other medals.

WWII fighter pilot, P-47, P-51s, four-and-a-half kills.

Ground fire downed on 67th mission. Captured, wounded in crashed aircraft, intense physical interrogations. Escaped, joined French Maquis and was later flown from behind enemy lines by MI-9 to England.

Korean War: covert and escape and evasion Intelligence duties with guerilla forces behind enemy lines. Conducted theatre E&E briefings and ran recovery center for downed F.E.A.F. Airmen. Taught E&E SAC Survival School, Air Force advisor, security service, research, development, etc. Ended military career in 1968.

Established, ran, and retired a successful housing construction business for 10 years. No plans to ever retire. Health and happiness is now enjoyed traveling, hunting, fishing. Living part time in Colorado and Texas.

"Winning is not luck. It's knowing how to fight."

GEORGE C. PADGETT, was born June 10, 1922 in Greenleaf, KS. Joined the Aviation Cadets in Jan. 1942 and graduated as a bombardier from San Angelo, TX. Completed combat training by gunnery school at Fort Meyers, FL and third phase

B-17 training at Blythe, CA and Dyersburg, TN.

Flew with the 379th BG, 525th Sqdn., from Kimbolton, England. Shot down and bailed out over La Chapelle-Thoirault near Rennes, France on Sept. 23, 1943. Evaded throughout France until captured at the Toulouse Train Station Feb. 2, 1944 while attempting to cross the Pyrenees into Spain.

After the war graduated from Kansas University as a petroleum engineer. Spent most of career working in Kuwait and Saudi Arabia as a manager for Getty Oil Co. Retired in Feb. 1985.

As a widower, met Guilaine Toreau in Paris and married in January 1987. Now headquartered in Sacramento, CA, but spend several months each year near Guilaine's family in Biarritz, France.

RALPH K. PATTON,

RALPH K. PATTON, was born Aug. 16, 1920 in Wilkinsburg, PA. Enlisted in the U.S. Army Air Corps April 17, 1942. Received pilots wings and commission as a second lieutenant at Altus, OK, class 43E, May 23, 1943.

First duty station, Pyote, TX, co-pilot B-17 June 1943. Assigned to the 331st Sqdn., 94th BG, 8th A.F. at Bury Saint Edmonds, England, Oct. 21, 1943. Flew first combat mission to the Renault factory near Paris Nov. 26, 1943.

Shot down on ninth combat mission to Merignac Air Field east of Bordeaux. Parachuted from crippled B-17 in the center of the Brittany Peninsula of western France at noon Jan. 5, 1944.

Lived with various members of the French Underground in the villages of Plouray, Langonnet, and Guingamp until March 18, 1944. Departed the French coast the night of March 18th from the town of Plouha via British motor gunboat 503 under the control of British Military Intelligence Service's Reseau Shelburn. Reseau Shelburn was under the command of two Canadian Intelligence officers, Lucien Dumais and Raymond LaBrosse.

Returned to the U.S. April 20, 1944 and served until the war's end as an instructor pilot B-17 at Columbus, OH and Sebring, FL.

Married to the former Bette Lou Hopkins May 1, 1944. Two children: Geoffrey L. Patton of Washington, D.C. and Beverly Patton Wand of Madison, NJ. Two grandchildren: Christopher and Elizabeth Wand.

Returned to civilian life in October 1946 as manager, Order Dept., Consolidation Coal Co., Pittsburgh, PA. Served in various managerial positions in Buffalo, NY, Rochester, NY and Detroit, MI. Retired in 1983 as vice president of eastern sales of Consolidation Coal Co., a subsidiary of the Dupont Co.

Founded the Air Forces Escape & Evasion Society in 1964 and served as its president from that time until the present. Served eight years as a director of the 8th Air Force Historical Society, including one year as president. Currently a director of the 8th Air Force Memorial Museum Foundation.

ARNOLD O. PEDERSON,

ARNOLD O. PEDERSON, was born Aug. 12, 1922 in Isle Royale, MI. Joined Army Air Corps Aug. 10, 1942. Took basic training at Sheppard Field, TX and Tyndall Field, FL.

Took combat training at Ephrata, WA, Rapid City, SD, Walla Walla, WA and Pyote, TX.

Flew as flight engineer with 729th Sqdn., 452nd Grp. at Deophum Green, England.

Shot down over northern France on returning from Frankfurt in February 1944. With aid of French Resistance, escaped over Pyrenees and returned to England May 6, 1944.

Returned to U.S. and assigned to Army Intelligence in Pentagon. Then as instructor at Alexandria, LA. Discharged on Nov. 27, 1945. Retired as railroad conductor on D.M.I.R. Railroad, Two Harbors, MN.

He and his wife, Irja, reside in Duluth, MN and have three children: Mary, Sandra and Lori and two grandchildren.

JOSEPH O. PELOQUIN,

JOSEPH O. PELOQUIN, S.Sgt., was born Nov. 10, 1923 in Saco, ME. Joined military Oct. 1, 1942 and attended airplane mechanic school at Sheppard Field, TX and airplane engine school at Wrights Aeronautical in Patterson, NJ and on to Wendover Aerial Gunnery School in Wendover, UT. Trained on B-24 Liberator as flight engineer.

At Alamogordo, NM, Langley Field, VA on sub-patrol prior to being assigned to 8th A.F. at 44th BG in England.

Bailed out on second mission over France May 11, 1944. Evaded until Aug. 13, 1944 after being liberated by American troops.

Separated from service April 26, 1945. Now retired from Portsmouth Naval Shipyard as a submarine pipefitter after 28 years of government service.

He and wife reside in Biddeford, ME.

JOSEPH M. PERRY, JR.,

JOSEPH M. PERRY, JR., was born in San Leandro, CA on Sept. 20, 1924. Inducted on April 6, 1944. Took basic training in Fresno, CA and went to armament school in Lowry Field, Denver, CO for nine weeks. Went to gunnery school in Laredo, TX for six weeks and became an A.P. armorer gunner.

Air crew was made up in Salt Lake City, UT and overseas flying training was at David Monthan Field, Tucson, AZ. Went to Mountain Home, ID for more training and to make bomb group.

In April of 1944, flew B-24 to England by way of Trinidad, Brazil and Africa, arriving May 12, 1944.

Group was in the battle of Normandy and north France. First mission was D-Day. On June 22, 1944, while bombing the Marshalling Yard, plane was hit by flak, sending the landing wheel through the hole in the wing and cutting all controls to the outboard motor. They dropped out of formation, throwing out all their ammunition and dropping their bombs on an air field, on way back to England. Fighters attacked them, forcing bail-out. Pilot Lt. David Kilpatrick was hit, seriously wounded and died after bail-out in the arms of a Frenchman. Roland Holwegner, the nose gunner, was wounded, as was the co-pilot, Lt. Allardt.

Once on the ground, the French took Perry to their farm. There, with Germans all around, he asked to be taken to a forest to hide. He slept there and started walking south. Came upon a village, early in morning, not knowing if they were friendly, and went around village until he came to a turn in the road and encountered a German on a motorcycle. He went by him and he decided he needed help. The second man he met was a Frenchman whom he asked for help.

Was taken to a school where the Gendarmes (police) helped him. They took Perry to Fouquet's farm to wait. In a day or two they brought tail gunner Koch and ball gunner Woodruff to the farm. There was a British soldier, John Vallely, who had been there for four years. He told them the best thing to do was to wait because all escape routes were closed due to the invasion.

They next took them to Huby's house in town where he met up with the rest of his crew. The seven men were placed with different French people on different farms to wait for liberation. Perry was put on the Le Grain farm and after many encounters with Germans while working there for two months, finally was liberated. Arrived back in England Sept. 13, 1944, just in time for his 20th birthday.

Discharged Oct. 9, 1944. Left service as a staff sergeant, 490th BG, 848th Sqdn.

Retired carpenter with five children, eight grandchildren, two step-children and two step-grandchildren.

Received Air Medal GO 237 HQ3 BG 1944, Distinguished Unit Badge, Victory Medal, American Theatre Ribbon, E.T.O. Ribbon with three Bronze Stars, and Good Conduct Medal.

NICHOLAS J. PETERS, was born Nov. 15, 1920 in Wyandotte, MI. Joined the service in March 1942 Ft. Custer, Battle Creek, MI. Basic training (Infantry) at Camp Livingston; 112th Infantry, H Co., 28th Div. Alexandria, LA. Transferred to Army Air Force, San Antonio, TX, Nov. 18, 1942 and went to Aviation Cadet Center for pre-flight (pilot) training Jan. 19, 1943-March 20, 1943. Elementary flying at Cimarron Field, Yukon, OK, 310 A.A.F.C.F.S., March 21, 1943-June 25, 1943 and basic flying June 27, 1943-Sept. 28, 1943 at Strother Army Air Field, Winifield, KS. Was a

Other schools and training at: Childress Army Air Field (bombardier), Childress, TX; Lowry Army Field (armament school), Denver, CO; Buckingham A.A.F. (flexible gunnery school 23 A.T.U.) Fort Meyers, FL; Drew Army Air Field (327 A.A.F. Base Unit R.T.U. HB) Tampa, FL; Hunter A.A.F. (3 A.A.F. staging wing) Savannah, GA; Goose A.A.F., Goose Bay, Labrador; Goodfellow Air Force Base (A.T.C.) San Angelo, TX; Webb A.F.B., (missile training wing) Orlando, FL. Stationed at numerous other and various locations stateside, in Europe, the Pacific and Asia.

Shot down on 11th mission Jan. 5, 1945 over Germany. Completed 35 missions.

Achieve rank of staff sergeant. Discharged in July 1945. Reenlisted. Discharged in July 1965.

Awarded Air Medal with Silver Oak, WWII Victory Medal, E.T.O. with four Bronze Stars, Army Good Conduct Medal, Distinguished Unit Badge with Bronze Oak, Air Force Longevity Service Ribbon with four, Air Force Good Conduct with three Bar Loops, Navy Good Conduct with one star, Navy Expert Pistol Medal, American Campaign Medal and National Defense Medal.

Retired from Air Force and Post Office.

THEODORE MELVIN (TED) PETERSON, was born Oct. 24, 1919 in Bountiful, UT. Entered U.S. Army Air Corps Aviation Cadet training Jan. 28, 1942. Pilot training at Cal-Aero Academy, Ontario, CA and Luke Field, AZ. B-17 combat pilot training Spokane, WA, Pyote, TX and Salina, KS.

E.T.O. 526th Sqdn., 379th BG, Kimbolton,

England, April 16, 1943. Shot down bombing submarine pens at St. Nazaire, France May 29, 1943. Escaped capture, aided by French Underground via Plourhan, St. Quay-Portrieux, St. Brieux, Paris, Toulouse, Folix, in France. Over the Pyrenees to Barcelona, Madrid, Gibraltar and back to England Aug. 16, 1943.

Returned to the U.S. Sept. 29, 1943. Instructor pilot at Columbus, OH, Galveston, TX and Sioux City, IA. Separated from the military service Sept. 29, 1945.

In 1987 was invited to dedication of monument in Plourhan, France (made from engine and propeller from his plane that had been submerged in ocean for 42 years), a tribute to honor the airmen and Resistance fighters who helped them escape.

Married Ileann Wendrich (Ann) Dec. 26, 1942. Parents of six children. Was real estate broker and developer 1946 to 1980. Retired and now resides in Bountiful, UT.

JOHN W. (BILL) PETTY, was born March 22, 1918. Joined Air Force Nov. 11, 1942. Served 1943, Cochran Field, GA on basic training planes as mechanic. Gunnery school, 1944 at Harlingen, TX. Overseas combat training on B-24 bomber in Casper, WY.

Nose gunner, B-24 *Dinah Might*, 761st Sqdn., 460th BG, 15th A.F., Spinazzola, Italy, Lt. Gerald S. Armstrong, pilot.

After his bomber crashed in enemy territory, Petty evaded capture and was rescued by two men (still alive) in Yugoslavia. Two other crew members and he were hidden by a lady for five days and nights. They walked through enemy territory for 72 days, two-to-three hundred miles. Later flown out of Yugo. back to friendly territory in south Italy.

In 1969, while in Venice, Italy, he wanted very much to find the lady, Mrs. Amaleja Faletic, to thank her for saving him from capture by the enemy and possibly from freezing in the Alps. What once was Caporetto, Italy was now Kobarid, Yugoslavia, the boundary being changed after the war. He found the lovely 88-year-old lady on a return trip to Yugoslavia in 1969.

Currently resides in Carthage, TN.

ROBERT PIPES, native of Dallas, Texas, attended schools in Dallas. Entered active military service in 1940 with 112th Cavalry. Enlisted Army Air Corps in May 1941. Assigned to Lt. Franklyn V. Cotner's crew in Boise, ID in July 1943. Transferred to Casper, WY in August 1943 with 331st BG, receiving three months training on B-24D aircraft. Transferred to Alamogordo, NM Nov. 1943, 466th BG. Further training on B-24s, crew assigned B-24H, S.N. 41-29399, named *Playboy*.

Transferred to Attlebridge, England via Herington, KN, Puerto Rico, British Guiana, Bra-

zil, Africa and Wales, Feb. 1944.

Flew 10 combat missions. Shot down by flak and FW190s on 11th mission to Berlin.

Bailed out of aircraft in Holland April 29, 1944. Evaded capture along with H.L. Heafner, Jr. until April 1945.

Retired U.S.A.F. Nov. 1960. Retired Solar Turbines, Inc. 1983.

JAMES W. POWELL, Sgt., was born Nov. 16, 1921 in St. Marys, KS. Joined Army Sept. 8, 1942 at Toledo, OH. Trained, then served as a B-17 mechanic. After gunnery school, received B-25 air crew training as an engineer-gunner.

Flew with 71st Sqdn., 38th BG, 5th A.F., Lingayen, Luzon, PI, WWII. During fourth mission, March 29, 1945, plane disabled over Formosa and crash landed in Japanese-occupied southeastern China. Evaded westward through China, reaching 14th A.F. HQ, Kunming, China April 2, 1945.

Returned to combat duty at Lingayen. On ninth mission, May 17, 1945, was wounded in action over Formosa. Returned to U.S., given a medical discharge Dec. 7, 1945.

Graduated as mechanical engineer June 1949. Served various aerospace firms as propulsion systems engineer. Retired from Hughes Aircraft Co. Feb. 27, 1987.

Married Jeanne A. Racy Sept. 2, 1944. Children: Thomas J., Michelle L., and Cheri M. (deceased). Grandchildren: Jeffrey, Jamey, Tia and Ross. Reside in Newhall, CA.

JOHN E. (JACK) PURDY, was born in Wyandotte, MI, June 17, 1919 and has resided in Dayton, OH since the end of WWII.

In June of 1941, he was drafted into the Army, and served his basic training in the Cavalry at Fort Riley, KS. After completing his basic training he was sent to Fort Snelling, MN where he remained until the outbreak of WWII in December of 1941, at which time he applied for and was accepted into the Army Air Corps Flying Cadet Program. He graduated from Luke Air Force Base at Phoenix, AZ in May 1943.

After extensive stateside training in P-40s, P-

39s, and P-38s, he was sent to the Southwest Pacific Theater for combat duty, assigned to the 475th Fighter Grp., 433rd Sqdn., 5th A.F., stationed in New Guinea, flying the Lockheed Lightening P-38.

Capt. Purdy, during the next 18 months, flew 184 combat missions from New Guinea bases at Port Moresby, Dobo-Dura, Finschhafen, Nadzab, Hollandia, Biak, and Philippine bases at Leyte, Mindoro and Luzon. While stationed at Mindoro he was appointed operations officer of the 433rd Sqdn. and subsequently led many of the squadron missions.

Tally record: seven kills, two probables, all air.

Survived four crash landings: one in the San Francisco Bay while flying a P-39; three in P-38s, one off the end of Dobo-Dura air strip in New Guinea, one in the Leyte Gulf, Philippine Islands, and the last in Cavite Province, southeast of Manila, Philippine Islands. In Cavite crash, Purdy was behind enemy lines and spent 16 days with Philippine guerrillas, recovering from injuries, before being transported to the coast for eventual pick up by an air-sea rescue PBY.

Awards: Distinguished Flying Cross with two Oak Leaf Clusters, Air Medal with six Oak Leaf Clusters and Purple Heart.

DOID K. RAAB, 1st Lt., was born Feb. 19, 1921 in Lancaster, OH. Enlisted Army Air Corps Sept. 18, 1942. Commissioned and earned pilot's wings May 23, 1944. Discharged Nov. 29, 1945. Flew with the 15th A.F., 450th BG, 721st Sqdn. Manduria, Italy.

Jan. 31, 1945, mission was Vienna flying a B-24 *Hubba Hubba*. With two inboard engines out we headed for Russian territory and safely landed at Srspka Crnja, Yugoslavia. Rescued by one of Tito's Partisan commanders, Djuro Knezevic and English speaking Ziva Popov. Taken by truck to Timosoara, Rumania and by train to Bucharest. The British flew them back, having been missing only 28 days. Flew 14 more missions, totaling 21.

In 1985 the veterans of Yugoslavia invited them back for a forty-year reunion. They were

royally entertained; placed a wreath on Marshal Tito's tomb, made honorary citizens, reunited with Djuro Knezevic, then 76 years old and Ziva Popov, then 95 years old. It was really a memorable experience.

FRANCIS C. (FRANK) RAMSEY, was born Feb. 11, 1921 in Gaffney, SC. Joined the Army Air Corps Aviation Cadet Program June 18, 1942.

Took basic training at Keesler Field in Biloxi, MS; aerial gunnery training at Laredo, TX and airplane mechanics at Keesler Field, MS.

Assigned out of Salt Lake City, UT as a member of the original 464th Heavy Bomb Group. Took combat training at Pocatello, ID. Flew overseas by the southern route with stops in Puerto Rico; British Guiana; Blehm and Natal, Brazil; Dakar, Senegal; Marrakech, Morocco; Tunis, Tunisia. Flew first mission out of Gioia del Colle, Italy and later moved to permanent base at Panatella, Italy.

On third trip to Ploesti, 39th mission, had to bail out over Yugoslavia. Spent 39 days there as an evader. Got help from the Partisans and was eventfully flown out by the Russians.

Returned to States and trained at the engine specialist school at Chanute Field, IL. After graduating as an engine specialist on flying status, was sent to the B-29 base at Savannah, GA. Stayed there until release from the service on Aug. 29, 1945.

Obtained the rank of technical sergeant. Awarded the E.T.O. Ribbon, with seven Battle Stars; two Presidential Unit Citations; the Purple Heart; Air Medal with two Oak Leaf Clusters and the Distinguished Flying Cross.

After discharge, attended Clemson University and graduated in 1948 with a B.S. Degree in Textile Engineering. Married to his wife, Hazel, in 1949. They have two children. Retired from the textile business in 1980. Retired from golfing the same year.

BERNARD W. RAWLINGS, Capt., was born June 24, 1920 in Sioux City, IA. Joined the Army April 18, 1942, pilot training in Texas. Assigned as B-17 co-pilot, joined 427th Sqdn., 303rd BG, 8th A.F., stationed at Molesworth, England.

Shot down on Jan. 29, 1944, during combat

mission to Frankfurt, Germany. Evaded through Belgium and France to Spain. Returned to England through Gibraltar May 28, 1944.

Was B-17 pilot instructor at Lockbourne Army Air Base, Columbus, OH. Released from active duty Sept. 1, 1945, and was then employed as pilot by Trans World Airlines.

Flew for TWA until retirement in 1988, with brief recall to active duty as C-46 pilot instructor with 514th Troop Carrier Wing, U.S.A.F., at Mitchel Field, NY, in 1951-52.

Married Cecile Elaine Shelton, June 27, 1942 and has three children. Resident of Long Island, NY.

CHESTER RAY, 1st Lt., was born Sept. 21, 1919 in Fitzgerald, GA and moved to Detroit, MI at age two. Was in the Air Corps from April 1941 to Aug. 1945. Service schools: air mechanic at Chanute Field; pilot, class of 43H, Southeast training command; B-24 at Maxwell Field; instrument pilot instructor at Lubbock, TX. Served with the 484th BG and transferred to the 461st at Cerignola, Italy.

Shot down July 12, 1944 in southern France. Helped by Mr. and Mrs. Edward Cassien of Nice, France and the French Underground. Aug. 12th, three days before invasion, a British pilot flew evadees to Italy in a C-47.

Returned to U.S. and married Doris Williams. Had five children: Larry, Patricia, Robert, Joan and William and six grandchildren: Michael and Jennifer Peters, John, Linda, Michael and David Ray.

Was an inspector for the City of Detroit Building and Safety Engineering 30 years. Now live in Tampa, FL.

EUGENE J. REMMELL, was born Aug. 8, 1920 in Baltimore, MD. Joined U.S.A.F. Sept. 2, 1941.

Sent to Sheppard A.F.B. in Texas in September 1941 for six months aircraft mechanics school training. Completed aircraft gunnery training at MacDill A.F.B., Tampa, FL. Joined the 91st BG, (H) at MacDill in April 1942 and after training there and several other places left for England in October 1942 to join the 8th A.F. Completed 25 missions as a flight engineer top turret gunner on

B-17s. Credited with shooting down four enemy aircraft. Was a gunnery instructor in England for several months and returned stateside in October 1923.

Was assigned to train B-24 gunners and volunteered for another tour of combat in August 1944. Sent to 15th A.F. in Italy in August 1944. Flew as flight engineer (50 missions) and top turret gunner with 450th BG, 720th Sqdn. Wounded and bailed out returning from a combat mission to Vienna, Austria Oct. 7, 1944. Got back to Italy with the help of Marshall Tito's Partisan soldiers after walking many miles across Yugoslavia.

Discharged May 1, 1963, rank of master sergeant.

Awarded Distinguished Flying Cross, Air Medal with nine Oak Leaf Clusters, Purple Heart, E.T.O. Ribbon with seven Battle Stars and Presidential Unit Citation.

Married Ruth Osborn, April 1953 and they have three children: Harry, Nancy and Peggy.

Assistant golf pro 1963-66. U.S. letter carrier 1967 to 1977. Retired.

CLARENCE B. RICH, 1st Lt., was born in Dean, MT March 6, 1919. Went to Army Air Corps May 15, 1942. Accepted for navigation training school in San Marcus, TX and commissioned as a second lieutenant and navigation rating from there Jan. 15, 1944. Sent to Springfield, MA, Westover Field, for Replacement Training Unit in B-24 Heavy Bombers. Finished in early April 1944 and was sent immediately overseas for replacement in the 8th A.F. Assigned to 392nd BG, 577th Sqdn. at Wendling, England.

Started bomb raids immediately. On June 23, 1944, crew lead the squadron and the squadron lead the group in an attack on a German fighter base outside Laon, France. Just after "bombs away", they received a flak hit in the hydraulic accumulators behind the navigation-bombardier compartment and the plane caught fire. All the crew was able to bail out except for the tail gunner, who burned with the plane. Rich's parachute burned and he had to go back to under the flight deck to get a spare to jump in, so he rode the plane from about 23,000 ft. to 9,000 ft., made free fall to 1000 ft. and landed in an area at the edge of a swamp. Hands, face, and some of back were badly burned. Hid in swamp tall grass for three nights and four days, but when eyes gradually closed, crawled to edge of swamp and watched a French farm and asked a small French boy (had watched him being whipped by German overseer) for help. Head of English spy ring took him to Laon for treatment for my burns.

Aided by French who helped him cross the Seine River to a little village where he met a French black market butcher (worked with him for 40 days) and helped deliver meat all over France. When the American Army advanced out of the Bulge and on in to France, borrowed a jeep and driver and made it back to 1st Army Headquarters. Next day went to 9th A.F. advance unit where some 110 evading American Airmen gathered. It was an impressive sight and all cried like babies knowing they were back under the American flag.

A C-47 cargo plane took them to Bovington, England. They traveled to bases around England talking about evading capture. After 30 days, caught a boat, Italian liner, S.S. Saturnia, spent 17 days on North Atlantic and ended up at Camp Kilmer, NJ. Went by train to Salt Lake City, UT, by plane to

Butte, MT and on by train to home town, Columbus, MT. Had spent 70 days behind enemy lines and lost 50 lbs. Five crew members were killed, five others had been taken prisoner. Rich was only one to evade capture and get away.

Awarded: E.T.O. Ribbon with three Battle Stars, Air Medal with Oak Leaf Cluster, Purple Heart.

Member of English and American Caterpillar Clubs and English Silver Winged Boot Society.

Lives in Montana and is a real estate broker at Seeley Lake, Montana. Part-time outfitter and guide for horse trips in the Bob Marshall wilderness.

CLYDE C. RICHARDSON, (EE #497), Lt.Col. U.S.A.F. Res. (ret.), was born Sept. 9, 1919 in Portage, PA. Appointed Aviation Cadet March 1942. Graduated Big Springs Bombardier School class 43-3 Feb. 1943. Graduated San Marcos Navigation School class 43-9 June 1943. Assigned as navigator on B-17 and shipped to England November 1944.

Member of 388th BG until shot down on 15th mission to Frankfurt on Jan. 29, 1944, in the vicinity of Cambrai, France. Walked for three days before a farm family took him in. About 10 days later, a courier took him to J.P. Morgan's castle at Blerancourt where he was interrogated by Mrs. Morgan's French secretary.

His travels then took him to Chauny, where he met my pilot, Frank Hennessey. On to Creil and to Paris to the apartment of Countess Bertranne de Hespel. The next stop was the Brittany Coast and the beach of Plouha, where the British MGB 503 made the pick-up under "Operation Bonaparte". Richardson maintained his affiliation with the military and retired in 1970 as a lieutenant colonel in the A.F. Reserve.

Retired in 1980 from Johnstown Works, U.S. Steel Corp. After 32 years as melter in hot metal department and inspector of mechanical products. Now living in Summerhill, PA.

JOSEPH E. RIPLEY, was born April 18, 1922 in Pawnee, OK. Joined the military Feb. 3, 1943. Took training at Shepherd Field, Wichita Falls, TX; gunnery school at Laredo, TX; flight engineer school at Keesler Field, MS; crew training at Tucson, AZ. Served in 15th A.F., 376th BG, 513th Sqdn. in Italy as a flight engineer, rank of technical sergeant.

On seventh mission, bailed out over Yugoslavia. Helped by Partisans and O.S.S. Returned after evasion to finish 28 more missions, two of them crashes.

Returned to U.S., Jan. 28, 1945 and served at Vance Air Base, Enid, OK until discharged Oct. 8, 1945.

Worked as a salesman for Firestone for seven years, then self-employed as distributor for Mid-

Continent Permanent Cookware Co. for 37 years.

Married Betty L. Cockrum, May 3, 1945. Two sons: Ron L. Ripley, attorney, and Joe Michael Ripley, teacher and coach.

Five grandchildren: Travis A., Trent D., Shannon L., Erika B. and Jessica L. Ripley.

MANUEL M. ROGOFF, was born Feb. 11, 1917 in Mt. Pleasant, PA. Joined military June 24, 1940. Motor School instructor, Infantry, Ft. Benning, GA. Joined Air Force July 1942, commissioned bombardier Midland Air Base, TX 1943.

Trained at Davis Monthan, Tucson, AZ and Casper, WY Air Base. Joined 389th BG, 567th Bomb Sqdn., 8th A.F., B-24s, Norwich, England.

On first mission blew up Heavy Water Plant, Rjukan, Norway.

Bailed out Jan. 7, 1944 south of Paris, France. Severely burned on face and hands. Patient at Valley Force General Hospital.

Assigned to the Greater Pittsburgh Air Force Command. Released Jan. 16, 1946.

Awarded Purple Heart and Air Medal.

Still active. President Leetsdale Auto Inc. Married Irma E. Schaffer Sept. 5, 1944. Two children: Lawrence J. and Cynthia R. Abrams. Resides in Pittsburgh, PA.

JOHN C. RUCIGAY, 1st Lt., was born Jan. 25, 1925. Joined the U.S.A.A.F. April 8, 1943. Completed pilot training Jan. 1944 in the Southeast training command. Assigned as B-24 copilot with crew training at Davis-Monthan Field, Tucson, AZ.

With the crew, they picked up combat aircraft at Topeka, KS and ferried the B-24 to Italy via South America and Africa. Assigned to 778th Bomb Sqdn., 464th BG, 15th A.F.

Bailed out with crew in occupied northern Yugoslavia on the 17th combat mission while returning from Munich, Germany July 19, 1944. Rescued by Partisans and returned to Italy after 40 days.

Completed active military service stateside September 1945 after serving as flight instructor flying AT-6s. Flew C-46s in the reserve.

Graduated as an Aeronautical Engineer from Polytechnic Institute of Brooklyn and employed as a helicopter flight test engineer with Vertol. Retired in 1986 after 30 years with General Electric as a flight control systems engineer and gas turbine project manager.

Married Dorothy Kaune in 1950 and has two daughters, one son and one grandson. Currently resides in Ballston Lake, NY.

KENNETH E. RUPPERT, was born Dec. 24, 1916. Was instructor in aerial mines and munitions at "O.T.U. School" at MacDill Field, FL 1942-43. Cadet pilot training at Maxwell Field, AL and

gunnery at Panama Field, FL.

Flew with the 464th H. BG, 776th Sqdn. based at Pantanella Field near Foggia, Italy. Was flying as a replacement nose gunner with another crew on first mission before regular crew was ready.

Plane was shot down over Florisdoff, Austria, but managed to make it to a field near Szarvas, Hungary and crash landed. Was hid two days by Hungarian Partisans until Russians moved up.

With the aid of the Partisans and Russians, the crew worked their way to Bucharest, Rumania. On Feb. 28, 1945, they were picked up and flown back to Italy. Staff sergeant Ruppert flew 20 more missions with his own crew.

Married to Marjorie Nichols at Davis Monthan Field Sept. 23, 1944 and they have three children: James, Gail and Kenneth, Jr.

Retired from teaching in Buffalo, NY in 1981. Resides in Treasure Is., FL.

HERBERT G. RUUD, was born June 20, 1920 in Osnabrock, ND. Joined the military August 1942.

Attended Air Force technical schools at Shephard Field, TX; flexible gunnery school, Fort Meyers, FL; B-25 training Myrtle Beach, SC and B-29 schools Chanute Field, IL and Seattle, WA.

Joined B-17 Group in Pyote, TX and flew to Prestwick, Scotland. Assigned to Snetterton Heath Air Base in England, with the 96th BG, 337th Sqdn. Served as engineer top turret gunner.

On his first mission, Jan. 5, 1944 was shot down by Germans and crash landed 40 Kilometers

from Bordeaux, France. Three of the crew walked to a farm where the French people helped them get into the French Underground. They guided them across the Pyrenees Mountains to Spain. A month later was released to U.S.A.F. in England for interrogation, and returned to the U.S. April 1, 1944.

Was assigned to Luke Field, AZ and Kingman, AZ training pilots and gunners for the B-17 replacement program.

Discharged from Roswell Air Base, Roswell, NM Oct. 27, 1945. Retired from the Hoover Co. with 43 years service as service manager Feb. 28, 1989.

Married Florence June 14, 1947 and has one daughter, Kathy, and four grandchildren.

BENJAMIN H. ST. JOHN, T. Sgt., was born July 4, 1913 in Downsville, NY. Married Mary E. Rosekrans on Nov. 21, 1940. Drafted from Oneonta, NY on Aug. 21, 1942. Basic training Miami Beach, radio school at Scott Field, gunnery at Laredo, TX. Assigned to B-17 flight crew, trained at Seattle, Ephrata and Walla Walla, WA.

Flew new B-17 from Kearney, NE to England. Assigned to 379th BG, 527th Sqdn., 8th A.F., at Kimbolton, England.

Shot down in a new B-17, *Duffy's Tavern* on Jan. 29, 1944, target Frankfort. Parachuted into Luxembourg, walked into Belgium. Contacted the Underground, harbored in Liege, Namur, Dinant, Belgium. Also Ardennes Forest, Sedan, Nancy, Epinal, Dijon, Besancon, France. Crossed into Switzerland at LaChaux deFond on May 11, 1944.

The American Legation billeted them in a hotel at Glion, Montreux. Flown back to base in England after General Patton liberated southern France. Back to U.S. and discharged Aug. 16,1945.

Awards: Winged Boot, Caterpillar, E.T.O. with three Bronze Stars, Air Medal with three Oak Leaf Clusters, Purple Heart, and Distinguished Unit Badge.

He and Mary have a son and daughter, James G. and Janet Duell. Retired as president of two small oil companies. Resides in Palm Harbor, FL.

SOLDIER EDWARD SANDERS, a full-blooded Cherokee Indian, was born Sept. 20, 1918 in Stilwell, OK. Entered military service May 14,

1942, assigned to 8th A.F. Composite Command.

Overseas September 1942, stationed near Belfast, Northern Ireland until 1943, then attended gunnery and communication schools near Kings Lynn, England.

Participated in air offensive, European campaign with B-17 Pathfinder Group and 390th BG, 571st Sqdn. as a gunner with staff sergeant rank.

Received the following awards: Distinguished Unit Citation, Air Medal with one Oak Leaf Cluster, E.A.M.E. Ribbon with one Bronze Star.

Crew was shot down by fighter attack over Magdeburg, Germany, May 28, 1944. Spent eight months at Luft IV, three months at Stalag XIII D Nuremburg. April 1945, on forced march somewhere between Nuremburg and Moosburg, he and a fellow P.O.W. escaped.

He made contact with the American Army approximately two weeks later, alone, as he and his partner had become separated three days before.

He was then flown to Paris, France hospital, where he was recuperating when the war in Europe ended.

Retired 1983 from government service after 43 years.

He and wife Catherine reside in Cherokee, NC. They have two sons, (both veterans of the Vietnam War era), two daughters and four grandchildren.

ANTHONY SAVASTANO, 2nd Lt., was born Nov. 5, 1916 in Brooklyn, NY. Enlisted in 1939 at Mitchel Field, NY. Training at Maxwell Field, AL, gunnery school at Amarillo, TX. Spent one year at France Field, Panama Canal Zone.

After Pearl Harbor sent to England in April 1942. Trained with R.A.F. Sqdn. (volunteer).

Flew missions in June and July. Got five Me109s. Downed by flak July 4, 1942, taken prisoner, escaped Aug. 18, 1943. Spent 17 days in woods. Helped by French, then Greek helpers back to England. Discharged in 1945.

Married, one son, Tom. Am now a widower. Two grandchildren: Damon and Kirrsten.

Awarded Purple Heart, Distinguished Flying Cross, Air Medal and P.O.W. Medal.

LEONARD J. SCHALLEHN, was born March 2, 1921 in Saratoga Springs, NY. Joined the military in fall of 1942.

Single-engine pilot training, Southeast training command. Assigned to 405th Fighter Grp., Christ Church, England.

Shot down June 16, 1944, over Mayenne, France. Following successful landing, three days and 30 miles later, arrived in Domfront. Helper was Andre Rougeyron, Resistance leader in that area of Normandy and mayor of Domfront. Rougeyron later arrested by Gestapo within Schallehn's vision. Sixty-five days later, rescued by Patton's Third Army.

Following Rougeyron's escape from Buchenwald, he and Schallehn embraced at first reunion in 1961. He remains in close contact with family.

Released from duty Jan. 1946, joined New York Telephone Co., (retiring 35 years later), and married Eunice Waite in July 1946. They have two married daughters, Cynthia and Sandra and two granddaughters, Kelly and Emily. Along with his family, golfing and skiing continue to be main interests. Resides in Saratoga Springs, NY.

ADOLPH F. SCHULTZ, was born March 5, 1921 in Gackle, ND. Entered Army Air Force June 15, 1943. Top gunner on A-20 night-intruder missions.

Shot down on 11th mission, along with Lt. Dowdell (bombardier-navigator) and S/Sgt. Boward (lower gunner), Nov. 12, 1944 while destroying a German bridge over Po River. Parachuted and joined Italian Partisans and evaded southward through U.S. Army front lines Nov. 20, 1944.

Discharged Oct. 18, 1945 at Hill Field, UT. Received Purple Heart.

Founded and successfully operated Ace Rental and Equipment Sales in Rock Springs, WY.

Married Donna on June 28, 1941 in Las Vegas, NV. Deceased Feb. 2, 1970. Survived by wife Donna and son, Larry.

ROBERT A. SCHWARTZBURG, was born Jan. 25, 1919 in Appleton, WI. Joined A.A.F. Oct. 26, 1942. Trained and stationed at Sioux Fall, SD; Kingman, AZ and Bury Saint Edmunds, England.

Shot down Jan. 5, 1944, Brest, Peninsula. Escaped, hidden and passed through French Underground to England.

Discharged Nov. 16, 1945 as staff sergeant. Awarded Purple Heart and Air Medal.

Married Betty Louise Papez and has two children and one granddaughter.

Retired from automobile dealership management.

RICHARD M. SCOTT, was born in Lancaster City, PA April 28, 1918. Graduated from Lancaster Boys High School, 1936, and from the United States Military Academy, 1942. WWII fighter (P-38) pilot in Europe. Failed to return to the U.K on 13th mission; then in Underground as an evadee in Holland, Belgium, and France for four months; captured and imprisoned in Stalag Luft III for ten months, escaped through Allied lines successfully on third attempt in April 1945.

Remained in the Air Force and served in a variety of assignments worldwide: Fighter test pilot (Florida); cold weather test pilot (Alaska); jet fighter pilot (F-86, Korea); entered nuclear weapons field in 1956; Chief of Weapons Production, Atomic Energy Commission; Chief Nuclear Plans, Allied Command Europe; and Deputy Assistant to the Secretary of Defense for Atomic Energy. Retired from Air Force in 1970 at rank of brigadier general.

Returned to Lancaster in 1970. General manager of Lancaster Auto Club and mayor of Lancaster 1974-79.

Appointed Adjutant General of Pennsylvania in 1979 with rank of major general by Governor Dick Thornburgh. Remained in that position as head of the Pennsylvania Army and Air National Guard and the Commonwealth's Veterans Programs. Left military service in 1987 with rank of lieutenant general, PA Nat. Guard.

Holds a B.S. Degree, U.S.M.A. and a Master's Degree, George Washignton University. Among his decorations are two U.S. Air Force Distinguished Service Medals, the U.S. Army Distinguished Service Medal, the Legion of Merit and the Pennsylvania Distinguished Service Medal.

Resides in Lancaster, PA with his wife, Flora. They have three children and six grandchildren.

CHARLES B. SCREWS, Lt. Col. (ret.), was born Dec. 7, 1921 in Sipe Springs, Comanche County, TX. Joined Army Air Corps July 7, 1941. Crewed BT-13 Trainers until July 1942. Pilot training, Maxwell A.F.B.; primary, Helena, AK; basic, Bush Field, Augusta, GA; advanced, Spence Field, Moultrie, GA, graduating April 29, 1943, class of 43D.

Fighter pilot training, P-47, Richmond, VA. Joined 361st Fighter Grp., 374th Sqdn., Camp

Springs, MD, June 1943. Group sailed to England Nov. 23, 1943 for combat missions out of Bottisham.

Belly landed in France Jan. 29, 1944 from flak damage over Dunqureque. Evaded capture, sought help from the French, evaded to Spain and returned to England May 25, 1944.

Assigned training command, and SAC. Flew T-6, C-45, C-47, P-47, P-40, P-51, B-29, B-36, KC-135 and B-52 during Air Force career.

Married Marguerite Allison July 14, 1944. Two children, David and Beverly. Grandchildren: Katie, Josh and Lacy. Two great-grandchildren: Kelsey and Molly.

Retired U.S.A.F. May 1, 1971. Resides in Abilene, TX.

EDWIN G. SECHRIST, was born April 3, 1921 in Elmira, NY. Joined the military as a glider pilot in August 1942. Transferred to Cadets and received wings and commission Oct. 1, 1943 in Stuttgart, AK.

Flew combat in E.T.O. and was shot down June 8, 1944 while pilot of a B-17, 390th BG.

Back in the U.S. instructed B-17s and flew many types of aircraft for the ferry command.

After active service, October 1945, went back to college and then flew 32 years as a captain for U.S. Air Airlines. Retired in 1981 and have been flying a HS-125 (small British jet) ever since.

Married, one daughter, one grandchild. Live in Horseheads, NY and Keuka Lake, NY.

ROBERT SEIDEL, was born July 20, 1925 in Euchart, IN. Entered Aviation Cadet Training Program May 1943. Completed combat air crew training June 1944. Served with 15th A.F., 55th Combat Wing, 460th BG, 763rd Bomb Sqdn. Air combat: Alpennines, Rhineland, Balkans.

M.I.A./P.O.W. Nov. 16, 1944 Munich, Germany. Hit over target, struggled to Salzberg, Austria. Bailed out in heavy snow storm and separated from rest of crew. Captured Nov. 29, 1944. Interned Stalag IV and I. Returned to U.S. June 1945.

Awards: WWII Victory Medal, Euro-African-Middle Eastern, American Service Air Medal, Purple Heart, Presidential Unit Citation, P.O.W.

Medal Korean Conflict.

Reassigned to MATS. Released from active duty to Reserves November 1946. Have a B.S. Mech/Aerospace Engineering. Various aerospace programs.

Activities: A.F.A., Ex P.O.W.s, V.F.W., C.A.F., A.F. Evasion Society, Caterpillar Assn., B-24 Club.

Married to wife Helen for over 43 years. Has three children, five grandchildren and resides in Dallas, TX.

KEN D. SHAVER, was born Nov. 16, 1921 in Richfield, NC. Joined the U.S. Air Force on July 5, 1942.

The service took him to Fort Bragg, NC; Miami Beach, FL; Amarillo, TX; Kingman, AZ; Seattle, WA; Pyote, TX; Dyersburg, TN; Nettahaule, England. Stationed with the 8th A.F., 388th BG.

Shot down on Nov. 5, 1943 and was taken prisoner by the Germans. Later escaped with the help of the Underground from the countries of Holland, France, Belgium and Spain.

After returned to 388th, made lectures to airmen at other bases on how to escape the enemy and to survive. Returned to U.S. and went to Pentagon in Washington, D.C., where continued lectures.

After returning to U.S., discovered he had been reported as killed in action and has three deaths certificates to confirm this.

Discharged Sept. 26, 1945, and took a job in a trucking company. After being employed there for 14 years, decided to start his own trucking company. Still work in that company started with two trucks. Now prospered to over 400 trucks. Resides in Lake Wylie, SC.

GILBERT S. SHAWN, Lt. Col., was born July 25, 1921 in New York City, NY. Joined the Air Force directly as cadet in class 43E. Took pilot training in Gulf Coast training command.

Flew as first pilot in B-24, C-47, C-54, B-25. Served in two wars, WWII and Korean. Reserve pilot in peace time with heavy time in C-47s.

Retired from Air Force in 1980.

Flew combat with the 445th BG, 702nd Bomb Sqdn., which was headed by Jimmy Stewart. In Korea flew C-47s with Hq. Sqdn. of 5th A.F.

In WWII flew B-24s and was shot down on mission to Zwickau. Parachuted into Belgium where with friends and the Underground worked his way to Sedan, France (before the invasion). Time behind enemy lines was six months.

Civilian employment: president of Warsaw Studio. Retired in 1981. Joined the Peace Corps and served in Kenya, Africa.

Married to beautiful actress, Melba Rae (deceased) and has one son, Eric. Currently resides in New York, but has lived in Portugal and Africa.

MILTON V. SHEUCHIK, was born June 1, 1918 in Ellsworth, PA. Joined service Nov. 20, 1940 at Pittsburgh, PA, Air Corps. Served five different branches.

Shot down in enemy territory Feb. 8, 1944, wounded and missing in action for two months. Spent two months with the French Underground.

Awards: Air Medal with two Oak Leaf Clusters, Presidential Unit Citation, Eastern Defense Medal with Oak Leaf Cluster, Western Defense Medal with Oak Leaf Cluster, and Britain Battle Citation.

Discharged as captain.

Crew members: pilot - 1st Lt. Milton Shevchik; co-pilot - 2nd Lt. Thorson; bombardier - 2nd Lt. Periolat; navigator - 2nd Lt. Williams; crew chief - S/Sgt. Stump; radio man - S/Sgt. Sidders; ball turret gunner - Sgt. VanSealus, D.F.C.; waist gunners - Sgt. Krabe, Sgt. Scanlon; and tail gunner - Sgt. Higgens.

ERNEST C. SKORHEIM, was born July 11, 1917 in Canton, SD. Grew up in Breckenridge, MN. Entered service June 23, 1941. Basic training Fort Leonardwood, MO. Transferred Army Air Corps, West Coast training command, Nashville, TN and Santa Anna, CA. Graduated Roswell A.F.B., class 43-3, Feb. 13, 1943 as second lieutenant. Joined Plummer Provisional Grp., Blyth, CA. Assigned as bombardier on B-17s.

Upon completing phase training, departed

Grand Island, NE June 1943 with assigned B-17 crew via Newfoundland/Scotland/England to Tunisia, Africa, where they joined the 49th Bomb Sqdn., 2nd BG, 12th A.F. Completed 32 missions, 250 combat hours, covering targets in France, Italy, Austria and Greece.

Aboard on two crash landings. Shot down on 33rd mission over Athens, Greece. Crash landed on island of Corfu, Nov. 18, 1943. After four-and-a-half months with Underground (on island and mainland), escaped via Italian fishing boat.

Returned to U.S. April 1944. Married Juanita Louisa G. Klinger of Breckenridge, MN April 27, 1944 and has one daughter, Lona Lee.

Assigned to Midland, TX as bombardier instructor. Transferred to Albuquerque, NM, assigned to Truax Field, Madison, WI, McCord A.F.B., WA, Bliss A.F.B., TX, Mather A.F.B., CA. Completed 1037 in 1949. Assigned to Castle A.F.B., CA, completed 10 years as SAC combat crew member in B-50's, B-47s, and B-52s as radar navigator, select crew and instructor, earning Master Navigator rating. Other assignment included Special Weapons, A&E Sqdn. commander, Court Marshal Board president.

Awarded: Air Medal with five Oak Leaf Clusters, Purple Heart, E.T.O. with four Stars, P.U.S., A.F. Commendation Medal, Army Commendation Medal, and Presidential Unit Citation.

Retired with rank of lieutenant colonel. Attended Healds Business College, receiving degree in accounting. After 13 years as deputy clerk, U.S. District Court, retired Oct. 30, 1979. In retirement: travel, take care of rental properties, garden, golf and keep busy with club activities and grandchild, Tyson. Live in Sacramento, CA.

RALPH L. SMATHERS, was born Nov. 29, 1918 in Canton, NC. Accepted for Aviation Cadet training in December 1941. Graduated at Craig Field, Selma, AL, class of 43D. R.T.U. training at Sarasota in P-40s. O.T.U. at Myrtle Beach in P-39s. Combat out of Winkton, England in P-47s, 508th Sqdn., 404th BG, 9th A.F.

Completed 20 missions bombing, strafing and escorting. Shot down on 21st mission by AA near Carentan on the Cherbourg Peninsula. Hid with two elderly French sisters in their duplex house shared with German soldiers. Ten days later U.S. Forces took the area.

Returned to U.S. September 1944. Stationed at Deming, NM, then at Abilene, TX teaching new P-47 pilots, then at Brownsville teaching P-47 aerial gunnery. Resigned October 1945.

Awards: Purple Heart, Air Medal, French Croix de Guerre avec Palm.

Married Joyce in June 1945. Has three children (doctor, lawyer, movie maker) and four grandchildren.

Returned to Florida in 1946. Career includes 15 years in consumer finance and 35 years in real estate overlapping 20 years as president/general manager Better Business Bureau of South Florida.

Now only managing real estate interests and acting in little theatre productions. Resides in South Miami, FL.

AUTLEY B. SMITH, was born Dec. 13, 1921 in Stone County, MS. Enlisted in Aviation Cadets Aug. 20, 1942.

Completed aerial gunnery school, Laredo, TX; engineering school, Keesler Field, MS; assigned to 486th, BG, 832nd Sqdn., 8th A.F. Flew from Sudbury, England; shot down returning from mission to Leipzig May 28, 1944. Evaded capture in Belgium Underground until liberated Sept. 6, 1944. Discharged October 1945, rank of sergeant.

Forestry degree, L.S.U., 1948. Worked in forest industry 1948-78, retired as manager of 600,000 acre industrial forest. Consultant, 1978-88.

Hobbies: hunting, (veteran of three African safaris); custom knife making; scrimshaw; winemaking. Has written book, *A Place Remembered*, on experiences as evadee.

Married Nettie Hickman Feb. 5, 1942. Two children: Merlin and Annette, seven grandchildren and three great-grandchildren. Lives in West Monroe, LA.

RICHARD M. SMITH, Capt., was born Sept. 8, 1921. Enlisted Fort Wayne, IN Feb. 15, 1942. Cadet class 43B. Kelly Field, Sikeston, MO, primary; Enid, OK, basic; Pampa, TX advanced; Boise, ID for B-17 phase training. Got my own crew. Trained until August. Received new B-17 at Grand Island, NE. and flew to Prestwick, Scotland via the North Atlantic.

Commenced combat missions Oct. 8, 1943. Had never been in a formation of more than three planes, to that date. Made runs to Norway and Gydnia, Poland, along with a few to Germany.

Shot down on 13th mission, Dec. 30, 1943, northeast of Paris, near St. Just enChaussee. Helped by three, as yet unknown, young men and a young farm couple. Then by Paul and Yvonne Beque.

Went by automobile to Paris, and 23 Rue Madelaine, train to Brest Peninsula, and Plouha. Returned to England on first British sea rescue mission, Jan. 29, 1944.

Spent 18 months at Fort Meyer, FL. Flew with Eastern Airlines for short time, then went back to college. Married with three children.

PHILIP SOLOMON, 1st Lt., was born June 2, 1917 in New York; lived in New Jersey and later in Washington, D.C. Was a civilian employee in the Office of Quartermaster General.

Enlisted in the Army Air Force March 1942. Trained at Maxwell Field, AL; Bennetsville, SC and Monroe, LA, where he received navigator's wings in June 1943. Remained there as an instructor until assigned to 445th BG, part of a new B-24 wing forming at Sioux City, IA, where he met Capt. Jimmy Stewart also joining the 445th.

After training at Watertown, SD, they flew their own planes to England via the southern route (South America and Africa), arriving in December 1943.

On April 12, 1944, on 24th mission, they were shot down over eastern Belgium where Solomon bailed out and landed on a cow. Fortunately he made immediate contact with the Underground, minutes before arrival of a German search party.

He eventually got down to the Swiss border, which he crossed about midnight of June 1st, in time for his birthday, June 2nd.

Received: Air Medal with three Oak Leaf Clusters and a Purple Heart.

After relief from active duty Sept. 1945, worked in New York office of the FCC until moving to Los Angeles in 1953. Retired as controller of Paramount Paint Co. in 1982.

He and Claire were married May 4, 1943. For their first anniversary Solomon was M.I.A. in Belgium. They had two sons; their one surviving son, Barry, now lives in Salt Lake City. They have two grandchildren, a boy and a girl.

EDWARD JOSEPH SPEVAK, Lt. Col. (ret.), was born Oct. 14, 1919 in Wheatland, WY. Joined Army Air Force while a student at

the University of Wyoming in January 1942, at Cheyenne, WY as a cadet.

Pilot training, Williams Field, AZ, Visalia, Merced and Victorville, CA. Flew B-24s at Davis Monthan, Tucson, AZ, B-17s at Biggs Field, El Paso, TX, B-29s at Sioux City, IA, Pueblo, CO and Salina, KS.

Sent to the 8th A.F. Bury Saint Edmunds, England as B-17 pilot in April 1943. Shot down May 17, 1943 on mission to submarine pens at St. Lorient in the Brest Peninsula. After evading Germans for four months, Spevak escaped through France, the Pyrenees Mountains to Andorra, then Barcelona, Madrid and eventually Gibraltar. Returned to England for interrogation then to Mitchell Field, NY.

Sent to rest camp in Arizona then to Kearney, NE as air inspector and eventually Sioux City and Pueblo, CO and Salina, KS as a B-17 and B-29 instructor. Retired from the Air Force in Dec. 1945 and from the Reserves in Oct. 1979.

Spevak met his wife, Aylene, while stationed in Sioux City and was married in May 1944. He entered the agriculture-business with his father-in-law in 1946 and remained active in that business for 40+ years. Now semi-retired, but still involved in agriculture with his two sons, Richard and Bradley and son-in-law Steve David. They have a daughter, Elizabeth, and four grandchildren. Reside in Watertown, SD, their home for the past 45 years.

DR. GEORGE W. STARKS, was born Nov. 20, 1923 in Mayo, FL. Enlisted in Aviation Cadets May 2, 1942. Trained at Southeastern Air Corps Training Command, Maxwell Field (preflight), Union City, TN (primary), Newport, AK (basic), Freeman Field, Seymour, IN (advanced), Lockbourne A.A.F., Columbus, OH (B-17 transition), Pyote, TX (all three phases operational training in Sturdivant, Provisional Grp., attached to 19th BG).

Assignments: ferried a B-17G from Grand Island, NE to Nuts Corner, Ireland via Presque Isle, Maine and Goose Bay, Labrador. With 92nd BG, 407th Sqdn., 8th A.F., Poddington, England.

Shot down March 16, 1944 near Vitry-le-Francois, France (near Reims), on Augsburg mission. Parachuted seconds before plane exploded. Crew was scattered. All survived as P.O.W. or escaped to Spain or Switzerland. Aided and sheltered by M. Paulin Crete and Mme. Josefa Wilcynska, Starks escaped by walking alone the 300 miles to Pontarlier, France through occupied territory. Twenty-five miles from the Swiss border, he was taken in by M. Henri Chambelland who contacted the French Underground. From there on he was guided and accompanied by Maurice Baverel, a Free French agent, code name "Victor", the bravest man Sparks had ever known. He had escaped from German prisons three times. He stayed with his uncle, M. Henri and Mme. Boillot for many days. Hidden in the small Peugeot of Dr. Paul Charlin under medical books, the good doctor drove him through several road blocks to a house on the border. Maurice skiied in and they went together into Switzerland. Turned himself in to the police was interned, then classed as an evadee and assigned to Glion above Montreux, Switzerland.

Three months later, Maurice also helped him and three evadees, Harold Killian, Ralph Potter and Hubert Trent, to escape from Switzerland in Aug. 1945. Starks joined a Maquis unit and eventually was flown back to England via north Africa.

Returned to unit September 1944, but was not allowed to fly in that theatre again. Back in U.S. was assigned as an instructor at Hendricks Field, FL. Separated Sept. 3, 1945 and enrolled at the University of Florida in January 1947. He began Dental School at the University of Louisville and graduated in June 1950.

Went to Korea as a dental officer with 52nd Transportation Battalion and made the landings at Inchon and at Wonsan, and the withdrawal at Hungnam on Christmas Day, 1950. Transferred to 121st Evacuation Hospital and became chief of Dental Services, 20 months in Korea during the war.

Private practice of pediatric dentistry, June 1952 to Dec. 1981. Now on faculty at the College of Dentistry, University of Florida.

Achieved rank of captain. Awarded: Bronze Star, Purple Heart, two Unit Citations, E.T.O. Ribbon, Korean Service Medal with six Service Stars, U.N. Service Medal.

CHARLES A. STRACKBINE, was born March 9, 1919 in St. Paul, MN. Married to wife Ruth June 22, 1942. Joined the military Oct. 23, 1942.

Took basic training and aircraft mechanics school at Sheppard Field, Wichita Falls, TX; B-25 flight engineer course at North American Aviation Factory, Inglewood, CA; then on to gunnery school at Tyndall Field, FL. Was assigned to 95th Grp., 335th Sqdn. as flight engineer, T/T gunner on a B-17.

Shot down on third mission, Berlin raid, March 4, 1944. Bailed out near St. Quentin, France and was helped by French family the next day. Joined the French Maquis and eventually joined up with Patton's Third Armored Div. at Ham, France, Sept. 3, 1944. Returned to 95th BG Sept. 6, 1944.

After return to U.S. was assigned to Las Vegas, NV gunnery school as instructor. Discharged, rank of technical sergeant, November 1945. Returned to St. Paul, MN and resumed career as musician with traveling bands and show bands. Relocated to San Diego, CA in 1953 and continued in the band business. Retired in the San Diego area in 1985. Has three children and eight grandchildren, all living within a ten-mile radius of San Diego.

WARREN KEITH SUTOR, was born Jan. 12, 1922 in Zurich, KS. Joined the service September 1942. Took training in Panama City, FL, Denver, CO, Tucson, AZ, Casper, WY. Flew as a tail gunner with the 567th Sqdn., 389th BG, out of Norwich, England.

Shot down Jan. 7, 1944 over Ludwishafen, Germany. Picked up Jan. 12, 1944 by French Underground and the Shelburn Line, going through Plouha and Bonaparte Beach. Picked up March 23, 1944 by British Coastal Forces Gun Boat #503. Returned to England and U.S.

Worked with military Intelligence and was assigned to the 4th A.F. B-25s in Muroc, CA, known now as Edwards Air Force Base. Mustered out Sept. 9, 1945.

Married Betty L. Campbell in 1942, have a daughter, Barsha Jo Miletello, and three grandchildren. I currently reside in Kansas City, MO.

ROBERT H. SWEATT, was born May 9, 1922 in Lovington, NM. Entered U.S. Air Force September 1942. Took aerial gunnery and armament training; assigned to 389th BG, Tucson, AZ.

Overseas assignments took him to Norwich, England, then Africa on detachment service. Was interned in Lisbon, Portugal; rejoined 389th BG in Africa. Returned to Hethel Air Base, Norwich, England.

Shot down in southern France on 17th mission, Jan. 7, 1944, after raid on Ludwishafen. Rescued by Kiebler Duplant; aided by French Underground survivor of crew.

Returned to U.S. 1944. Sent to Florida as instructor. Met and married Mary Davidson Feb. 6, 1945. Discharged Oct. 11, 1945. Entered college, received degree in geology. Had five children. Retired from teaching in 1981. Now ranching in Burton, TX.

DEAN W. TATE, was born April 7, 1920 in Portland, OR. Educated at Newberg High School, Newberg, OR, graduate of George Fox College 1942 (official graduation was after entering Air Force).

Entered Air Force May 16, 1942 at Portland, OR, became an Aviation Cadet. Entered bombardier training, pre-flight at Ellington Field, TX;

flight training at Big Springs, TX. Commissioned second lieutenant May 13, 1943. Pre-combat training on B-17s at Moses Lake, WA; Walla Walla, WA and Madras, OR.

Sent to England with 8th A.F. as a replacement crew. Arrived at Kimbolton, England, 379th BG, 525th Sqdn., Oct. 15, 1943.

Flew 13 missions with Martin's crew, (targets: Bremen, Kiel, Frankfurt, Stuttgart, French coast, Norway, Munster and Hamburg). On Feb. 8, 1944, 14th mission, was flying as a substitute bombardier with a strange crew, going to Frankfurt. On the way were shot down by FW190 German fighters. Co-pilot was killed in aircraft. Four escaped capture and came out through Underground movement. Five were taken prisoner, including first pilot, Lt. Beam.

Returned to England March 17, 1944 via Operation Bonaparte with crew member S/Sgt. Bill Lessig, top turret engineer and others from other aircraft. During the spring and summer of 1944, lectured on evasion and escape in Northern Ireland and U.S. to incoming airmen.

Spent some time as a bombardier instructor and was then operated on for a herniated disc and ultimately retired as a first lieutenant in January 1946.

Awarded: Air Medal with three Oak Leaf Clusters and Presidential Unit Citation with one Oak Leaf Cluster.

Since retirement have been a public high school teacher, principal and assistant school superintendent. Retired from school work in 1980, then taught in a community college until permanent retirement.

He and his wife Lillian have one daughter, Susan. She and her husband, Joel, have two youngsters, Aimee and Alexander Ankeny. They live in Portland, OR. Hobbies: reading and playing golf.

JACK TERZIAN, Lt. Col., was born (Armenian descent) July 28, 1919 in Adana, Turkey. Attended schools and worked in New York City before enlisting in the Army Air Corps March 11, 1941. Entered pilot training, Gulf Coast, in January 1942 and gradated class 42J as a second lieutenant and pilot Nov. 10, 1942.

Went to England with the 353rd Fighter Grp.,

351st Fighter Sqdn. in June 1943 flying the P-47. Shot down by ground fire over Belgium May 22, 1944. Evaded capture through the Belgium Underground until July 12, 1944 when he was captured by the Gestapo and imprisoned in St. Gilles prison in Brussels.

When the Germans tried to evacuate the city by rail Sept. 3, 1944, train was derailed and he and 40 other Allied prisoners escaped.

Remained on active duty and retired from the Air Force Oct. 1, 1963. Awards include the Distinguished Flying Cross with Oak Leaf Cluster, Air Medal with four Oak Leaf Clusters, Purple Heart, Air Force Commendation Medal and the P.O.W. Medal.

He has flown the P-40, P-47, P-39, P-51, P-63, F-80, F-86, T-6, T-28, T-33, C-47, the Gloster Meteor and the C-130 for a total of 4,800 hours.

He married the former Martha (Marty) Tait in Chester, VA on Oct. 15, 1944. They have three children: Robert P., Toni T. Locke, and Charles L.

Joined the New York Life Insurance Co. in Abilene, TX in October 1963 and retired after 25 years with the company in 1988.

THOMAS S. THOMAS III, was born Oct. 31, 1924 in Morristown, NJ. Joined Army Air Corps June 1943. Commissioned as navigator July 1, 1944. Flew over in October 1944 to Africa and Italy in a B-24 with combat crew, attached to 464th BG in 15th A.F.

Shot down over Slovakia Dec. 6, 1944. Wounded but able to evade Nazi troops. Hid out until he met the Russian troops April 5, 1945 at base of Carpathian Mountains. Later flown by Russians to Kiev and met Dunquerque holding force survivors on train to Odessa.

Returned to U.S., graduated Yale, 1949, and entered insurance business in New Jersey.

Married Mary Ann Williamson Oct. 14, 1950. Has four sons and a daughter and five grandchildren. Still active in business. President of 464th BG Assn. Lives in Mendham, NJ.

ROBERT A. TITUS, was born March 8, 1915 in Marion, IA. Drafted Aug. 19, 1941 into Field Artillery, but later became an Aviation Cadet. Completing navigator's training, October 1942, was assigned to the 95th BG (H) which, after training at Rapid City, SD, flew to England in April 1943.

On his third combat mission, May 29, crew had to bail out over Brittany. Helped by farmer Leandre Rochelle to escape to Switzerland with two crew members (first Americans to arrive there). While there worked in Intelligence with Allan Dulles (O.S.S.) Repatriated March 1944 and reassigned to the Ferry Command and later that year made two trips to England delivering A-26s.

Enroute to Australia by C-47 Jan. 18, 1945, engine failure resulted in ditching, 900 miles from

the California coast, but all crew members were rescued from the raft.

After the war, resumed teaching career. Retired in 1981 after thirty-some years on faculty at Ohio State University.

JOHN L. TONEY, was born Feb. 14, 1919 in Ohio. Enlisted service February 1942, Wright-Patterson Field, Dayton, OH.

Attended airplane/engine mechanic school at Parks Air College, St. Louis, and Packard Engine Plant, Detroit. Assigned as staff sergeant gunner on B-17 crew.

Departed for E.T.O. January 1944 from Goose Bay, Labrador. Flew five of 20 missions to Berlin.

Shot down on 20th mission. Parachuted into northern Belgium, near St. Nicholas. One of five crew members to escape through the Belgium Underground. Five others were captured by the Germans.

Traveled by foot, bicycle, and train, guided by Belgian friends. Spent last weeks in Ardennes Forest. Liberated by American Rangers. In northern France, met his brother, Col. Robert M. Toney, with 5th Armored Div. Rode by jeep into Germany, on mail truck to Paris and was flown to England.

Received E.T.O. Ribbon, two Bronze Stars, Air Medal, two Oak Leaf Clusters. Discharged October 1945, Chanute Field, IL.

Farmed Preble County, OH; departed for Alaska 1953. Worked 31 years for Pacific Northern and Western Airlines. Retired in 1984. He and his wife Dorothy continue to reside in Anchorage, AK.

RICHARD M. TRACY, Lt. Col., was born Jan. 14, 1922 in Seattle, WA. Enlisted Aviation Cadets Sept. 12, 1942. Commissioned second lieutenant navigator, U.S.A.A.F. Feb. 5, 1944, Western training command. Combat training Ardmore A.A.B., OK. Assigned May 1944, 379th BG (H), 8th A.F., Kimbolton, England, WWII.

Lead B-17 received flak damage, Leipzig, July 7, 1944 and crew parachuted over Holland. Aided by Underground, evaded capture during Germans' continuous attempts to control audacious Underground activities as Allied Forces approached. Rescued by Canadians advancing into

Germany near Weert, Holland, Nov. 18, 1944.

Returned to U.S., refresher training, then assigned Walla Walla A.A.B., WA; combat navigation instruction, then flight test navigator. Released from active duty Dec. 12, 1945 and returned to Seattle.

Married Dorothy Brown April 30, 1945. Two children: Marilyn and Michael and two grandchildren: Joseph and Elizabeth.

Engineering graduate of University of Washington Dec. 1948. Retired 1984 following worldwide professional civil/structual consulting engineering career.

GARNETT T. TUNSTALL, 1st Lt., was born Nov. 5, 1919 in New Kent County, VA. Enlisted in Army Air Corps in 1942 after graduation from College of William and Mary.

Attended pre-flight, Ellington Field, navigation school, San Marcos. Was navigator on B-17s at 385th HBG in England and flew 16 mission over Germany.

On mission over Karlsruhe, Pathfinder B-17 was shot down and crash landed in Switzerland on May 27, 1944. Crew was interned. In September 1944 attempted to escape and return to Allied control. After several arrests and imprisonment, escaped to France in November and with help of the French Underground, returned to England and U.S. in December 1944.

Married Helen Holbrook. Graduated from William and Mary Law School, admitted to Virginia Bar and joined F.B.I. in 1947. Retired in 1977.

Has a son who is an attorney in Philadelphia and a daughter in U.S. Navy as lieutenant commander.

Now lives and serves on the Community Council in Leisure World of Maryland, Silver Spring.

HOWARD TURLINGTON, was born May 13, 1919 in Dunn, NC. Joined Air Force in May 1942. Gunnery training Las Vegas, NV; Kessler Field, MS. Boeing, Seattle, WA, Gowen Field, ID, Wendover, UT, Sioux City. Assigned to 384th BG, 547th Sqdn. Went to England in June 1943.

Shot down on 14th mission, Sept. 16, 1943, near Rennes, France. Walked 14 days before being aided by several French people. Crossed the Pyrenees into Spain June 1, 1944.

Returned to States and was an instructor with 2nd Air Force Training Command. Later transferred to Troop Carrier Command.

Discharged November 1945 at rank of master sergeant.

Married Kay Wotli in February 1946. Has two sons and four grandchildren.

Retired from St. Louis Post Dispatch newspaper after 33 years. Now lives in Spring Hill, Florida.

RAYMOND D. VITKUS, was born June 16, 1921 in Chicago, IL. Joined U.S.A.F. March 2,

1943. Flew as tail gunner with 381st BG, 535th Sqdn., 8th A.F. Shot down on second mission north of Paris.

In May 1944, while in hiding near Orleans, two British agents came to see him. They explained that since there were so many Allied airmen in hiding and the invasion was imminet, they were sent to organize a camp behind the German lines to house evadees and were to be supplied by the French Underground air drops.

DON W. VOGEL, Capt., was born Feb. 1, 1921 in Standish, MI. Military service: U.S.M.C.R. April 1938-March 1941, pvt.; R.C.A.F. March 1941-November 1943, F/O; U.S.A.A.C. November 1943-July 1945, 1st Lt.; U.S.A.F.R. July 1945-April 1961, capt.

Civilian flying, 1939-40, Aeronca Chief. R.C.A.F. training at St. Catharines, Ontario and Aylmer, Ontario in Fleets and Harvards. Operational training in England in the Mustang I. Operational assignment, R.A.F. Reconn., Sqdn. 268 flying in the Mustang I. U.S.A.A.C. operational assignment, 362nd Fighter Sqdn., 357th Grp., 8th A.F., flying P-51B out of Leiston, England.

Shot down in dog-fight near Ste. Quentin, France July 1, 1944. Walked about 150 miles in the first 10 days and was picked up by the French Underground in a small town near Louviers. Hid out until the end of August when area was liberated.

Worked for the C.A.A./F.A.A. as an air traffic control specialist unitl retirement in February 1977.

Married Maureen in England, Sept. 11, 1945; have a daughter, Wendy. Resides in Brandon, VT.

JOSEPH (NMN) VUKOVICH, (1st Lt.) was born March 14, 1924 in Glennie, MI. Enlisted in Army Air Corps in 1943. Pilot training in class 44-A, Avon Park, FL, Greenville, MS, Seymour, IN and B-17 operational training at Drew Field, Tampa, FL.

Parachuted from a burning B-17G over Raleigh, NC en route to England. Was hospitalized and separated from crew.

Assigned to 8th A.F., 91st BG, 322nd Sqdn. at Royton, England. Shot down on first mission on Aug. 13, 1944 and parachuted into occupied France. Was hidden by the French Underground. Com-

pleted pilot instructor training and taught flight cadets in UC78 and checked out returning combat bomber pilots in the AT-6. Discharged November 1945.

Completed Engineering and Business degrees and worked in the personnel profession until retiring in 1987 from the LINK Flight Simulation Co.

Married Georgia Cassimus and live in San Jose, CA.

IRA J. WALTER, S/Sgt., was born Jan. 27, 1922 in Elm Grove, WV. Inducted into U.S. Army Oct. 22, 1942 at Fort Thomas, KY. Trained as armorer gunner at A.A.F.T.T.S. Buckley Field, CO and Tyndall Field, FL. Was tail gunner in a B-17E Bomber with the 360th Sqdn., 303rd BG, 8th A.F. Molesworth, England, WWII.

His plane, *Career Girl*, was downed on its third mission, Dec. 1, 1943. Parachuted to safety near Lille, France and evaded capture until Dec. 7th. Was sent to Stalag 17B near Krems, Austria. April 8, 1945, as P.O.W., was marched across Austria to Braunau, where he was liberated by the 13th Armored Div., 3rd Army on May 2, 1945.

Discharged Nov. 17, 1945. Awarded American Defense Service Medal, American Campaign Medal, EAME Campaign Medal, WWII Victory Medal, Air Crew Member Badge, Air Medal and later the P.O.W. Medal.

Retired from Norris Industries, tool and die supervisor, Jan. 31, 1987.

Married Betty J. Marshall Feb. 19, 1946; one daughter, Sandra Kay and three grandchildren.

Died Oct. 9, 1990. Interned Riverside National Cemetery, Riverside, CA.

JOHN J. WARD, was born May 6, 1917 in Brooklyn, NY and was reared in Tucson, AZ. University of Arizona 1935-39. Commissioned U.S. Army Air Corps May 1942. Flew combat as a B-17 navigator in LeMay's 305th BG out of England, 1942-43.

Shot down over Kiel on 19th mission May 1943. P.O.W. 23 months in Stalag Luft III. Escaped and returned to Allied control April 1945. Twenty-seven years military service with A.A.F., U.S.A.F., MATS navigator, U.S.A.F. Reserve.

Retired lieutenant colonel May 1977.

In civilian life employed October 1946 as security agent with Manhattan District Corps of Engineers at University of California Radiation Laboratory. Subsequently, chief, Los Angeles Branch, U.S. Atomic Energy Commission. Investigator with U.S. Nuclear Regulatory Commission, Denver and Arlington, TX. Retired March 1979.

Married Helen Munro, R.N. (sister of fellow P.O.W.) November 1946; six children, nine grandchildren. Resides in Arlington, TX.

GEORGE WATT, was born Nov. 5, 1913 in New York City. Inducted into U.S. Army Aug. 18, 1942. Discharged with rank of technical sergeant, Sept. 18, 1945. Flew B-17 waist with 563rd Sqdn., 388th BG, 8th A.F.

Shot down Nov. 5, 1943 on seventh mission, after Gelsenkirchen raid. Protected by villagers in Zele and Hamme in Belgium and evaded with help of the Comet Line through Belgium, France and Spain. Returned to England Dec. 20, 1943.

Prior to WWII in 1937-39, had served as an infantryman with the Abraham Lincoln Brigade in the Spanish Civil War. After WWII, worked as a printer and later an administrator of a community mental health center.

Retired in 1982. Lives in Northport, Long Island with wife, Margaret. Has two sons, four grandchildren and two great-grandchildren.

Author of *The Comet Connection - Escape From Hitler's Europe*, published by University Press of Kentucky, 1990.

GEORGE RYAN WEINBRENNER, Col. (ret.), was born June 10, 1917 in Detroit, MI, son of George P. and Helen Ryan Weinbrenner. Attended parochial schools in Detroit and the Hall of the Divine Child in Monroe, MI. Graduated from Northwestern Military and Naval Academy, Lake Geneva, WI in 1936.

Commissioned as second lieutenant, Infantry Reserve, U.S. Army in 1939. In 1940 he received a B.S. degree from the Massachusetts Institute of Technology and the following year, 1941, received a M.S. degree in Economics and Engineering from the same university, and completed the Harvard Business School Advanced Management Program in 1966.

During WWII, he served a combat tour with the 8th A.F. in the European Theater of Operation, including several months of duty in enemy-occupied territory. Shot down by German fighters Feb. 22, 1944 while returning from raid in Germany. Evaded for seven months in Belgium and France, assisted by Belgium and French Patriots. Worked with Maquis.

Returned to civilian life in 1946 to take over the direction of family-owned enterprises. In April 1951, he was ordered back to active duty at Selfridge A.F.B., MI as deputy commander, 439th Troop Carrier Wing (M).

Following the Korean War the majority of his assignments were in the field of technical and scientific intelligence and research and development. Served as defense and air attache, U.S. Embassy, Prague, Czechoslovakian Socialist Republic from 1959 to 1961, when he was assigned to the newly activated Headquarters A.F. Systems Command at Andrews A.F.B., MD, where he served as assistant deputy chief of staff, plans and as deputy chief of staff, Intelligence. In November 1968 he was appointed commander, Foreign Technology Div., A.F. Systems Command, the major aerospace scientific and technical intelligence agency of Dept. of Defense. In September 1974 he assumed command of Brooks A.F.B., TX, remaining there until his retirement Sept. 1, 1975, completing a career that spanned 37 years of commissioned service.

Authored numerous articles on foreign science and technology and is considered a leading authority on foreign military capabilities. He is an Associate Fellow of the American Institute of Aeronautics and Astronautics.

Decorations: Distinguished Service Medal, Legion of Merit, Bronze Star, Air Medal, Purple Heart, and the French Order of National Merit, Resistance Medal and Croix de Guerre.

Married to the former Billie Elwood of San Antonio, TX. Col. and Mrs. Weinbrenner reside in San Antonio, TX.

ALFRED E. WENDT, (S/Sgt.) was born July 27, 1920 in Oak Harbor, OH. Drafted Dec. 1, 1942 at Camp Perry, OH. Gunnery training at Harlingen, TX. Joined B-17 crew at Moses Lake, WA as a tail gunner with the Col. Wm. Lawley crew.

Overseas with the 305th BG, 364th Bomb Sqdn. Shot down over enemy territory with the Lathrop crew, Jan. 7, 1944. Never captured. Walked alone to central France. Took three months, went down to 80 lbs. Picked up by the F.F.I. with Col. Weinbrenner. Escaped with Col. Weinbrenner when the southern invasion came through. Fought with F.F.I. for six months.

Returned to U.S. in October 1944. Married Doris Schubel April 27, 1946. Became a factory engineer. Built his own home and greenhouse. Have seven children and 10 grandchildren. Retired in 1978 due to health condition, but still playing in flowers.

WILLIAM B. (DICK) WHITLOW, was born June 8, 1918 in Monkey's Eyebrow (Ballard County), KY. Joined the Army Air Corps Cadet Program March 17, 1942 at Battle Creek, MI. Indoctrination and flight training at Santa Ana, CA; Oxnard, CA; Taft, CA; and Douglas, AZ. Commissioned and placed on flying status Jan. 4, 1943.

Assigned to Blythe, CA for B-17 flight training as co-pilot. Followed crew through staging period, then re-assigned to Boise, ID for further crew training as pilot. Joined Bowman Provisions Grp. at Spokane, WA and completed stateside training at Grand Island, NE.

Flew with crew to Bangor, Maine, Novia Scotia and on to Scotland in late August. Assigned to 385th BG at Great Ashfield in mid-September, 1943.

Shot down on sixth mission over Munster, Germany on Oct. 10, 1943. Immediately taken to safe hiding by Mr. Joop Noest, who now resides in Ruinen, Holland. Evaded capture and escaped through Holland, Belgium, France and Spain. Returned to London, Jan. 4, 1944.

After return to U.S. assigned to Wright Field, Dayton, OH. Discharged Oct. 31, 1945.

Married Pauline (Duffy) Matherly of Dearborn, MI on May 14, 1944. They have three sons, ages 45, 42, and 31.

Retired from private practice of law in 1989 and now resides in Newport Beach, CA.

THOMAS C. WILCOX, T/Sgt., was born May 27, 1923 in Youngstown, OH. Drafted into military service Feb. 16, 1943. Took radio operator mechanic training at Scott Field, IL; gunnery training at Buckingham A.A.F. Ft. Myers, FL. Was assigned to the 344th BG, 496th Sqdn. at Lakeland, FL, where he received his overseas training in the Martin B-26 Marauder.

Flew with the plane via the southern route to base at Stansted Airfield, near Bishop's Stortford,

England. Was shot down on 67th mission over Venlo, Holland Sept. 23, 1944. With help of Dutch Underground, escaped on Nov. 24, 1944.

Returned to U.S., entered pilots training at S.A.A.C., TX. Completed ten week training course when war with Germany ended. Pilots training was discontinued. Discharged July 15, 1945.

Married E.L. (Pat) Shepard Aug. 12, 1945. Children: David T., Rebecca E., Deborah G. and Melody E. Grandchildren: Michele and Mark Wilcox, Seth and Justin Gang, Rayne, Brianna and Dani Smith. First wife died May 1985. Remarried May 1987 to Mary Hudson. Presently residing in Ft. Myers Beach, FL.

CLIFFORD ODELL WILLIAMS, 1st Lt., was born Oct. 17, 1921 at Village Mills, TX. Enlisted Army Air Corps Oct. 1940. Completed airplane mechanic school, Chanute Field, IL October 1941. Assigned 55th Fighter Grp., 38th Sqdn. at Portland, OR; McChord Field, WA and Payne Field, WA. Crew chief on P-43 and P-38, rank technical sergeant.

Pilot training west coast, class 43H, at Blythe, CA; Bakersfield, CA and Williams Field, AZ. Combat training P-38 west coast at Salinas, CA; Glendale, CA; and Ontario, CA. Assigned 55th Fighter Grp., 343rd Sqdn. at Wormingford, England, March 1944.

Shot down May 27, 1944 over north France on 10th mission. Evaded capture with help of French Resistance. Returned to England, Sept. 15, 1944 and to U.S. October 1944.

Assigned as instructor AT-6 west coast at Marana, AZ December 1944. Assigned as instructor P-38 at Ontario, CA, June 1945 until released from active duty November 1945. Resides in Nederland, TX.

JAMES REECE WILSON, Major, was born June 30, 1924. Volunteered for military service Nov. 11, 1942. Was with Air Corps, as flight engineer on B-17C, 8th A.F., 379th BG, 525th Bomb Sqdn., Kimbolton, England.

Lost service of two engines on May 7, 1944, one was on fire. Four bailed out over Holland and

were picked up by the Underground. Spent a year evading the Germans, May 7, 1945 to liberation May 7, 1946.

Discharged from Air Force in 1946, rank of master sergeant.

Awarded Purple Heart and Air Medal with Oak Leaf Cluster.

Married and have two sons and six grandchildren. Worked at Chamber of Commerce. Retired, busy playing bridge, golf, riding Gold Wing motorcyle and volunteering. Lives in Waterloo, IA.

JOHN W. WILSON, was born Feb. 20, 1920 in Ellensburg, WA. Educated at Chico High School (graduated 1938), University of Southern California (B.S. Business 1955), post graduate study at University of Southern California (M.B.A.).

Enlisted California National Guard, Chico, CA in 1937. Army Air Corps Cadet June 1942. Graduated navigator-gunner Hondo Navigation School August 1943; phase training in Alexandria, LA. December 1943, assigned to 96th BG, 339th Bomb Sqdn., 8th A.F. Snetterton-Heath, England.

M.I.A. Berlin March 4th mission, landed in Belgium and remained until Sept. 19, 1944. Nov. 1944, assigned to Air Transport Command, Long Beach, CA until released from active duty April 1946.

Recalled to active duty March 1951, assigned to 22nd Bomb Wing, 2nd Bomb Sqdn., B-29, until March 1953. Retired from Air Force Reserve Feb. 1963.

Married Evelyn Moore August 1945.

Civilian employment: wallcovering contractor, residential and commercial projects in California, Arizona, Nevada, Disney Parks, California and Florida. Resides in Los Angeles, CA.

EUGENE A. WINK, JR., Lt. Col., was born Oct. 19, 1920 in Biloxi, MS. Pilot training in Texas, class 42K. Commissioned second lieutenant, U.S. Army, at West Point, NY, class January 1943.

Went to England with 365th Fighter Grp. after P-47 training at Richmond, VA. Bailed out over northern France March 2, 1944 after fighting FW190s. Evaded enemy in France with help of Etienne Capron, a courageous Frenchman from Graincourt-les-Havrincourt. Crossed Pyrenees into Spain, arriving England April 17, 1944.

Performed variety of operational and staff duties in U.S.A.F. Flew Air Rescue missions during Korean War and KC-135 sorties with SAC during Vietnam War.

Became a banker after U.S.A.F. retirement September 1969. Retired as senior vice president, Frost Bank Corp. in 1985.

Married 1947. Wife: Dr. Irma June Wink. Children: Sue Karen Wink, M.D., Robin Wink and Bruce Wink. Resides in San Antonio, TX.

HENRY C. (HANK) WOODRUM, Lt. Col., was born June 15, 1918, Redding, CA. Joined U.S. Army July 1940. Stationed at Wheeler Field, HI Dec. 7, 1941.

Took pilot training at Stockton, CA, class 43D. Arrived in England Jan. 1944. Stationed with the 344th BG (M), 495th Sqdn., flying B-26s.

While on 35th mission, shot down over Paris. Evaded capture by contacting French Underground and remaining with them for over 90 days. Returned to England after the liberation of Paris. Released from service October 1945.

Recalled to active duty September 1946. Flew C-47s and C-54s during Berlin Air Lift. Retired from U.S.A.F. as director of Air Borne Electronics School at Keesler A.F.B., Sept. 4, 1964.

After returning to Redding in 1964, employed by Shasta County as emergency services director; 1978, employed by City of Redding as airport manager. Retired in 1984.

Married Alberta Sneed Feb. 9, 1946; three sons, Henry C. Jr., Stephen L. and Michael R.

Passed away Feb. 11, 1990.

MARSHALL D. WORD, was born June 28, 1915 in Elk City, OK. Graduated from Oklahoma University Law School in 1940. Entered service as Aviation Cadet Aug. 28, 1941.

Received pilot wings and commissioned second lieutenant April 18, 1942, Stockton Field, CA. Instructed BT-13s Gardner Field, CA, until Aug. 7, 1943; B-24 instructor one year at Kirtland Field, NM; then sent to Italy Aug. 1, 1944 with 451st BG, 727th Sqdn., operations officer.

Shot down Osweicim mission Dec. 26, 1944; M.I.A. 23 days. Yugoslav Partisans aided return to Italy; completed 26 missions earning Distinguished Flying Cross and Air Medal with Clusters; was squadron commander of the 725th Sqdn. prior to return to U.S.

Remained in Air Force Reserve serving in SAC and later in OSI for summer tours; retired 1976 as lieutenant colonel.

Except for military service, practiced law since 1940, retiring 1980. Married Elta Hibler, May 16, 1942; two sons, Bill and Richard, five grandchildren. Resides in Arnett, OK.

ARNOLD T. WORNSON, was born July 29, 1917 in Mankato, MN. Joined the Army Air Force in April 1942. Had his pilot training in the West Coast training command, graduated from Williams Field, Phoenix, AZ in twin-engine training. Joined the 379th Grp., 525th Sqdn., 8th A.F. as a co-pilot on a B-17.

Shot down on second mission Sept. 23, 1943 near Rennes, France. Spent appoximately four months in the French Underground and in the Brittany area of France, to Paris, to Lyon, to Perpignan on the border of France and Spain. Walked across the Pyrenees Mountains into Spain. Returned to England by way of Gilbraltar.

After returning to the U.S. was assigned to Yuma, AZ Air Force Base, and flew P-39s and P-63s. Ended military career as an instructor in P-51s at Ft. Myers Air Force Base, FL in September 1945, with rank of captain.

Spent his post-war years as co-owner of Wornson-Polzin Dental Laboratories, Mankato, MN, at which time he and his partner owned and flew a Beechcraft Bonanza.

Married in January 1947 and has three daughters and three grandchildren.

JOHN M. WYLDER, was born Dec. 17, 1920 in Kansas City, MO. Enlisted in the U.S.A.A.F. Aug. 27, 1942 in Los Angeles, CA.

Bombardier training: Carlsbad, NM, 43-18, December 1943. Commissioned second lieutenant

June 1, 1944, 13th A.F., 5th BG, 23rd Bomb Sqdn. Flew mission when 5th BG, 23rd Sqdn. sunk Japanese cruiser "Kuma Natori" class Battle of the Philippine Sea.

On 18th mission to a "milk-run" target shot down Nov. 1, 1944. M.I.A. Floated off shore Bacolad Air Field. Strafed in shark infested waters. Rescued by Philippine guerillas in broad daylight. Fought with guerillas under Lt. Col. Cirilo B. Garcia. Walked 150 miles to submarine rendezvous area. Rescued by USS Hake (SS-256) Dec. 5-16, 1944. Depth charged, dive bombed at scope depth and chased on surface at night while running a mine field at flank speed.

Awarded: Purple Heart, Presidential Unit Citaion, Asia-Pacific Service Medal with four Clusters, Air Medal with Oak Leaf Cluster, Philippines Liberation Medal and Star.

Wife, Kay; children: Linda and Robert. Noise control consultant and distributor of noise control materials, Van Nuys, CA. Resides in Van Nuys, CA.

JOHN M. YANDURA, was born March 26, 1921 in East Vandergrift, Westmoreland, PA. Joined the military July 22, 1942.

Military service took him to locations in Africa and Italy. Flew 38 missions during WWII, between the military bases of Deppiene, Tunisia and Cerignola and Amendola in Italy. During his Air Force career, he was a radio operator on the following planes: B-17, C-47, AT-18, B-34 and C-54.

Served in the 12th and 15th Air Forces and achieved the rank of technical sergeant. Retired Sept. 5, 1945.

On Yandura's 39th mission, March 24, 1944, he bailed out over Yugoslavia.

Retired in 1981 from a bricklayer position with Allegheny Ludlum Steel Corp., Brackenridge, PA. He and his wife, Ethel, reside in East Vandergrift. One child, one grandchild.

THOMAS L. YANKUS, SR., was born Aug. 5, 1923 in Richmond Hill, NY, second son of William and Margaret Yankus.

After moving to Dearborn, MI at age seven, returned to Laurelton, Long Island, NY, attended Andrew Jackson High School and lived in Laurelton until 1941. Worked at Sperry Gyroscope Co. for two years.

Enlisted U.S. Army Air Corps Dec. 4, 1942. Inducted Camp Upton, NY; basic training, Miami Beach, FL; radio school, Scott Field, IL; B-17 crew training Moses Lake, WA. Picked up B-17 in Nebraska. Flew north Atlantic route to England, arrived 95th BG, 335th Bomb Sqdn., Horham, England January 1944.

Shot down on third mission, March 4, 1944, first bombing of Berlin. Helped to evade capture by the French Underground, Comete Line. Liberated Aug. 13, 1944 by Patton's 3rd Army.

Returned to States September 1944. Trained radar operators Langley Field.

Married teenage sweetheart April 21, 1945. Discharged November 1945. Settled on Long Island and worked for United Parcel until 1953. Owned motel, Adirondack, Mountains, NY until 1955.

Moved to St. Petersburg, FL. In construc-

tion business for 32 years. Had two children: Thomas, 43, principal, Georgia, four children; Margaret Jane, 33, loan officer, two children.

Retired 1987. Lives in Crystal River, FL.

RICHARD L. FELMAN, (Maj., USAF, Ret'd), born May 29, 1921, New York City. Enlisted in Army Air Corps July 24, 1942, retired July 18, 1968. Master Navigator.

Flew combat tours in WW II (B-24), Korea (B-29), Air Refueling (KC-97, KC-135). Received 27 awards and decorations. Proudest of Purple Heart. Decorated personally by King Peter II of Yugoslavia.

During WW II, shot down over occupied Yugoslavia and was one of over 500 flyers rescued by Gen. Draza Mihailovich and his Chetnik guerillas in the largest air rescue of American MIAs from behind enemy lines in history.

Submitted documentation to Encyclopedia Britannica and Encyclopedia Americana which corrected their previous erroneous accounts on Mihailovich.

Appeared many times before US Congress seeking a memorial to Mihailovich which is nationally supported by the American Legion, Veterans of Foreign Wars and the Air Force Association. Permission to erect a Mihailovich Memorial has twice been granted by the Senate but opposed by the State Department and communist Yugoslavia. His group is still trying and currently have two bills before the 1991-1992 Congress. He is President of the National Committee of American Airmen Rescued by Gen. Mihailovich, Inc.

(L to R): Edward O'Leary, Marcel Trubert, Frank McDonald, Minvielle, Donals Girard. O'Leary, McDonald and Girard are three American crew members helped by Marcel Trubert. This photo was taken at his home in Locq, Bas DePyrenees, France the day before Minveille was to guide them to Spain. Trubert was arrested May 4 and deported to Germany. At the end of the war, he returned to France where he died six months later.

AFEES Roster of Members

This is the official roster of the Air Force Escapes and Evasions Society as provided to the Publisher. It was the most current version available at press time. The Publisher is not responsible for errors or ommissions.

A

LOUIS H. ABBOTT
DR. PRESTON S. ABBOTT
CHARLES E. ADCOCK
DAVID G. ALFORD
IRA R. ALLEN
*JARVIS ALLEN
WILLIAM R. ALLISON
ALBERT C. ALT
DWIGHT F. ALVERSON
JOHN T. AMERY
F. EARL ANDERSON
LESTER E. ANDERSON
ROBERT O. ANDERSON
JAMES A. ANGELUCCI
JAMES R. ANSLOW
ALEX ANTANOVICH
THOMAS B. APPLEWHITE
JAMES E. ARMSTRONG
*HAROLD ASHMAN
JOHN ATHERTON
ROBERT ATKINS
RUDOLPH AUGARTEN
ROBERT C. AUGUSTUS
ROYCE F. AUSTIN
GEORGE M. AVDEK
LESLIE M. AVERY

B

LAWRENCE BABCOCK
JOSEPH P. BAGLIO
F. M. BAILEY
JOSEPH C. BAKER
WILLIAM M. BAKER
LEON "BUD" BALLARD
MABRY D. BARKER
JOHN F. BARNACLE
STUART K. BARR
LEONARD L. BARTON
ARTHUR BEACH
CHARLES D. BEARD, JR.
ALBERT E. BEAUCHEMIN
JOSEPH F. BEAULIEU
JENNING B. BECK
JAMES K. D. BECKER
REV. CLAUD W. BEHN
WILLIAM E. BENDT
GLEN E. BENEDA
EUGENE E. BENNETT
GEORGE F. BENNETT
WOODROW J. BERGERON
ELMO BERGLIND
JOHN F. BERNIER
COL. DAVID C. BESBRIS
J. M. BICKLEY
*JOSEPH A. BIRDWELL
HARRY E. BISHER
CLARE A. BLAIR
GLENN F. BLACKBURN
ROBERT B. BLACKBURN
ROGER J. BLAKE
MILO E. BLAKELY
ROBERT W. BLAKENEY
CHARLES W. BLAKLEY

JOHN A. BLATNIK
THORNTON BLINE
ARLIE J. BLOOD
*KENNETH O. BLYE
WAYNE C. BOGARD
MAGNUS G. BOLKEN
JOSEPH P. BONCZEK
WILLIAM H. BOOHER
WILLIAM H. BOOTH
ROBERT G. BORST
RICHARD R. BOSTER
EUGENE B. BOWARD
JOHN J. BRADLEY
EMERSON BRANSON
LOUIS H. BREITENBACH
ADOLPH F. BREMER
GEORGE F. BRENNAN
WALTER T. BRESSLER
HERBERT BRILL
JACOB "BILL" BRINN
JESS W. BRITTON
JOHN L. BRIXIUS
HAROLD C. BROOKS
GEORGE JOSEPH BROOKS
NELSON E. BROTT
LT. COL. KENNETH A. BROWER
LT. COL. JOHNNY BROWN
LESTER BROWN
DEWEY C. BROWN
JOHN R. BROWN, JR.
JOE L. BRYANT
GUS E. BUBENZER
GEORGE P. BUCKNER
JOHN R. BUCKNER
EDWARD R. BURLEY, JR.
*ROBERT L. BURNETT
LAWRENCE F. BURT
*LLOYD C. BUSBOOM
DAVID L. BUTCHER
JOHN A. BUTLER
ROBERT K. BUTLER

C

JOSEPH W. CAGLE, JR.
GLENN STERLING CALL
WILLIAM T. CAMPBELL
DENVER M. CANADAY
HOWARD W. CANNON
THOMAS W. CANNON
JOHN M. CARAH
CLAUDUS E. CARTER
CLELL M. CARD
FLOYD M. CARL
THORNTON L. CARLOUGH
CHARLES V. CARLSON
*DENNIS CARLSON
JOHN PHILLIP M. CARLSON
REGIS R. CARNEY
E. M. CARNICELLI
THOMAS J. CARROLL
KENNETH CARSON
COL. LAWRENCE R. CASEY
JAMES C. CATER
H. PHILLIP CAUSER
MARTIN CECH
ALLEN J. CHAPLIN
JOHN J. CHAPMAN

WALTER E. CHAPMAN
ROY A. CHEEK
JOHN CHERNOSKY
EVERETT L. CHILDS
*KENNETH P. CHRISTIAN
COL. STONE CHRISTOPHER
MILTON L. CHURCH
JAMES P. CLARENDON
BENJAMIN L. CLARK
DONALD CLARK
FORREST S. CLARK
*GEORGE F. CLARK
JACK C. CLIFFORD
LEECROY "CLIFF" CLIFTON
ALBERT M. COBB
JAMES M. COCHRAN, JR.
ALTON WARD COCKRELL
J. D. COFFMAN
SIMON COHEN
CLIFFORD E. COLE
LEONARD COLLEN
*CHARLES W. COMPTON
JOSEPH M. CONNABLE
*EUGENE W. CONNOR
THEODORE G. CONVERSE
GEORGE D. COOKSEY
KERMIT Q. COOKSEY
*FRANKLIN D. COSLETT
*JOSEPH D. COSS
WESLEY G. COSS
*ROBERT L. COSTELLO
RUSSEL J. COTTS
ROBERT D. COUTURE
FORD C. COWHERD
HARVEY G. COX
COL. WILLIAM L. CRAMER, JR.
SILAS M. CRASE
DONALD H. CRAWFORD
WILLIAM F. CROWE
CLEO R. CRUTCHFIELD
*TOM CULKIN
WILLIAM L. CUPP
COL. ED. C. CURY

D

ELDON H. DAHL
NEIL F. DALEY
EDWARD M. DALY
NED A. DAUGHERTY
ROBERT L. DAVEY
LT. COL. CLAYTON C. DAVID
EUGENE L. DAVILA
CLAYTON E. DAVIS
GLENDON V. DAVIS
*JACK C. DAVIS
WILLIAM M. DAVIS
FRANK M. DEASON
CURTIS L. DEATRICK
ALBERT H. DeBACKER
GERLAD P. DECHAMBRE
DR. WM. B. DEHON
*EDWARD H. DECOSTE
HOWARD R. De MALLIE
RAOUL de MARS
FREDERICK DEMATTEIS
ROBERT O. DENISON
ALEXANDER J. DEWA

PAUL F. DICKEN SR.
CO. THOMAS I. DIGGS
EUGENE W. DINGLEDINE
LAWRENCE J. DISSETTE
JEROME W. DIX
IRA JAMES DOBBIE
HARRY A. DOLPH
DAVID A. DONOVAN
ROBERT H. DOOLAN
EUGENE H. DORR
CLEMENT D. DOWLER
CHARLES O. DOWNE
WILLIAM W. DRISCO
*HOWARD DROLLINGER
DOUGLAS R. DRYSDALE
W. C. DuBOSE
ELMER E. DUERR
HERBERT DULBERG
KENNETH P. DUNAWAY
DANIEL E. DUNBAR
LLOYD F. DUNCAN
CHARLES W. DUNGAN
ATHUR L. DUNN
DONLAD A. DURANT
*DALE G. DURKES

E

*CURTIS EASLEY
ROBERT H. EASLEY
*HARRY L. EASTMAN
DONALD E. EBERHARDT
ROBERT W. ECKMAN
MALCOM L. EDWARDSEN
ROBERT EIDENMILLER
MORRIS ELISCO
LT. COL. SIDNEY J. ELSKES
*GORDON B. ERICKSON
JERRY ESHUIS
JAMES C. ESTEP
LT. COL. GEORGE W. EVANS
COL. I. WAYNE EVELAND

F

EUGENE E. FARROW
RICHARD J. FAULKNER
JAMES R. FAUTH
LEE FEGETTE
R. LOUIS FEINGOLD
*STANLEY E. FELIX
MAJ. RICHARD L. FELMAN
FORREST S. FENN
VICTOR J. FERRARI
WILLIAM FERREIRA
REUBEN FIER
WILLIAM L. FINCH
PHILIP J. FINK
CARROLL L. FISHER
ROY D. FISHER
E. B. FITZPATRICK
HENRY FLESH
WESTWOOD H. FLETCHER,JR.
WILLIAM M. FOLEY
RICHARD M. FORTNER
KENNETH W. FOSTER
COL. JAMES FOWLER
ARNOLD E. FRANTZ

LT. COL. E. S. FRASER
ELMER C. FREEMAN
*HAROLD O. FREEMAN
ROBERT K. FRUTH
DWIGHT A. FRY
ROBERT D. FULKS

G

JOHN R. GABRIEL
GEORGE H. GAGNE
FRANK E. GALLAGHER
BRUNO M. GALLERANI
*DELMAR J. GALLOWAY
COL. PAUL E. GARDINER
RICHARD F. GARLAND
*JOHN W. GEORGE
ALBERT L. GESE
BEVERLY C. GEYER
OLIN E. GILBERT
ROBERT LeROY GILBERT
WILLIAM J. GISE
*HENRY H. GLADYS
DR. CARL I.GLASSMAN
ERNEST P. GLEASON
FRED P. GLEASON
T. JACK GLENNAN
FRED R. GLOR
LT. COL. JOHN F. GOAN
JAMES J. GOEBEL
DR. MARVIN T. GOFF
MILTON M. GOLDFEDER
COLEMAN GOLDSTEIN
JOSEPH P. GONET
LEE C. GORDON
ROBERT J. GRACE
LARRY E. GRAUERHOLZ
JAMES A. GRIBBLE
THOMAS J. GRIMA
ROBERT Z. GRIMES
WILMONT C. GRODI
JOSEPH GROSS
CHARLES L. GURNEY,II
*ROBERT E. GUSTAFSON

H

CARROLL F. HAARUP
CHARELS A. HADFIELD
KENNETH L. HAINES
ALBERT P. HALL
ERSEL L. HALL
LESTER W. HALL
MARION A. HALL
RALPH HALL
EDWARD W. HALLIBURTON
LOUIS L. HALTOM
OSCAR K. HAMBLIN
WILBUR W. HAMPTON
*THOMAS A. HAMILTON
LT. COL. J. F. HAMMOND
ROBERT J. HAMRICK
ROBERT J. HANNAN
GEORGE HANLON
MARINO HANNESSON
DONALD W. HANSLIK
FRED HARGESHEIMER
FRANCIS X. HARKINS
CHARLES C. HARPIN
ROBERT W. HARRINGTON
DELBERT E. HARRIS
HOWARD M. HARRIS
ALFRED B. HARRISON JR.
J. C. HART
WALTER L. HARVEY

*PAUL H. HASSLER
WILBUR T. HAUGEN
CHARLES HAUPT
*FRANK B. HAWKINS
WILLIAM C. HAWKINS
ROBERT W. HAWKINSON
WILLIAM B. HAYES
DR. LOUIS R. HEAD
DONALD E. HEADRICK
H. L. HEAFNER,JR.
JAMES J. HEDDLESON
FRANCIS X. HEEKIN
COL G. A. HEINICKE
WALTER R. HELDORFER
LESTER J. HENDERSON
*FRANK P. HENNESSY
JOHN E. HENNESSY
ROBERT F. HENRY
JAMES H. HENSLEY,JR.
JAMES CARL HENSLEY
*HERMAN F. HERMANSON
WALTER S. HERN JR.
LOUIS R. HERNANDEZ
ROBERT O. HERSCHLER
DAVID HESSLER
EARL W. HEUER
JOHN F. HICKMAN
L. D. HICKS
ERIC HILDITSCH
JAMES E. HILL
JAMES M. HILLER
RICHARD HOBBY
JAMES B. HODGIN
HENRY J. HODULIK
DOUGLAS C. HOEHN
WILLIAM A. HOFFMAN
PETER B. HOGAN
WILLIAM L. HOLLOWAY
FRANZ F. HOLSCHER
CHARELS V. HOLT
ROLAND L. HOLWEGNER
GEORGE HOOPER
ODELL HOOPER
THAYER HOPKINS
WILLIAM F. HOPMAN
LAURIE S. HORNER
ARUTHR J. HORNING
KENNETH N. HOUGARD
DOULAS K. HOVERKAMP
ORLAND T. HOWARD
ELTON HOYT,III
JOHN HRIBAR
JOHN K. HUGHES
ERNEST H. HUGONNET
JOE HUMBLE
LLOYD HUNT
JOHN K. HURST
G. GERALD HYSON

I

JACK ILFREY
JIM INKS
*LT. COL. BENJAMIN C. ISGRIG
ELMER P. ISRAELSON
STANLEY M. IVERSON
ASHLEY IVEY
BOB IZAARD

J

EDGAR J. JACOBUS
GEORGE A. JANOS
JAMES L. JARED
WILBUR L. JARVIS

ROLAND H. JENKINS
WALTER D. JENSEN, JR.
RUSELL N. JEVONS
*STEPHEN W. JEZERCAK
HANS C. JOHANSSON
GLENN B. JOHNSON
ROBERT H. JOHNSON
*WILLIAM R. JOHNSTON
CHARLES O. JONES
L. RAY JONES
*VIRGIL W. JONES
CLYDE S. JUDY
E. A. JURIST
JOHN K. JUSTICE
HOWARD J. JUSTIN

K

DEMETRIOS KARNEZIS
WALTER E. KASIEVICH
PAUL P. KASZA
JOHN KATSAROS
HECTOR A. KAUFMAN
JAMES H. KEEFFE
THEODORE R. KELLERS
E. ROBERT KELLEY
FREDERICK C. KELLY
NORMAN P. KEMPTON
JAMES L. KENDALL
PAUL E. KENNEY
ROBERT R. KERR
CONRAD J. KERSCH
JACQUES KESHISHIAN
IKE K. KILLINGSWORTH
ERNEST C. KING
NORMAN R. KING
*WILLIAM C. KINNEY
DR. JOSEPH L. KIRKNER
ELLIS H. KLEIN
THEODORE H. KLEINMAN
KENNETH KLEMSTINE
*BERTRAM D. KNAPP
EDWARD L. KNAPP, III
DONALD C. KOCH
*RAYMOND KOCH
HAROLD C. KORNMAN
WILLIAM KOSSEFF
ANTHONY KOSINSKI
JOSEPH Z. KRAJEWSKI
FRANK X. KREBS
RICHARD H. KRECKER
FRED KRIESBERG
ROBERT KRENGLE
THEODORE J. KROL
A. RAY KUBLY
FREDERICK D. KUHN
ERNEST J. KULIK
JOHN A. KUPSICK
JOSEPH J. KUREK
EDWARD F. KUTCH

L

WILLIAM R. LaFORCE
DR. JOHN L. LaFOUNTAIN
JOHN F. LACY
RICHARD A. LAMIE
BILL M. LANE
JOSHUA D. LANE, JR.
JOSEPH A. LANTIGNE
P. C. LARGENT JR.
JOHN C. LARKIN
CLARENCE L. LARREW
FRANCIS J. LASHINSKY
*ROBERT V. LAUX

JAMES P. LAW
DUANE J. LAWHEAD
VINCENT LAYBE
JOHN PARKER LAYNE
ALFRED LEA
EDWIN O. LEARNARD
DALE V. LEE
ARMIT W. LEWIS
DONALD M. LEWIS
JOHN L. LEWIS
LEON E. LEVENS
JOSEPH WILLIAM LINCOLN
DR. ERNEST V. LINDELL
MIKE LITTLE
ROBERT M. LITTLEFIELD
WILLIAM B. LOCK
*DARIUS A. LOGAN
EDWARD F. LOGAN JR.
WARREN E. LORING
GLEN LOVELAND
LT. COL. CHARLES M. LOWE
THOMAS LOWE
JACK O. LUEHRS
JAMES A LUTON
HAROLD G. LYNCH

M

JAMES D. MAHAFFEY
LAYMON M. MAHAN
DR. R. HOWARD MAHANES
WALKER M. MAHURIN
JOHN J. MAIORCA
JOSEPH L. MALONEY
A. F. MALTBIE
*NICHOLAS MANDELL
PAT N. MANN
JOSEPH E. MANOS
ANDREW MARCIN
VIRGIL R. MARCO
JOHN M. MARR
FREDERICK T. MARSTON
ADRIAN A. MARTIN
BENJAMIN T. MARTIN
CLYDE J. MARTIN
JOHN W. MARTIN
MERLE E. MARTIN
ROY A. MARTIN
FRANCIS C. MARX
WILLIAM E. MASSEY
WILLIAM R. MATTSON
OWEN L. MAYBERRY
*ROBERT L. MAYS
COL. CHARLES C. McBRIDE
GLEN A. McCABE
ROBERT H. McCARTHY
MELVIN L. McCARTNEY
WILLIAM H. McCHESNEY
CHARLES J. McCLAIN
PAUL H. McCONNELL
HOMER McDANAL
CLOVIS W. McDONALD
FRANK G. McDONALD
EUGENE P. McDONNELL
JAMES D. McELROY
WILLIAM C. McGINLEY
FRANK P. McGLINCHEY
JOHN A. McGLYNN
JACK McGOUGH
JOHN R. McKEE
RALPH D. McKEE
WILLIAM R. McKILLOP
THOMAS D. McMAHON
JOSEPH PAUL McMENIMEN
LLOYD E. McMICHAEL

JOSEPH S. McMINN
WENDEL S. McMURRAY
CHARLES H. McNEMAR
*SAMUEL J. MELANCON
HARRISON CLAY MELLOR
HOWARD E. MELSON
GEORGE F. MESSICK
ROBERT WILLIAM METLEN
EUGENE J. METZ
IRVING MEYER
EDGAR W. MICHAELS
GEORGE W. MICHEL
WILLIAM F. MIDDLEDORF
PETER P. MILASIUS
GILBERT MILLAR
*CHARLES P. MILLER
EDWARD C. MILLER
KARL D. MILLER
ROBERT M. MILLER
ROSSWELL MILLER
VINCENT N. MILLER
WILLIAM J. MILLER
MILTON J. MILLS
MARTIN G. MINNICH
BOBBY D. MITCHELL
GLENN A. MITCHELL
WALTER A. MIZE, JR.
MICHAEL A. MODICA
HOWARD E. MOEBIUS
MILTON MOEN
HERMAN MOLEN
THOMAS R. MONACELLI
GEORGE S. MONSER
RICHARD T. MOONEY
CHARLES L. MOORE
GOFFRED F. MORETTO
EVERETT E. MORGAN JR.
ERNEST T. MORIARTY
PAUL F. MORITZ
GILBERT L. MORRIS
LOWELL D. MORROW
NORMAN C. MOSHER
WILLIAM E. MOUNTAIN
JAY MUELLER
JACOB J. MULLER
*CHARLIE H. MULLINS
JAMES R. MUND
JOHN P. MULVIHILL
JAMES S. MUNDAY
MAJ. JOSEPH P. MURPHY
CLAUDE MURRAY
JAMES R. MURRAY
JACK ALLEN MURRELL
CLARE M. MUSGROVE
EDWIN R. MYERS

N

CARL T. NALL
CHESTER NATANEK
DONALD G. NAUGHTON
JOSEPH NAVARRO
WILLIAM F. NEAL
KENNETH E. NEFF
ROBERT G. NEIL
CHALES M. NEKVASIL
ROBERT E. NELSON
*WALTER T. NELSON
EDWARD F. NEU
JACK E. NOSSER

O

DAVID W. O'BOYLE
ROBERT B. O'CONNELL

EDWARD F. O'DAY
BENJAMIN L. O'DELL
RAWLIN E. O'LEARY
GEORGE H. OGBURN
CHARLES S. OLDFIELD
JOHN H. OLIPHINT
WILLIAM L. OLSEN
CLINTON H. OREAN
LT. COL. DAVID B. OSBORNE

P

GEORGE C. PADGETT
MAX PALENICA
JOHN J. PARIS
RALPH K. PATTON
HEYWARD A. PAXTON, JR.
RONALD PEARCE
*JONATHAN PEARSON
ARNOLD O. PEDERSON
JOSEPH O. PELOQUIN
RAYMOND F. PENCEK
LT. COL. W. C. PENSINGER
JOSEPH M. PERRY
NICHOLAS J. PETERS
ALVIN E. PETERSON
COBERN V. PETERSON
DONIS A. PETERSON
THEODORE M. PETERSON
JOHN WILLIAM PETTY
KARL A. PFISTER
JAMES W. PHILLIPS
WAYNE E. PHILLIPS
JOHN W. PIDCOCK
ROBERT F. PIPES
ALFRED G. PLATT
LEONARD A. POGUE
JEFFERSON D. POLK
BERNARD L. POOLE
DONALD A. PORTER
JOSEPH E. PORTER
GEORGE J. POWELL
JAMES W. POWELL
WILLIAM POWELL
JOSEPH E. POWERS
JOEL D. PUNCHES
JOHN E. PURDY

Q

JOHN L. QUAIL
JAMES N. QUINN
JOSEPH F. QUIRK

R

DOID K. RAAB
GERALD RAHL
MERLE C. RAINEY
FRANCIS C. RAMSEY
BERNARD W. RAWLINGS
CHESTER A. RAY
CHARLES A. REED
QUILLA D. REED
*EUGENE REEDY
THOMAS REICH
DONALD A. REIHMER
EUGENE J. REMELL
WILLIAM A. RENDALL
LT.COL. McCALLISTER B.RHODES
*ROY J. RICE
ALEXANDER RICHARD
*LAWRENCE RICHARDS
THOMAS C. RICHARDS
LT. COL. CLYDE RICHARDSON

HERSCHELL RICHARDSON
HOWARD E. RICHARDSON
WILLIAM K. RICHMOND
RICHARD RICKEY
EWELL M. RIDDLE
CLELL B. RIFFLE
LT. COL. H. D. RIGNEY
JOSEPH E. RIPLEY
ROBERT RIPPS
GEORGE J. RITCHIE
LOUIS RITT
ALVIS D. ROBERTS
JOHN W. ROBERTS
SAMUEL W. ROBERTS
JOHN M. DES ROCHERS
ROBERT L. RODGERSON
LOUIS RODRIGUEZ
*GEORGE M. ROGERS
LEONARD ROGERS
MANUEL M. ROGOFF
ARTHUR P. ROHR
ALBERT ROMERO
CHARLES W. ROOF
WOODIE M. ROSE
SEYMOUR L. ROSENTHAL
OTTO V. ROSKEY
HAROLD B. ROSS
WILLIAM O. ROSS
JOHN C. RUCIGAY
GOERGE F. RUCKMAN
ROBERT E. RUGH
DONOVAN W. RULIEN
CARL F. RUNGE
KENNETH E. RUPPERT
DR. JOHN F. RUSSELL
MICHAEL RUTA
HERBERT GILMAN RUUD
RICHARD G. RYAN

S

MYRON E. SABIN
CHARELS J. SALIVAR
ALFRED M. L. SANDERS
LEE SANDERS
SOLDIER E. SANDERS
*ROBERT D. SANDUSKY
VIRGIL E. SANSING
HENRY P. SARNOW
TONY SAVASTANO
SAMUEL W. SAYER
ROBERT L. SCANLON
WILLIAM J. SCANLON
CHARLES B. SCARBOROUGH
EUGENE B. SCERBO
WILLIAM E. SCHACK
FRANK N. SCHAEFFER
RICHARD SCHAFER
LEONARD SCHALLEHN
PAUL H. SCHLINTZ
FRED T. SCHMITT
RICHARD J. VON SCHRILTZ
JOHN H. SCHUFFERT
CARL T. SCHUNEMAN JR.
ROBERT A. SCHWARTZBURG
PETER P. SCOTT
GEN. RICHARD M. SCOTT
LT. COL. CHARLES B. SCREWS
ROBERT A. SEAMAN
EDWIN G. SECHRIST
EARL J. SEAGARS
ALLEN E. SEAMANS
ROBERT S. SEIDEL
JOHN SEMACH
EDWARD R. SHAFFER

JOSEPH SHANDOR
HENRY SHANE
ELIOT H. SHAPLEIGH
KENNETH D. SHAVER
J. KELLY SHAW
JOHN SHAW
GIL SHAWN
*WILLIAM C. SHEAHAN
EDWARD J. SHEDLOCK
RICHARD S. SHEEHY
A. C. EARL SHEPHERD
HOWARD W. SHERMAN
MORTON B. SHERWOOD
MILTON V. SHEVHICK
HUGH C. SHIELDS
JAMES G. SHILLIDAY
PAUL F. SHIPE
DAVID SHOSS
ORION H. SHUMWAY
IRVING H. SHWAYDER
JACK B. SICKELS
HARRY J. SIEMENS
HERBERT SIMON
OLIVER S. SIMONS
JOSEPH W. SKARDA
ERNEST C. SKORHEIM
CHARLES R. SLINGLAND
JAMES R. SLOAN
RALPH SMATHERS
A. B. SMITH
BERT I. SMITH
RALPH D. SMITH
RICHARD M. SMITH
ROBERT E. SMITH
*ROBERT D. SMITH
RONALD O. SMITH
DAVE O. SNOWDEN
HOWARD J. SNYDER
WALTER R. SNYDER
*STANLEY A. SOKOLOWSKI
PHILIP SOLOMON
DAVID W. SOUDER
JOHN WILSON SPENCE
WILLIS E. SPELLMAN
EDWARD J. SPEVAK
*HEYWARD CLAUDE SPINKS
*WILLIAM H. SPINNING
HENRY ST GEORGE
BENJAMIN H. ST. JOHN
THEODORE R. STABLEIN
LLOYD A. STANFORD
DR. GEROGE W. STARKS
ROBERT STARZYNSKI
JACK W. STEAD
FLOYD M. STEGALL
NORMAN STEPHENS
LT. COL. STANLEY E. STEPNITZ
RICHARD W. STONES
CHARLES A. STRACKBINE
GEORGE R. STRICKER
J. R. STUEBGEN
EVERETT E. STUMP
DAVID C. SULLIVAN
IRWIN L. SUMPTER
GOV. BRUCE G. SUNDLUN
ALFRED F. SUTKOWSKI
WARREN K. SUTOR
ELMER J. SUTTERS, JR.
JOHN E. SWAIN
JAMES A. SWANSON
LT. COL. ART M. SWAP
WALTER W. SWARTZ
ROBERT H. SWEATT
RAY SWEDZINSKI
DMITRI A. SWEETAK

JOHN L. SWENSON
RICHARD T. SYKES
FRANCIS R. SYLVIA

T

DAVID R. TALBOTT
HAROLD C. TALLING
WOODROW W. TARLETON
DEAN W. TATE
STANLEY TAXEL
EDGAR M. TAYLOR
ORVIN VERLE TAYLOR
GEORGE W. TEMPLE
LAWRENCE H. TEMPLETON
THOMAS J. TERRILL
JACK TERZIAN
BUFORD THACKER
RICHARD V. THIRIOT
MAURICE S. THOMAS
THOMAS S. THOMAS, III
HAROLD E. THOMPSON
EARL THORNSEN
CHARLES H. THORNTON
ROBERT F. THOURSON
WILLIAM A. THURSTON
RUSSEL TICKNER
ROBERT A. TITUS
JOHN L. TONEY
*ED TOVREA
JAMES E. TRACY
HOBART C. TRIGG
WILLIAM W. TRIMBLE
GEORGE I. TRIPP
JAMES T. TRONSON
DAVID EDGAR TROUP
GERALD H. TUCKER
ROBERT C. TUCKER
GARNETT T. TUNSTALL
THEODORE A. TURBAK

HOWARD J. TURLINGTON
DAVID H. TURNER
ROBERT E. TUTHILL
FREDERICK A. TUTTLE
ALBERT P. TYLER

U

KASMIR ULAKY
BERNARD UNGER

V

JAMES J. VALLEY
ROBERT R. VANDEGRIFF
JOHN D. VECCHIOLA
ISADORE C. VIOLA
RAYMOND E. VITKUS
JOHN S. VITZ
DON W. VOGEL
*GEORGE W. VOGEL
CLYDE K. VOSS
JOSEPH VUKOVICH

W

JAMES M. WAGNER
ROY M. WALKER
*FRANCIS C. WALL
ROY E. WALLER
RAYMOND E. WALLS
*IRA J. WALTER
JOHN J. WARD
ROBERT L. WARD
DAVID WARNER
*ROBERT E. WARNER
RAYMOND H. WARNS
CHARLES R. WARREN
C. JOSEPH WARTH
DONALD A. WATERS

CODY U. WATSON
GEORGE WATT
LOUIE F. WEATHERFORD
*CHARLES H. WEAVER
WILLIAM A. WEBER
DONALD S. WEBSTER
COL. GEORGE R. WEINBRENNER
GLEN WELLS
R. JOSEPH WELLS
LT. COL. EDWARD G. WELSH
JOSEPH E. WEMHEUER
ALFRED E. WENDT
*CHARLES L. WENSLEY
EDWIN WEST
CHARELS H. WESTERLUND
THOMAS R. WESTROPE
RUSSEL S. WEYLAND
CARL WHITE
HARRY E. WHITE
*LONNIE E. WHITE
LAMAR H. WHITTIER
ROBERT B. WILCOX
THOMAS C. WILCOX
*VIRGIL WILCOX
BURT K. WILLIAMS
CLIFFORD O. WILLIAMS
FRANK E. WILLIAMS
KENNETH R. WILLIAMS
LEO WILLIAMS
WALTER R. WILLIAMS
SIDNEY H. WILLIG
ALBERT G. WILLING JR.
*ALAN R. WILLIS
JAMES S. WILSCHKE
CLAY W. WILSON
HENRY F. WILSON
JAMES R. WILSON
JOHN W. WILSON
ROBERT I. WILSON
EUGENE A. WINK, JR.

*CHARELS B. WINKLEMAN
LEROY R. WINTER
FRANCIS J. WITT, JR.
HENRY W. WOLCOTT
EARL J. WOLF
LT. COL. PAUL L. WOLFF
WILLIAM E. WOLFF
JOHN B. WOOD
EARL E. WOODARD
*HENRY C. WOODRUM
MERLE E. WOODSIDE
H. D. WOOTEN
MARSHALL D. WORD
ARNOLD T. WORNSON
THEODORE WOZNICKI
COL. DONALD B. WREN
*NORMAN J. WRIGHT
PHLEMON T. WRIGHT
RICHARD E. WRIGHT
WILLIAM E. WYATT
JOHN M. WYLDER

Y

JOHN YANDURA
THOMAS L. YANKUS SR.
WILLIE B. YATES
ALFRED YAVOROSKY
ORLANDO J. YEMMA
*DALLAS F. YOUNG

Z

WILLIAM D. ZAHRTE
EDMOND ZELLNER
*JAMES E. ZENGERLE
ALFRED J. ZEOLI
AUGUSTUS di ZEREGA
BERNARD F. ZYGLOWICZ

Joe Gross received this photo for Christmas 1945. It is from John, Wilson, Mum and Dad Bell of Kirkcaldy, Scotland. The photo was taken August 1944 upon John's return from France.

AFEES Index

Printed in the USA
CPSIA information can be obtained
at www.ICGtesting.com
JSHW051959150824
68134JS00058B/2655